Asian-Americans
Psychological Perspectives

DATE

DISCARD

Contributors

Elizabeth Lee Abbott, M.A.
  Past Director of the Chinese Branch of the YWCA, San Francisco, Calif.

Kenneth A. Abbott, D.S.W.
  Associate Professor of Social Welfare, Smith College, Northampton, Mass.

Ransom J. Arthur, M.D.
  Psychiatrist, San Diego, Calif.

Timothy R. Brown, Ph.D.
  Director of Research and Evaluation, Resthaven Psychiatric Hospital, Los Angeles, Calif.

Lowell Chun-Hoon, B.S.
  Editor, *Amerasia Journal*, University of California, Los Angeles, Calif.

Fred Cordova, B.S.S.
  Director of Public Information, Seattle University, Seattle, Wash.

Donald F. Duff, M.D.
  Psychiatrist, San Diego, Calif.

Russell Endo, Ph.D.
  Assistant Professor of Sociology, University of Colorado, Boulder, Colorado

Stanley L. M. Fong, Ph.D.
  Assistant Professor of Psychology, California State University, Long Beach, Calif.

Irene Fujitomi, B.S.
  Graduate Student in Clinical Psychology, University of Illinois, Chicago, Ill.

Darrel E. Harris, M.A.
  Staff member, Resthaven Psychiatric Hospital, Los Angeles, Calif.

Katherine Huang, M.S.W.
  Psychiatric Social Worker, Resthaven Psychiatric Hospital, Los Angeles, Calif.

Richard A. Kalish, Ph.D.
  Visiting Scholar, Graduate Theological Union, Berkeley, Calif.

Harry H. L. Kitano, Ph.D.
  Director, University of California Education Abroad Program, Tokyo, Japan

Stanford Lyman, Ph.D.
  Professor of Sociology, New School for Social Research, New York, N.Y.

Gary M. Matsumoto, M.D.
  Surgical Resident, Tufts University Medical School, Medford, Mass.

Minoru Masuda, Ph.D.
  Professor of Psychiatry, University of Washington School of Medicine, Seattle, Wash.

Connie G. W. Meredith, M.A.
  Assistant Professor of Human Development, University of Hawaii, Honolulu, Hawaii

Gerald M. Meredith, Ph.D.
Chief Evaluation Officer, University of Hawaii, Honolulu, Hawaii

James K. Morishima, Ph.D.
Chairman of Asian-American Studies, Associate Professor of Higher Education, and Director of Institutional Educational Research, University of Washington, Seattle, Wash.

Dennis Ogawa, Ph.D.
Assistant Professor, American Studies, University of Hawaii, Honolulu, Hawaii

Harvey Peskin, Ph.D.
Professor, Department of Psychology, San Francisco State University, San Francisco, Calif.

Lindbergh S. Sata, M.D.
Director, Psychiatry Department, Harborview Hospital, and Associate Professor, Department of Psychiatry, University of Washington, Seattle, Wash.

Kenneth M. Stein, Ph.D.
Director, Community Program, Resthaven Psychiatric Hospital, Los Angeles, Calif.

Derald Wing Sue, Ph.D.
Assistant Professor of Psychology, University of Santa Clara, Santa Clara, Calif.

Stanley Sue, Ph.D.
Assistant Professor of Psychology, University of Washington, Seattle, Wash.

Nathanial N. Wagner, Ph.D.
Professor of Psychology and Director of Clinical Psychology Training, University of Washington, Seattle, Wash.

Melford S. Weiss, Ph.D.
Associate Professor of Anthropology, Sacramento State University, Sacramento, Calif.

Diane Wong, B.A.
Graduate student in Higher Education, University of Washington, Seattle, Wash.

Samuel Y. Yuen, M.A.
Director, Self-Help-for-the-Elderly Program, San Francisco, Calif.

Asian-Americans
Psychological Perspectives

Edited by:

Stanley Sue, Ph.D.

Nathaniel N. Wagner, Ph.D.

Science and Behavior Books, Inc.
Ben Lomond, California 1973

Library of Congress Card Number 72-84064
ISBN 0-8314-0033-1

Table of Contents

Foreword   xi

Preface   xiii

Acknowledgments   xv

Part One

Introductory Section

   Introduction   1

1. The Jap Image
   Dennis Ogawa   3

2. The Evacuation: Impact on the Family
   James K. Morishima   13

3. Red Guard on Grant Avenue: The Rise of Youthful Rebellion in Chinatown
   Stanford Lyman   20

4. A White View of American Racism
   Nathaniel N. Wagner   45

5. Passive Discrimination: The Normal Person
   Harry H. L. Kitano   54

Part Two

Assimilation and Sex Roles

   Introduction   63

6. Ethnic Identity: Honolulu and Seattle Japanese-Americans
   Gary M. Matsumoto, Gerald M. Meredith, and *Minoru Masuda*   65

7. Modern Perspectives and Traditional Ceremony: A Chinese-American Beauty Pageant
   Melford S. Weiss 75

8. Sex Role Strain and Personality Adjustment of China-born Students in America: A Pilot Study
   Stanley L. M. Fong and *Harvey Peskin* 79

9. Selective Acculturation and the Dating Process: The Pattern of Chinese-Caucasian Inter-racial Dating
   Melford S. Weiss 86

10. Sex Temperament among Japanese-American College Students in Hawaii
    Gerald M. Meredith 95

Part Three

Personality

   Introduction 103

11. Acculturation and Personality among Japanese-American College Students in Hawaii
    Gerald M. Meredith and *Connie G. W. Meredith* 104

12. Chinese-American Personality and Mental Health
    Stanley Sue and *Derald Wing Sue* 111

13. Jade Snow Wong and the Fate of Chinese-American Identity
    Lowell Chun-Hoon 125

14. The Filipino-American, There's Always an Identity Crisis
    Fred Cordova 136

15. Ethnic Identity: The Impact of Two Cultures on the Psychological Development of Asians in America
    Derald Wing Sue 140

16. Musings of a Hyphenated American
    Lindbergh S. Sata 150

Part Four

Mental Health

   Introduction 159

17. Japanese-American Crime and Delinquency
    Harry H. L. Kitano 161

18. Juvenile Delinquency in San Francisco's Chinese-American Community: 1961-1966
    Kenneth A. Abbott and *Elizabeth Lee Abbott* 171

19. Japanese-American Mental Illness
     Harry H. L. Kitano   181

20. Between Two Worlds: Filipinos in the U.S. Navy
     Donald F. Duff and *Ransom J. Arthur*   202

21. Mental Illness and the Role of Mental Health Facilities in Chinatown
     Timothy R. Brown, Kenneth M. Stein, Katherine Huang, and *Darrel E. Harris*   212

Part Five

Contemporary Issues
     Introduction   235

22. Americans of East Asian Ancestry: Aging and the Aged
     Richard A. Kalish and *Samuel Y. Yuen*   236

23. The New Asian-American Woman
     Irene Fujitomi and *Diane Wong*   252

24. Division and Unity: Social Process in a Chinese-American Community
     Melford S. Weiss   264

25. Community Intervention: Implications for Action
     Stanley Sue   274

26. Whither Ethnic Studies: A Re-examination of Some Issues
     Russell Endo   281

27. Filipinos: A Minority within a Minority
     Nathaniel N. Wagner   295

Appendix: 1970 Census Bureau Tables   300

Foreword

It is a difficult and painful recognition for most members of minority groups to become aware that they know only the barest essentials about members of other minority groups. What they do know often is information from the mass media which at its worst perpetuates racial stereotypes, and at its best, in its attempts to educate the masses, oversimplifies past and present. Even friendships between different minority group members do not often reveal many of the hidden dynamics which determine value systems and behaviors of various cultures. There is so much pain and anguish associated with the existence of being a minority group member in America that we cannot often share our feelings and perceptions easily except with our own.

It is from this perspective that I, as a Black American, read this book about the Asian-American experience. It is basically unimportant what my previous conceptions of Asian-Americans were. What is important is that after reading this anthology I not only had a better understanding of Asian-Americans, but my capacity to identify with the anger of the Asian-American, who is crying out against American racism, was greatly enhanced.

There are some striking similarities and some striking contrasts between experiences of Blacks in America and experiences of the different Asian-American groups. No other minority culture has had the hardship,

brutalism, destruction of family structure, and shameful sexual abuse that Blacks experienced during their period of slavery in America. However, White America almost destroyed the Chinese immigrant family by restrictive anti-Chinese immigration laws which ultimately not only limited the numbers of Chinese laborers entering the United States, but also prevented Chinese women from joining their men who had entered the country prior to 1882. No other minority group has had the shameful experience of forced confinement and evacuation as did the 110,000 Japanese residing on the West Coast in 1942. However, many Black Americans have wondered if history would repeat itself concerning them.

When one reads passages from the article by Ogawa (Chapter 1) which describes the stereotypes of Japanese-Americans, the similarity of these racist views to Black stereotypes is chilling. The highly sexualized aspects of White racism also are familiar.

The maintenance of cultural traditions, the stability of the family unit, and the strong pressures for conformity and suppression of individual, strong passions in the Asian community make for the most striking differences between Blacks and Asians. The two minorities, however, could be viewed as learning from each other. Blacks are recapturing a pride in their African heritage. Blacks are struggling to build strong family units while young Asian-

Americans are modifying the tendency to suppress outrage and are speaking out forthrightly and militantly against discriminatory practices.

When I read the article by Sue and Sue (Chapter 12) on "Chinese-American Personality and Mental Health," I could not help but reflect upon the sometimes-bitter struggle within the Black community between Blacks who wish to be integrated into White society (marginal man) and Blacks who wish to preserve certain Black value systems in the formation of a new identity (Asian-American). The personality conflicts for individuals in comparable categories within each group are very similar.

Facility in the language of the majority culture makes life less complicated for the minority member. I had never before realized the asset the Black American possesses vis-á-vis the Chinese-American as an exit from poverty and ghetto life.

The minority female, whether Asian-American or Black, asks a similar question in today's society. Can she obtain her own libera-tion from racist and sexist views without getting into a major conflict with her minority male? It is ironic that, although the historical perspective and traditional role of the Black woman and Asian woman are almost polar opposites, the contemporary struggle for these two women is the same.

My thoughts could continue for several more pages, but a foreword should only be a small hors d'oeuvre in preparation for the main course. I would like to thank Drs. Sue and Wagner for the opportunity to add the personal reflections of a Black American to their book. It is my dream that some future day minority Americans will be able to link hands and march as one against the common enemy, racism. That dream also includes minority Americans joining with White Americans to eradicate racism. I think I now am better prepared to help in achievement of this dream than before reading this book.

William M. Womack, M.D.
Assistant Professor
Department of Psychiatry
University of Washington

Preface

The growing interest in the experiences and problems of minority groups has not resulted in much greater understanding of Asian-Americans (Chinese, Filipinos, Japanese, Koreans, etc.). To a considerable extent, Asian-Americans are still members of an "invisible" minority. Our dissatisfaction with the lack of knowledge and systematic study of these minority groups provided us with the impetus to organize this book. The task of developing courses on Asian-Americans without adequate resource materials has been one steeped in frustrations. In the study of Asian-Americans, students have had to rely upon essays, the anecdotal experiences of some Asians, and the few published studies which are often difficult to obtain. Furthermore, the general understanding of Asian-Americans has been based upon stereotypes, contact with a few members of these minorities, or personal experiences in "Chinatowns" and "Little Tokyos" as tourists and sightseers.

We have a singular purpose in this book: the integration of research findings with impressionistic material to provide a better understanding of Asian-Americans. This task has been both easy and difficult. Selection of articles for this book was facilitated by the relatively small number of articles from which to choose. The paucity of literature, however, has limited the scope and depth of the book. Coverage of Asian groups other than Chinese and Japanese has

been particularly inadequate. We know it is a cliché, but it is still true: more research is needed!

Selections in this volume are diversified. Topics range from racism to mental health and from assimilation to community intervention. Content varies according to the specific Asian group being discussed. Writing styles of contributors are also quite different. Conversational articles, as well as more technical reporting, have been included. Contributors have used different data sources. Some have reported personal and impressionistic observations; others have reviewed and integrated existing literature. Many have presented findings of their own research. It is interesting to note that almost all research data on Asian-Americans are descriptive or correlative. Experimental studies would not be very fruitful in the absence of more basic knowledge. Compared to White Americans, Asian-Americans have only begun to be researched. The reason for these deficits in our knowledge is probably the fact that experimenters have lacked interest in Asian-Americans or have encountered problems in obtaining an adequate Asian sample, in overcoming language problems, and in reducing the reluctance of Asian subjects to participate in research.

We have included writings and research of both Asian-Americans and non-Asian-Americans. We have looked for the best scholarship we could find. It is our strongly held belief that, while being a member of a particular minority group sensitizes that individual to the problems and experiences of that group, sensitivity, understanding, and scholarship run deeper than skin color.

We feel indebted to Timothy Brown, Russell Endo, Irene Fujitomi, Darrel Harris, Katherine Huang, James Morishima, Lindbergh Sata, Kenneth Stein, Derald Sue, Melford Weiss, and Diane Wong for their original contributions and to the authors and publishers who have given their permission to reprint their articles and book chapters. We also wish to thank our publishers, Science and Behavior Books, Inc., for their encouragement and willingness to venture into this neglected area.

Stanley Sue, Ph.D.
Assistant Professor of Psychology

Nathaniel N. Wagner, Ph.D.
Professor of Psychology &
Director of Clinical
    Psychology Training

Acknowledgments

Part One

1. Reprinted by permission from *From Japs to Japanese: The Evolution of Japanese-American Stereotypes*, written by Dennis Ogawa. Copyright 1971 by Dennis Ogawa and published by McCutchan.

3. Reprinted by permission from *The Asian in the West*. Copyright 1970 by Desert Research Institute.

5. Reprinted by permission from the *Journal of Social Psychology*, 1966, 70, 23-31. Copyright 1966 by the Journal Press.

Part Two

6. Reprinted by permission from *Journal of Cross-Cultural Psychology*, 1970, 1, 63-76. Copyright 1970 by the *Journal of Cross-Cultural Psychology*.

8. Reprinted by permission from the *Journal of Abnormal Psychology*, 1969, 74, 563-567. Copyright 1969 by the American Psychological Association.

9. Reprinted by permission from the *Journal of Marriage and the Family*, 1970, 32, 273-278. Copyright 1970 by the National Council on Family Relations.

10. Reprinted by permission from the *Journal of Social Psychology*, 1969, 77, 149-156. Copyright 1969 by the Journal Press.

Part Three

11. Reprinted by permission from the *Journal of Social Psychology*, 1966, 68, 175-182. Copyright 1966 by the Journal Press.

12. Reprinted (with modification) by permission from *Amerasia Journal*, 1971, 1, 36-49. Copyright 1971 by the Yale Asian-American Student Association.

13. Reprinted by permission from *Amerasia Journal*, 1971, 1, 52-63. Copyright 1971 by the Yale Asian-American Student Association.

14. Reprinted by permission from the *Seattle Times*, July 5, 1970. Copyright 1970 by the *Seattle Times*.

Part Four

17. Reprinted by permission from the *Journal of Psychology*, 1967, 66, 253-263. Copyright 1967 by the Journal Press.

ACKNOWLEDGMENTS

18. Reprinted by permission from the *Journal of Sociology*, 1968, 4, 45-56. Publication of National Taiwan University.

19. Reprinted by permission from *Changing Perspectives in Mental Illness*, edited by Stanley Plog and Robert Edgerton. Copyright 1969 by Holt, Rinehart, and Winston, Inc.

20. Reprinted by permission from the *American Journal of Psychiatry*, 1967, 123, 836-843. Copyright 1967 by the American Psychiatric Association.

Part Five

22. Reprinted by permission from *The Gerontologist*, 1971, 2, 36-47. Copyright 1971 by the Gerontological Society.

Part One: Introductory Section

Introduction

In the minds of most individuals, Asian-Americans cannot be identified with oppressed minorities such as Native Americans, Blacks, and Chicanos. High levels of education and low official rates of mental illness, juvenile delinquency, and divorce characterize Chinese and Japanese in the United States (Sue & Kitano, in press). In fact, Chinese and Japanese have been labeled as members of a model minority.

The proclamation of Asians as being a successful minority is premature at best and totally inaccurate at worst. Certainly Filipinos do not even share the apparent success of Chinese and Japanese. In addition, the relatively high level of educational attainment has not resulted in superior financial income. Daniels and Kitano (1970) note that, for comparable levels of education, White Americans have a greater median income than that of Asian-Americans. Although divorce rates among Asians in America are quite low, there is evidence that they are increasing; and the number of "emotional divorces" (i.e., those not legally obtained) is not a part of official statistics. Asian cultural values strongly dictate against formal divorces. As for mental illness, there is general agreement that official rates, again, do not accurately reflect the psychological well-being of Asian-Americans. Cultural factors often make the individual reluctant to seek mental health services. Statistics based on the number of persons seeking treatment severely underestimate the number of Asian-Americans actually needing help. In order to provide a better estimate of mental health problems, one research strategy would be to observe the frequency and severity of emotional and behavioral difficulties in non-patient groups. In a study of "normal" Chinese-American students at the University of California, Berkeley, Sue and Kirk (1972) found that they exhibited greater feelings of loneliness, isolation, anxiety, and discomfort than other students in the general student body. Finally, recent killings in San Francisco's Chinatown, the rise of Chinese youth-gangs, and the militancy of Asian-Americans at colleges and universities all indicate that feelings of frustration, dissatisfaction, and oppression which were previously rarely aired are now surfacing.

The papers in this introductory section discuss prejudice and discrimination. Understanding of the experience of Asian-Americans would not be complete without an analysis of historical and contemporary forms of racism. In the first paper, Ogawa (Chapter 1) presents the past stereotypes of Japanese-Americans. From a review of early literature, he concludes that Japanese were considered highly un-American, inferior citizens, sexually aggressive, and part of an international menace. So negative were these stereotypes that the period prior to 1942 can be characterized as fostering a "Jap" image. These negative stereotypes helped to provide a

1

rationale for one of the greatest atrocities committed in American history — the internment of over 110,000 Japanese during World War II. Japanese were "sneaky," "conniving," and "un-American" and therefore deserved imprisonment. The fact that massive acts of sabotage did not happen or that many, many Japanese fought patriotically during the war made no difference. Morishima (Chapter 2) discusses the effects, based on an informal survey of Japanese in the Los Angeles area, of the internment on Japanese-Americans.

The immigration of Chinese to this country also resulted in a series of discriminatory acts and laws. Lyman (Chapter 3) provides an historical account of the problems encountered by the Chinese. He also presents an interesting description and analysis of youthful gangs in Chinatown. Disillusioned with the "American Dream" and dissatisfied with the poverty of Chinatown, many Chinese youths have organized to demand social reform.

The final two papers focus on racism as a strong part of culture. Wagner (Chapter 4) analyzes American racism from an historical perspective. Factors perpetuating prejudice and discrimination are so pervasive that flagrant examples of the oppression of minorities can be found in institutional practices, as noted by Wagner. A study by Kitano (Chapter 5) indicates that Japanese-Americans exhibit "passive" discrimination toward other groups because of the internalization of, and the conformity to, dominant values in the Japanese subculture. The significance of this finding, however, is not that Japanese exhibit discrimination. Rather, discrimination is often perpetuated by the folkways, customs, and values of *any* society.

References

Daniels, R., and Kitano, H. H. *American Racism.* Englewood Cliffs, N.J.: Prentice-Hall, 1970.

Kitano, H. H. *Japanese-Americans. The Evolution of a Subculture.* Englewood Cliffs, N.J.: Prentice-Hall, 1969.

Sue, D. W., and Kirk, B. A. "Psychological Characteristics of Chinese-American Students." *Journal of Counseling Psychology,* 19, 1972, 471-478.

Sue, S., and Kitano, H. H. "Stereotypes as a Measure of Success." *Journal of Social Issues,* 1973, in press.

1. The Jap Image

by Dennis Ogawa

Anglo-Americans have been notorious for their ill-treatment of non-Anglos. The American Indian, the Catholic, the Irish, the Negro, the Mexican, the Spanish, the East European have all felt the heavy hand of Anglo discrimination and stereotyping. The Japanese immigrant to America was no exception.

Actually, however, the stereotype which the Japanese-American first generated was quite positive. Although there was considerable anti-Chinese sentiment in California, this sentiment was not transferred to the Japanese immigrant of the late nineteenth century. In the *San Francisco Chronicle* on June 17, 1869, an editorial pointed out that "the objections raised against the Chinese ... cannot be alleged against the Japanese ... they have brought their wives, children and ... new industries among us."[1]

Even in 1893 newspapers still carried favorable Japanese stereotypes. The *Sacramento Bee* in that year was referring to Japanese as "more docile and obedient than the Chinese."[2]

Inevitably, as the anti-Chinese movement waned, and Japanese immigration numbers rose, Anglo wrath turned to the Japanese. No longer "docile and obedient," new labels and images came to be associated with the Japanese. These new and highly negative stereotypes were to circulate in the Anglo community throughout the first forty years of the twentieth century, and result in the passage of a 1924 immigration law excluding Oriental immigrants from the United States. This sentiment climaxed with the wholesale imprisonment of Japanese-Americans in 1942.

To facilitate an analysis of the Japanese-American stereotype which existed prior to 1942, four major stereotypes are presented: highly un-American, inferior citizens, sexually aggressive, and part of an international menace. None is mutually exclusive of the other, but all four, nebulously combined, comprised the portrait of the Japanese-American in the Anglo mind.

Highly Un-American

A certain degree of prejudice is characteristic of any cultural group; foreign customs and traditions are naturally thought inferior or undesirable by the natives. The alien must always encounter the cultural transformation inherent in immigration, and realize that, if he wishes to become a member of that society, he must be assimilated into its cultural milieu.

The Japanese immigrant in 1900 encountered a culture, social system, and language radically different from his former experience. The color of his skin, his slanted eyes, his small stature, his diet, his language, and his religion were so different from the Anglo that he aroused nationalistic feelings. He was little; he looked different; he talked funny.

Consequently, one of the most predominate

stereotypes that developed about the Japanese-American was that he was highly un-American; the Japanese were unassimilable into the mainstream of American society.

James Duval Phelan was mayor of San Francisco in 1900, and, like many Californians, saw Japanese as unassimilable and alien creatures. The *San Francisco Examiner* and *Chronicle* of May 8, 1900, ran the following quotation from Phelan:

> The Chinese and Japanese are not bona fide citizens. They are not the stuff of which American citizens can be made.... Personally, we have nothing against Japanese, but as they will not assimilate with us and their social life is so different from ours, let them keep at a respectful distance.[3]

This same stereotype of the Japanese appeared in the *San Francisco Chronicle* on February 23, 1905. Maintaining the same spirit of excluding Japanese from American society, the *Chronicle* argued that the Japanese laborers had no inclination to assimilate, and were, by reason of their race, habits, mode of living, disposition, and general characteristics, culturally undesirable:

> The Asiatic can never be other than an Asiatic, however much he may imitate the dress of the White man, learn his language, and spend his wage for him. Nor will he ever have the slightest concern with our laws except to evade them, nor with our government except to cajole it and to deceive it. The Japanese in California is just as though he had never left Yokohama or the rice fields of his native country.[4]

The prevailing mood throughout the first few decades of the 1900s was that, as far as Anglos were concerned, a Jap was a Jap. Whether from Tokyo or Los Angeles, the Japanese was culturally, racially, and ethnically a Jap, despite any attempts at assimilation.

In 1909, *The Valor of Ignorance* was published. It was a book devoted to analyzing the Japanese problem in California. Its author, Homer Lea, argued that "a nation may be kept intact only so long as its ruling element remains homogeneous ... [racial similarity was the cornerstone of national security]. Assimilation was out of the question since racially there existed no relationship between the people of Japan and of the U.S."[5] Hence, by Lea's logic, Californians were led to believe that, in order to protect America and keep her strong, the unassimilable Japanese had to be eliminated.

The originator of the move to exclude Japanese-Americans was the Asiatic Exclusion League. The major argument by the League was that since Japanese were so un-American they had no place in America. A May 1910 bulletin stated that:

> 1. We cannot assimilate them [Japanese] without injury to ourselves.
> 2. No large community of foreigners, so cocky, with such distinct racial, social, and religious prejudices, can abide long in this country without serious frictions.[6]

In 1924, the Japanese-American exclusion movement culminated in a new immigration law that prohibited Oriental immigration to the United States. Again, the predominate stereotype perpetuated was that of the unassimilable Jap. Before the United States Senate, V. S. McClatchy, leader of a three-man exclusionist delegation lobbying for the immigration law, testified that:

> The Japanese are less assimilable and more dangerous as residents in this country than any other of the peoples ineligible under our laws.... With great pride of race, they have no idea of assimilating in the sense of amalgamation. They do not come here with any desire or any intent to lose their racial or national identity. They come here specifically and professedly for the purpose of colonizing and establishing here permanently the proud Yamato race. They never cease being Japanese.[7]

The racists had achieved their goals in the twenties and consequently could find no new issues to arouse public opinion against the Japanese-Americans, and stereotypes lay dormant in the Anglo mind and media throughout the thirties. However, with the Japanese attack on Pearl Harbor, these dormant impressions were reawakened and found new means of expression and new aims. If Japanese-American stereotypes had been used prior to 1924 to exclude new Japanese, the same stereotypes were now used to place the existing Japanese-Americans in concentration camps.

That the Japanese-American was unassimilable, loyal to Japan and not to America, was a stereotype frequently employed after December 7, 1941. The *Contra Costa Gazette*, for example, emphatically stated that "a Jap is a Jap and will never be anything else, whether he is born in California or Tokyo. He is taught from infancy that his first duty is to the Mikado." The paper also asserted:

> Many of the Jap aviators shot down in the attack on Pearl Harbor were discovered to be American born and graduates of various schools in this country. Therefore, there is ample evidence that the American-born Japanese owe their first allegiance to the "Son of Heaven" ruler of their parents.[8]

Military commander for the West Coast, General J. L. DeWitt, testified before the House Naval Affairs Subcommittee in 1943 on the relocation of Japanese-Americans. Two of his most-often-quoted remarks will suffice to illustrate the General's viewpoint on Japanese unassimilability:

> A Jap's a Jap. They are a dangerous element, whether loyal or not. There is no way to determine their loyalty.... It makes no difference whether he is an American; theoretically, he is still a Japanese and you can't change him.... You can't change him by giving him a piece of paper.
>
> The Japanese race is an enemy race and, while many second- and third-generation Japanese, born on United States soil, possessed of United States citizenship, have become "Americanized," the racial strains are undiluted.[9]

Following World War II, the War Relocation Authority did a study on contemporary myths concerning Japanese-Americans. Again the stereotype of the Japanese as being unassimilable and highly un-American was evident: "The religion of the Japanese, no matter where they live, binds them to the Emperor. They all have Shinto shrines in their homes."

Equally widespread in the West Coast states was the myth: "Japanese language schools were maintained in many communities on the West Coast before the war to inculcate American-born Japanese with the national ideals of the Japanese Imperial Government."[10]

Inferior Citizens

Naturally, to the Anglo-American, the un-American Japanese would make an inferior citizen. He possessed many undesirable personality traits and he was a dangerous agrarian neighbor.

To the American mentality, certain behavior traits have been traditionally abhorred. The Protestant ethic stressed hard work, honesty, integrity, and frugality, as well as a sense of sportsmanship. Laziness, dishonesty, untrustworthiness, spendthriftiness, and connivance have always been undesirable social traits. And so it was that Americans, prior to 1942, consistently stereotyped Japanese-Americans as lazy, dishonest and untrustworthy. Japanese had none of the admirable personal qualities which characterized good citizens like Benjamin Franklin or Horatio Alger.

The *Pacific Rural Press* in 1906 expressed the inferiority of the Japanese personality when it emphatically pointed out that "the Chinese are the most skillful, trustworthy, and devoted laborers California ever had, while the Japanese are careless, preoccupied, and untrustworthy."[11]

The next year, Wallace Irwin published "Letters of a Japanese Schoolboy," which was serialized and widely read on the West Coast. These letters stereotyped the Japanese as: bucktoothed, bespectacled, tricky, wordy, arrogant, dishonest figures. Coined also was "Jap" speech, especially honorifics such as "Honorable Sir" and "so sorry, please." Both the "Jap" speech and image were later promulgated in comic strips and pulp magazines. To have this sort of individual as a neighbor seemed inconceivable to an Anglo community saturated with these negative images of the Japanese-American.

The Asiatic Exclusion League, in its attempts to stir public opinion against the Japanese, perpetuated the stereotype of the inferior citizen. In its 1910 position paper, the League claimed that "we cannot compete with a people having a low standard of civilization, living, and wages."[12]

Anglos often viewed the Japanese-Americans as being filthy and ignorant of personal hygiene. The publication of the Native Sons of the Golden West, the *Grizzly Bear*, stated in February, 1920, that Japanese were unclean and "if people knew how Japs raised their garden truck, they would never let a bit of it pass their lips."[13]

This stereotype reappeared in 1935 in the *American Defender*, a magazine put out by an anti-Japanese group, the Committee of One Thousand. In it they related that:

> [Wherever] the Japanese have settled, their nests pollute the communities like the running sores of leprosy. They exist like the yellowed, smoldering, discarded butts in an over-full ashtray, vilifying the air with their loathsome smells, filling all who have misfortune to look upon them with a wholesome disgust and a desire to wash.[14]

The general Anglo attitude towards the Japanese-American personality was expressed in a 1920 hearing before the Senate Committee on Immigration and Naturalization, when the then-Senator Phelan stated that "Japanese are an immoral people ... (who lead) California toward mongrelization and degeneracy."[15] One California legislator went so far as to describe Japanese as "bandy-legged bugaboos, miserable, craven, simian, degenerated, rotten little devils."[16]

This stereotype was also evident in the statements and literature concerning the Japanese farmer who, on the West Coast, was in a precarious situation: the American and Japanese values taught him to be industrious and hard-working, but the harder the Japanese farmer tried to be successful, the more he was hated by his Anglo neighbors.

In 1905, the *San Francisco Chronicle* asserted that at least 100,000 of "the little brown men" were undercutting White labor and in a subsequent article, it pointed out that "the Chinese are faithful laborers and do not buy land.... The Japanese are unfaithful laborers and do buy land."[17]

In 1920, Wallace Irwin published another highly anti-Japanese novel, *Seed of the Sun*, which was serialized in the *Saturday Evening Post*. In this novel, a Baron Tagumi slyly masterminds Japanese land acquisitions as part of the Mikado's plan for world sovereignty.

In the same year, the American Legion produced a movie, the *Shadows of the West*, which portrayed lurid Japanese characters, among them one who controlled the statewide vegetable market over a wireless apparatus. Other Japanese were shown dumping vegetables into the harbor to maintain high prices.

This stereotype, motivated by a fear of Japanese economic success, was enhanced by the governor of California, William Stephens, who declared in 1920, that "Japanese operate 623,752 acres of the very best lands in California,"[18] insinuating that the best lands were being held and consequently ruined by Japanese. The low standard of living of the Japanese farmer was noted by Congressman E. A. Hayes, who proclaimed:

> As is well known, no White man can compete with the Japanese laborers. They are satisfied to be housed in such cramped and squalid quarters as few White men ... could live in, and the food that keeps them in condition would be too cheap and poor to satisfy the most common laborer in this country.[19]

Thus, especially to those Anglos in California, before 1942, the Japanese possessed traits as a person and a farmer which rendered him an undesirable neighbor and an inferior citizen.

Sexually Aggressive

To some extent, ethnic and racial stereotyping follows a pattern. Different groups share many of the same stereotyped characteristics: they are viewed as too different to be assimilated into American society, and they are often viewed as sexually aggressive. It is true of the welfare-collecting Black rapist, the lazy Mexican pimp, and the Japanese-American before 1942.

One of the most visceral images in the Anglo mind is that of intercourse between a White woman and a man of another race. Nothing strikes more at the White man's heart than his women being molested by Blacks, Browns, or Yellows.

As early as 1892, the *Sacramento Daily Record Union* was portraying Japanese "as men who know no morals but vice, who sit beside White daughters and debauch and demoralize them."[20]

The image of the sexually aggressive Japanese was also propagated by quite a few political figures. In 1909, Grover Johnson, father of Hiram Johnson, regularly and publicly denounced the Japanese in his speeches with statements such as:

> I am responsible to the mothers and fathers of Sacramento County who have their little daughters sitting side-by-side in the school rooms with matured Japs, with their base minds, their lascivious thoughts, multiplied by their race and strengthened by their mode of life.... I have seen Japanese twenty-five years old sitting in the seats next to the pure maids of California ... I shudder ... to think of such a condition."[21]

One concerned mother, writing in the March, 1913, *Grizzly Bear*, warned that "it is not unusual these days to find ... Japanese casting furtive glances at our young women.

They would like to marry them."[22] The *San Francisco Chronicle* in 1920 editorialized:

> The Japanese boys are taught by their elders to look upon ... American girls with a view to future sex relations.... What answer will the fathers and mothers of America make ...?
>
> The proposed assimilation of the two races is unthinkable. It is morally indefensible and biologically impossible. American womanhood is by far too sacred to be subjected to such degeneracy. An American who would not die fighting rather than yield to that infamy does not deserve the name.[23]

As often is the case, perpetuation of sexually aggressive stereotypes occurs in news reports of current events. The *San Francisco Examiner* in 1920 ran a headline which stated "Jap attacks girl, beaten by mother."[24] A Los Angeles paper published a story of an alleged Japanese attempt to poison a "society woman." "There were placed in her food," so the story went, "a dozen small pieces of sharp bamboo splinters, each enclosed within a binding gut."[25]

The 1920 movie, *Shadows of the West*, depicted two White girls being kidnapped by a group of Japanese men. Fortunately, however, they were rescued by a posse of American Legionnaires in the end.

Another stereotype which enhanced the sexually aggressive image of the Japanese-American was that the Japanese birth rate was tremendous, and thereby a threat to the purity of the Anglo race. Grover Johnson was warning Californians in 1909 that the greatest danger of the Japanese was their high birth rate. These fears were also expressed by exclusionist McClatchy who stated that "the biological fecundity of the Japanese is so great that in a limited time, I think sixty-four years, the entire state will be Japanese."[26]

On January 20, 1942, a Dr. W. R. Livingstone told a group at Oxnard, California, that "unless adequate preventive measures are enforced, the Japs will eventually overrun California and the Pacific Coast just as the rabbits, brought to Australia, have overrun that

Island."[27] Even after the Japanese were relocated, separation of the sexes was often advocated so that relocation centers would not become "breeding farms."[28]

Part of an International Menace

Not only was the Japanese-American stereotyped as an internal threat to Anglos but also as an international threat to America. From the victory of Japan in the Russo-Japanese War to the attack on Pearl Harbor, Japan was considered an increasingly menacing power in the Pacific. And as Japanese power grew, the unrest and fears of those on the West Coast of the United States, who might be affected by this Yellow Peril, grew. Logically, or illogically, this mistrust of the Japanese power was extended to the Japanese-American. Somehow the Japanese immigrant became part of an international conspiracy to turn the West Coast into a bastion of the Japanese Empire.

The first evidence of this stereotype of the Japanese-American as being part of a Yellow Peril appeared on December 20, 1906. The *San Francisco Examiner* began warning people that Japanese laborers were spies; its headline page read: "Japan Sounds Our Coast, Brown Men Have Maps and Could Land Easily."[29] In 1907, the *Examiner* insisted that the Japanese were "the most secretive people in the world" and that they were "rushing forward with feverish haste, stupendous preparation for war ... the war ... to be with America."[30]

During the years 1911-1915, many myths circulated about the threat posed by Japan and the part played by Japanese-Americans. Carey McWilliams reports some of the false rumors which abounded at this time:

> In 1911, it was widely reported in this country, with thrilling details, that Japan was taking steps to secure from Mexico a naval base at Magdalena Bay, in Lower California. This had followed a report in 1910 that the Japanese had sunk our drydock Dewey in Manila Bay, after planting mines which imperiled our navy at the station. They also had secretly

charted our California harbors. Then there were numerous plottings with Mexico for a position from which this country could be attacked. A combination with Germany to destroy the Monroe Doctrine was the pabulum served up to the American public in 1912. In the same year, Japan was forming an alliance with the West Coast Indians to gain a military foot-hold in this country. In 1915, Japanese spies were seen in the Panama fortifications, and, in the next year, Japan was found conspiring to get a foot-hold in Panama by getting control of the San Blas Indian lands. Japan's diplomats penned Carranga's protests against our invasion of Mexico, after there had been landed in that country two hundred thousand Japanese troops, who had already fired on American troops at Mayatton.[31]

Throughout 1915 and 1916, sensational anti-Japanese stories were perpetuated by the news and principally the Hearst Press. A "Hymn of Hate" popularizing these stories was circulated on July 23, 1916, in the *Los Angeles Examiner.* One stanza read:

> They've battleships, they say,
> On Magdalena Bay!
> Uncle Sam, won't you listen when we
>   warn you?
> They meet us with a smile
> But they're working all the while,
> And they're waiting just to steal
>   our California!
> So just keep your eyes on Togo,
> With his pockets full of maps,
> For we've found out we can't trust
>   the Japs![32]

In 1916, the International Film Corporation, part of the Hearst Empire, produced a motion picture called *Patria.* It was described by a Captain George Lester to a Senate Investigating Committee as one with:

> ... three barrels. Its principal excuse was preparedness. But by the time the first episodes were released [it was a ten-part serial] the country was already committed to that. Therefore, only the other two elements, anti-Mexican and anti-Japanese propaganda, remained

active. These showed the attempt by Japan to conquer America with the aid of Mexico. A Japanese noble, at the head of the secret service of the Emperor in America, was the chief villain. Japanese troops invaded California, committing appropriate atrocities [the chief of which was the attempted rape of the heroine, played by Irene Castle].[33]

The 1920 movie, *Shadows of the West*, also depicted Japanese involved with spying for Japan, and it should be remembered that in *Seeds of the Sun* (1920), Baron Tagumi was in the employ of the Mikado.

On February 21, 1940, William Randolph Hearst wrote in the *Los Angeles Examiner*:

Come out to California and see the myriads of little Japs peacefully raising fruits and flowers and vegetables on California sunshine, and saying hopefully and wistfully: "Someday I come with Japanese army and take all this. Yes, sir, thank you." Then ... see the fleets of peaceful little Japanese fishing boats, plying up and down the California coast, catching fish and taking photographs.[34]

This statement, though uncomplimentary, was mild compared to the Fifth Column rumors and fears vigorously circulated by newspapers after the bombing of Pearl Harbor. On December 16, 1941, the official Knox report on the Pearl Harbor disaster was headlined in the *San Francisco Chronicle*, "Secretary of Navy Blames 5th Column for the Raid";[35] in the *San Francisco Examiner*, "Fifth Column Prepared Attack";[36] and in the *Los Angeles Examiner*, "Fifth Column Treachery Told."[37] Headlines about the Japanese in Hawaii, however, were exceeded by those concerning West Coast Japanese: "Pacific Coast Jap Spying Exposed; Dire Peril Told";[38] "Feared ... Deadly Nest of Saboteurs on Edge of Huge ... Navy Yard";[39] "Alien Danger—L.A. County, City Dismiss Jap Workers";[40] "Immediate Evacuation of Japanese Demanded—Southern Californian. Call for Summary Action by Army after Submarine Attack."[41]

The *San Francisco Chronicle* announced that contraband goods, seized after a raid on a Jap spy ring, included a "complete set of U.S. Navy signal flags, at least five illegal radios, at least two guns, at least two illegal cameras."[42] Reporting another raid, the *San Francisco Examiner* stated that "more than 60,000 rounds of rifle ammunition, 14,900 rounds of shotgun ammunition, 378 pistol bullets, eleven still cameras were uncovered."[43] The same paper reported on December 29, 1941: "A beautiful field of flowers on the property of a Japanese farmer ... had been plowed up because the Jap was a Fifth Columnist and had grown his flowers in a way that, when viewed from a plane, formed an arrow pointing the direction to the airport."[44] The *Los Angeles Evening Herald* printed a story of Japanese placing ground glass in shrimp they were canning and spraying overdoses of arsenic on vegetables.[45]

Charges made by the press of course further impressed the Fifth Column image on the minds of the American public. The editor of the *Monterey Park Progress* asserted that Japanese were "tricky and treacherous ... scarcely a community along the Pacific Coast from Canada to Mexico but has its positive evidence of the fact that we are but inviting dire trouble by continuing to harbor those yellow creatures in our midst."[46] Between January 20 and March 16, 1942, the *San Diego Union* pointed out that there was "too much time ... wasted ... in palavering about the 'rights' of Fifth Columnists" and demanded: "What about the rights of those killed at Pearl Harbor?" The paper went on to admonish, "We are confronted on both sides by enemies who have devoted their entire careers to ... treachery, deceit, and sabotage. We can be neither soft-headed nor soft-hearted in dealing with them or their agents."[47]

Nationally syndicated columnists also devoted space to the danger of resident Japanese. Damon Runyon reported on January 4, 1942:

It would be extremely foolish to doubt

the continued existence of enemy agents among the large alien Japanese population. Only recently city health inspectors looking over a Japanese rooming house came upon a powerful transmitter, and it's reasonable to assume that menace of a similar character must be constantly guarded against throughout the war.[48]

Like Runyon, but more intemperate in his view of West Coast Japanese, was Henry McLemore, who wrote from Los Angeles on January 29, 1942, that California, because of its airplane industry and invasion-prone location, was the key state of the Union: yet "what does the Government do about the tens of thousands of Japanese in California? Nothing." What the Government should do, according to McLemore, was remove the Japanese

> to a point deep in the interior. I don't mean a nice part of the interior, either. Herd 'em in the badlands. Let 'em be pinched, hurt, hungry, and dead up against it.... If making one million innocent Japanese uncomfortable would prevent one scheming Japanese from costing the life of one American boy, then let the million innocents suffer ... let us have no patience with the enemy or with anyone whose veins carry his blood.... Personally, I hate the Japanese. And that goes for all of them.[49]

Even one of the most conscientious and liberal American political commentators was vulnerable to the hysterical stereotyping. Walter Lippmann, in a column written from San Francisco on February 20, 1942, said:

> ... the Pacific Coast is in imminent danger of a combined attack from within and from without.... It is true ... that since the outbreak of the Japanese War there has been no important sabotage on the Pacific Coast. From what we know about the Fifth Column in Europe, this is not, as some have liked to think, a sign that there is nothing to be feared. It is a sign that the blow is well organized, and that it is held back until it can be struck with maximum effect ... I am sure I understand fully and appreciate thoroughly the unwillingness of

Washington to adopt a policy of mass evacuation and internment of all those who are technically enemy aliens. But I submit that Washington is not defining the problem on the Coast correctly.... The Pacific Coast is officially a combat zone: some part of it may at any moment be a battlefield. Nobody's constitutional rights include the right to reside and do business on a battlefield. And nobody ought to be on a battlefield who has no good reason for being there.[50]

Basing a column of his own on what Lippmann had pointed out, Westbrook Pegler, the Scripps-Howard commentator, argued that:

> ... the Japanese in California should be under guard to the last man and woman right now and to hell with habeas corpus until the danger is over.... Do you get what Mr. Lippmann says? ... The enemy has been scouting our coast ... the Japs ashore are communicating with the enemy offshore and ... on the basis of "what is known to be taking place" there are signs that a well-organized blow is being withheld only until it can do the most damage....[51]

The stereotype of the Japanese-American being part of an international menace was also brought to the public's attention by political leaders. On January 30, 1942, Attorney General Earl Warren publicly declared: "I have come to the conclusion that the Japanese situation as it exists in this state today may well be the Achilles heel to the entire civilian defense effort. Unless something is done it may bring about a repetition of Pearl Harbor."[52] A few days later on February 2, 1942, Warren freely said to the Tolan Committee:

> I want to say that the consensus among the law-enforcement officers of this State is that there is more potential danger among the group of Japanese who were born in this country than from the alien Japanese who were born in Japan.

He went on to talk about the "disturbing situation" of Japanese being close to defense plants, "within a grenade throw of coast defense guns," and in the vicinity of key beaches, air fields, railroads, power lines, gas and water mains, and so on.[53]

Warren also stereotyped the Japanese as tricky and conniving. Following the same line of reasoning as Lippmann and Pegler, he stated:

> It seems to me that it is quite significant that in this great state of ours we have had no Fifth Column activities and no sabotage reported. It looks very much to me as though it is a studied effort not to have any until the zero hour arrives.[54]

Warren, however, was not the only political leader holding this stereotype. Los Angeles Mayor Fletcher Bowron on February 5, 1942, publicly announced:

> If there is intrigue going on — and it is reasonably certain that there is — right here is the hotbed, the nerve center of the spy system, of planning for sabotage. Right here in our own city are those who may spring to action at an appointed time in accordance with a prearranged plan wherein each of our little Japanese friends will know his part in the event of any possible attempted invasion or air raid.

Bowron, like Warren, did not look for isolated acts of sabotage, for the Japanese were "too smart for that."[55]

Typical of the type of stereotype statements which abounded in 1942 and which ultimately played a major part in the relocation of Japanese-Americans was one made by the deputy district attorney of Los Angeles County on February 2, 1942:

> You can't draw a distinction between the alien enemy and a Nisei; they all look alike, act alike, and think alike. . . . We have got to make a drive to do something about the American-born Japs, not the alien Jap, but the American-born. He is the danger.[56]

From 1900 to 1942 Japanese-Americans could best be termed "Japs" in terms of how Anglos viewed them. Inherent in such a word as "Jap," "kike," or "nigger" is a sense of utter inferiority; someone less than equal to the Anglo. The "Jap" before 1942 was an unassimilable, un-American creature, who was

sly, dishonest, dirty, sexually promiscuous, and aggressive. In addition, he was intimately involved with a foreign power to invade the West Coast. Indeed, the Jap was an animal, something to be kept out or caged. Yet, somehow, after 1942, this highly negative and fairly consistent stereotype disappeared, and what emerged in its place was a quite different stereotype.

Chapter Notes

1. *San Francisco Chronicle*, June 17, 1869.

2. Bradford Smith, *Americans from Japan* (New York: J. B. Lippincott Co., 1948), p. 202.

3. Daniels, *The Politics of Prejudice* (New York Atheneum, 1968), p. 21.

4. *San Francisco Chronicle*, February 23, 1905.

5. Carey McWilliams, *Prejudice* (Boston: Little, Brown & Co., 1944), p. 42.

6. Daniels, p. 28.

7. Daniels, p. 99.

8. *Contra Costa Gazette*, March 2, 1942.

9. Smith, p. 274.

10. War Relocation Authority, *Myths and Facts about the Japanese-American* (Washington, D.C.: Department of Interior, 1945), p. 7.

11. Smith, p. 204.

12. Daniels, p. 28.

13. McWilliams, p. 59.

14. *American Defender*, April 27, 1935.

15. McWilliams, p. 59.

16. McWilliams, p. 96.

17. McWilliams, p. 19.

18. K. K. Kawakami, *The Real Japanese Question* (New York: Macmillan Co., 1921), p. 25.

19. Morton Grodzins, *Americans Betrayed* (Chicago: University of Chicago Press, 1949), p. 9.

20. Daniels, p. 20.

21. Daniels, p. 47.

22. Daniels, p. 85.

23. *Los Angeles Times,* July 15, 1920.

24. *San Francisco Examiner,* November 1, 1920.

25. Kawakami, p. 140.

26. Kawakami, p. 34.

27. Grodzins, p. 49.

28. Grodzins, p. 61.

29. Kawakami, p. 83.

30. *San Francisco Examiner,* November 3, 1907.

31. McWilliams, p. 39.

32. McWilliams, p. 53.

33. Daniels, p. 76.

34. *Los Angeles Examiner,* February 21, 1940.

35. *San Francisco Chronicle,* December 16, 1941.

36. *San Francisco Examiner,* December 16, 1941.

37. *Los Angeles Examiner,* December 16, 1941.

38. *Los Angeles Times,* February 28, 1942.

39. *San Francisco Chronicle,* February 6, 1942.

40. *San Francisco Chronicle,* January 28, 1942.

41. *Los Angeles Times,* February 25, 1942.

42. *San Francisco Chronicle,* February 6, 1942.

43. *San Francisco Examiner,* February 12, 1942.

44. *San Francisco Examiner,* December 29, 1941.

45. *Los Angeles Evening Herald,* December 9, 1941.

46. *Monterey Park Progress,* February 20, 1942.

47. *San Diego Union,* February 3, 1942.

48. Grodzins, p. 386.

49. *San Francisco Examiner,* January 29, 1942.

50. *New York Herald Tribune,* February 20, 1942.

51. Grodzins, p. 388.

52. Grodzins, p. 94.

53. Allen Bosworth, *America's Concentration Camps* (New York: W. W. Norton & Co., Inc., 1967), p. 73.

54. Grodzins, p. 94.

55. Grodzins, p. 103.

56. Grodzins, p. 129.

2. The Evacuation: Impact on the Family

by James K. Morishima

The Evacuation

Although the bombing of Pearl Harbor ushered the United States into World War II, only the time and place were surprises. The United States had been gearing itself for entry into the war in Europe, and many felt the probability of war with Japan approached 1.0, particularly after Japan and the Axis joined forces and the United States froze Japanese assets in the United States in July, 1941.

In view of the history of anti-Japanese feeling exhibited by groups on the West Coast (see, for example, Daniels, 1962; Daniels and Kitano, 1970; and Ogawa, 1971), it is particularly perplexing that for six weeks following Pearl Harbor there were few voices raised against the Japanese-American (Nikkei). Organized campaigns on the West Coast against the Nikkei began in mid-January, championed by the Native Sons and Daughters of the Golden West, the Grange, the A.F. of L., the C.I.O., the American Legion, syndicated columnists, the mass media and many others. Partly as a reaction to these voices, President Roosevelt signed Executive Order 9066 on February 19, 1942.

Executive Order 9066 ushered in a shameful era, the era of the forced confinement of 110,000 Nikkei residing on the West Coast. By virtue of birth in the United States, two-thirds were American citizens. (The majority were 18 or younger.) The remainder were alien — not necessarily by choice but by American naturalization laws which prohibited their naturalization until the laws were changed in 1952. The only crime the evacuees were guilty of was being of Japanese descent.

The Nikkei from Washington, Oregon, California, and Arizona were initially removed to fifteen assembly centers located conveniently on the West Coast near Nikkei population centers. These centers, e.g., Puyallup Fair Grounds in Washington, the Santa Anita Racetrack in Los Angeles, and the Livestock Exposition Hall in Portland, Oregon, were way stations in which the Nikkei lived while awaiting the completion of their new "luxurious" quarters.

The maximum population in the assembly centers ranged from 245 in Mayer, Arizona, to 18,719 at Santa Anita. (It is interesting to note that while some justifications for evacuation were potential Fifth Column activity and proximity to the war theater, no proven cases of Fifth Column activity by Nikkei were uncovered and Hawaiian Nikkei were *not* evacuated en masse.)

Meanwhile, the Army and Nikkei volunteers worked very hard at completing the ten permanent relocation centers in such salubrious California areas as humid Rohwer and arid Tule Lake. Meyer (1971) indicated that:

> The period of moving in and getting settled ranged from May, 1942, to March, 1943. For the most part, the dazed,

confused, and frustrated evacuees arrived amidst the turmoil of partly completed, wood and tar-paper centers constructed by the Army. The buildings were like temporary barracks constructed to house soldiers in dormitory style. No cooking or plumbing facilities existed in these barracks. In each block were a mess hall and a building that provided latrines, showers, and laundry facilities.

Most centers were surrounded with woven-wire and barbed-wire fences, with watch towers for the Army guards. These centers, located in out-of-the-way places, largely desert or wastelands, were desolate and forbidding — especially during the early months. (pp. 31-32)

Photographs in such publications as Conrat and Conrat (1972), Hosokawa (1969), and Spicer (1969) strikingly illustrate Meyer's verbal description.

Introduction

While the remainder of this paper establishes the importance of the family institution, reviews the literature, and cites some previously unpublished research conducted by the author, it does not purport to be definitive.

The evacuation resulted in a wealth of literature on the experiences of the Nikkei (see, for example, Girdner and Loftis, 1969; Kitagawa, 1967; Okimoto, 1971; Okubo, 1946; tenBroek, Barnhart, and Matson, 1954; Thomas and Nishimoto, 1946; and many others). In view of the abundance of written materials and the recognized importance of the family and familial traditions among the Nikkei, it is surprising to find that very little literature exists on the impact of the evacuation on the Nikkei family.

The central role of the family in the socialization of the child and the development of his later personality is a truism. The role of the family has, however, been analyzed from a number of diverse theoretical viewpoints.

Sears, Maccoby, and Levin (1957) in a fairly atheoretical approach conducted a field study on child-rearing practices. Utilizing a role process approach, Kirkpatrick (1955) analyzed family interaction as that of the teaching and learning of roles. Bandura and Walters (1963) described the family environment as embodying the learning of behavior through imitation and modeling. Bijou and Baer (1961, 1965) utilize a Skinnerian analysis to study the behavior of children.

Throughout these publications, often written from vastly different theoretical approaches, the one factor which stands out clearly is that the family and interactions within the family effectively mold the personality of the child. These early experiences with family surrogates and peers, then, have lasting impact.

The importance of the family and familial traditions to the Nikkei also has been established by anecdote and research. Law enforcement agents are prone to ascribe the low rate of juvenile delinquency among Asian-Americans to a close-knit family which teaches "correct" values. Miyamoto (1938) and Benedict (1946) both indicate the critical nature of the family in the development of social solidarity and personality among the Nikkei.

Despite the recognition of the importance of the Nikkei family, the literature pays, in the main, little attention to that social institution. Meyer (1971) and Daniels (1971) mention the family infrequently. Hosokawa (1969) and Leighton (1945) devote slightly more space to the family, while Spicer, et al. (1969), Kitano (1969), and Petersen (1971) devote more attention to that institution. The University of California, Berkeley, series on the evacuation develops the family issue in passing but devotes little attention to the question of the effects of the evacuation on child-rearing.

Bloom (1943a, 1943b, and 1947), Broom (Bloom) and Kitsuse (1956), and the Bureau of Sociological Research (1943) have written extensively on the impact of the evacuation on the Japanese-American family. The emphasis, however, was on the adult and not on the children.

The Impact on the Adult

There is little doubt that the evacuation permanently affected the adult in the family. Some of the effects recorded in the literature, however, may not have been as pervasive as has been implied. For example, much has been made of the loss of prestige by the adult male who was no longer the sole or primary provider for the family. The data reported by Bloom and Reimer (1949) indicate that, even in an urbanized area such as Los Angeles, a large number of women were in the labor force. In proprietary businesses such as groceries, hotels, etc., women undoubtedly made contributions to the family equivalent to those made by their husbands. In many of these small businesses, the occupations of the women often went unrecorded although they made substantial income contributions. Wives in agricultural areas worked just as long and hard in the fields as did the husbands, child-rearing having been left in the hands of the older children. While the evacuation did result, then, in some husbands' losing their role as sole or primary provider, the emphasis in the existing literature may overstress the extent of the loss.

While some families may have been disrupted by the abrupt incarceration of the Issei (immigrant) males immediately after Pearl Harbor, interviews conducted by the author indicate that other families were brought together. Children who had married and left often returned home to help their parents conclude their affairs. The extended family was maintained in the relocation centers. One interviewee in Los Angeles, for example, indicated that he and his bride had moved to the Midwest where he had found a high-paying job. After the war began, he attempted to bring his parents and siblings to the Midwest but failed. The interviewee then left his job and moved to Los Angeles with his wife to help his parents divest themselves of their remaining property. He was subsequently evacuated with his parents and siblings and has been unable to break away from his parents again. While one could speculate about the potentiality of permanence of the move to the Midwest, it is clear that the war and the evacuation served as a stimulus for getting that family together again.

The relocation centers encouraged many adults to find ways of coping with an unaccustomed phenomenon — leisure. They had time to learn *go, shogi,* bridge; time to gossip, to brood, to think. Time and ennui — these were also prime ingredients for camp disruptions described by Daniels (1971).

Privacy, a sacrosanct ingredient to the Nikkei, disappeared. The ceilingless barracks transmitted sound from one end to the other. Thin partitions between units also provided little privacy. (Despite this loss of privacy, a large number of children were born during the war.) Communal showers and toilet facilities did little to encourage privacy. There was no sanctum sanctorum for a family to unwind. All was public. The Nikkei were in a glass menagerie — a small (20' x 20') room with cots and a potbelly stove.

Interview data collected by the author also reveal that, in retrospect, respondents recall that the mounting social pressures to conform — so pervasive in the Nikkei community — became almost unbearable in camp. The impact of the "Japanization" of the more assimilated Nikkei cannot be treated here. Suffice it to say that many of the interviewees felt their "Americanization" retarded and many never recouped.

As a result of the evacuation, one-fourth of those interviewed indicated that they had made conscious efforts after the war to be more American. Having ascribed the evacuation to the relative isolation of the Nikkei community and the "alien" customs of the community, these interviewees felt that, were they more American, the evacuation would not have taken place. They consequently decided that they would act more like Americans and raise their children as Americans. (Because of cultural differences, this would lead to the development of different personality types in their children.)

Many evacuees are perhaps understandably cynical about democracy as a result of their experiences. This cynicism has in many instances been transmitted to their children, but it is, perhaps, surprising to note that many students indicate their parents are unwilling or reluctant to discuss the evacuation.

The foregoing is obviously not meant to be an exhaustive iteration of the impact of the relocation and its impact on the adults in the family institution. It is meant, rather, to illustrate that the literature does not present all facets of the effects of the evacuation. This is understandable in view of the fact that the family institution was rarely the focus of the reports. Suffice it to indicate that the reports of the effects on the adults are only indicative and, like the visible surface of an iceberg, reveal only a small portion of the story. While the author reports the recollections of some Nikkei in the late 1950s, he well recognizes that memories become distorted over time and that the examples may not reflect the composite experiences of a large number of evacuees.

The Impact on the Child

For many children, the evacuation was one of the happiest periods in their lives. For the first time, many had no scarcity of friends to play with and discipline was lax. School was no longer as traumatic because the emphasis on upward mobility through education often diminished in the face of an uncertain future.

Adult interviewees, for example, recalled playing from sunrise until breakfast, going to school, playing until dinner, and then playing to a point of physical exhaustion, only to repeat the pattern every day for three years. Children tended to band together with minimal adult supervision in the relatively safe confines of a barbed wire enclosure. (There were no vehicles to keep a wary eye out for, few potential child molesters, no family enterprise to assist with, etc.)

The diminution of supervision did have a

deleterious effect on discipline. Many children ran roughshod and saw their parents only infrequently. Under these conditions the importance of the peer group increased and reliance upon the family concomitantly decreased.

For the first time in their lives, some children had Nikkei peers. Having lived in relative isolation from other Nikkei, they had had Caucasian peers in school, but now, in the isolated setting of the relocation centers, they found their peers were primarily Nikkei. These individuals had to learn a new set of values, norms, roles, etc., to interact successfully with their Nikkei peers.

For these individuals, the assimilation process was negatively impacted. The values they had learned from White peers no longer applied, and Nikkei values replaced White values. Under these conditions, then, the relatively homogeneous Nikkei value system (see Miyamoto, 1938) became the dominant theme — a theme which would retard the Americanization of many Emikos.

Mealtime, often the only time many families had to exchange experiences and opinions, virtually disappeared from the family institution. As Meyer (1971) indicated, each block had a mess hall. The communal dining facilities were not conducive to carrying on meaningful social intercourse. Spicer, et al. (1969) indicates that "family solidarity was difficult to maintain in the enforced communal living, with all 250 residents of a block eating in the same mess hall." (p. 104)

The availability of mealtimes as stimuli for interaction, then, largely disappeared. Sharing a table with other families and with other tables in propinquity does not normally encourage candid conversation. Here again, however, there were exceptions. One interviewee whose parents had owned a grocery store indicated that camp had allowed the family to eat together for the first time. Gone were the interruptions of customers and the need to keep an eye on the store. While the interviewee was able to eat with his entire family, however, conversation was generally innocuous.

The disciplining of children took on an increasingly Japanese look. More and more psychological punishment was utilized, and physical punishment was relied upon less and less. Children crying at night were cuddled to prevent disturbing other families in the barracks. The infants soon learned to control their parents' behavior through crying. The lasting impact of discipline in the camp setting cannot be measured at this time. It is unfortunate more attention was not focused on the effects of increased reliance on psychological disciplinary techniques — techniques which can be expected to extract their toll on the later, functioning adult.

Many youngsters, then, spent part of the formative periods of their lives devoid of non-Nikkei peers, imbued with Nikkei values, raised by disciplinary techniques which were mostly psychological, and with minimized meaningful interaction with adults. The exact effects are difficult to measure some twenty-five years after the event but some things are clear. The effects, of course, varied from person to person.

For example, the author inquired about the phenomenon of striving for mobility via formal higher education. When children the same age and raised in the same camp were asked to recall their attitudes toward higher education, resultant data points, when plotted, displayed more of a bimodal than a unimodal distribution at the two extremes — negative and positive. On the other hand, distribution of attitudes among those who spent significant portions of their early lives outside the concentration camps tends to exhibit a more unimodal distribution with the attitudes being much more positive. Unfortunately, this author did not have the techniques in hand to explore this phenomenon more deeply when he conducted this study as a Cal Tech undergraduate some fifteen years ago.

What some data collected by the author do reveal is that, while the means of some of the recall measures for those raised outside the camp environs do not appear different from the means of those raised in the camps, the distributions are often different. Or, put in more statistically oriented jargon, the means are not significantly different but the variance for the camp-raised group is larger than the variance for the non-camp-raised groups.

Suffice it to indicate again that the current literature is, on the whole, fairly accurate. The effects of the relocation on children reported in the evacuation literature did happen in all too many cases. Children were neglected by their parents more frequently in camp than out. Attitudes were "Japanicized" and many youths grew up more "Japanesee" than their older or younger siblings.

The proportion who entered a formalized, higher educational tract was smaller for evacuees within certain age brackets. Whether these effects will last longer than just that one generation is, of course, open to empirical test. Anecdotal information would indicate that the lasting effects were restricted to the impacted generation, and their children are little different from those of other Nikkei.

Like the data on the effects of the relocation on adults, the data on the lasting impact of the evacuation on children are sadly lacking in depth and scope. Longitudinal measures which might have been taken are also lacking. The greatest hope for a deeper understanding of what transpired lies in reading scores of diaries. Unfortunately, children do not keep diaries, and many adults have long since discarded theirs. The author's research data are not in great enough depth, do not tie loose ends together very well, and are based solely on recollections which were distorted by ten to fifteen intervening years. Were recall measures taken now, it would mean twenty-five or more years would have intervened between the events and the reporting.

The evacuation, then, is an historical event, an event on which behavioral scientists cannot get a firm handle with today's tools. Unfortunately, at the time of the evacuation the more recent research techniques did not exist, and there was minimal effort expended to utilize the tools which did. The author, of course, recognizes and applauds the efforts of a small handful of men to chronicle and understand the experiences of the evacuees. Reports on the evacuation should be read in light of the inadequacies which underlie them.

Chapter Notes

This paper has been especially written for this volume. It is based on a literature review and the author's previously unpublished research.

The author is currently Chairman of Asian-American Studies, Associate Professor of Higher Education, and Director of Institutional Educational Research, University of Washington, Seattle, Washington.

References

Bandura, A., and Walters, R. H. *Social Learning and Personality Development.* New York: Holt, Rinehart, and Winston, Inc., 1963.

Benedict, R. *The Chrysanthemum and the Sword.* Boston: Houghton Mifflin, 1946.

Bijou, S. W., and Baer, D. M. *Child Development I: A Systematic and Empirical Approach.* New York: Appleton-Century-Crofts, Inc., 1961.

_____ *Child Development II: Universal Stage of Infancy.* New York: Appleton-Century-Crofts, Inc., 1965.

Bloom, L. "Familial Problems and the Japanese Removal." *Proceedings of the Pacific Sociological Society, 1942.* Pullman, Washington: Research Studies of the State College of Washington, XI, 1943.

_____ "Familial Adjustments of Japanese-Americans to Relocation: First Phase." *American Sociological Review* 8, 1943, 551-560.

_____ "Transitional Adjustments of Japanese-American Families to Relocation." *American Sociological Review* 12, 1947, 201-209.

_____ and Riemer, R. "Removal and Return: The Socio-Economic Effects of the War on Japanese-Americans." *University of California Publications in Culture and Society* 4, 1949, 1-260.

Broom, L. (Bloom), and Kitsuse, J. I. "The Managed Casualty: The Japanese-American Family in World War II." *University of California Publications in Culture and Society* VI, 1956, 1-226.

Bureau of Sociological Research, The (War Relocation Authority). "The Japanese Family in America." *Annals of the American Academy of Political and Social Science* 229, 1943, 150-156.

Conrat, M., and Conrat, R. *Executive Order 9066: The Internment of 110,000 Japanese-Americans.* Los Angeles: Anderson, Ritchie, and Simon, 1972.

Daniels, R. *Concentration Camps USA: Japanese-Americans and World War II.* New York: Holt, Rinehart, and Winston, Inc., 1971.

_____ *The Politics of Prejudice.* Berkeley, California: University of California Press, 1962.

_____ and Kitano, H. H. L. *American Racism: Exploration of the Nature of Prejudice.* Englewood Cliffs, New Jersey: Prentice-Hall, Inc., 1970.

Girdner, A., and Loftis, A. *The Great Betrayal.* New York: The Macmillan Company, 1969.

Hosokawa, B. *Nisei: The Quiet Americans.* New York: William Morrow and Company, Inc., 1969.

Kirkpatrick, C. *The Family as Process and Institution.* New York: The Ronald Press Company, 1955.

Kitagawa, D. *Issei and Nisei: The Internment*

Years. New York: Seabury Press, 1967.

Kitano, H. H. L. Japanese-*Americans: Evolution of a Subculture.* Englewood Cliffs, New Jersey: Prentice-Hall, Inc., 1969.

Leighton, A. H. *The Governing of Men: General Principles and Recommendations Based on Experience at a Japanese Relocation Camp.* Princeton, New Jersey: Princeton University Press, 1945.

Meyer, D. *Uprooted Americans.* Tucson, Arizona: University of Arizona Press, 1971.

Miyamoto, S. F. *Social Solidarity Among the Japanese in Seattle.* Master's Dissertation, Seattle, Washington: University of Washington, 1938. Later published in abbreviated form under the same title in *University of Washington Publications in Social Sciences* II, December, 1939, 57-130.

Ogawa, D. *From Jap to Japanese: The Evolution of Japanese-American Stereotypes.* Berkeley, California: McCutchan, 1971.

Okimoto, D. *American in Disguise.* New York: John Weatherhill, Inc., 1971.

Okubo, M. *Citizen 13660.* New York: Columbia University Press, 1946.

Petersen, W. *Japanese-Americans: Oppression and Success.* New York: Random House, Inc., 1971.

Sears, R. R.; Maccoby, E. E.; and Levin, H. *Patterns of Child Rearing.* Evanston, Illinois: Row, Peterson, and Company, 1957.

Spicer, E. H.; Hansen, A. T.; Loumala, K.; and Opler, M. K. *Impounded People: Japanese-Americans in the Relocation Centers.* Tucson, Arizona: University of Arizona Press, 1969.

tenBroek, J.; Barnhart, E. M.; and Matson, F. W. *Prejudice, War, and the Constitution.* Berkeley, California: University of California Press, 1954.

Thomas, D. S., and Nishimoto, R. *The Spoilage: Japanese-American Evacuation and Resettlement During World War II.* Berkeley, California: University of California Press, 1946.

3. Red Guard on Grant Avenue:
The Rise of Youthful Rebellion in Chinatown

by Stanford Lyman

On May 7, 1969, visitors to San Francisco's historic Portsmouth Square were startled to see the flag of the Peoples' Republic of China flying over the plaza. The occasion was supposed to be a rally to commemorate the fiftieth anniversary of the May 4th Movement in Peking, an event during which Chinese students demonstrated and protested against ignominious foreign treaties and criticized China's traditional institutions and moribund philosophy. In San Francisco a half century later, however, a group of disaffected Chinatown youth took over the rally from its original sponsors to protest against the community's poverty and neglect and to criticize its anachronistic and conservative power elite. Calling themselves the "Red Guards," these youths listed eleven demands, asserted their right to armed self-defense against the city police, and called for the release of all Asians in city, state, and federal prisons on the ground that they had had unfair trials. On a more immediate and practical level, the Red Guards announced plans for a remarkably unradical petition campaign to prevent the Chinese Playground from being converted into a garage, and for a breakfast program to aid needy children in the Chinatown ghetto. A spokesman for the Red Guards stated, "The Black Panthers is the most revolutionary group in the country and we are patterned after them."

To most San Franciscans the rise of youthful rebellion in the Chinese quarter of the city must have come as a surprise. For the past three decades, Chinese-Americans have been stereotypically portrayed in the mass media as quiet, docile, and filial, a people who are as unlikely to partake of radicalism as they are to permit delinquency among their juveniles. In the last few years, however, there has been mounting evidence to suggest a discrepancy between that favorable, if somewhat saccharine, imagery, and reality. Not only is there an unmistakable increase in delinquent activity among Chinese young people, there is also a growing restlessness among them. Chinatown's young people are experiencing a gnawing sense of frustration over the recalcitrance of local institutions, the powerlessness of youth, and their own bleak outlook for the future. The politics as well as the "crimes" of Chinatown are coming to resemble those of the larger society with alienation, race consciousness, and restive rebelliousness animating a new generation's social and organizational energies.

The Demographic Equation

A basic cause for the emergence of youthful rebellion among the Chinese is the increase in the youth population itself. In an absolute sense there are simply more Chinese young people in the ghetto now than there ever have been before. Two sources for the increase are discernible: an increasing birth rate among the indigenous population, and a sudden rise in immigration from Hong Kong and other Asian centers of Chinese population.

Except for a few sailors, merchants, actors, and itinerants, Chinese immigration to the United States did not get underway until 1850. Then, occasioned by the twin developments of disaster in China and opportunity in California, a steady movement of Chinese across the Pacific populated first San Francisco, then California, and later the urban areas to the east with Chinese laborers and merchants. The great majority of these were young men eager to try their luck in the "Gold Mountain" and then return, wealthy and esteemed, to wives, sweethearts, and kinsmen in their home villages. During the entire period of unrestricted immigration (1850-1882), a total of only 8,848 Chinese women journeyed across the Pacific to San Francisco. Many of the women could not withstand the rigors of life in America and died or returned to China. By 1890, only 3,868 Chinese women were reported to be in the country. During the same period, the number of Chinese men emigrating from China to America was much larger. The census reported 33,149 male Chinese in 1860; 58,633 in 1870; 100,686 in 1880; 102,620 in 1890; 85,341 in 1900. The sex ratio, that is, the number of males for every 100 females, reached alarming proportions among the Chinese in America in this period. In 1860 it was 1,858; 1870, 1,284; 1880, 2,106; and, in 1890, it reached its highest point, 2,678. In other words, before the turn of the century there were about twenty-seven men for every woman among the Chinese in America.

The settlement abroad by Chinese men unaccompanied by wives was not confined to the United States. Chinese communities in the Straits Settlements, New Zealand, Thailand, Hawaii, Peru, and Trinidad were also conspicuous for their superfluity of males. A basic reason for this was the Chinese custom and family law which required that a wife remain in the home of her husband's parents even if her husband sought work elsewhere. Should his parents die during his absence, the wife was expected to perform the appropriate burial and mourning rites in place of her husband.

Villages in Southeastern China were for the most part communities of lineage groups tracing their origins from a common male ancestor. Loyalty to the lineage was expected and encouraged. Often enough, village headmen secured an additional insurance of that loyalty by requiring all departing males to marry before they left. Then, it was assumed, these emigrating husbands would be sure to return to their wives in the village, and, furthermore, would send remittances to their patiently waiting families throughout the duration of their sojourn abroad. Absences often proved to be far longer than the spouses had anticipated. Not infrequently, several decades passed before a husband returned to his wife. Some men became birds-of-passage, returning just so long as it took to sire a child, hopefully a son, and then going back to the immigrant communities abroad. Later, the son sometimes followed in his father's footsteps and joined the lonely and homeless men that constituted the Chinese diaspora.

The Chinese custom of leaving the wife behind had begun to erode by the late nineteenth century. However, a new American immigration law brought about a similar result and left Chinese men to work and wait for the great promise of wealth in America — alone. In 1882, under pressure of an anti-Chinese movement that had reached national proportions, Congress passed a law prohibiting Chinese laborers from coming to America for ten years. That prohibition, together with numerous and even more restrictive amendments, was renewed decennially until it became a permanent feature of the law in 1904. It was re-enacted in the Immigration Act of 1924. In effect, Chinese immigrants, except for the few who fell under the exempt classes of merchants, students,

21

itinerants, and religious leaders, could not enter the United States legally until the exclusion law was repealed in 1943 and a quota system was substituted in its stead.

In 1884, a United States Federal Court ruled that the Immigration Act of 1882 properly excluded not only a Chinese laborer but his wife as well, so that, under the law, no Chinese women, except the wives of those in the exempt classes and later the Chinese wives of certain American citizens, could enter the country. Since, according to subsequent judicial rulings and revisions in the Naturalization Act, Chinese immigrants were declared to be aliens ineligible for citizenship in the United States, a status they held until 1943, the lonely Chinese male was rendered helpless in effecting the entry of his wife by legal means.

Chinese men who remained abroad were left to form a homeless men's community within the confines of the Chinatown ghetto. Condemned to a life without intimate family relationships, they joined together in clan associations, *Landsmannschaften*, and secret societies that provided them with a sense of familiarity and solidarity. They participated in Chinese versions of the kinds of recreation that typically arise among men without immediate ties of home and family — gambling, opium-smoking, and prostitution. And, just as typically, in a society known for its hostile racial stereotypy, the Chinese came to be identified with these vices, and, in the minds of many White Americans, were regarded as lowly, immoral, and dangerous.

One important effect of the low number of females in the Chinese communities in the United States was the near inability to produce a second generation of American-born Chinese. In 1890, forty years after Chinese had begun to migrate, the American-born constituted only 2.7 percent of the Chinese population in America. In 1920, this had risen to only 30 percent, and it was not until 1950 that American-born Chinese numbered more than one-half of the total Chinese population in the United States. In 1960, 93,288 Chinese, or more than 35 percent of the total Chinese population in the United States, were still foreign born.

American naturalization laws allowed only those Chinese born on American soil to become citizens of the United States. Thus, inability to procreate in the United States acted as a powerful deterrent to the creation of any sizable body of Chinese-American citizenry who, had they existed, might have been able to stem the tide of anti-Chinese legislation and discrimination, remove the burdens of non-acculturation which afflicted the immigrants, and partake more fully and completely of those benefits that are automatically bestowed on citizens of the United States.

The current increase in the number of Chinese youth in San Francisco's Chinatown is in part a product of the balancing of the sex ratio and the formation of families among America's Chinese in the last three decades. Table I below shows the sex ratios for those ten-year periods.

TABLE I		
RATIO OF CHINESE MEN TO WOMEN 1930 — 1960		
	Chinese in U.S.		Sex Ratio Males per
Years	Females	Males	100 Females
1930	15,512	59,802	394.7
1940	20,115	57,389	285.3
1950	40,621	77,008	189.6
1960	101,743	135,549	133.1

The increase in the number of females by 1950 was made possible by relaxation of restrictive immigration measures against the Chinese. The figures again jumped by 1960, bringing the ratio of males to females to only 1.3. In the San Francisco-Oakland metropolitan area, the sex ratio was slightly lower at 128.0. A sufficient balance had been achieved by 1960, however, so that one could predict with fairly good reliability that most Chinese men and women would indeed be able to marry, settle down, and rear families in the United States.

The increase in the young among America's Chinese was noticeable even before 1960. Between 1920 and 1940, in part as a result of the illegal immigration of Chinese females to the United States, a small American-born population had been produced. The quota system that was substituted for absolute exclusion in 1943, and a few additional laws in the next fifteen years, resulted in the admission of many more Chinese women. In the six years after 1956, the number of births among America's Chinese was significantly higher than during the half-dozen previous years. From 1950 until 1955, there was a total of 28,058 births, of which 14,542 were boys and 13,516, girls. But, from 1956 to 1961, there was a total of 31,106 births, including 15,694 boys and 15,212 girls. And, during the next three years, 19,964 Chinese were born in the United States, comprising 10,686 boys and 8,018 girls. In San Francisco, the total Chinese births between 1941 and 1947 was 2,383. However, in the next decade, the number of Chinese births in San Francisco rose to a total of 9,673.

Enrollments of Chinese in San Francisco's elementary schools numbered 4,995 in 1958; seven years later, they had risen to 5,789, of whom 3,174, or nearly 55 percent, were attending six schools in or near Chinatown. In 1968, San Francisco's Chinese student population numbered 3,351 in high schools; 2,905 in junior high; and 2,645 in elementary schools. Another 1,120 were distributed in various special, vocational, private, continuation, and nursery schools, while 6,863 attended public and private colleges. Of San Francisco's total Chinese population in 1968, believed to be 47,700, no less than 23,984, or about 50 percent, were estimated to be under twenty-one years of age.

A second source for the increase in youthful Chinese was the relaxation of immigration restrictions. After World War II, a number of special laws effected the entry of brides, refugees, displaced persons, and scientific or technically trained personnel of Chinese ancestry. Between 1956 and 1961, the number of Chinese children entering the United States increased slightly. If we look at the age group of males five to fourteen in that period — i.e., those who would be eighteen to twenty-seven in 1969 — the following figures are revealing: 1956, 380; 1957, 362; 1958, 164; 1959, 589; 1960, 289; 1961, 332; for a total during those six years of 2,126. The number of females in that age group admitted for that period totaled 1,772. In 1965, President Johnson signed into law a new immigration act, to become fully effective in July, 1968, which repealed the entire system of quotas based on national origins and substituted in its place an entry procedure based on skills, and a means for the reuniting of families.

Fear that San Francisco would be "swamped" with Chinese proved unfounded, but the increase since July, 1968, suggested to District Immigration Director C. W. Fullilove that the number entering San Francisco with the intention of remaining there would be approximately 1,200 per year. Although official statistics show that 4,496 Chinese between the ages of ten and nineteen entered the United States in 1967-1968, Fullilove has pointed out that the "problem ages" for Chinese youth are between sixteen and nineteen, and that this comprises about 40 percent of the total group. Moreover, since about half of those officially listed as arriving immigrants were already residents of the United States who earned the statistical status of "arriving" because of an "adjustment" of their status, Fullilove concluded that the "problem youth," i.e., newly arrived immigrant youth, number less than 20 percent of that age group, or about 900 adolescents. Although not all of these remain in San Francisco, a significant portion do become a part of the burgeoning Chinatown population.

Sheer numbers alone do not, of course,

account for the rise of rebelliousness among young Chinese in San Francisco. A more significant factor is that conditions of life in Chinatown are by no means pleasant, productive, or promising. We must distinguish, however, from among the Chinese those who have escaped the ghetto, those who are American born but still inhabit Chinatown, and those foreign-born youth who reluctantly find themselves imprisoned within a ghetto not of their own making. Of the first group, there are the scholars, scientists, intellectuals, and professionals — many of whom hail from regions other than Southeastern China, the original home of the bulk of America's Chinese immigrants — who have found work and residence within the larger society. In university, corporation, professional, or government communities, these Chinese do not, for the most part, feel themselves to be a part of Chinatown and journey there only occasionally for a banquet or for a brief sense of their ethnic origins.

A second and much larger group, although actually quite small in relation to the total number, consists of those American-born Chinese who have successfully completed high school and college and gone on to enter the professions, most frequently pharmacy and engineering. They have joined the American middle class and, when they can evade or circumvent the still-prevalent discrimination in housing, the finer neighborhoods or the suburbs. This "gold bourgeoisie" — to paraphrase E. Franklin Frazier, whose concept of and eloquence on the Black bourgeoisie has so richly informed sociology about middle-class life amongst Negroes in America — is also estranged from Chinatown. Proud of his own achievements, wary of any attempt to thrust him back into a confining ghetto existence, and alternately angered, embarrassed, or shamed by the presence of alienated, hostile, and rebellious youth in Chinatown, the middle-class American Chinese holds tenaciously to his newly achieved material and social success.

Middle-class, native-born Chinese are discovering, however, that the American dream is not an unmixed blessing. On the one hand, the "Gold Mountain" of American bourgeois promise seems somehow less glittering now that its actual pinnacle has been reached. Chinese, like other descendants of immigrants in America, are discovering that the gold is alloyed more heavily than they had supposed with brass, but, like their second- and third-generation colleagues among the Jews and Japanese, they are not quite sure what to do about it. The price of success has been great, not the least payments being the abandonment of language, culture, and much of their ethnic identity.

For some in this class, there is a new search for cultural roots in Chinese history, a strong desire to recover the ancient arts, and a renewed interest in speaking Chinese — at least at home. Others emphasize, perhaps with too much protestation, their happiness within the American middle class — they engage in conspicuous consumption of leisure to prove it. Finally, a few recognize their Chinatown roots and return there with a desire to somehow aid in the advancement of the Chinese ghetto-dwellers. Sometimes their proferred assistance is rejected with epithets and insults, and they begin to wonder about their own motives and, also, to re-evaluate their abilities to help.

It is this presence of a growing number of restive Chinatowners that constitutes another challenge to the comfort of bourgeois existence among the Chinese. In its most primordial sense, the visible contrast between the style of life of the impoverished ghetto-dweller and that of the middle-class professional promotes a gnawing sense of guilt and shame in the latter. Somehow, it seems wrong that one's ethnic compatriots should suffer while one enjoys the benefits of success. Yet, in estimating the sources of their own success, middle-class Chinese are quite ready to attribute it to their own diligence, their proverbial habits of thrift and hard work, and their conscious avoidance of delinquent or other kinds of unruly behavior. In the face of this analysis, some middle-class Chinese charge the angry Chinatown youth with indolence, impropriety, and impiety. They sometimes urge the youths to cultivate the old virtues as a sure cure for their personal and social ailments. Yet, some perceive that there is more to these problems than can be solved by the careful nurturance of Confucian or Protestant ethics. The issues of poverty, cultural deprivation, and discrimination are seen as more obdurate barriers to the advancement of these ghetto-dwellers of today than they were to the more Americanized and less alienated Chinese of the fifties. Moreover, there is an ever deeper and more profound problem. In line with the orientations of other alienated youthful minorities, the youth of Chinatown appear to have adopted a perspective which rejects just that dream which inspired and activated the now bourgeois Chinese. For the middle-class Chinese, then, the peak of the "Gold Mountain" seems to have been just reached when those still below shouted up that the arduous climb wasn't worth the effort.

Among Chinatown's rebellious groups, there are two distinguishable types: those who are American born but have dropped out of school and form part of the under-employed or unemployed proletariat of the Chinese community; and those recently arrived immigrant youths who, speaking little or no English and having little to offer in the way of salable skills, find themselves unable to enter the city's occupational and social mainstream. Both native- and foreign-born Chinese are included among the ranks of the quasi-criminal and quasi-political gangs that are accused of contributing to the mounting incidence of delinquency in the Chinese quarter. Culture, language, and background have divided the native- from the foreign-born Chinese in the past, and it is only recently that there is any sign of a common recognition between the two. (In the 1950s, native- and foreign-born Chinese

on the University of California campus at Berkeley formed two clubs: the Chinese Students' Club for the American born and the Chinese Students' Association for the foreign born. In addition, there was a Chinese-American social fraternity, Pi Alpha Phi, which drew its membership primarily from American-born Chinese.)

It is traditional to focus on Chinatown gangs as an unfortunate form of juvenile delinquency among a people otherwise noted for their social quiescence and honesty. A more fruitful approach, however, would adopt the perspective taken by E. J. Hobsbawm in his discussion of social bandits and primitive rebels. According to Hobsbawm, who has studied these phenomena in Europe, social banditry is a form of pre-ideological rebellion which arises among essentially agrestic, unskilled, and unlettered peoples who are at great cultural distances from the official and oppressive power structure. It is led by those who enjoy a certain amount of local notoriety or awe.

Often enough, social banditry remains at a stage of petty criminality, evoking only the attention of police to what appears to be local acts of homicide, assault, larceny, and property damage. A more refined stage includes the formation of predatory gangs that confine their criminal activities to attacks on strangers and officials, and the sharing of any loot obtained thereby with local community members who, though not a party to the depredations, identify with and protect the robbers. Further, bandit gangs may adopt a populist or conservative style: the former represented by a "Robin Hood" ideology of robbing the rich to feed the poor, and an attack on civic or state officialdom who are regarded as intruders in the community's traditional way of life; the latter indicated by the co-optation of bandit gangs as the toughs and thugs defending local satrapies and powerful petty interests.

Social banditry may exist side by side with ideologically rebellious or revolutionary elements, but it is usually untouched by them except for particular reasons of strategy or tactics. Essentially, social banditry is separated from ideological politics by its deep involvement with local, rather than cosmopolitan, ethnic and class interests. It is not, however, impossible for class and ethnic interests to merge, and for the liberation of local groups to become enmeshed within the revolutionary aims of a radically politicized sector of a modern party-state.

Looked at under the perspective of "primitive rebellion," Chinatown's gangs take on a greater significance for the understanding of loosely structured, pluralistic societies like the United States. Gangs in Chinatown are by no means a new phenomenon, but their activities in the past describe mainly the early stages of social banditry. For the most part, Chinatown's traditional social banditry has been of a particularly conservative type, identified with the recruitment of young toughs, thugs, and bullies into the small criminal arm of Chinatown's secret societies. In this capacity, these young men formed the "flying squads" of paid and contracted mercenaries who "protected" brothels, guarded gambling establishments, and enforced secret society monopolies over other vice institutions of Chinatown. From their number came assassins and strong-arm men who fought in the so-called "tong wars" that characterized Chinatown's internecine struggles of a half-century ago and which still occasionally threaten to erupt today. Social banditry was an exclusive and private affair of Chinatown. Insofar as Chinatown's violent altercations were circumscribed, not only by the invisible wall which separated the ghetto from the metropolis, but also by the limited interests of the contending parties for women, wealth, and power, the community was isolated by its internal conflicts and, whether manifested in fearful acquiescence or active participation, bound together in a deadly kind of "antagonistic cooperation."

Since 1943, a progressive cycle of rebellion among Chinatown's youth has metamorphosed from crime to politics, from individual acts of aggression to collective acts of rebellion, and from non-ideological modes of hostility to the beginnings of a movement of ideological proportions. From 1943 until 1949, juvenile crime in Chinatown was largely the activity of a small number of native-born boys about fifteen years of age who experienced some sense of deprivation through unemployment, difficulties in home life, or inadequate income. The crimes were typical of the most individualized and inarticulate forms of primitive rebellion. Burglary, auto theft, robbery, larceny, hold-up, and assault and battery constituted 103 of the 184 offenses for which Chinese male juveniles were referred to San Francisco's juvenile court in those years. There were also gangs of native-born youth, apparently sponsored by, or under the protection of, secret societies, which occasionally assaulted and robbed strangers in Chinatown, not a few of whom, incidentally, were Japanese-Americans recently returned from war-time internment camps and also organized into clubs, cliques, and gangs.

Petty criminal gangs emerged more frequently among both the native- and foreign-born youth in Chinatown from 1958 to 1964. In some cases, these gangs were composed of young men sponsored in their criminal activities by secret societies. Such an instance was found in the "cat" burglary ring, broken up by police in 1958 and discovered to be a branch of the Hop Sing Tong. Three years later, two gangs — the "Lums" and the "Rabble Rousers," the first composed of boys aged fourteen through seventeen, the second of those aged seventeen to twenty-two — were reported to be engaged in auto thefts, extortion, street fights, and petty larcenies. In January, 1964, members of a San Francisco Chinatown gang were charged with the $10,000 burglary of a fish market in suburban Mountain View. A year later, the police broke up the "Bugs," a youthful criminal gang dressing entirely in black, with bouffant hair style and raised-heel boots, who, over a period of six months, committed forty-eight burglaries and made off with $7,500 in cash and $3,000 in merchandise. The "Bugs," who capitalized on an otherwise-stigmatizing aspect of their existence — their short stature — re-emerged a year later, despite an attempt by Chinatown's leaders to quell juvenile gangs by bringing in streetworkers from San Francisco's Youth for Service, a program begun a half-dozen years earlier to channel delinquents toward constructive activities. By the mid-1960s, Chinatown's burglary gangs had begun to branch out and were "working" areas of the city outside the Chinese quarter.

The present stage of a more politicized rebellion may be dated from the emergence in May, 1967, of Leway, Incorporated. In its history to date (August, 1969), the Leways experienced almost precisely the pattern of problems and responses that typically gives rise first to non-ideological rebellion and, under certain conditions, to the development of revolutionary ideology. Leway, standing for "legitimate ways," began as a public-spirited, self-held group among American-born Chinese teenagers. Aged seventeen to twenty-two, these young men organized to unite Chinatown's youth, to combat juvenile delinquency, and to improve conditions in the poverty-stricken Chinese ghetto through helping youths to help themselves. In its first months, it gained the support of Chinatown luminaries such as Lim P. Lee, now San Francisco's postmaster and a former probation officer, and other prominent citizens. Through raffles, loans, and gifts, these youths, many of whom constituted the delinquent members of Chinatown's younger generation, raised $2,000 to rent, temporarily, a pool hall near the Chinatown-Filipino border area and, with the help of the Chinese YMCA and Youth for Service, to outfit it with five pool tables, seven pinball machines, some chairs, and a television set. "This is a hangout for hoods," said its president, Denny Lai, to reporter Ken Wong. "Most of us 'cats' are misfits, outcasts with a rap sheet. What we're

trying to do is to keep the hoods off the streets, give them something to do instead of raising hell."

Leway was a local, autochthonous group seeking to employ its own methods and style to solve its own members' problems; it was precisely this that caused its downfall. Police refused to believe in the efficaciousness of methods that eschewed official surveillance, sporadic shakedowns, and the not-always-occasional beating of a youth "resisting arrest." Leway tried a dialogue with the police, but it broke down over the rights of the latter to enter Leway's headquarters — a tiny piece of "territory" which the young Chinese had hoped to preserve from alien and hostile intrusion — and to search and seize members there. Leway claimed it wanted to be left alone by this official arm of a society which it saw as already hostile and generally ill-disposed toward it. "We are not trying to bother them (the police) . . . and we won't go out of our way to work with them either."

In addition to continuing problems of police harassment, Leway failed to establish itself as a legitimate association in Chinatown. The Chinese Chamber of Commerce refused it official recognition, and, as a result, Leway could not gain access to the local Economic Opportunity Council to obtain much-needed jobs for Chinatown youth. The Tsung Tsin Association, which owned the building in which Leway had established its headquarters, threatened to raise the rent or lease the premises to another renter. Finally, whether rightly or not, the members of Leway, together with other Chinatown youth groups, were blamed for the increasing violence in Chinatown. Throughout 1968-1969, reports of violent assaults on tourists and rival gangs and during festivals emanated from Chinatown. Police increased their intrusive surveillance and other heavy-handed tactics. Chinese youth charged them with brutality, but the police replied that they were only carrying out proper procedures in the line of a now-more-hazardous duty.

In late summer, 1969, the combination of police harassment, rent hikes, its [Leway's] failure to secure jobs for its chronically unemployed members, and its general inability to establish itself as a legitimate way of getting Chinatown youth "straightened out" took its final toll. Leway House closed its doors. Smashed were its dreams of establishing on-the-job training for the unskilled, new business ventures for the unemployed, a pleasant soda fountain for Leway adolescents, and an education and recreation program for Chinatown teenagers. The bitterness of its defeat stung deep into the hearts of Chinatown young people. "Leway stood for legitimate ways," a fifteen-year-old youth told reporter Bill Moore. "Helluva lot of good it did them." The closing of Leway did away with many Chinatown young people's faith in the official culture and its public representatives.

The stage was set for the next phase in the development of rebellion. Out of the shambles of Leway came the Red Guards. It is composed of the so-called "radical" elements of the former Leway. But now, Leway's erstwhile search for legitimacy is turned on its head. The Red Guards flout the little red book, *Quotations from Chairman Mao Tse-Tung*, as their credo, make non-negotiable demands on the power structure of Chinatown and the metropolis, and openly espouse a program of disruption, rebellion, and occasionally, it seems, revolution.

Leway had been modeled after other San Francisco youthful gang reform groups, but the Red Guards have adopted the organizational form, linguistic style, and political mood of the Black Panthers. Cooperation between Chinese and Black youth has not been frequent in the past. In the 1960s, there were frequent bloody clashes between youthful gangs of Chinese and Negroes; interracial incidents at Samuel Gompers School — a kind of incarceration unit for Black and Oriental incorrigibles — had not encouraged friendly relations between the two groups. Nevertheless, it was just these contacts, combined with a growing awareness of Panther tactics and successes and some not-too-secret proselytization by Panther leaders among the disaffected Leway members, that effected an adoption of the Black militant style. Whatever prejudices Chinese might harbor against Negroes, Black Panther rhetoric seemed to describe perfectly not only the Black, but also their own, situation. After all, Leway had tried to be good, to play the game according to the White man's rules, and all it had gotten for its pains was a heap of abuse and a few cracked skulls. Now it was time to be realistic, "to stop jiving" and "to tell it like it is." The Panthers provided a language that not only depicted, but also evaluated, the situation properly. Police were "pigs," White men were "honkies," officially developed reform programs were attempts to "shine" on credulous Chinese youth, and the goal to be attained was not integration or material success, but power. "We're an organization made up mainly of street people, and we're tired of asking the government for reforms," said Alex Hing, a twenty-three-year-old Chinese who is the Minister of Information of the Red Guards. "We're going to attain power, so we don't have to beg any more."

The Red Guards are a populist group among Chinatown's "primitive" rebels. They stand against two power structures in their opposition to oppression and poverty, that of old Chinatown and that of the larger metropolis. Ideologically, they are located somewhere between the inarticulate rumblings of rustic rebels and the full-scale ideology of unregenerate revolutionaries. They cry out for vengeance against the vague but powerful complex of Chinese and White elite that oppresses them. They dream of a world in which they will have sufficient power to curb their exploiters' excesses; meanwhile, they operate as best they can to right local wrongs and to ingratiate themselves with the mass of their Chinatown compatriots. The free breakfast program for indigent youngsters, a copy of a similar program utilized by the Black Panthers, provides a ready means of obtaining popular support among Chinatown's poor at the same time that it shames Chinatown's elite for allowing the community's children to go hungry.

The demand for the release of all imprisoned Asians seems to place the Red Guards squarely on the side of all those "little people" of Chinatown who feel themselves victimized by an alien and oppressive police system. However, their ethnic consciousness usually supersedes and sometimes clashes with their alleged attachment to a class-oriented ideology, as it did when the Red Guards accepted the invitation to guard a meeting of the Chinese Garment Contractors' Association against a threatened assault by Teamsters Union men who sought to organize Chinatown's heavily exploited dressmakers. But it is precisely their parochial dedication to a sense of Chinese ethnicity — which eludes exact definition but encloses individual identity in psychic security against the *angst* of alienation — that limits their political effectiveness at the same time that it endears them to the less hardy of young Chinatowners who secretly share their dilemmas and dreams.

Below this level of semi-articulated ideology are the still-existent gangs and social cliques that, although angry and alienated, have not yet thrown in their lot with the Red Guards. Three gangs, the Baby Hwa Ching, the Raiders, and the Junior Raiders, attempt to maintain some sense of autonomy despite the fact that they did congregate at Leway's pool hall and youth center. Two other gangs, the Brothers Ten and the Country Club Boys, represent particular school and residential areas, respectively. The Project 895s and the 880s congregate at the addresses represented by their number names. The Drifters, a group of about twenty young men, seem to find their own special outlet in motorcycles. In all these cases, there are represented the elementary stages of rebellion, stages that may never progress beyond the limited activities described by social cliquishness, youthful exhuberance, and petty criminality. But, it could also happen that some or all of these groups will be absorbed into the new ethnic, radical, and populist forms of rebellion that today characterize the Red Guards.

Populist rebellion is not the only form of social politics in Chinatown. In the evolution of the Hwa Ching and the Junior Hwa Ching is illustrated a conservative type of rebelliousness. Hwa Ching emerged in 1967 as a loose association made up mostly of Hong Kong-born youth in Chinatown. Estimates of its size vary from 25 to 300; this fact alone testifies to its low degree of cohesiveness and the sense of drift that characterizes its members. Until very recently, Hwa Ching was represented in most public discussions by a "spokesman" (its looseness of organization prevented any greater clarification of title), George Woo, a former photographer who took on the task of bridging the communication gap between the largely Chinese-speaking youths and the officials of the metropolis. What the aims of the association were are difficult to ascertain exactly, partly because common agreement among its members was not great, and because spokesman Woo usually tended to a polemical and scare-producing speaking style in order to call attention to Chinatown's immigrant problems. Like many multi-problem groups, Hwa Ching had less of a perfected program than a set of practical problems, less of a coherent perspective than a prevalent condition. Hong Kong youth were insufficiently educated and skilled to obtain jobs besides Chinatown's dreary positions of waiter, bus boy, and sweated laborer; unequipped linguistically to enter the metropolis; and, in the beginning, unwilling to accept confinement in a congested, poverty-stricken, and despotically ruled ghetto.

Hwa Ching seemed to form itself around El Piccolo, an espresso coffee house opened in Chinatown in 1967 and operated by Dick and Alice Barkley. Alice Barkley, herself a Hong

Kong-born Chinese, turned the coffee house into a haven for foreign-born Chinese youth. There they could meet in peace and with the freedom to discuss, argue, complain, and occasionally plan some joint activity. Reaction to the clubby fraternization that existed at El Piccolo was mixed. Traditional Chinatowners accused the Barkleys of offering asylum to raffish criminal elements; a newly aroused college and university group of Chinese-Americans praised the establishment of such a place for impoverished immigrants to congregate; most San Franciscans didn't even know the Hwa Ching existed.

Early in 1968, Hwa Ching approached the Human Relations Commission, the Economic Development Council, and the Chinese Six Companies to ask for their aid in establishing an educational program for alleviating the misery of Chinatown's immigrant youth. Their approach was frank and practical; it indicated both the growing frustrations and the general problems of these youth, frustrations and problems arising out of a vicious circle of poverty, illiteracy in English, and crime — from all of which they wished somehow to extricate themselves. At the January, 1968, meeting of the Human Relations Commission a spokesman presented their case in Cantonese:

> The crime rate in Chinatown is increasing. We are partly responsible. We seek a chance to change and be a productive member of the community:
> Frustration is our lot. Housing, job opportunities, recreation facilities in Chinatown are poor. We live in an age of technical advance that requires skill and training to survive.
> We are under the same pressures as other youths. In addition, we are subjected to some that are unique because we are foreign born.
> We are frustrated in our pursuit of an education because they do not know how to reach us. As long as we are under-educated and under-trained, we will remain under-employed.
> The burgeoning crime rate is largely the result of these problems.

In order to remedy the situation, Hwa Ching proposed the establishment of a comprehensive two-year educational program to provide Chinatown's young immigrants with a high school diploma and vocational training in auto repair, business machine operation, construction, sheet metal, electrical installation, and plumbing. They closed with a statement that was unfortunately taken as a warning and a threat: "We've been hearing too many promises. The rise and fall of our hopes is tragic and ominous."

The Hwa Ching, unsuccessful in their first bid, spoke to the Chinatown Advisory Board of the Human Relations Commission in late February. Represented this time by the fiery George Woo, the Hwa Ching was more modest in its request for a comprehensive program but more militant in its presentation. Hwa Ching wanted $4,322 to build a club house. Although Woo reiterated the same arguments as other Hwa Chings had presented in January, the tone was different. Speaking of the youths whom he represented, Woo said, "There is a hard core of delinquents in Chinatown who came from China. Their problems are the problems of all poor with the addition that they don't speak English." Then he added, "They're talking about getting guns and rioting. . . . I'm not threatening riots. The situation already exists, but if people in Chinatown don't feel threatened they won't do anything about it."

The mention of guns and the warning of possible riots was too much for John Yehall Chin, former president of the Chinese Six Companies, principal of St. Mary's Chinese Language School, and member of the Rights Commission's Chinatown Advisory Board. With respect to the Hwa Ching's request, he gave this advice to the Commission and, indirectly, to the youth. "They have not shown that they are sorry or that they will change their ways. They have threatened the community. If you give in to this group, you are only going to have another hundred immigrants come in and have a whole new series of threats and demands."

Although the Commission expressed its interest, Hwa Ching's demand was rejected.

In March, the Hwa Ching's President, Stan Wong, presented the immigrant youths' case before the Chinese Six Companies, the oligarchy that controls Chinatown. Speaking in Cantonese, Wong repudiated the threat of riots made at the February meeting. "We made no threats," he said. "They were made by non-members. We need to help ourselves. We look to the future and are mindful of the immigrant youths who will be coming here later. We hope they do not have to go through what we've been through." Later, he answered a question about possible Communist affiliation: "Hwa Ching is not involved with any political ideology." Although Commissioner Chin pointed out that the Hwa Ching had mended its ways, the Six Companies refused them help, while the Human Rights Commission, under the direction of Chin, organized an establishment-controlled Citizens for Youth in Chinatown. The Hwa Ching felt utterly rejected.

In their bitterness and anger, however, the Hwa Ching did not turn to populist revolt, as had the angry former Leways. Instead, they fragmented even more. Their loose coalition at El Piccolo ended when that establishment closed its doors in August, 1968. The Hwa Ching had never, in fact, professed an ideology. What seemed like such was more a product of the fervid imaginations of alarmed Whites and of the fiery invective of George Woo than it was any coherent line of political or revolutionary thought. The Hwa Ching had had a few minor successes outside of Chinatown. They received advice and help from the Mission Rebels, a youth group in San Francisco's Latin-Negro-Oriental area, and almost got their club house built. Woo spoke wherever anyone would listen. (He harangued my race and ethnic relations course at Sonoma State College, fifty miles north of San Francisco, and so impressed the mostly White students in the classroom that they spontaneously took up a collection during

his talk, and at the end of the hour presented him with an envelope filled with small change and a few bills.) A meat packer offered them an abandoned building, but more than $5,000 in repairs would have been required to put it in habitable condition.

By the end of the year, Hwa Ching was suffering even more than it had in the beginning. All of its demands for help had been rejected or given only token support. The Chinese-American Democratic Club had helped a little, and Hwa Ching had developed some limited cooperation with Leway. But, like the latter group, it had neither established its legitimacy in Chinatown nor was it able to provide its own members with satisfaction. Its spokesman, George Woo, ineffective in his attempts to win substantial support for those for whom he orated so eloquently, if polemically, enrolled at San Francisco State College and became an active member of Intercollegiate Chinese for Social Action (ICSA), a college-based education and community action group. In January, 1969, he addressed the "Yellow Identity" Conference at the University of California at Berkeley with a rousing call for the students to come away from their books and help in the rehabilitation and liberation of Chinatown.

Hwa Ching's interests could not be channeled into an ideological movement, nor could its restive members be organized into a disciplined cadre of revolutionaries. Their practical needs were too immediate, their literacy in English too low, and their limited but practical political experience in Hong Kong and Chinatown was too great for them to accept an organization that used Mao's red book and which, hence, ran the risks of attracting political persecution and possible deportation. As Tom Tom, a twenty-three-year-old immigrant who had been one of the earliest members of Hwa Ching, explained to a reporter, the immigrant youth were independent of the Leway and all other Chinatown groups, effected none of the hippie-Che-Raoul-Panther styles, and wanted little more than jobs, girls, and to be left alone. The Hwa Ching found themselves oppressed by their supposed allies nearly as much as by their condition. Leway boys and other American-born Chinese called them "Chinabugs" and attacked them in gang rumbles; Negroes picked on the diminutive Chinese until they learned to retaliate in numbers and with stealth, strategy, and tactics; college students sought to tutor and evangelize them with secular and sometimes political ideas, but succeeded mostly in making them feel inferior and ashamed, and in frightening them with a kind of politics which they abhorred.

By mid-1969, the Hwa Ching had split into three factions. One portion of the short-lived coalition returned to the streets, to fight, burglarize, and assault all those available symbols and representatives of the seemingly monolithic power structure that had scorned them; two other factions apparently accepted co-optation into Chinatown's two most powerful, though age-ridden, secret societies, the Suey Sing and Hop Sing Tongs. There, their anger could find outlet at the same time that their strength could be utilized for traditional aims. The secret societies could pay for the immigrant youths' basic needs and with the same expenditure buy the muscle to keep control of their own interests and institutions. And, since the Tongs were part of the complex congeries of associations that make up Chinatown's power elite, it is not surprising that leaders of this same elite gave tacit approval to the Tongs' recruitment of what had appeared in early 1968 to be a serious threat to the old order. Unlike the Leway youth, who could not join the old order and may have been too Americanized to accept secret society patronage, the immigrant youth find in it [the Tong] a perhaps temporary expedient in their dilemma. They are not a politicized body of young people. Thus, they can more readily join in the protection of old Chinatown. They have assumed a posture typical of a Chinatown a half

century ago. They form the conservative wing of Chinatown's complex structure of conflict and rebellion.

In other areas of primitive rebellion, conservative and populist factions often fought each other as much as their respectively professed enemies. In traditional nineteenth-century China, for example, the several secret societies that had existed for centuries in Kwangtung and Fukien Provinces fell out with one another over their respective support for wealthy landlords or rebellious peasants during the course of several popular uprisings and the catastrophic Tai Ping Revolution (1850-1864). Similarly in Chinatown, the young toughs who have become paid guards of the secret societies' meetings are not infrequently arrayed against the Leway-Red Guard gangs and on occasion against the ICSA youth as well. In this sense, young Chinatown recapitulates a structure of conflict that characterized that of its earlier generations. Conservative-populist conflicts isolate the contending parties from outside groups and larger issues. The violent fights and smoldering feuds appear to non-comprehending outsiders to be exclusively Chinese in their nature and content. And this intramural conflict in turn circumscribes Chinatown and once again cuts it off from the metropolis.

Connections to the larger society of San Francisco in particular and the United States in general do, however, exist. For the youth, the most important one is the Intercollegiate Chinese for Social Action. This group was formed at San Francisco State College from among the more socially concerned and politically aware Chinese-American students. For a while, it managed the special program by which Chinese students from the ghetto were recruited to the college. This activity, however, had an unintended effect on the originally education-interested ICSA leaders. It forced them into reconsidering the whole relationship of college to community and, eventually, into re-evaluating their priorities of education and service.

Several facets of this relationship came to a head during the long student strike at San Francisco State College in 1968-1969. A loose coalition of non-Anglo and non-White student groups formed under the banner of the Third World Liberation Front. Among the Oriental students, two groups stood out. One was the Asian-American Political Alliance (AAPA) which, on other campuses around California, had a more radical rhetoric and more Chinese-American representatives than at State. Although it had its leftward-leaning and radical members, AAPA at San Francisco State College came to be more a Japanese-American group and less an outlet for radical expression. Eventually, a few of its leaders put together the Japanese portion of the College's incipient Ethnic Studies Program. ICSA contributed a program for Chinese ethnic studies, and, like many of the other programs offered in the Third World proposals, it sought to link the educational experience to community development.

The strike, with its violence, terror, and excitement, propelled ICSA members into even greater contact with the Chinatown community. They became socially conscious and actively oriented toward conditions about which previously they had been only vaguely aware. For one thing, San Francisco State's language program taught only Mandarin, while the bulk of San Francisco's Chinese spoke one or another of the several dialects of Cantonese. In addition, ICSA asserted with loud emphasis what had been but an open secret for decades: Chinatown was a racial ghetto, poverty-stricken, disease-ridden, over-crowded, under-developed, and with a population growing in Malthusian proportions. Finally, they pointed out that no course, major, or program existed to deal specifically with the history, culture, problems, and identity of the Chinese in America. They dedicated themselves to the remedy of all these defects and established offices not only in the college but in Chinatown itself.

ICSA functions today as a dualistic communication and cultural bridge. On the one hand, it has re-created contacts between the originally bourgeois-oriented Chinese-American college students and the Chinatown dropouts. "The generation before us moved out to the Richmond District and the suburbs," says Jeffrey Chan, a young English instructor at State who supports ICSA. "Now we're moving back into the ghetto." ICSA provides tutoring services to Chinatown's less-educated youth and urges that San Francisco State College establish even more programs for community rehabilitation. The community-oriented Chinese college youth will not openly attack Leway or the Red Guards and remain in communication with them as well as with the erstwhile Hwa Ching. But, observes George Woo, now an ICSA member, "We can also see the pitfalls in using too much of the blarney, as the Red Guards did. As a result, they alienated immigrant youths and the whole community in three months' time." ICSA, by keeping open contacts between the native- and foreign-born, between Hwa Ching and Leway-Red Guards, between status-conscious diploma-bearers and socially stigmatized delinquents, and between the legitimated and the lowly, may yet be able to blunt the deadly edge of conflict and build a durable community for Chinatown.

Such a community, if it is built, will be ethnic without being necessarily Confucian, adaptive without being conformist, race conscious without being bigoted, and economically efficacious without being uncritically bourgeois. What this means, specifically, is by no means clear, even to the ICSA members themselves. Chinese-Americans in particular, and youthful ethnic minority members in general, are going through an identity crisis of fundamental cultural and psychological proportions. At this moment, it is easier for them to state what they are not, and what they will refuse to become, than it is to indicate precisely the content of an appropriate identity. Echoing the inner nagging question of most of his compatriots, a twenty-one-year-old college student complained, "I'm still trying to figure out what I am suppose to be as a Chinese-American." And George Woo replied, "I know how you feel. I don't identify with China either, and I certainly don't identify with the petty American middle-class values of my aunts and uncles."

In some ways, ICSA's approach is reminiscent of an idea for the emancipation of Negroes, formulated over a half-century ago by W. E. B. du Bois, that the minority community must be lifted up and guided by its "talented tenth"; i.e., its educated and professional leaders. "The college students are the only hope," argues Mason Wong, twenty-nine-year-old ex-Marine and ICSA leader, "because we live in a society where you have to have credentials to do anything." In contrast to the elitist implications that plagued the old program of du Bois, however, ICSA seems to emphasize a two-way learning process between the lettered and the drop-outs and to call for the formulation of a new ethic to replace the Confucian-Protestant ethos of Chinese-America. As Mason Wong has said, "Our generation here will no longer accept the old and still-prevalent Confucian doctrine of success coming only from hard work and humility." What that ethic will be is not yet known. In the meantime, the Chinese must still contend with the traditional social order that is Chinatown's establishment.

The Old Order . . .

Any person at all conversant about San Francisco's Chinatown will have heard of the Chinese Six Companies. In a vague sense, he might know about some of its activities, be able to point out its headquarters, and note that it is a benevolent, protective, and representational body of Chinese who enjoy unofficial but influential standing at City Hall. Beyond this, he may know very little, but offer the familiar litany: the Chinese take care of themselves; they contribute little if at all to the welfare rolls or to the city's alarming rate of juvenile

delinquency; while the Chinese were perhaps at one time a troublesome minority, they are now safely ensconced in their own quarter of the city where they enjoy a modicum of freedom to practice the peculiar cultural expressions derived from a China that is no more. To him, the Six Companies is one aspect of that cultural freedom.

Like many stereotypic images that arise in racist societies, this perspective on the Chinese Six Companies and on Chinatown contains some kernels of truth. The Chinese in San Francisco, like the Chinese in Calcutta, Singapore, Bangkok, Saigon, Manila, and, indeed, in almost every large city to which Chinese have migrated, enjoy a measure of home rule that far exceeds that of any other minority group in a metropolis. During the colonial period in Southeast Asia, the British and Dutch formalized their practices of indirect rule into a specified system of titles. "Kapitan China" was the Dutch designation for the uniformed and be-medaled Chinese who represented his people in the colonial councils at Batavia, and the "Captain China" system prevailed in British Malaya and other colonies as well.

Indirect rule was for the colonial powers an expedient way of maintaining sufficient control over restless and hostile native peoples in a precariously pluralistic society and a means by which to extract their labor and the colony's natural resources without having to contend with their local tribal and customary ways and woes. For the subject peoples, it meant that they could organize their lives with impunity in accordance with a modicum of traditional practices and customary modes, as long as none of these interfered with the rather limited interests of the imperial powers. Besides the colonial area, the Chinese immigrant elite also managed to establish a kind of cultural extra-territoriality. They legitimated their traditional control over their fellow-migrants by winning unofficial recognition from the White civic elite. In Vancouver, British Columbia, and in

New York City, the Chinese Benevolent Association has obtained such prerogatives; in San Francisco it is the Chinese Six Companies. In some cities, the leader of this body of Chinatown elite is unofficially referred to as "The Mayor of Chinatown," a perhaps suitable surrogate sobriquet for the more formal and more formidable title of "Kapitan China" that prevailed more than a half-century ago in Southeast Asia.

To more fully understand Chinatown's power structure, it is necessary to analyze the several kinds of traditional associations from which it is composed. There are three basic types of traditional associations established in Chinatown; in addition, there are subsidiary and ancillary groupings, including occupational guilds. At the apex of this complex associational pyramid is a confederation of associations which tends to govern the community.

First, there are clan associations, or "family associations," as Occidental journalists and sociologists usually term them. Clan associations ideally unite all persons descended from a common male ancestor and derive from the lineage communities so prevalent in Kwangtung. Overseas, however, the more manageable lineage unit was replaced by a kinship network with wider influence than that which originally enclosed but a compact village. The clan association includes all who bear the same surname. Its function, with respect to kinship, is to provide the boundaries of the incest taboo by prohibiting marriage within the same surname group. (When I was in high school, a Chinese-American friend confided to me that he was dating a girl of the same surname as his own, a fact, he said, which would anger and shame his parents.)

In the early days of Chinese immigration, clan leaders established headquarters and hostelries, and the more formalized association of kinsmen became a particularized kind of immigrant-aid society, providing the newcomer with food, shelter, employment, protection, and advice. Clan leaders reminded the immigrant of his obligations to parents and family in the home village, and, in the absence of the village elders, assumed a role *in loco parentis*, settling disputes, arbitrating disagreements, and, in general, containing intraclan differences within the kinship fold. Some clan associations exercised a monopoly over a trade or profession in Chinatown, effectively resisting encroachments by ambitious Chinese upstarts from other clans. Until the recent arrival of large numbers of immigrants from Hong Kong, the clan associations had been declining in power and authority as a result of the aging of their members and the acculturation of American-born Chinese. However, even their new life-blood of immigrants is less acquiescent than the former sojourner members. Chinatown clan associations are now challenged to provide something more than a paltry benevolence in exchange for their petty despotism.

In addition to clans, however, there developed among overseas Chinese a functionally similar, but structurally different, type of association. The *hui kuan* united all those who spoke a common dialect, hailed from the same district of origin in China, or belonged to the same tribal or ethnic group. (It is a mistake to suppose, as many Occidentals do, that the peoples of China are culturally homogeneous. In the tiny area around Canton from which most of America's immigrants have come, there are numerous dialects which, while they have a common script, are nearly mutually unintelligible when spoken.) Like the clan association, the *hui kuan* originated in China where, by the middle of the nineteenth century, associations of that type had sprung up in urban areas throughout the empire to minister to the needs of students, merchants, and other migrants from China's many rural villages. Overseas, the *hui kuan* was but one more extension of this provincial form of solidarity. In many ways, these Chinese associations were similar to those immigrant-aid and benevolent societies established by

Germans, Irish, Jews, and other Europeans in America, and the German name which has been applied to the latter, *Landsmannschaften,* is applicable to them as well.

In San Francisco and other cities in which Chinese dwelt, the *hui kuan,* like the clan association, maintained a headquarters and served as caravansary, hostelry, credit association, and employment agency. In all these matters, it exercised authoritarian control, and, since most of the Chinese in America were debtors, directly or indirectly, to their *hui kuan,* its officers were not infrequently suspected of garnishing an excessive interest or corrupt profit from their charges. The *hui kuan,* again similar to the clan, conducted arbitration and mediation hearings between disputing members, adjudicated conflicts among its factions, managed and collected the debts of its members, and, in addition, charged them various fees for its services. The seniority of its membership and the flight of the American-born to the middle-class districts of the city and to the suburbs tended to undermine *hui kuan* authority, but the old businesses in Chinatown still affiliate with them and accept their mediation and arbitration services. They are especially important in the ownership and control of Chinatown property which they administer in a traditional way, quite contrastive to real estate management in the Occidental parts of the city.

The third major type of association in Chinatown is the secret society. Like the clan and the *hui kuan,* the secret society originated in China where for centuries it served as a principal agency for popular protest, violent rebellion, and social banditry. The overseas migrants from Kwangtung included not a few members of the Triad Society, the most famous of China's clandestine associations. In nearly every overseas community of significant Chinese population, they established chapters of, or models based on, that order.

In the United States, secret societies among the Chinese were established by the early immigrants in the cities and also in those outlying areas where clans and *hui kuan* could not form a solid base. Inside Chinatown, the secret societies soon took over control of gambling and prostitution, institutions which flourished in the absence of wives and domestic habitation and in the presence of the "frontier spirit" that characterized the early West in general. It is with these pursuits, rather than with their political or eleemosynary activities, that they are most often associated in the minds of non-Chinese in America. Clans, *hui kuan,* and the several chapters of secret societies often fell out with one another over their competition for women, wealth, and power inside Chinatown, and these so-called Tong wars raged intermittently until a Chinatown Peace Association established a still-perilous peace between the warring factions in the 1920s. The charitable works of secret societies were confined for the most part to the giving of mutual aid to their own members, the establishment of headquarters and hostelries, and in recent years the building of club houses where their aged bachelor members might find fraternity.

The political activities of the secret societies have consisted of their intermittent interest in the fortunes of China's several regimes, but they have not shown any particular interest in upsetting the national politics of the United States. A vague commitment to restoring the Ming Dynasty in China (deposed in 1644 by the Manchu conquerors), coupled with a pronounced hostility to the Manchu rulers, made it possible for Sun Yat Sen to tap them for financial contributions to his republican revolution in 1911. A few hundred young men (at the most) were even inspired to form eventually abortive drill teams in rural California in anticipation of the fateful day when the revolution would call upon their help. Factionalized again after Sun's Republic proved unable to establish a consensus in China, the overseas secret societies remained only occasionally interested and never effective in solving China's problems. The Triad Society reorganized as a political party in 1947, and, led by aging delegates from the United States and Canada, made a totally unsuccessful attempt to mediate between Chiang Kai-Shek and Mao Tse-Tung. Since then, its political interests have subsided considerably. Meanwhile, the secret societies' most successful source of revenue in Chinatown — the control over gambling and prostitution — diminished as the Chinese bachelors aged and died, and interest in these vices declined amongst the American born. The recruitment of the newly arrived and disaffected immigrant youth from Chinatown has undoubtedly done much to rejuvenate these societies, but it remains to be seen whether this will lengthen their institutional life in America or change their function in accordance with new interests and current developments.

At the top of the community power structure of Chinatown is the Chinese Benevolent Association, commonly known as the Chinese Six Companies. It was formed in the late 1850s as a confederation of *hui kuan*. Later, it incorporated clans, guilds, and, reluctantly, secret societies in order to provide community-wide governance, to promote intracommunity harmony, and to present at least the appearance of a common Chinese front before the White society. Until the 1870s, it functioned as an agency of international diplomacy and as a consulate as well, since the Chinese Empire did not provide a specific overseas office for those duties. The Six Companies has been the principal spokesman for the Chinese to White America. It has protested against anti-Chinese legislation, helped fight discriminatory laws in the courts, petitioned federal, state, and local governments in behalf of the Chinese, and generally afforded Chinatown a modest respectability in the face of Sinophobic stereotypy. One of its more recent efforts in defense of Chinese in America was a protest against Secretary of Transportation Volpe's omission of the role that Chinese

played in the building of the Transcontinental Railroad when he spoke at the centenary celebration of the railroad's completion.

Gradually, the Six Companies established its legitimacy as rightful representative of the Chinese in San Francisco. Composed of merchants and traders, the confederation's leaders seemed to inspire assurance among civic leaders that the Chinese were not a threat to the city's economic base. The anti-Chinese movement in America was largely made up of small farmers and laborers who acted against what they described as the "unfair competition" of Chinese laborers. Once labor agitation had succeeded in driving Chinese workers out of the city's industries and into the confines of Chinatown, a movement that had largely completed its work by 1910, civic functionaries were quite prepared to negotiate with the Six Companies whatever agreements might have to be reached between the ghetto and the metropolis. For its part, the Six Companies, although it protested the excesses of the movement, must have realized the gain to be made in its own power by having the great majority of Chinese housed and employed in Chinatown. The final establishment of Chinatown as an unofficial, but nonetheless fixed, quarter of the city, consolidated and enhanced the power of the Six Companies over its denizens.

In effect, the Six Companies' authority over Chinese in San Francisco was, until the advent of the American born and the rise of intracommunity rebellion, an institutionalized version of the kind of control Booker T. Washington and his "Tuskegee Machine" exercised over Negroes in America from 1890 until 1915. The slow growth of a second generation prevented an effective counteraction to its powers by an acculturated group demanding a new politics. To be sure, Chinatown's Six Companies had its "du Boises," men who opposed the despotic benevolence which it exercised, the containment of Chinese in the ghetto which it tacitly espoused, and the corruption in its offices which they exposed from time to time. But they were too few in number to be effective, too readily coopted into the controlled violence of Chinatown's secret societies, or too easily frightened into silence by threats of financial loss, deportation, or, perhaps, conviction of trumped-up crimes in the White man's courts, where Chinese interpreters could be bought and witnesses willing to perjure themselves were easily obtainable. When the American-born generation did reach maturity, many of its members went to college, entered the professions, and departed from Chinatown. This caused the Six Companies some loss in the totality of its constituency, but, since the bourgeoisified Chinese-Americans did not challenge the authority of the Six Companies, it did not undermine their control over Chinatown.

Today, in addition to the "illegitimate" rebellion of youth in Chinatown, there is a "legitimate" counteraction of adults against the community-wide authority of the Six Companies. This loyal opposition includes several intra-Chinatown associations composed of "respectable" members of the American born, and, occasionally, a foreign-born Chinese leader who opposes the associational oligarchy. Until 1956, the only significant organization among the American-born Chinese was the Chinese-American Citizens' Alliance (CACA), a group so small that, in its early days, more than a half-century ago, it was little more than a name promising assimilation. Unlike its Japanese counterpart (the Japanese-American Citizens' League, which, in the 1930s, supplanted the old immigrant organizational federation, the Japanese Association of America), the CACA has never been able to overturn or replace the Six Companies. Since the mid-1950s, however, a new association has arisen, the Chinese-American Democratic Club (CADC). This organization of politically minded and socially conscious Chinese-Americans heralds a shift from communal-oriented traditionalism to civic-minded cosmopolitanism in Chinatown. Through its affiliation with the Democratic Party, CADC has helped to place prominent Chinese-Americans in municipal judgeships and other politically appointed posts in the city and has sponsored some of the candidates for city supervisor that for the first time are coming from Chinatown. Still another organization outside the domination of the Six Companies is the Concerned Chinese for Action and Change (CCAC), a loose and informal association of middle-class Chinese-Americans who live out of the ghetto and who can be counted on to mass for support of more liberal social action in Chinatown. It sponsored a reformist demonstration in Chinatown in August, 1968, fielded one of the two unsuccessful Chinese-American candidates in the 1969 election for municipal supervisor, and may become an even greater force in Chinatown, if it can continue to muster support. Third, the Chinatown-North Beach Area Youth Council, a product of the Economic Development Agency in Chinatown, seeks to link up the respectable middle-class Chinatowners with the less respectable youth groups. With a coalition of fifteen different youth groups in the area, including ICSA, Leway, and some of the street gangs, the Council hopes both to legitimate youth power and to effect communication between generations in Chinatown, between native- and foreign-born in the city, and between the ghetto and the metropolis in general.

Finally, there is one aging Chinese, J. K. Choy, who almost alone has opposed the old order in Chinatown without effective reprisal. A Columbia-educated banker and a professed disciple of Fabianism, Choy has exposed the poverty and neglect hidden beneath the tinseled glitter of Chinatown's neon-lit ghetto. He organized a reading room and English classes for immigrants in the offices next to the branch bank which he oversees as general manager. When, in October, 1966, he advised the women employed in Chinatown's sweatshops to organize for better wages, shorter hours, and improved conditions, and offered a devastating criticism of the ghetto's poverty program, rumors were started in the community which resulted in a three-day run on the bank. Unlike the old Chinese boycotts, which were used so effectively in the early days of the economically isolated Chinatown, this attempt to destroy a Chinatown reformer failed because the bank was protected by its connections to the larger banking system of the state. The failure to silence Choy by traditional methods is an unobtrusive measure of the ghetto's growing interdependence with the nation, and a testimony to the decreasing power of traditional sanctions available to intra-community elite.

The battle arena between the new opposition and the old order in Chinatown has been the poverty board organized under the community action program of the Economic Opportunity Act of 1964. As in other poverty-stricken areas, major competition arose for seats on the board representing the poor in Chinatown. The poor never were effectively represented. The interim board, composed of Chinatown elite and charged with the task of providing "maximum feasible participation of the poor," emerged eventually as the permanent board. Including two EOC members and representatives from the Chinese Six Companies, the Chinese-American Citizens' Alliance, the Chinatown-North Beach District Council, the Greater Chinese Community Service Organization, the Chinese Chamber of Commerce, the Chinese Christian Union, and the North Beach Place Improvement Association, the board actually was dominated by the traditional power holders who continued their conservative stewardship over the Chinatown poor.

The Chinatown Board offered no significant opposition to Mayor Shelley during San Francisco's "revolt of the poor" in 1965, and instead favored the immediate establishment of a rather limited area improvement program and

an equally limited drive for teaching English to immigrants. To the charge that it failed to involve the poor in solutions to their own problems, a mandate of the original program, the Board replied that an admission of poverty was too shameful for a Chinese to bear, that the Chinese poor worked long hours, that they could not afford the additional time to attend Board meetings, and, finally, that many of the Chinatown poor were non-English-speaking immigrants who could not participate effectively in the planning of community programs.

When, after much liberal pressure, the Board expanded to include representatives of the Italian and Filipino communities, a few Chinese-speaking immigrant poor, the ILGWU, and, remarkably enough, representatives from two veterans' organizations, policies changed but little. Of the four representatives elected to the Board from the Ping Yuen Improvement Association, in April, 1966, the first grass-roots group formed in response to the original EOC mandate, only one, an eighteen-year-old college freshman, could speak English. In the next three years, and especially following the emergence of the Intercollegiate Chinese for Social Action, the public meetings were tinged with great drama but few developments. The English-speaking Board controlled the outcome of business by its clear mastery of parliamentary procedure; the Chinese-speaking members rarely contributed to the discussions, but regularly voted in silent but ineffective opposition to most proposals; the audience, which included a vociferous element of angry youths and ICSA members, hurled epithets and obscenities at the Board; and the more traditional-minded Chinese were either scared off by these improprieties or shamefully silenced by their humble position before Chinatown's elite.

In April, 1969, after three years of internecine in-fighting, the liberal opposition, composed largely of the members of the CADC, was finally able to depose the Six Companies board member, and to replace him with a chairman more to their liking. The Six Companies charged that the EDA Board was dominated by "left-wing militants," but they were unable to secure complete control over Chinatown's poverty program. However, the Chinatown program, a part of the national policy that Daniel Patrick Moynihan has labeled a "maximum feasible misunderstanding," was to be budgeted only to the beginning of 1970. If the program were scrapped, the arena of conflict and opposition in Chinatown might shift to some other plane.

Another challenge to the old order was hurled by ICSA. In August, 1969, a news reporter interviewed Foo Hum, tea merchant, mogul in the Chinese Six Companies, and representative on the Chinatown EDA, concerning Chinatown's social problems. In addition to denying that the community's problems were either exclusive or very grave, Hum refuted the assertion that they were attributable to newly arrived immigrants. He then launched into an attack on the native-born youth, especially the Red Guards and the ICSA, and was quoted in the press as saying, "The Red Guards and the Intercollegiate Chinese for Social Action — theirs are Communist activities. They should not be blamed on the new immigrants." ICSA promptly filed a slander suit against Hum for $100,000 general damages and $10,000 punitive damages. Hum, backed by a Six Companies legal defense fund of $10,000, refused to settle out of court an offer made by Mason Wong, ICSA President, that the suit be dropped in return for Hum's writing a letter of apology and publishing it in all local papers, paying all legal fees that had arisen so far, and donating a "Lai-sze," a token gift of money, to ICSA. The suit is still pending at this writing [1970].

The edge of Chinatown's cake of customary control may be beginning to crumble. The old order must contend not only with the mounting opposition of the community's respectable, professional, and American-born younger and middle-aged adults, but also with the militant organization of Chinatown's disaffected youth. In addition, it is by no means clear that the new immigrants will acquiesce to Chinatown's traditional power elite in the future as they have in the past. Whatever the outcome among the parties in the continuing competition for community power, there still remains the burgeoning social problems of the ghetto.

... And the New Problems

Chinatown is not only a brightly lit avenue of restaurants and shops, not only a cultural preserve of some institutions of old Cathay, not only a tourist attraction of major civic and economic proportions — it is also a poverty-ridden, over-crowded slum. Similar to Michael Harrington's descriptions of the poor, Chinatown's indigents are not quite visible. They are hidden behind the grandeur of Chinese *objets d'art*, the glitter of Grant Avenue's neon lights, and the gastronomic delights of the ghetto's modestly priced restaurants. Nevertheless, in the recesses of Chinatown's alleys and side streets, in the buildings that rise above the tourist-crowded avenue, and in the basements buried below street level, exist all the elements of poverty and neglect that usually evoke concern, compassion, and condemnation when discovered elsewhere. Chinatown suffers from conditions of exploited labor and unemployment, ill health, bad housing, and educational impoverishment. Chinatown is a pocket of poverty secreted within a gilded ghetto.

Chinatown's problems are cultural, social, and economic, and they are all rendered more difficult of solution because of the traditional politics that prevail in the ghetto. Linguistically, Chinatown is composed of sub-ethnic groups speaking several dialects of Cantonese. Even before the arrival of the new immigrants, the language barrier interfered with educational advancement and occupational opportunities. In 1960, the median education of persons over twenty-five years of age was 1.7 years, which compared unfavorably with a city-wide average of 12 years. New immigrants find themselves trapped in the ghetto because they do not speak English, and the current attempts to teach English have not yet proven effective. Meanwhile, the American born, imbued with a new sense of ethnic consciousness, have discovered that their own speech defects in English are matched as well with their difficulties in communicating in Chinese, and, no longer regarding their native language as inferior, are demanding that Cantonese be taught in public schools and colleges.

Beyond the language barrier is that created by a slum hemmed in by century-old real estate discrimination. Population density in Chinatown is greater than in any other part of the city and is second only to that in Manhattan. City-wide the density is 24.6 persons per gross acre; for Chinatown it ranges from 120 to 179.9 persons per gross acre. Seventy-seven percent of Chinatown's buildings are substandard; most are nearly a half-century old; 60 percent of the housing lacks bathrooms, many are without heat, closed off from natural light, and without facilities for cooking. Electricity is antiquated, and any space inside the tiny apartments or single rooms for indoor working or studying is poorly lit and cramped.

The poor housing is inhabited by Chinatown's disproportionately large number of aged bachelors and new immigrants, two groups which, either because of age and indigence or newness and non-literacy in English, or both, are unable to make effective claims for better habitation. Medical facilities in Chinatown are inadequate and in some cases substandard, and attempts by committees of compassionate Chinese-American physicians to remedy the defects have only just begun. The Chinese Hospital has only sixty beds; it was not founded until 1924 and did not receive accreditation until 1967. Filth and refuse are still exposed on the streets of Chinatown, and rats are not infrequently seen in the alleys and

cellars. Chinatown has the highest suicide and tuberculosis rates in the nation. Finally, the occupations which Chinese have held since their forcible expulsion from the jobs protected by labor unions are for the most part menial, non-competitive with those held by Whites, and highly subject to exploitation. All these conditions are enclosed in the brightly lit ghetto and were, until recently, insulated against exposure by an anachronistic system of community politics that does not prevail in any other ethnic community in the United States.

No institution better reveals the scope of Chinatown's seemingly insurmountable problems and its encapsulation within an almost-closed community than its garment-making sweatshops. At one time, Chinese were employed in many phases of city-wide industry in San Francisco. Cigar-wrapping, gunpowder manufacture, slipper-making, woolen-milling, and embroidery were the most significant modes of Chinese employment in the city's industries. Then, in the face of labor's open policy of Sinophobia, Chinese were driven out of these industries in a wave of race-baiting strikes and exclusionary contracts that swept over the city from 1875 until 1910. Chinese workers, most of them sojourners beginning to age, fled into Chinatown where, without much choice, they became the exploitable victims of Chinese contractors. One industry which began in this way is garment-making. Today, that industry continues in much the same form as it began, in tiny shop-factories, employing immigrant women at rates that are estimated to range from thirty-five to seventy-five cents per hour (although official reports present a higher wage), and under conditions of piece-work and "sweated" labor that would make all but an early nineteenth century liberal recoil in horror. In 1921, San Francisco's supervisors established the Chinatown area by ordinance as a place where these shops might continue to operate with impunity, absolutely unprotected by unionization, largely unsupervised by civic inspectors, but occasionally improved because of the benevolence or compassion of the garment contractors. In 1958, an amendment to the city's zoning ordinance legalized those shops that operated outside the specified area of the 1921 zone. The number of factories is hard to ascertain precisely because some are too well hidden from view and a few are actually mobile, but it is estimated today to be between 120 and 180 in the Chinese quarter. The Chinatown garment industry is estimated to be worth $1,500,000.

In the past three years, both major newspapers of San Francisco have exposed the conditions that prevail in these workshops, and there have been several claims that the evils would be remedied by quick and coercive trade union action. A few Chinese have been signed up by the ILGWU, there was one short-lived and abortive strike by a few workers, and fresh claims of unionization drives have recently been made by joint teams of ILGWU and Teamster leaders. However, the situation looks less than promising. First, Chinese have good reason to distrust and disbelieve the blandishments of trade union organizers. The labor movement in the West was built upon the exploited and overworked bodies of the Chinese, who were excluded from almost every trade union organized, vilified mercilessly as the major source for White workers' woes, and employed as scabs by a skillful management that took good advantage over a racially divided labor force. Labor's long hostility to the Chinese is not likely to be forgotten by Chinatowners who know their own history and are properly suspicious of the working-class solidarity propaganda put forth by newly aroused union organizers from the White metropolis.

Second, precisely because of their location inside Chinatown and their employment of immigrant women, the shops are less susceptible to unionization or even union control after successful membership drives. These shops have taken on something of a cultural orientation and social character reflecting their Chinese environment. The

language in them is Cantonese, the women often work with their pre-school children playing at their feet, and the managers extend a paternalistic benevolence over their despotic exploitation that is hard for the more traditional Chinese to oppose. Attempts by civic officials or union investigators to discover the real wages, actual hours, and existent worker benefits are by no means easily successful. The non-English-speaking women are defeated by the language barrier, disciplined by Confucian tradition, and demeaned in the face of their interrogators. Most often they remain silent, providing mute confirmation of the sometimes-false reports turned in by the garment shop contractors.

Finally, Chinatown's more liberal-minded leaders may be self-defeated by their ambiguous support of both progressive policies and a new racial consciousness. The former may call for a need to push for the introduction of unionization and other characteristic features of White America into Chinatown's anachronistic institutions. But the new ethnic consciousness, a consciousness that in its extreme forms opposes both the old order of transplanted Cathay and the middle-class ways of White America, may forbid cooperation with those institutions, progressive or not, that are dominated by Caucasians.

It is in this possible paralysis that Chinatown's old order coalesces with its new rebels. Both seem to oppose the imposition of the metropolis upon the ghetto, but for quite different reasons. For the old elite, any more intrusion might undermine their exclusive and "extra-territorial" power; for the new rebels, any intrusion might wrest away their newly discovered desire for ethnic self-determination. It would not be impossible for Chinatown's garment workers, as well as the community's other unprotected and impoverished denizens, to be caught helplessly in the vise of this excruciatingly cultural conflict.

Discrimination and National Oppression

Beyond the problems of the ghetto itself loom the attitudes and actions of the larger society. Chinatown's myth of social propriety, communal self-help, familial solidarity, and a low crime rate was carefully nurtured and designed to counteract the vicious stereotypy of coolie laborers, immoral practices, murderous Tong wars, and inscrutable cunning that characterized the American White man's perspective. As a pervasive mystique coloring most reports of Chinatown for the past three decades, it has succeeded to a point in its original purpose: to substitute a favorable stereotype for an unfavorable one. It had other latent functions as well, not the least of which was to protect the community's social and political structure from excessive scrutiny and destruction. So long as Chinatown could "contain" its problems, circumscribe its para-governmental institutions with bourgeois or innocuously exotic descriptions, and control its members, the community was safe, and the city adopted a relaxed attitude toward its own cosmopolitan character.

But Chinatown's safety rests also on America's foreign relations with China. The repeal of the exclusion laws in 1943 was a gesture of reconciliation toward the country's ally during the war against Japan, just as the incarceration of Japanese-Americans during that same war was a hostile move against those Americans who had the misfortune to be physically identifiable with America's enemy. Aware of the vicissitudinal character of America's friendliness toward her racially visible peoples, Chinatown has presented a picture of cultural identity with nineteenth-century Cathay and of moral sympathy for the Nationalist Regime in Taiwan. This is not a false picture, for the political identity of the aged aliens is of very low intensity. But, if it must be linked to old China, it is most probably attuned to the Republic founded by Sun Yat Sen and continued under Chiang Kai-Shek. American-born Chinese are not "zionists" to

any degree and, therefore, feel themselves to be Americans politically and socially. They do not identify with either China. Even the Red Guards' rhetorical usage of Mao's book is more a symbol of an American rebellion than the substance of communist affiliation. And the new immigrants have shown a profound disinterest in associating even with the symbols of Maoism.

Nevertheless, the fires of fear and prejudice are still kindled in America. Not only are acts of prejudice and discrimination still visited upon Chinese-Americans in everyday life, in jobs, housing, schools, and interpersonal relations, but at least one agency of the government itself is still not wholly satisfied with the loyalty of Chinese in America. On April 17, 1969, J. Edgar Hoover testified before a Subcommittee of the House Committee on Appropriations that "the blatant, belligerent, and illogical statements made by Red China's spokesmen during the past year leave no doubt that the United States is Communist China's Number One enemy." Hoover went on to warn the Subcommittee that Chinese Communist intelligence functions in ways "overt and covert, to obtain needed material, particularly in the scientific field." After hinting darkly that a Chinese-American who served a sixty-day prison sentence for making a false customs declaration about electronic parts being sent to Hong Kong might have been an agent of a Communist country, Hoover asserted, "We are being confronted with a growing amount of work in being alert for Chinese-Americans and others in this country who would assist Red China in supplying needed material or promoting Red Chinese propaganda." "For one thing," he continued, "Red China has been flooding the country with its propaganda, and there are over 300,000 Chinese in the United States, some of whom could be susceptible to recruitment either through ethnic ties or hostage situations because of relatives in Communist China." "In addition," he added, "up to 20,000 Chinese immigrants can come

43

into the United States each year, and this provides a means to send illegal agents into our Nation." Hoover concluded his testimony on this point by asserting, "There are active Chinese Communist sympathizers in the Western Hemisphere in a position to aid in operations against the United States."

Thus, the Chinese in America were reminded that perhaps all their efforts at convincing White America that they were a peaceable, law-abiding, family-minded, and docile people who contributed much and asked little in return had gone for naught. In time of crisis, they too might suffer the same fate that overtook the highly acculturated Japanese-Americans a quarter-century before — wholesale incarceration. When Hoover's remarks are coupled with the widespread report in 1966 that China's atomic bomb was "fathered" by Dr. Tsien Hwue-shen, an American-educated Chinese who was persecuted here for five years ʻduring the McCarthy era and then allowed to return to the country of his birth and citizenship, and with the fact that, under Title II of the Emergency Detention Act of 1950, any person or group who is deemed to be a "threat to the internal security of the United States" may be incarcerated in the same detention camps in which the American Japanese were imprisoned, the safety of the Chinese in America from official persecution is by no means assured. The Chinese, of course, protested Hoover's comments, and one San Francisco paper labeled his testimony an irresponsible slur on "a large and substantial segment of American citizens." Meanwhile, Japanese-American, Chinese-American, and several other kinds of organizations have joined together to attempt to get Congress to repeal the infamous Title II.

Race prejudice, as Herbert Blumer has reminded us, is a sense of group position. It arises out of the belief, supported and legitimated by various elite, that a racial group is both inferior and threatening. Such a belief may lie dormant beneath the facade of a long-term racial accommodation, made benign by a minority group's tacit agreement to live behind the invisible wall of an urban ghetto. Then, when circumstances seem to call for new meanings and different explanations, the allegedly evil picture and supposedly threatening posture may be resuscitated to account for political difficulties or social problems that seem to defy explanation.

History, however, does not simply repeat itself. There is a new Chinatown and new sorts of Chinese in America. The old order holds its power precariously in the ghetto; the new liberals and the now-vocal radicals bid fair to supplant them and try new solutions to the old problems. Finally, the experience of 1942 may not be repeated, either because the United States has learned that lesson too well, or because too many Americans would not let it happen again.

4. A White View of American Racism

by Nathaniel N. Wagner

Having lived for a considerable period of time in other parts of the world, I am more than ever committed in my belief as to the benefits of living in America. I can think of no other country where such opportunity and freedom exist for so many people. Despite these strongly held feelings, there is much in America that can and must be improved! Next to the question of limiting our numbers so that a quality of life and environment can be developed and maintained, prejudice and racism should have our highest priority.

Racism in America begins with the "discovery" of this continent by Columbus and his party. If Columbus "discovered" America, what was the relation of the natives inhabiting these shores to their own land? The obvious ethnocentrism of "discovering" America is matched only by the atrocious misnaming of the inhabitants of the Western Hemisphere as "Indians." Columbus thought he had found the short route to India, and this inaccurate name is only now beginning to disappear as the indigenous people of this continent begin to prefer "Native American" to "Indians," just as "Black" is preferred to "Colored" or "Negro," and "Chicano" is preferred to "Mexican-American." Racism is as American as hot dogs, Sunday football on T.V., and the National Rifle Association. We need to acknowledge that, for only after the acceptance of historical truth can we plot our course.

Definitions

When topics such as racism and prejudice are discussed, the emotionality is often so intense as to preclude objective, honest scholarship. Only topics such as abortion and euthanasia bring the intensity of feeling that race, racial intermarriage, and school busing do. Some clear definitions will help. For the purposes of this chapter, racism means very simply the belief that one or more races are innately superior over other races. For America, this translates as the superiority of Whites over non-Whites as the most destructive and important form of racism. Non-Whites are not immune to developing racist attitudes, although historically these attitudes seem to have come largely in response to White racism. Even the term non-White suggests the racist position. If you doubt that, then think about the term non-female as the appropriate description for males.

Racism is a particular form of prejudice. Prejudice means pre-judgment. Prejudice or pre-judgment is necessary for survival in a world as complex as ours. As you walk down a long flight of stairs talking to your companion, you do not look down to make sure each step is there; you pre-judge the staircase. When you enter a room and decide to sit in a chair, you do not need to inspect the chair to be sure it has four legs in good condition. You are prejudiced in favor of chairs and their possessing four legs, although your pre-judgment may not always be correct. Prejudice is a way of ordering data and simplifying our lives. For chairs and stairs, it helps; for long-hairs and Asian-Americans, it can be deadly.

Discrimination is the application of prejudice in behavior. Someone can be prejudiced and not discriminate or discriminate and not be prejudiced. The White basketball coach who hates Blacks, but wants to win, will play his Black players if they are the best on his team, even though he may wish things were different. The non-prejudiced White basketball coach may refuse to play five Black players at one time for fear of the White alumni, and because of his wish to maintain his job. Discrimination and prejudice are correlated in most instances, but by no means is that correlation a perfect one.

American Racism

In March, 1968, the National Advisory Commission on Civil Disorders, appointed by President Lyndon B. Johnson, published its findings, basically twofold. First:

> What White Americans have never fully understood, but what the Negro can never forget, is that White society is deeply implicated in the ghetto. White institutions created it, White institutions maintain it, and White society condones it. (1968, page 2)

Second:

> Of the basic causes, the most fundamental is the racial attitude and behavior of White Americans toward Black Americans. Race prejudice has shaped our history decisively; it now threatens to affect our future. White racism is essentially responsible for the explosive mixture that has been accumulating in our cities. . . . (1968, page 10)

How is it possible to integrate this view of American racism with the traditions of America so thoughtfully and beautifully stated in the Declaration of Independence, the Bill of Rights, and all of the American libertarian traditions? I believe that an historical analysis will indicate

that our democratic traditions combined with some other factors to sabotage the essential freedoms of peoples in America who are not White.

The European development of racism seems intrinsically tied to their undeniable technological success that came with the Industrial Revolution. A few centuries before that revolution, Marco Polo, in the late thirteenth century, had written of his visit to China from the perspective of a member of an underdeveloped nation visiting a developed one. By the end of the seventeenth century, the European belief in their racial superiority was fully developed. This is the period of the conquest and colonization of America.

Slavery and racism intertwined in America with unfortunate results. The vastness of the North American Continent made slavery economically viable. As slavery developed in America, there came a clash of traditions. The English, the main colonizers of this continent, had been the first European peoples not only to do away with chattel or property slavery, but also to codify the rights of ordinary men. The Magna Carta is considered by many to be the most significant document in man's evolution to political freedom, and the Magna Carta was born and bred in English traditions. The Portuguese and the Spanish, the colonial powers of South America, had no such democratic traditions and had long-continuing experience with slavery. The English had ended chattel slavery, although the concept of bonded indebtedness was still alive in England. In fact, many slaves, in the early days of the English colonization of America, earned their freedom from their masters by hard and loyal work. As more and more slaves were brought to America, the concept of slavery slowly moved to a chattel one.

The religion of the early English settlers aided in this movement to chattel slavery. The Church of England (in America, after independence, the Episcopal Church) was never a missionary or proselytizing church. In South

America, the Roman Catholic Church, in contrast, baptized boat loads and has long been a missionary church.

For slaves in North America who were not baptized, the sacraments of the church were not available. Importantly, the sacrament of marriage was not available to slaves; the consequences of this are hard to imagine with a twentieth-century consciousness.

To recap: The English did not have a tradition of slavery as did the Portuguese and the Spanish, nor did the English make their religion available to their slaves. They could not reconcile the principles of freedom so beautifully stated by Thomas Jefferson and the reality of American slavery. Their resolution, horrendous in its consequences, was to dehumanize their slaves. This made it possible for Jefferson, at the time he was writing the Declaration of Independence, to own slaves, and to boast and brag of his personal abilities in increasing his slave population by his sexual exploits. Slaves were not people; therefore, neither the Magna Carta nor the Declaration of Independence applied to them. This position was restated by the United States Supreme Court in the instance of Dred Scott, a runaway slave. In 1856, the Court ruled that Dred Scott was property and, therefore, could not sue for his freedom. A fortuitous marriage of capitalistic ideology, animal husbandry, and male sexual desire combined to make a period of American history difficult to acknowledge in its cruelty to the females, or in its effects upon the male slaves.

If the National Institute of Mental Health had convened a conference with the avowed purpose of keeping Blacks in slavery, the results would probably have suggested following colonial slave practice. Keep the young male slaves away from male models of strength. Punish adult males who act in strong and positive ways. This discomfort with Black male aggressiveness continues to this day and is seen clearly in the "crime" of Muhammad Ali (Cassius Clay) of being an "uppity nigger." In 1971, a Supreme Court not known for its liberalism unanimously found that Ali's rights had been unconstitutionally taken from him.

But racism in America is not just directed at our Black brothers. Here are some contemporary examples to indicate its pervasiveness. The first was discovered while being a good, White, middle-class father and reading to my oldest son when he was quite young. I was reading from a book entitled *A Child's Garden of Verses* by Robert Louis Stevenson, copyrighted originally in 1929 and again in 1956. The book was given to my son by one of his aunts in 1959. Here is the poem, "Foreign Children." It needs no comment.

> Little Indian, Sioux or Crow,
> Little frosty Eskimo,
> Little Turk or Japanee,
> O! don't you wish that you were me?
>
> You have seen the scarlet trees
> And the lions over seas;
> You have eaten ostrich eggs,
> And turned the turtles off their legs.
>
> Such a life is very fine,
> But it's not so nice as mine:
> You must often, as you trod,
> Have wearied *not* to be abroad.
>
> You have curious things to eat,
> I am fed on proper meat;
> You must dwell beyond the foam,
> But I am safe and live at home.
>
> Little Indian, Sioux or Crow,
> Little frosty Eskimo,
> Little Turk or Japanee,
> O! don't you wish that you were me?

The second example is more current. Quoted in its entirety is the public record of Judge Gerald S. Chargin of the Superior Court of California.

IN THE SUPERIOR COURT OF THE STATE OF CALIFORNIA
IN AND FOR THE COUNTY OF SANTA CLARA
JUVENILE DIVISION

HONORABLE GERALD S. CHARGIN, Judge

Courtroom No. 1

In the matter of
PAUL PETE CASILLAS, JR.,
 a minor

No. 40331

STATEMENT OF THE COURT

San Jose, California

September 2, 1969

APPEARANCES:

For the Minor:

FRED LUCERO, ESQ.
Deputy Public Defender

For the Probation Department:

WILLIAM TAPOGNA, ESQ.
Court Probation Officer

Official Court Reporter:

SUSAN K. STRAHM, C.S.R.

September 2, 1969

10:25 a.m.

STATEMENTS OF THE COURT

The Court: There is some indication that you more or less didn't think that it was against the law or was improper. Haven't you had any moral training? Have you and your family gone to church?

The Minor: Yes, sir.

The Court: Don't you know that things like this are terribly wrong? This is one of the worst crimes that a person can commit. I just get so disgusted that I just figure what is the use? You are just an animal. You are lower than an animal. Even animals don't do that. You are pretty low.

I don't know why your parents haven't been able to teach you anything or train you. Mexican people, after thirteen years of age, it's perfectly all right to do that to a stranger, let alone a member of your own family. I don't have much hope for you. You will probably end up in State's Prison before you are twenty-five, and that's where you belong, anyhow. There is nothing much you can do.

I think you haven't got any moral principles. You won't acquire anything. Your parents won't teach you what is right or wrong and won't watch out.

Apparently, your sister is pregnant; is that right?

The Minor's Father, Mr. Casillas: Yes.

The Court: It's a fine situation. How old is she?

The Minor's Mother, Mrs. Casillas: Fifteen.

The Court: Well, probably, she will have a half a dozen children and three or four marriages before she is eighteen.

The County will have to take care of you. You are no particular good to anybody. We ought to send you out of the country — send you back to Mexico. You belong in prison for the rest of your life for doing things of this kind. You ought to commit suicide. That's what I think of people of this kind. You are lower than animals and haven't the right to live in organized society — just miserable, lousy, rotten people.

There is nothing we can do with you. You expect the County to take care of you. Maybe Hitler was right. The animals in our society probably ought to be destroyed because they have no right to live among human beings. If you refuse to act like a human being, then, you don't belong among the society of human beings.

Mr. Lucero: Your Honor, I don't think I can sit here and listen to that sort of thing.

The Court: You are going to have to listen to it because I consider this a very rotten, vulgar human being.

Mr. Lucero: The Court is indicting the whole Mexican group.

The Court: When they are ten or twelve years of age, going out and having intercourse with anybody without any moral training — they don't even understand the Ten Commandments. That's all. Apparently, they don't want to.

So if you want to act like that, the County has a system of taking care of them. They don't care about that. They have no personal self-respect.

Mr. Lucero: The Court ought to look at this youngster and deal with this youngster's case.

The Court: All right. That's what I am going to do. The family should be able to control this boy and the young girl.

Mr. Lucero: What appalls me is that the Court is saying that Hitler was right in genocide.

The Court: What are we going to do with the mad dogs of our society? Either we have to kill them or send them to an institution or place them out of the hands of good people because that's the theory — one of the theories of punishment is if they get to the position that they want to act like mad dogs, then, we have to separate them from our society.

Well, I will go along with the recommendation. You will learn in time or else you will have to pay for the penalty with the law because the law grinds slowly but exceedingly well. If you are going to be a law violator — you have to make up your mind whether you are going to observe the law or not. If you can't observe the law, then, you have to be put away.

STATE OF CALIFORNIA
COUNTY OF SANTA CLARA   ss

I, SUSAN K. STRAHM, do hereby certify that the foregoing is a true and correct transcript of the STATEMENTS OF THE COURT had in the within-entitled action taken on the 2nd day of September, 1969; that I reported the same in stenotype, being the qualified and acting Official Court Reporter of the Superior Court of the State of California, in and for the County of Santa Clara, appointed to said Court, and thereafter had the same transcribed into typewriting as herein appears.

Dated: This 8th day of September, 1969.

SUSAN K. STRAHM, C.S.R.

One can take some solace from the fact that Judge Chargin's colleagues publicly expressed disapproval of his racist statements and that he publicly apologized for his outburst. Nonetheless, as of this writing he sits in judgment of his fellow citizens in the State of California.

Racist attitudes against Asian-Americans have existed almost as long as Asian immigration to this country. Chinese were the first to immigrate, attracted by the advertisement and need for labor at the time of the finding of gold in California. In the 1850s, they started to arrive, and, in 1856, the following law was enacted in California's Columbia mining District:

Neither Asiatics nor South-Sea-Islanders shall be allowed to mine in this district, either for themselves or for others. . . .

(Shinn, 1965, p. 246)

The anti-Chinese movement gained momentum in the 1860s and 1870s; the following quote from an editorial in an Arizona newspaper communicates the flavor:

The Chinese are the least desired immigrants who have ever sought the United States ... the almond-eyed Mongolian with his pig-tail, his heathenism, his filthy habits, his thrift and careful accumulation of savings to be sent back to the flowery kingdom.

The most we can do is to insist that he is a heathen, a devourer of soup made from the fragrant juice of the rat, filthy, disagreeable, and undesirable generally, an incumbrance that we do not know how to get rid of, whose tribe we have determined shall not increase in this part of the world. (Smith, 1967, p. 31)

Or the words of the governor of Montana, James M. Ashley, addressing a combined session of the Montana Legislature on December 11, 1869:

> It will be conceded by all practical men who have given the subject any thought that Montana is better adapted to the hardy races of men and women from Great Britain and Northern Europe. . . . I am . . . opposed to the importation of laborers from any of the barbarous or semi-civilized races of men, and do not propose to co-operate in any scheme organized to bring such laborers into Montana, or into any part of the country. (Quinn, 1967, p. 83)

These attitudes culminated in the Chinese Exclusion Act of 1882 which prohibited any further immigration of Chinese. It is remarkable that the Encyclopaedia Britannica, an eminent reference work not usually considered a racist book, describes these Congressional actions in the following way:

> Prior to World War I, the laws of the United States permitted immigration without numerical limitation and were concerned chiefly with barring undesirables. The initial federal limitation upon immigration prohibited the importation of Oriental slave labour, prostitutes, and alien convicts, pursuant to laws enacted in 1862 and 1875. The mentally ill, epileptics, physical defectives, tubercular persons, anarchists, beggars, those likely to become public charges, Chinese labourers (sic), contract labourers, those suffering from loathesome or dangerous diseases, polygamists, paupers, persons whose passages were paid by others, and aliens convicted of crimes involving moral turpitude were added by successive enactments in 1882, 1885, 1891, 1903, and 1907. (Encyclopaedia Britannica, Vol. 11, 1965, Wm. Benton, p. 1102)

The story of the Japanese was similar. James Morishima has more than adequately documented the effects of the inhumane and tragic evacuation of all persons of Japanese ancestry from the West Coast of the United States. A colleague of mine, Professor Minoru Masuda of the Department of Psychiatry at the University of Washington, relates a particularly poignant incident in relation to that shameful period of American history. At the time of Pearl Harbor, Masuda, who had been born in Seattle, was twenty-six years old. He told his Japanese-born, alien father — whom United States laws at that time prohibited from becoming a citizen — that he was concerned about the reaction of the United States to the war. He warned his father that he might be interned, but was not concerned for himself, as he was a citizen of the United States, protected by the Constitution and the Bill of Rights. Early in 1942, Minoru Masuda, citizen of the United States, and his alien father were incarcerated by the United States Government for the crime of Japanese ancestry. The Government dealt with the problem of citizenship in the following manner:

> Pursuant to the provisions of Civilian Exclusion Order No. 57, this headquarters, dated May 10, 1942, all persons of Japanese ancestry, both alien and non-alien (sic), will be evacuated from the above area by 12 o'clock noon, P.W.T., Saturday, May 16, 1942.

The order was signed by J. L. DeWitt, Lieutenant General, U.S. Army Commanding, and dated May 10, 1942, Headquarters, Western Defense Command and Fourth Army, Presidio of San Francisco, California.

Almost a quarter of a million individuals of Japanese ancestry stayed in Hawaii throughout the war. They were not interned because of the tremendous cost and effort in relocating such an enormous number of people by boat, compared to the 110,000 persons of Japanese ancestry who were evacuated by train away from the Pacific coast. In Hawaii, not a single act of treason or sabotage occurred during the entire war by these quarter-million people of Japanese ancestry, either alien or non-alien (citizen)!

The Effects of Racism

The effects of racism are twofold. First have

been the effects upon the Native Americans, Blacks, Chicanos, and Orientals. Of course, prejudice and discrimination have been felt by Catholics, Jews, Mormons, Poles, Irish, Italians, and other minority groups. For reasons that go beyond the scope of this chapter, these White European groups have been able to overcome much of the prejudice and discrimination, and have generally shared in the American dream and wealth beyond that of their non-White countrymen. It is particularly the Native American, the Black, the Chicano, the Asian who have suffered most severely the results of racism. Whether one looks at the statistics of longevity, infant mortality, maternal deaths, alcoholism, poverty, poor educational achievement, or annual income, it is clear that Native Americans fare the worst. They are usually followed by Blacks and then the other racial minorities. Either these races are inferior, or inequality is deeply imbedded in the American experience. More of this later.

The second effect of racism is upon the White majority. Increasingly segregated in their White suburbs, the majority of Americans are shut off from significant portions of the American experience, from the experience of interacting with their non-White countrymen. The more major effect, however, is upon the strength of the American democracy and its institutions. Racism, and the hate it breeds, is an infection in the bloodstream of American democracy, sapping its vitality and forcing it to deny and ignore important aspects of its own experience.

The Continuation of Racism

When the reality of the economic and social position of racial minorities in America is juxtaposed with the stated principles of American democracy, there are only two explanations possible. Either these racial groups — in particular Blacks, Native Americans, and Chicanos — are, in fact, inferior to the White majority, or racism and discriminatory treatment are part of the fabric of the American experience. Many

Americans, in all probability the majority of White Americans, maintain a racist position — namely, that non-White Americans are in fact inferior to the majority of White Americans. These people are not overt racists and, in many instances, have little contact with non-Whites. In those limited and superficial contacts, they are often polite and thoughtful and would never think of calling anyone a "Nigger" or a "Jap" — at least, not to their face.

They are able, however, to maintain their racist belief in non-White inferiority (White superiority sounds too coarse) through the operation of a well-understood psychological principle — cognitive consistency. This concept describes the tendency of all human beings to wish to appear to be consistent in their thinking. Beyond this consistency is the tendency to avoid or deny information that is inconsistent with the central belief, and to look for and quickly integrate any information that is consistent with the central belief. In relation to the continuation of racism in America, something like this occurs in the minds of many Americans.

This is the greatest and best country in the world. Success is available to all Americans if they will work hard, be polite, and dress properly. Shaggy beards and long hair are signs of laziness and disrespect. If these simple principles of hard work and good manners are followed, everyone can share in the American dream and in American wealth. There are other components of this belief system for particular subgroups. A belief in a God, saying "Yes, Sir" and "Yes, Ma'am," and "not drinking, swearing, smoking, or screwing" are some of the variations on the theme.

But the racial minorities in America do not practice the twin virtues of hard work and good manners, or they practice them in an inferior way. That is the only conclusion to be drawn as one drives through East St. Louis, or the South Side of Chicago, or the North Side of Philadelphia, or through Black Watts, or Brown East Los Angeles, or one of the many rural reservation areas of Native Americans. If they don't practice those twin virtues, then they are either lazy or dumb or both. It is not our fault; it is theirs; and the American dream comes out red, white, and blue, and unscathed. And we can feel self-righteous and good and clean in our middle America.

It sounds vicious and cruel, and it is. But its cruelty is not the cruelty of lynchings and Nigger and Jap or Chink. Its cruelty is in the gentle looking-away; in the continuation of "color-blind" practices that do not take into account the color-related history of America; in the stratification of the society into White suburbs and Black inner-city; in the continued belief that America's racist history is exaggerated by emotional and irresponsible people who really don't even like this country. Of note is the fact that the critics of America and its racism, in pursuit of their cognitive consistency, have often been unable to accept the truth of aspects of the American dream and the truth that, with all its misery, America has been the land of opportunity for Whites and for many non-Whites.

Solutions

The cognitive position that holds the solutions for America is, I believe, that stated in the first paragraph of this chapter: America is a country with extraordinary opportunities and freedom for many people. It is also a country with a terrible racist history and institutions that have coagulated the consequences of that racist history. It is difficult for White Americans to live with such contradictory views, just as it is difficult for non-White Americans. The non-White situation is best stated in "Things are getting better every day and they are worse than ever." As conditions improve for racial minorities, the individual members of each racial group will get stronger and more outraged by anything short of genuine equality. It is all so beautifully summarized by a Black college student of mine, angered at the police treatment of the Black Panthers. The situation, he

told me, was intolerable, and he cited as his source *Time* magazine. What a strange irony that he cites *Time* for his data, never questioning its honesty, and apparently oblivious to the changes in America that make it possible for such an established, majority publication as *Time* to report the killing of Black Americans by the police or anybody.

The cognitive position that this is a great country but that many, many things must be improved is one that *is* consistent with American traditions. Historically, White minorities have succeeded to a remarkable degree, and we need to provide the conditions which can make these solutions work as well for non-Whites. The major solutions for non-White minorities in America have been in employment, education, and politics. Any one of these avenues, although the political arena has often been used as a facilitation for opportunities in employment and education, can provide the solution for any particular group.

What is needed is, first, the commitment to the solution of the problem, based on an understanding of our racist history, so that the removal of racial inequalities becomes as important as containing the spread of Communism in Southeast Asia. The importance of this priority cannot be overstated! Second is the courage of our convictions so that a new set of inequalities and racist positions is not just substituted for the old ones. Very personally, in my own area of specialization, we are encouraging the entrance of minority candidates into graduate training in psychology, providing every possible aid and tutoring assitance, but irrevocably demanding that, although entrance requirements need to be adjusted to allow minority students to enter, existing standards must be maintained! This is an absolute, both for the minority candidate (or else a racist position is implied) and for the public who is to be served by the minority psychologist or physician or nurse or teacher. This is more easily stated than implemented, but the success of remedial education programs rests upon the firm commitment not to lower existing standards. The fact that we need more Black, Chicano, and Native American doctors, engineers, lawyers, and nurses cannot be debated unless one wants to argue the essential inferiority of those races. With our racist history, at the very least we need a few generations of non-discriminatory treatment, a condition not yet available in this country, before a racist superiority position can even be seriously considered.

With a growing commitment to right the wrongs of the past, it is easy for minority groups to fall into all the same errors and stupidities as the majority group. Great care is needed to separate these new idiocies from the main thrust of the removal of racial inequalities. I remember poignantly the disappointment of a minority teaching assistant at having terrific pressure put upon him to change grades because someone was a "brother" or a "sister," and not because they had done the work or been graded unfairly. Or the minority student who was appalled at being asked to serve on the Board of Directors of a minority action group the first time she attended a meeting. No one knew anything about her except that she was from the right minority. Racial minorities should be expected to make as many foolish mistakes and be guilty of an equal number of stupidities as their White brothers and sisters. Let us not be racists! Let all groups be allowed errors. It is human, and it is our humanity that eventually becomes most important of all.

It is my fervent hope that one day a chapter on racism will not be needed in a volume such as this. When that day arrives, we can just talk about people without regard to racial membership, unless a particular individual wishes that to be a part of his or her identity. That day probably will never come, but we need to work toward it.

References

Encyclopaedia Britannica. Vol. 11, 1965; Wm. Benton, publisher; p. 1102.

Quinn, Larry D. " 'Chink, Chink, Chinamen,' The Beginnings of Nativism in Montana." Pacific Northwest Quarterly 58, 1967, 82-89.

Report of the National Advisory Commission on Civil Disorders. New York: Bantam Books, Inc., 1968.

Shinn, Charles H. Mining Camps: A Study in American Frontier Government. New York: Harper, 1965.

Smith, Duane A. Rocky Mountain Mining Camps: The Urban Frontier. Bloomington: Indiana University Press, 1967.

5. Passive Discrimination: The Normal Person

by Harry H. L. Kitano

Introduction

A common point of view found in both popular and research literature has centered around the relationship between emotional disturbance and discrimination. The idea that frustration, poor parent-child relationships, and extreme deprivation are behind prejudice and discrimination has led to studies of Hitler, the Nazis, and other racist groups. These studies support the point of view that the unstable and "sick" are the primary conveyors of prejudice and discrimination. Research evidence stemming from studies of the authoritarian personality, rigidity, and other personality variables also lends support to this type of analysis. It may very well be that those who go out of their way to practice segregation or to join known hate groups, such as the Ku Klux Klan, are emotionally disturbed and have identifiable personality patterns; however, it is difficult to ascribe pathology to all who practice acts of discrimination, no matter how tempting this approach.

Perhaps a different kind of conceptualization is needed for handling the "passive" discriminator. By passive, the author refers to the person who discriminates through limiting interaction and "input" from other groups but, when queried, might express non-discriminatory attitudes. He might verbalize the equalness of all groups, but, in the critical area of behavioral interaction, he would prefer that his friends and friends of his children be of his own reference group.

The purpose of this paper is to analyze the discriminatory behavior of a "normal group" in terms of their relationship to a cohesive, identifiable subculture and the resultant restriction of their outgroup interactions. It is the author's belief that the insulation of subgroups in our pluralistic society provides a perhaps unwanted, but nevertheless powerful, structure that fosters discriminatory behavior against outgroups.

The author is, therefore, presenting a social-psychological perspective on discrimination, with an emphasis on the effectiveness of subculture structure as a possible force fostering discrimination through restricting interaction, contact, and concern for other groups. Furthermore, from this point of view, the more normal personality — that is, the individual more fully integrated into the subculture — is hypothesized as the person who discriminates; and, conversely, the person less integrated and perhaps more alienated from his subculture is hypothesized as the individual with less discrimination. Specifically, the major hypotheses for empirical testing are:

1. That groups can be differentiated in terms of the degree of identification with a subculture;
2. That groups more identified with their subcultures will show more normal

3. That those groups more identified with their subcultures and exhibiting more normal personality patterns will practice discrimination at a higher level than the less identified and less integrated.

From this social-psychological perspective, the author is predicting the reverse of what is generally thought to be true — namely, the author hypothesizes that discrimination is practiced by the "more normal" and integrated; and, conversely, more democratic behavior is practiced by the less integrated and "less normal." The author is also suggesting that the pluralistic social structures of our society, with their various degrees of power, are a critical factor in the problem of social discrimination.

Methodology

The data are drawn from a larger research project by the author. (The study was supported by NIMH Grant, OM-476.) A comparison was made between a matched group of male, third-generation, adolescent, Japanese-American non-delinquents (called Group X) and delinquents (called Group Y) on answers to selected interview questions and a personality test: the Gough California Psychological Inventory, CPI.[1] The groups were matched in terms of ethnicity, age, schooling, area of residence, and sex. They were both similar in social-class background as measured by residence, occupation, and income of their parents. A comparison of parental responses was also tabulated.

Discrimination was measured in terms of friendship, dating, and marriage preferences. Social interaction on these levels appears to be an important concern for adolescents, especially since the appearance of many social structures, both formal and informal (e.g., gangs, secret societies, fraternities, and sororities), is readily apparent at this age. The author recognized that other indices of discrimination can also be used, ranging from the broad economic to the use of public service facilities. However, attitudinal and behavioral changes are probably more closely related to intimate areas of social interaction;[2] therefore, working side by side, although important, is not as effective for intergroup understanding as the voluntary social interaction that takes place after the office is closed.

The degree of ethnic identification and integration was measured through responses to group membership and participation in ethnic customs and activities. It was assumed that the availability of opportunities for ethnic activities was evidence of a subculture structure.

The data were tabulated through yes-no responses, and levels of significance are expressed in terms of p, derived from chi squares and Fischer's Exact Probability Test in cases where the expected cell frequencies fell below five.

Results

The data in Table 1 show the degree of ethnic identification between the samples. Members of Group X were clearly identified with their own group, they belonged to groups that were primarily of their own ethnicity, they participated in more activities and customs that were Japanese than were of other ethnic origins, and they preferred ethnic cuisine. Sixty percent of Group X belonged to Japanese groups only, as compared to only 16 percent of Group Y, and a chi square of 12.2, significant at the .01 level, was computed between the groups. In terms of friends, 100 percent of Group X, as compared to 75 percent of Group Y, had only Japanese friends. A p of .05, utilizing Fischer's Exact Test, was computed between the groups.

Sixty-two percent of Group X participated in Japanese activities, as compared to 32 percent of Group Y. A chi square of 4.3 is significant at the .05 level. Thirty-nine percent of Group X observed Japanese customs at home, as compared to none of Group Y, a difference that is statistically significant. Sixty-nine percent of Group X preferred Japanese food, as compared to 32 percent of Group Y. A chi

Table 1
Ethnic Identification Between Non-Probationer (Group X)
and Probationer (Group Y) Groups

| | Percent "Yes" Responses | | |
Adolescent Responses	Group X (N = 37)	Group Y (N = 25)	p
1. Belong to Japanese groups only	60	16	.01
2. Have Japanese friends primarily	100	75	.05
3. Participate in Japanese activities	62	32	.05
4. Observe Japanese customs	39	0	.05
5. Prefer Japanese food	69	32	.05

square of 5.4 is significant at the .05 level.

The data support the hypothesis concerning differences in ethnic identity between the groups.

Table 2 shows the differences in personality scores on the CPI between Groups X and Y. There were significant differences between the groups on the following scales: Responsibility (Re), Socialization (So), Tolerance (To), Achievement via Conformance (Ac), Achievement via Independence (Ai), Intellectual Efficiency (Ie), Flexibility (Fx), and Femininity (Fe).

Group X scores were more normal than Group Y scores, in that responses were congruent with the norms established for high school adolescents; Group Y scores were closer to the norms established for socially deviant populations (e.g., California delinquents) than Group X scores. Since lower mean scores indicate a lesser amount of the characteristic, the data support the hypothesis of less personality integration among Group Y adolescents than among Group X adolescents.

The data in Table 3 analyze responses in terms of social discrimination. Groups X and Y were asked questions regarding dating girls of various ethnic backgrounds. Both Groups X and Y would date other Japanese, other Orientals, and Caucasians in approximately equal proportions. However, statistically significant differences between the groups were found in terms of dating Mexican and Negro girls. Here Group Y responded in terms of much less discrimination: 68 percent of Group Y would date Mexican girls, as compared to only 27 percent of Group X. A chi square of 8.6 is significant at the .01 level. Thirty-six percent of Group Y would date Negro girls, as compared to only 8 percent of Group X. A chi square of 5.6 is significant at the .02 level.

The parents of both groups were also asked questions about social interaction. Even though the non-probationer parents (Group X) were generally more restrictive than were Group Y parents toward their sons' dating other Orientals and Caucasians (49 percent to 72 percent, 43 percent to 76 percent), the differences were not statistically significant.

However, in the area of their children's dating Negroes and Mexicans, significant differences were noted. Only 5 percent of Group X parents would allow the dating of Mexican girls, as against 60 percent of Group Y (p = .001); 3 percent of Group X parents would allow the dating of Negroes, as against 36 percent of Group Y (p = .01).

Parental responses were also similar in terms of friendship (see Table 2). Ninety-four percent of Group X parents preferred only Japanese friends for their children, as compared to 53 percent of Group Y. The difference was sig-

Table 2
Differences Between Japanese Non-Probationers (Group X) and
Japanese Probationers (Group Y) on the California Psychological Inventory (CPI)

CPI Variable	Group X (N = 30)		Group Y (N = 30)		p
	Mean	SD	Mean	SD	
Poise, Ascendancy, and Self-Assurance					
Dominance (Do)	21.3	6.7	21.3	5.1	
Capacity for Status (Cs)	15.4	3.4	14.1	3.0	
Sociability (Sy)	21.1	5.8	21.5	4.7	
(Social Participation)					
Social Presence (Sp)	33.2	6.4	32.7	3.5	
Self-Acceptance (Sa)	18.7	4.4	19.1	3.8	
Sense of Well-Being (Wb)	32.8	5.2	30.7	6.0	
Socialization, Maturity, and Responsibility					
Responsibility (Re)	26.4	4.4	20.4	6.1	.01
Socialization (Delinquency) (So)	36.6	6.2	28.3	7.1	.01
Self-Control (Impulsivity) (Sc)	25.1	9.2	22.1	9.9	
Tolerance (To)	18.8	4.9	15.2	5.0	.01
Good Impression (Gi)	13.4	6.9	12.7	6.0	
Community (Infrequency) (Cm)	24.8	2.7	24.2	3.1	
Achievement Potential and Intellectual Efficiency					
Achievement via Conformance (Ac)	23.0	3.4	20.7	5.2	.05
Achievement via Independence (Ai)	17.4	3.9	14.2	3.6	.01
Intellectual Efficiency (Ie)	34.8	5.1	30.9	6.3	.05
Intellectual and Interest Modes					
Psychological Mindedness (Py)	8.8	3.3	9.3	2.2	
(Psychological Interests)					
Flexibility (Fx)	10.7	3.8	8.0	2.9	.01
Femininity (Fe)	16.8	3.0	14.7	2.7	.01

nificant at the .001 level. The same proportion and the same significant difference were found in terms of friends for themselves.

Other variables (not included in the tables) also showed similar differences. For example, 72 percent of Group X parents would restrict marriages to only Japanese girls, as against 30 percent of Group Y parents, a difference that was significant at the .01 level.

The data support the hypotheses that the Group X adolescents and parents take a much more restrictive position in regard to intergroup interaction than Group Y adolescents and parents; and, conversely, the less ethnically identified population, Group Y, supports a much more liberal position than Group X. It should also be noted that both groups were in high agreement as to the desirability of intra-

Table 3
Social Discrimination: Differences Between Non-Probationers (Group X) and
Probationers (Group Y) and their Parents on Social Interaction

| | Percent "Yes" Responses | | |
Response	Group X (N = 37)	Group Y (N = 25)	p
Adolescent Responses			
Have or would date girls that are:			
1. Japanese	92	100	n.s.
2. Other Oriental	68	72	n.s.
3. Caucasian	65	68	n.s.
4. Mexican	27	68	.01
5. Negro	8	36	.02
Parental Responses			
Would permit sons to date:			
1. Japanese	97	92	n.s.
2. Other Oriental	49	72	n.s.
3. Caucasian	43	76	n.s.
4. Mexican	5	60	.001
5. Negro	3	36	.01
Parental Responses			
Would prefer friendship:			
1. Majority of Japanese friends for son	94	53	.01
2. Japanese friends for self	94	53	.01

ethnic interaction, which can be taken as evidence that Group Y respondents were not overtly rejecting their ethnicity.

Our data, then, lead to the acceptance of the overall hypotheses, that the ethnically identified and the "normal" practice social discrimination at a higher rate than do the less ethnically identified and the "less normal," at least as measured by the present study.

Generally, observations provided further validation for the empirical findings. Group X adolescents and parents considered themselves normal, non-discriminatory, democratic, and unbigoted. The parents, especially, would have been surprised had the author indicated (which he did not) that their responses were somewhat

inconsistent. Although professing the equality of all, they generally steered their children through the Japanese social structure — the all-ethnic church (Buddhist or Protestant), the all-ethnic YMCA or Boy Scout Troop, the all-ethnic Little League — and carefully screened out "other groups" from this structure.

Impressions gathered from members of other cohesive subgroups were also similar — for example, a Jewish girl noted that her father was for democracy and for integration, but carefully steered her through the Jewish social structure with the threat of "disowning her" if she dated or married out of her group. Possibly the greatest danger in this form of "passive discrimination" is the unawareness and the normality of those caught up in it.

Discussion

It is interesting and perhaps gratifying to note the relationship between conceptualizations and theories, and social preceptions and behavior. Although there have been many influences on theories of discrimination, bigotry, and prejudice, it would appear that much of our thinking in this area comes from studies of the authoritarian personality[3] and of Allport.[4] The weight of the evidence concerning the emotionally disturbed, the authoritarian personality, the rigid, the need for scapegoating, and other similar psychological phenomena is impressive, and undoubtedly reflects part of the problem of discrimination. However, the author strongly doubts that it explains the prevalence of discrimination over large sectors of the population; he believes that a social-psychological theory that analyzes the cohesion and structures of subcultural groups, their goals, attitudes, and behaviors, comes closer to striking at the larger significance of this problem.

Probably the most discriminatory and the most influential is the dominant White, Anglo-Saxon, Protestant group, since identification with and possession of its attribute-based criteria allow an individual the opportunity to participate in the major structures in our society. His social, economic, educational, political, and psychological needs are met through the dominant institutions; and, the more "normal" and integrated he is to his culture, the less opportunity he will have to interact and meet with members of other subculture groups on a voluntary basis.

Predictably, we find other integrated subgroups based on religion, ethnicity, or some other criterion providing structures and opportunities for its own membership. Those subcultures with a high degree of cohesion, structure, and integration may then face the same dilemma of turning inward that tends to strengthen a "we-they" dichotomy. This does not necessarily have to be so, and leadership in many instances can be effective in moving groups toward a much more sympathetic position in regard to problems of other groups. However, it does seem significant that many are couched in terms of "it could happen to you." It may be realistic recognition that the self-interest of a group is a more powerful motivating factor than appeals on a more idealistic level. It also appears that some groups that have faced overt discrimination in the past are much more sensitive and helpful towards others.

The problem of discrimination from our perspective calls for a different type of analysis. Gordon[5] uses the term "structural pluralism," since the existence of subsocieties, with their own networks, cliques, institutions, organizations, and friendship patterns, functioning not only for the immigrant generation but for succeeding generations as well, becomes the unit for analysis. The organized subculture can be viewed positively: it probably is a key factor in the control of mental illness, crime and delinquency, and the like; but it may also involve other risks — discrimination and prejudice, among others. The important question is how ethnic prejudice and discrimination can be reduced and conflicts kept to workable levels in our society, when separate structures for separate groups limit primary group relationships among persons of various ethnic or religious backgrounds.

The structures set up in late high school and college appear to be clear examples of the structural pluralism that attempts to control and limit social interaction to "desirable" groups. The dilemma is that, the more effective the subcultures, the higher is the probability of discrimination. (A common·observation of this phenomenon is the identification with a school through an athletic team, with its resultant bitterness toward all of its foes: "our team against theirs." An extreme identification might be the refusal to have any social interaction with members of the "enemy." The same observation might also be made of the superpatriot who will broach no dealings with "foreigners.") Conversely, marginal identification would be associated with an increasingly democratic outlook.

Summary and Conclusions

There is a story that concerns a former inmate of a concentration camp. When asked about the people who may have contributed to his plight, he was said to have answered: "I didn't mind my enemies because I knew who they were, and the worst they could do to me was to kill me. I didn't mind my friends because I knew who they were, and the worst they could do to me was to stab me in the back. I guess the ones that I was really concerned about were those who didn't care, or were too busy with their own affairs, because I never really knew who they were, and they would set the stage for the conditions which would enable my enemies to kill me, and my friends to stab me in the back." Although it may be a fictionalized account, the story makes the point that lies behind this article; for it is aimed more at the "normal," the integrated, and the comfortable than at the less-integrated or alienated as possible influences behind discriminatory behavior. And it suggests that their behavior is perhaps a consequence of a social structure that aids an individual in his socialization processes and serves a very valuable function. But the paradox may lie in the fact that, the more effective the subcultural integration is (e.g., the more need-satisfaction provided by the subculture), the less are the individual and family, caught in these strong influences, able to permit intimate social interaction with other groups.

The implications of the present study are important. If replicated studies confirm the data, we might begin to approach conflicts among groups through their structures, rather than through personality and the individual, per se.

There are hopeful signs to warrant a more optimistic point of view. Subcultural groups are changing, and the acquisition of the "American culture" through learning and interaction is proceeding at a pace that, although slow to some, is, nevertheless, progressing. Groups that may have previously emphasized boundary maintenance are becoming more permeable, and there are important groups in our society (e.g., the "intellectual and academic") wherein interest and achievement are more relevant for participation than ethnicity or religion. The verbal goals of most subculture groups include a more democratic society, and the current stage of ethnic isolation of certain groups may be thought of as stages in a developmental process.

However, the risks of structural pluralism should be made clear. Ethnic or religious subcultural integration can turn into parochialism and isolation as easily as it can turn to a process that aids individuals and groups through the difficult problems of socialization and acculturation.

Chapter Notes

1. H. Gough, *Manual for the California Psychological Inventory* (Palo Alto, Calif.: Consult. Psychol. Press, 1957).

2. M. Deutsch and M. E. Collins, *Inter-racial Housing* (Minneapolis, Minn.: University of Minnesota Press, 1951).

3. T. W. Adorno, et al., *The Authoritarian Personality* (New York: Harper, 1950).

4. G. W. Allport, *The Nature of Prejudice* (Cambridge, Mass.: Addison-Wesley, 1954).

5. M. M. Gordon, *Assimilation in American Life* (New York: Oxford University Press, 1964).

Part Two: Assimilation and Sex Roles

Introduction

As documented by Ogawa (Chapter 1) in the Introductory Section, Japanese were regarded as individuals incapable of assimilating the values and standards of America. The same attitude was held toward other Asian immigrants such as Chinese and Filipinos (Daniels and Kitano, 1970). Although the unassimilable nature was attributed to the inherent foreign and defective character of Asians, it is quite obvious that Americans were unwilling to extend the "melting pot" to include Asians. Segregation, restricted employment opportunities, laws prohibiting the ownership of land, anti-miscegenation laws, and denial of citizenship status kept them "foreigners."

To what extent have Asian-Americans remained unassimilable? Fong (1965) indicated that Chinese college students had largely assimilated Western values. The Chinese students could perceive most of the cultural expressions and possessed many of the same values as members of the dominant culture. The longer the individuals had lived in the United States, the greater the degree of assimilation. In the first paper, Matsumoto, Meredith, and Masuda (Chapter 6) studied the responses of Honolulu and Seattle Japanese-Americans. They administered a questionnaire to assess the degree of ethnic identity reported by students. Results indicated that second- and third-generation Japanese in Seattle and Honolulu exhibited less "Japaneseness" than those of the first generation. Furthermore, Seattle Japanese had stronger ethnic identification than their Honolulu counterparts. Assimilation often results in the adoption of the ceremonies and rituals of the dominant culture. Weiss (Chapter 7) describes the mixing of the aspects of two cultures — the celebration of the traditional Chinese Moon Festival with the American Beauty Contest. Although the ceremony is sponsored by Chinese and the contestants are Chinese, the dress, ritual, and even the food served follow a Caucasian pattern. Weiss is quick to add, however, that the beauty pageant does not have uniform approval. Some members of traditional Chinese associations feel the pageant is improper and immoral; a few young members of activist groups believe that public displays of Chinese females are sexist activities.

Obviously, the influence of Western values is often antagonistic to those of traditional Asian culture. Many Asians thus face a great deal of cultural conflict. Reasoning that Chinese values regarding educational achievement were more restrictive toward females than males, Fong and Peskin (Chapter 8) hypothesized that China-born female students would exhibit more conflict and alienation than their male counterparts. The results of their study confirmed this hypothesis. Weiss (Chapter 9) reports the findings of an anthropological field study on the dating patterns of Chinese-Americans. He found that Chinese females were adopting

Caucasian values to a greater extent than the males. As a result, Chinese females preferred their male dates to exhibit behaviors characteristic of Caucasians. They felt that Chinese males were "inept" and "childish" in their dating behaviors. Many Chinese girls dated Caucasians, who were described as being more fun, considerate, and confident. The results obtained by Weiss also reflect a differential pattern of acceptance by White Americans. Beliefs concerning the Chinese female as a submissive, sexy, and feminine individual are quite favorable; the Chinese male is more negatively stereotyped as a shy, introverted, but intelligent, person. Thus, it is perhaps easier for the Chinese female to date Caucasians than for the male.

In the final paper, Meredith (Chapter 10) analyzes the responses of Chinese-, Japanese-, and Caucasian-Americans on the attitude-interest test. Results indicated that Caucasian males tended to have the highest "masculine" score, followed by the Chinese. Japanese males exhibited the lowest scores. With respect to "femininity," Japanese females were highest, closely followed by Chinese, and, finally, by Caucasians.

References

Daniels, R., and Kitano, H. H. *American Racism.* Englewood Cliffs, N.J.: Prentice-Hall, 1970.

Fong, S. L. "Assimilation of Chinese in America: Changes in Orientation and Social Perception." *American Journal of Sociology* 71, 1965, 265-273.

6. Ethnic Identity: Honolulu and Seattle Japanese-Americans

by Gary M. Matsumoto, Gerald M. Meredith, and Minoru Masuda

This study[1] compared the magnitude of ethnic identification among three generations of Japanese-Americans in Honolulu, Hawaii. Ethnic identification was measured by a recently constructed Ethnic Identity Questionnaire. The first-generation Japanese immigrant (Issei) scored higher than the second (Nisei) and third (Sansei) generations. The EIQ scores between the Nisei and Sansei, although not significantly different, were in the hypothesized direction of attenuation with generations. This was attributed to intermingling of peer self-defined generation groups.

The Honolulu sample was then compared to three generations of Seattle Japanese-Americans on the same questionnaire. The former were seen to be less ethnically identified than their Seattle counterparts. Possible reasons for this unexpected result were discussed in terms of immigration and community history, greater structural assimilation in the areas of political and economic power and social inter-relationships, middle-class status conformity, personality differences, and varying definitions of ethnic identity.

Ethnic identification is held to be an important determinant of the behavior of Japanese-Americans. The magnitude of one's ethnicity is a function of the extent of the individual's incorporation into his total ego identity the sense of "Japaneseness." The latter is a reflec-

tion of all things, material or abstract, that are derived from Japanese culture. In a previous study (Masuda, Meredith, and Matsumoto, in press), an ethnic identity questionnaire was developed to quantify Japanese-American ethnicity and was applied to three generations in Seattle, Washington. The hypothesis of attenuation with generations was confirmed.

This study extends the quantification of ethnic identification to the same three generations of Japanese-Americans in Honolulu, Hawaii. It was hypothesized that (1) there would be a successive generational erosion of ethnic identification from the Issei to the Sansei; and (2) that the three generations of Japanese-Americans in Honolulu would exhibit higher ethnic identity scores than the Seattle sample.

Methods

The Ethnic Identity Questionnaire (EIQ) has previously been described (Masuda et al., in press). The EIQ consists of fifty items with which the respondent could agree or disagree on a five-point scale. The items were composed of preferences for Japanese things (e.g., foods, movies, etc.), personality characteristics (e.g., display of affection, spontaneity, etc.), child-rearing customs, family kinship items, community social relationships, discrimination, Japanese cultural heritage, sex roles, interracial attitudes, etc. Highest ethnicity for an item was given a score of five; the lowest, one. The total ethnic identification score for an individual was the sum of the scores on the fifty items.

After preliminary groundwork, one of the authors spent two months in Honolulu (Summer, 1968), gathering the data. This involved many local organizational contacts and explanations to various groups.[2] Questionnaires were mailed out or hand-distributed. The Nisei (second generation) and Sansei (third generation) received English versions of the EIQ, and the Issei (first generation) received the Japanese version. The Japanese translation of the EIQ was done by an Issei professional translator of the Far East Department of the University of Washington. Subsequent modifications were made after suggested changes by a younger Seattle Japanese-born businessman and a Honolulu Nisei language expert. Of the 700 questionnaires mailed, 287 were returned, an overall return rate of 41 percent. The sample is not necessarily representative of Honolulu Japanese-Americans. The Seattle Japanese-American sample is the same as that described in the previous study (Masuda et al., in press).

Results

The Honolulu Sample

Figure 1 shows the age distribution by generations of the original sample of 287. There is a considerable overlap in the age ranges. The Issei's ages ranged from twenty-seven to eighty-one years (N = 50); the Nisei's from twelve to sixty-three years (N = 109); and the Sansei's from eleven to fifty-three years (N = 128). The lack of distinctness in the age groupings of the three generations posed a difficulty, since the variables of age and generation are entertwined. The age groups in the three generations of Seattle Japanese-Americans had not shown such a distribution. To resolve the confounding of age and generation, and to be able to compare the Honolulu and Seattle samples, the former generations were restricted to the following:

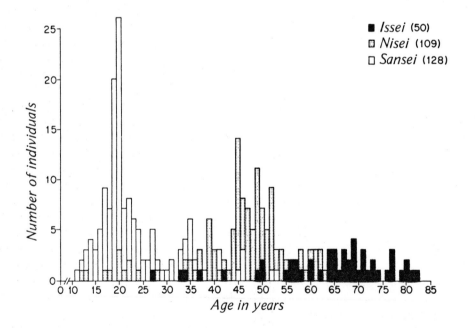

Fig. 1 — Age Distribution of Honolulu Japanese-Americans by Generations

	Table 1			
	Japanese-American Generations in Honolulu and Seattle			
Generation	*City*	*N*	*Age Range*	*Mean Age*
Issei	Honolulu	42	55-82	68.4
	Seattle	125	45-87	69.3
Nisei	Honolulu	97	34-63	47.8
	Seattle	114	23-66	41.6
Sansei	Honolulu	118	11-35	21.0
	Seattle	94	15-38	23.1

Issei, at least fifty-five years of age; Nisei, at least thirty-four years of age; and Sansei, age thirty-five years and under. With these age restrictions on generations, the final Ns were: Issei, 42; Nisei, 97; and Sansei, 118 (Table 1). The age characteristics of the Seattle sample are also shown in the table. All statistical data are based on this restricted sample.

In view of the age distribution within each generation, Spearman rank-order correlations of the total EIQ scores and age were computed. None of these intragenerational correlations was significant. The younger members of each generation were not apt to have lesser ethnic identification than the older members.

Although the mean total EIQ scores between the sexes within the generations showed the females as being consistently less ethnically identified, these differences were not significant (Mann-Whitney U test; see Table 2). There were thirteen items which were scored significantly differently by the sexes. As Table 2 indicates, these were not evenly distributed across the three generations, for the Sansei showed only one item as being scored differently. It is interesting to note that there was no item replication of sex differences among the generations. Only the Nisei males showed an indication of being more ethnically identified (four of five items).

In view of the absence of sex differences in the mean total EIQ scores, the males and females were combined in analyzing differences between generations. These results are shown in Table 3. While the mean total EIQ scores for the three Honolulu generations show attenuation with time, with Issei showing significantly higher scores than the Nisei and the Sansei, the difference between the latter two was not significant.

The lower section of Table 3 contains the thirty-two individual items that were scored significantly differently by at least one pair of generations. The table of probabilities shows that, of the sixty-two differences which appeared between generations, fifty-five were in the hypothesized direction of Issei. > Nisei > Sansei. Most of these differences were between the Issei and the Nisei and/or Sansei. The absence of a significant difference between the Nisei and Sansei in the total EIQ score is a reflection of the fact that only eleven of the fifty items were scored as significantly different in the hypothesized direction, in contrast to the other generation pair comparisons where at least twenty-one were so ordered. Five of six items (items 8, 10, 17, 18, 21, 46) that were not in the expected direction showed the Issei to have lower ethnicity scores than the two other generations. There were only six items that illustrated the hypothesis of attenuation of ethnic identification across all three generations (items 5, 13, 28, 33, 47, 50).

Comparison of Honolulu and Seattle Samples
Responses by the Honolulu and the Seattle

	Issei		Nisei		Sansei	
	Male (13)*	Female (29)	Male (69)	Female (28)	Male (29)	Female (89)

Table 2
Sex Differences Within Honolulu Generations
on the Ethnic Identity Questionnaire
Total and Individual Item Scores

	Issei Male (13)*	Issei Female (29)	Nisei Male (69)	Nisei Female (28)	Sansei Male (29)	Sansei Female (89)
*Mean Total EIQ Scores***	162.15	158.52	144.51	139.06	142.93	138.10
*Mean Item Scores**** *Item*						
1 Good child is obedient			3.61	2.77		
5 J background prevents delinquency			3.41	2.61		
6 Unlucky to be born J					4.18	4.58
9 Eldest son's duty to parents			2.69	2.00		
13 J-A's are deprived of opportunities			2.54	2.10		
18 Apt to hide feelings	2.23	3.07				
19 Shame that J-A's not know Japanese			2.77	3.52		
21 Disturbed if C's did not accept as equal	4.15	3.38				
36 Traditional J organizations not needed	1.77	2.26				
37 Unnecessary for J-A's to learn J culture	2.00	2.96				
38 Better without all-J communities	2.08	3.11				
40 J-A's unfavorable to J culture are wrong	4.23	3.74				
49 Family is let down when one lets down	4.31	3.65				

   * (N)
  ** None of the intragenerational sex comparisons was significantly different.
 *** Only differences of $p < .01$ are shown (Mann-Whitney U test).
   J = Japanese; J-A = Japanese-American; C = Caucasian.

samples to the EIQ are compared in Table 4. The mean total EIQ score of each Seattle generation was higher than the corresponding Honolulu generation, but only the Nisei were significantly different ($p < .01$). Table 4 also shows the twenty-three items that were scored differently by the Seattle and Honolulu samples. In generation comparisons of these items, the Honolulu sample scored lower on all but three of the items. The data indicate that, while only the Honolulu Nisei showed a significantly lower total ethnic identification, the Honolulu sample in general tended to have a lower ethnic identification than the Seattle sample (twenty-eight of thirty-two item differences).

In considering the individual items which distinguished the three generations of Honolulu and Seattle subjects, there were a total of thirty-two significant differences spread out over twenty-three items. These items covered every area of ethnic identification. It was interesting that the Honolulu Nisei and Sansei both said that they would feel more comfortable living in a neighborhood where there were at least a few Japanese-Americans

				Probability Levels of Pair Comparisons		
Table 3 Generation Analysis of Honolulu Japanese-Americans on the Ethnic Identity Questionnaire Total and Individual Item Scores						
	Issei	Nisei	Sansei	Issei vs Nisei	Issei vs Sansei	Nisei vs Sansei
Mean Total EIQ Scores	159.76	142.81	139.22	.001	.001	N.S.
Mean Item Scores						
Item						
1 Good child is obedient	4.23	3.36	3.37	.001	.001	
5 J background prevents delinquency	3.90	3.18	2.40	.01	.001	.001
8 I show my affection	2.20	2.52	2.62		.01*	
10 Expectation of discrimination in new places	2.70	3.36	3.02	.001*		.01
11 J-A's should retain part of J culture	4.44	4.06	3.85	.001	.001	
13 J-A's are deprived of opportunities	2.98	2.40	2.03	.01	.001	.01
14 Children may question parents	1.93	1.91	1.77			.01
15 Warmer relationships in J community	3.93	2.89	2.50	.001	.001	
16 No tendency to agree with Japan	2.54	2.06	2.18	.01	.01	
17 J-A's should feel 100% American	1.82	3.06	3.15	.001*	.001*	
18 Apt to hide feelings	2.77	3.12	3.45		.001*	
19 Shame that J-A's not know Japanese	3.72	3.00	3.27	.001		
20 J's have deep feeling for nature	4.13	3.06	3.08	.001	.001	
21 Disturbed if C's did not accept as equal	3.56	3.29	3.86			.001*
22 J-A's not allowed to be leaders	2.62	2.41	2.03		.001	.001
23 No strong attachment to Japan	3.56	2.29	2.17	.001	.001	
27 Less at ease with C's	3.89	2.97	2.89	.001	.001	
28 J's no better or worse	2.61	2.07	1.74	.01	.001	.01
30 J schools later appreciated	4.13	3.43	3.48	.001	.001	
31 U.S. life ideal for J-A's	4.11	4.02	3.66		.001	.001
32 Rely on relatives for help	3.55	2.57	2.87	.001	.001	
33 Better J-A's date only J-A's	3.38	2.11	1.80	.001	.001	.001
34 Companionable parents can have respect	1.97	1.76	1.60		.001	
35 Once a J, always a J	3.92	2.62	2.74	.001	.001	
41 Noble to repay debt of gratitude	4.33	3.49	3.34	.001	.001	
42 Avoid places of discrimination	3.76	3.42	2.85		.001	.001
43 Participation in group discussions	3.13	2.30	2.27	.001	.001	
46 Natural to wise-off at authority	2.63	3.32	3.14	.01*		
47 Questions interfere with group progress	3.58	2.70	2.18	.001	.001	.001
48 Prefer all-J church	3.47	1.98	2.02	.001	.001	
49 Family is let down when one lets down	3.87	3.46	3.21		.01	
50 J-A and C marriages to be discouraged	2.50	1.98	1.72	.001	.001	.01

*Scores not in hypothesized direction.
J = Japanese; J-A = Japanese-American; C = Caucasian.

	Issei		Nisei		Sansei	
	Seattle	Honolulu	Seattle	Honolulu	Seattle	Honolulu

Table 4
Comparison of Seattle and Honolulu Generations
on the Ethnic Identity Questionnaire

Mean Total EIQ Scores*	Seattle 163.34	Honolulu 159.76	Seattle 153.46	Honolulu 142.81	Seattle 143.76	Honolulu 139.22
Mean Item Scores *Item***						
2 Personal desires before family duty			3.82	3.32		
3 J-A's shouldn't disagree among C	2.35	1.88				
4 Especially like J foods			3.78	3.25	3.69	3.17
5 J background prevents delinquency			3.68	3.16	2.99	2.40
7 Comfortable in J-A neighborhood			2.76	3.28***	2.79	3.29***
9 Eldest son's duty to parents	3.35	2.80				
11 J-A's should retain part of J culture					4.16	3.85
12 Wife's career is as important as husband's			3.24	2.53		
13 Children may question parents	3.45	3.00	2.75	2.40		
19 Shame that J-A's not know J	3.86	3.00	3.62	3.27		
20 J's have deep feeling for nature			3.55	3.04		
24 Not spontaneous with people					2.37	2.72***
25 No need to promote J culture in children			3.43	3.00		
27 Less at ease with C's					2.27	2.89***
29 American first, J second					2.39	1.97
30 J schools later appreciated			3.85	3.45		
32 Rely on relatives for help			3.25	2.60		
33 Better J-A's date only J-A's	3.87	3.35	3.07	2.09	2.27	1.80
38 Better without all-J Communiites					3.54	3.13
40 J-A's unfavorable to J culture are wrong	3.91	3.49				
46 Natural to "wise-off" at authority			3.82	3.31		
48 Prefer all-J church			2.60	1.98	2.51	2.02
50 J-A and C marriages to be discouraged			2.94	1.97	2.17	1.72

* Only the Nisei are significantly different ($p < .01$).
** Only items with significant differences of $p < .01$ are shown.
*** Items on which Honolulu generation scored higher.
J = Japanese; J-A = Japanese-American; C = Caucasian.

than did the Seattleites. Both Seattle and Honolulu Sansei agreed that they were socially at ease with Caucasians but the latter were less so; in agreement with this, the Honolulu Sansei also admitted to less spontaneity with people. Although, in general, social psychologists indicate the essential similarity of Hawaiian and mainland Japanese-Americans (Kitano, 1968), the number of item differences in Table 4 indicates considerable dissimilarity in ethnic identification.

Discussion

The purpose of this study was a quantitative investigation of the ethnic identification of three generations of Honolulu Japanese-Americans and a comparison with Japanese-Americans in Seattle. It was hypothesized that the newly devised Ethnic Identity Questionnaire might reveal subtle differences between these two groups. This hypothesis was based on considerations of personal contacts as well as the differences in the political, social, cultural, and economic history, past and present, of the two regions.

In comparing the Honolulu and Seattle samples by sex and generation, the magnitude and the direction of the total EIQ scores of the Honolulu males were consistently higher across all generations than their female counterparts. This was not so with the Seattle sample. Further, the distribution of individual item differences was not the same. While the Honolulu Sansei males and females were the most homogeneous, in the Seattle sample it was the Issei who showed but one item as being scored differently. The items that were scored differently between sexes in Honolulu were not the same items as scored by the Seattle sample. The Seattle Nisei males, in comparison with females, said that they were less affectionate, outgoing, and spontaneous, and felt less certain that companionship with their children was compatible with respect. The Honolulu Nisei males appeared more authoritarian than the females; they said that a good child was an obedient child and that a "good Japanese background" would help decrease youth delinquency. The Seattle Sansei females were more ethnically identified than their male counterparts, but this was not seen in the Honolulu group. The Issei sexes of Honolulu disagreed on the most number of items, but there was no consistency as to the direction. The Issei males frowned on those who looked unfavorably on Japanese culture, felt more disturbed if Caucasians did not treat them as equals, and said that one could not let himself down without letting the family down. On the other hand, the female was more apt to hide her feelings and to feel more strongly the value of traditional Japanese organizations and an all-Japanese community. Thus, there were some qualitative differences between the Seattle and Honolulu sexes in their response to the EIQ.

The attenuation of ethnic identification with generations that had been found in the Seattle study was not completely confirmed in the study of Honolulu Japanese-Americans. The Nisei and Sansei did not show significant differences in ethnicity as measured by the EIQ. The similarity between the Nisei and Sansei is puzzling in view of the generation gap differences seen in the many areas of attitudes and behavior (Berrien, Arkoff, and Iwahara, 1967; Kitano, 1968; Meredith, 1965).

Hawaii's history of Japanese immigration stretches back a hundred years, when the first group was recruited to work on the sugar plantations. In Hawaii, the immigration from 1886 to 1899 was primarily contract labor and included men, women, and children (Ichihashi, 1932). The continuing but reduced influx of Japanese immigrants since 1924 has rendered more hazy the boundaries of generations as here defined. A correction was attempted by use of age boundaries. This confounding of generations was illustrated in Figure 1 where the age distributions of self-identified generations revealed considerable overlap. Further, there is the complication of intergenerational marriages. These tend to obscure the placement of the offspring into one generation, e.g., a son born to an Issei father and Nisei mother is "officially" a Nisei, but may be reared in an environment similar to one of a Sansei. He may, thus, have values, attitudes, and behavior more like a Sansei.

While it is recognized that the use of "generations" is a form of self-categorization in a particular language discourse, there is, in acutality a considerable overlap between the groups in their degree of commitment to shared patterns and values. In Honolulu, these categories of Nisei and Sansei seem to have broken down to the extent of yielding similarities in ethnic identification. This is presumably due to the Honolulu Nisei's showing a relatively low EIQ score (see comparison to Seattle Nisei). Arkoff (1959) used 137 Nisei and 183 Sansei undergraduate students at the Univeristy of Hawaii. Such an intermingling of generations at the University of Washington would be very low. While exact figures are not available, this can be inferred from the 1960 census of Seattle native and foreign born.[3] Such generational mixing as obtained in Honolulu would diminish attitudinal differences because of peer group associations.

All three generations of Honolulu Japanese-Americans exhibited lower ethnic identification than did the corresponding Seattle generations. These findings were at variance with the investigators' original impressions as well as the thinking of Kitano (1968), who said, "The Japanese in Hawaii also retain more 'Japanese ways' than their mainland counterparts because of a larger and more cohesive ethnic culture." It would seem that the Ethnic Identity Questionnaire is going beyond "Japanese Ways" and, perhaps, is measuring assimilation into American society. Kitano maintains that Hawaiians, of all regional Japanese-Americans, show the greatest degree of assimilation in cultural, social-marital, occupational, housing, and political spheres. The past and present history of the Japanese in Honolulu and in Seattle reveals differences which may relate to the Hawaiians' increased assimilation and lower ethnic identity.

The Japanese population in Hawaii has shown a linear upward growth from 1890 to 1960. There is, thus, not only a community cultural continuity but a continuing infusion of Japanese immigration. The Seattle Japanese population has not experienced such changing cultural infusions and, having known more severe discrimination, has been a solidified and isolated community (Miyamoto, 1939). While the severe disruption of evacuation and relocation during and after World War II has increased acculturation possibilities, the present West Coast Japanese-Americans are considered to show the least degree of structural assimilation (Kitano, 1969). There are four facets of the assimilation process which are seen to be different — the political, social-marital, occupational, and housing areas.

It is inevitable that, in those regions where the Japanese population has been in the racial plurality for many decades and constitutes a majority-minority (32 percent in 1960 [Kitano, 1968] and equal to the Caucasians, as contrasted to Washington's 0.6 percent in 1960 [Schmid and McVey, 1964]), the behaviors and attitudes of these two regional groups may well be different. The large bloc of Japanese in Hawaii represents strength in the fields of politics and economics. There are two Japanese-Americans in the halls of Congress and many in the Hawaiian legislature and judiciary. There is not even a glimmer of such political strength of Japanese-Americans in Seattle. The economic strength of the Japanese in Hawaii is seen in the history of plantation labor difficulties. In 1909 and again in 1920, when thousands of plantation workers struck for higher wages, the Japanese were at the forefront of these economic confrontations of strength (Lind, 1946). By 1920 and subsequently, the labor group had been supplemented by Japanese expansion into other areas of preferred occupations. Since World War II, the Japanese, gaining further economic strength in expanding areas of finance and business, have been important factors in Hawaii's economy.

In the area of social relations, the history of Japanese immigrants and their offspring in Hawaii with the other minority races has been one of cordiality. The intermingling of many different social immigrants in Hawaii has produced a degree of interracial marriage and hybrid offspring that is unusual. While the Japanese have intermarried less than other racial groups, the rate is increasing (Lind, 1946; Steiner, 1947). The intersocial relationship of the multiracial composition of Hawaii lends itself to a greater social mobility and assimilation.

In the assimilation process, the degree of interaction in the contacts between ethnic groups as well as the duration of interaction are important variables. The quality of the interaction is heavily influenced in a reciprocal fashion where the majority-minority can and does exercise considerable economic and political power. Such reciprocity in interaction leads to a consideration of the strength of Hawaiian-Japanese class identification and the desire for conformity to the middle-class norms as they see it as Hawaiian-Americans. Perhaps this strength of middle-class American status conformity is also reflected in lower ethnic identification of the Japanese in Hawaii.

There also exists the possibility of personality trait patterns that may be different between the Honolulu and Seattle groups. In testing Honolulu Nisei and Sansei on the Edwards Personal Preference Schedule (EPPS), Arkoff (1959) found only three item differences (two at $p < .05$) between the two generations on the fifteen-item schedule, although the Sansei showed scores intermediate between the Nisei and the normative Caucasian group, indicative of acculturation. Fujita (1956) applied the same instrument to fifty Nisei at the University of Washington. Comparative scanning of Arkoff and Fujita's data indicates that the Honolulu males tended to be more normative than the Seattle males on needs for aggression, autonomy, and order, while the latter were more normative in the need for achievement. In contrast, the Seattle females were more normative than the Honolulu females in six of the seven items that tended to be different. These were in the needs for deference, dominance, achievement, exhibition, change, and heterosexuality. Only in the need for intraception were the Honolulu females more normative. While personality trait patterns are not necessarily associated with ethnic identification, one cannot discount psychological need differences as determinants.

The greater visibilities of Japanese culture in Hawaii would lead to the apparently contradictory result that a larger, cohesive cultural group, while exhibiting greater ethnic pressures, can still exhibit a lesser ethnic identity. The answer, perhaps, lies in how we have defined ethnic identity or "Japaneseness." The ethnic identity items that are in the EIQ may be based on old Issei cultural attitudes and beliefs of the Meiji era which they brought with them when they emigrated. The greater ethnic cultural evidence seen in Hawaii may be less related to Meiji attitudes and beliefs but more to the contemporary ethnic scene. Postwar changes in Japan (cf., Vogel, 1963) indicate that Japanese values are undergoing modifications. Thus, the term "ethnic identity" may be all too inclusive, meaning "Meiji Japaneseness" as we conceived it in Seattle and "neo-Meiji Japaneseness" as we see evidenced in Honolulu. We shall be testing this notion on similar age groups in Japan.

Chapter Notes

1. This research was supported in part by Public Health Service Undergraduate Training in Human Behavior Grant No. 5-T2-MH-7871-06 and Undergraduate Training in Psychiatry Grant No. 5-T2-MH-5939-17 from the Institute of Mental Health; Stuht Psychiatric Research Fund; O'Donnell Psychiatric Research Fund; and the East-West Center, Honolulu, Hawaii.

2. 442nd Veterans Club, Club 100, Harris

Memorial Church, Nuuanu Congregational Church, Young Buddhist Association, Honpa Hongwanji Buddhist Church, and University of Hawaii students.

3. Personal Communication, C. F. Schmid, Office of Population Research, University of Washington, 1968.

References

Arkoff, A. "Need Patterns in Two Generations of Japanese-Americans in Hawaii." *Journal of Social Psychology* 50, 1959, 75-79.

Berrien, F. K.; Arkoff, A.; and Iwahara, S. "Generation Differences in Values: Americans, Japanese-Americans, and Japanese." *Journal of Social Psychology* 71, 1967, 169-175.

Ichihashi, Y. *Japanese in the United States.* Stanford, Calif.: Stanford University Press, 1932.

Fujita, B. "An Investigation of the Applicability of the Edwards Personal Preference Schedule to a Cultural Sub-Group, the Nisei." Master's thesis, University of Washington, 1956.

Kitano, H. L. *Japanese-Americans: Evolution of a Sub-culture.* West Nyack, N.Y.: Prentice-Hall, 1968.

Lind, A. *Hawaii's Japanese.* Princeton, N.J.: Princeton University Press, 1946.

Masuda, M.; Meredith, G. M.; and Matsumoto, G. M. "Ethnic Identity in Three Generations of Japanese-Americans." *Journal of Social Psychology*, in press.

Meredith, G. M. "Observations on the Acculturation of Sansei (Japanese-Americans) in Hawaii. *Psychologia* 8, 1965, 41-49.

Miyamoto, F. S. "Social Solidarity Among the Japanese in Seattle." *University of Washington Publications in Social Sciences* 11(2), 1939, 57-130.

Schmid, C. F., and McVey, W. W., Jr. *Growth and Distribution of Minority Races in Seattle, Washington.* Seattle Public Schools, 1964.

Steiner, J. F. "Recent Social Trends in the Pacific." *Social Process in Hawaii* 9, 1947, 7-17.

Vogel, G. F. *Japan's New Middle Class: The Salary Man and His Family in a Tokyo Suburb.* Berkeley, Calif.: University of California Press, 1963.

7. Modern Perspectives and Traditional Ceremony: A Chinese-American Beauty Pageant

by Melford S. Weiss

In the past thirty years, the Chinese minority in America has experienced dramatic upheavals in its family, organization, and community life. Many of these changes stem directly from the acculturation of the Chinese into modern American society. One indicator of this acculturation is the increasing importance of a local community celebration — the Moon Festival Beauty Pageant— a syncretic attempt to marry a traditional Chinese ritual, the Moon Festival, to a contemporary American phenomenon, the beauty contest.

Up until World War II, Chinese social organization was characterized by an overlapping and interlocking structure of surname, linguistic, and territorial groups which, generally speaking, controlled the warp and woof of Chinatown life. By the 1960s, decreasing discrimination and expanding occupational opportunities enabled many Chinese to leave their Chinatown ghettos and to pursue successful careers as professionals and businessmen. A substantial number adopted a cultural orientation that was contemporary, cosmopolitan, and middle class. As the Chinese became more involved in their American community, they became less dependent upon traditionist associations — associations which perpetuated Chinese exclusiveness and acceptance of a Chinese way of life — and not a few found them a "bit old fashioned" and unable to meet their social and political concerns. Excluded from some Caucasian organizations or uncomfortable as token Chinese members, they initiated the formation of new Chinese organizations that parallel their American counterparts both in form and function. These modernist clubs espouse a blending of the old with the new and a desire to enter more fully into the total community life. This attempt to merge the old with the new and re-establish Chinese community solidarity resulted in a joint sponsoring of the first Moon Festival Beauty Pageant in 1963. However, by 1970, divisions, resulting, in part, from differential acculturation, made even nominal joint sponsorship impossible. The pageant was now an exclusively modernist venture.

Traditionally, in China, the Moon Festival is celebrated on the 15th day of the eighth lunar month, late in September, on a day of the full moon. In one respect, it is a women's ritual and, as such, not the most spectacular of Chinese festivals. The women approach the family altar on which moon cakes of greyish flour, filled with spices, nuts, and sugar, are displayed, bow to the moon, light incense, and, if unmarried, contemplate marriage prospects. On the other hand, the Moon Festival is a harvest festival, marking, in the North, the end of work in the fields and the harvesting of crops and, in South and Central China, the planting of the second crop of rice.

In our local community, the only relic of

this traditional festival, apart from the name, appears to be the preparation or purchase of moon cakes by individual families. Unlike its historical predecessor, this rite of intensification, held in mid-October, is not so much a ritual to re-affirm social and ecological harmony within the Chinese community, but a conscious attempt to present a favorable image to the Caucasian society. As a community effort, it, without doubt, reinforces community solidarity, yet its most important function (and the one we have singled out for discussion) is to bind both communities together by their involvement in a shared experience, to promote and advertise the desired interdependence of Caucasian and Chinese business enterprise, and to inform the society-at-large that the Chinese are, indeed, a successfully acculturating minority.

This is accomplished by a rather noticeable display of Chinese beauties who easily convince the audience that Caucasian-Chinese "togetherness" can be pleasant. The contestants parade before the judges and audience in an assortment of costumes, including short and full-length cheong-sam and mini-skirted tennis outfits, pirouetting (and sashaying) on stage and on a walkway that extends part way into the auditorium. (Tennis outfits are preferred by the girls to swim suits which are thought to do less to disguise a small bustline.) Each contestant demonstrates her talent, usually by a song or a dance of contemporary rather than traditional vintage. Occasionally, a contestant may sing a Chinese song, and, in a recent contest, one hopeful performed a simulated gung-fu exhibition, but to modern musical accompaniment complementing her skin-tight leotards. While the performances are not always exceptional, the contestants are attractive and fit Caucasian beauty standards, and it is not only this researcher's opinion that the winners tend to be tall and big busted.

The director of the pageant, who is largely responsible for its planning and executing and who coaches the girls, is a Caucasian. The judges are also Caucasians, frequently including local television personalities. The local Chinese community is not so large as to preclude an affinal or consanguineous relationship between some Chinese judge and contestant; thus, using Caucasian judges minimizes claims of fraud, accusations commonly associated with the Miss Chinatown-U.S.A. pageant in San Francisco where the judges are often leaders in the Chinese community. There is both an English-speaking and Cantonese-speaking Master of Ceremonies, yet most explanations and commentaries are in English, and only the essentials are presented in Cantonese. The girls are also asked questions in both languages. While the English responses appear to be spontaneous, the Cantonese answers are well rehearsed and always in the Sam-Yap dialect, though it is common knowledge that many girls do not speak Cantonese. Often the questions are simple enough, such as: "What are you looking for in a husband?" "What will you do if you win?" "What are your goals in life?" and the answers are correspondingly adequate.

The parents of the girls are always introduced and applauded by the audience, as are the judges and invited state and local dignitaries whose presence acknowledges the growing political and economic importance of the Chinese community. Caucasian and Chinese individuals and businesses which make large contributions to the event are publicly recognized, and an elaborate program guide contains professional and business advertisements. The chairman of the highest level traditionist association appears but briefly and addresses the audience in both English and Cantonese.

As the pageant progresses, the excitement mounts, and, finally, a winner — Miss Chinatown, Sacramento — is announced. She is crowned by last year's queen and poses with her parents and the runners-up on stage. The audience adjourns to a buffet and bar downstairs in the gymnasium of the Confucian Church.

The food served (American cheese, salami, and pastries) appeals to an American, rather than a Chinese, palate. The dress of the men (suits and rented tuxedos) and of the women (gowns and pantsuits) is contemporary and chic, reflecting the largely middle-class status of both sponsors and audience. English is the primary language spoken, and it is only an occasional remark in Cantonese or an expensive cheong-sam that indicates the Chinese character of the event.

A coronation ball follows. A five-piece American combo plays both Lawrence Welk and rock music to a dwindling audience, who soon leave to spend the remaining evening with their Chinese or Caucasian friends. The majority of those attending appear to enjoy themselves and to look forward to returning next year. The monies collected, $6.00 per person, go to support the sponsors' charities.

The dominant symbols — indeed, the major focus of this annual rite — are the beauty-queen contestants, who serve as representatives, ambassadors of goodwill, of the Chinese community. Their walk, style, dress, talent, and demeanor are Asian facsimiles of their Caucasian counterparts in Miss America pageants. (The girls are coached and advised to use make-up and movements that primarily appeal to middle-aged Caucasian judges.) Thus, they purposely support and encourage an Americanized female image, something like Hollywood's tragic heroine "Suzy Wong," an image which emphasized the sensual and exotic components of the Asian female. The beauty contestants serve as models for young Chinese girls who attend the pageant in much larger numbers than their male counterparts. Indeed, the pageant is both an initiative and supportive agency of feminine beauty, sexuality, charm, and talent in which Chinese teen-agers learn how to appeal to Caucasian men.

Yet, while this image delights Caucasian guests, it is not acceptable to all segments of this Chinese community. Members of traditionist associations who support and

perpetuate a Chinese ethnic and historical identity — expressed by a publicly docile and subservient role for women — do not usually attend the pageant, although their associations contribute monetarily to the event (not to contribute would mean to lose face). While only a handful of traditionists think the pageant is shockingly immoral, many of them do not believe it is proper or ladylike, or even Chinese, to parade about in revealing outfits.

Young members of Asian activist groups similarly disapprove and view the pageant as an exploitation of Chinese women as a sex symbol, if you will, a dainty plaything for Caucasian men. They also consider such display as running contrary to the ideas of women's equality and liberation.

But, a large segment of the community considers the pageant a reflection of the Chinese taking their place, at long last, in the larger Caucasian world. For them, this public display of Chinese females is a positive statement. It is a clear indication that they have made it as Americans as well as Chinese.

Thus, the beauty pageant serves as a marker of the current status of the Chinese in America and gives an indication of things to come, namely, the increasing acculturation of the Chinese minority and their concurrent structural assimilation into White America at the secondary level. Indeed, the mother of this year's queen is presently married to a Caucasian. But, if the secondary contacts with Caucasians during the pageant do not develop into primary ties of a more intimate nature, it has served the purpose of demonstrating Chinese success in an historically American social production. (However, the Chinese do not seem to be particularly anxious to interact with Blacks and other minorities, and very few representatives of other racial and ethnic groups attend this event.)

Although the event takes place in the Confucian Church, this community center is owned and operated by the highest level traditionist group.

The beauty pageant is a challenge to traditionist claims to represent the Chinese to the larger community. The pageant has grown to become the most popular community attraction, while attendance at most traditionist functions is low. It is, more importantly, the one event which attracts a substantial non-Chinese audience. For many Caucasians, it is their only acquaintance with the Chinese community. In the future, modernist involvement in Chinese community structure is sure to increase, as it appeals to an expanding segment of the Chinese populace. As sponsors of the local Miss Chinatown Pageant, this modernist group participates in the Miss Chinatown-U.S.A. Pageant in San Francisco; and, as a Chinese branch of an international social fraternity, it is in contact with other Chinese branches across the country and with non-Chinese branches in the local community. We expect it to increase its stature, and its reputation as Americans of Chinese descent, with the larger dominant society; to sponsor more Chinese community events which appeal to Caucasians; and, in spirit if not in substance, to emerge as a legitimate spokesman for the Chinese community.

In conclusion, then: this festival plays a significant role in publicizing and endorsing a female image consonant with the dominant society's standards rather than with traditional Chinese ideals, and, as such, may be viewed as an indicator of the extent to which acculturation has taken place. At the same time, it serves as a vehicle for feedback from the Caucasian community, acknowledging this effort. The pageant also provides the Chinese with an important opportunity to not only publicly demonstrate their American character, but to interact on an equal level with more successful members. Finally, it is indicative of a change in Chinese social organization, in which traditionist leadership is challenged by modernists, whose primary objective is to bring the Chinese community into the mainstream of American life.

8. Sex Role Strain and Personality Adjustment of China-born Students in America: A Pilot Study

by Stanley L. M. Fong and Harvey Peskin

Since the role of student has been traditionally reserved for the male in Chinese society, it was hypothesized that China-born, female college students would feel generally alienated from, and in defiance of, norms of the parent culture. Results on the California Psychological Inventory (CPI) with forty-three male and forty-three female China-born college students supported this view, with females scoring lower on Socialization and Good Impression. The Chinese model of the feminine role (reserve, patience, modesty, etc.) was most rejected by the subsample of females on student visas and most accepted by the naturalized females (including permanent residents), as reflected on the CPI Femininity Scale. Regardless of sex, naturalized and resident students clearly outranked visa students on important aspects of psychological health.

People migrating to another society can be expected to carry over the culturally ingrained emotional meanings of essential social roles. When two cultures are as different as the Chinese and the American, new role meanings often come into conflict with traditional ones, with evident implications for personality adjustment under the new circumstances. Moreover, such discrepancies may be greater for one sex than the other and, thus, pose interesting questions relating to sex roles. This study[1] is concerned with the differential adjustment of China-born male and female students in America.

In the role of student, the sexes doubtless face differential role strain in Chinese culture. Since the sixth century, males only, rich or poor, were allowed to take the imperial examinations based on the Confucian teachings (Hsu, 1955). In 1905, the imperial examinations were abolished before the decline of the Manchu dynasty and the establishment of the people's republic. But the traditional respect for the male's scholarship is still very much in evidence, with the college degree replacing the imperial ones. Education for the woman was seen to endanger feminine virtue. Her status in life was to be a devoted helper to the future mother-in-law and a bearer of many grandchildren for her, preferably male ones. It was only in the last century, with the aid of missionaries, that the emancipation of Chinese women began, and a number of Christian schools and colleges were established. As late as 1910, these schools alone provided women with the same educational opportunities as men (Liu, 1963). Although their educational ambitions have enlarged, Chinese girls may still find that their emerging role is not fully accepted by all segments of Chinese society (DeVos and Abbott, 1966; Wright, 1964).

From this brief analysis, it is reasonable to suppose that females in college will feel alienated from, and rebel against, traditional expectations of what is appropriate for Chinese females.

A host of sociopsychological factors may either mitigate or aggravate such sex differences. Certainly, length of residence in America would be expected to facilitate the incorporation of the new culture. Over and above residence, the Chinese eligibility for naturalization, under liberalized immigration policy, has conferred the constitutional and psychological security of full membership in American society. Thus, it may be expected that the naturalized Chinese (or those eligible for citizenship) would be noticeably more in tune with significant American norms and, thus, with themselves, in terms of well-being and self-esteem, than a disenfranchised Chinese group. For this study, the latter will be represented by Chinese holding student visas.

Method

Subjects

The Chinese Ss were students, living and attending colleges in the San Francisco Bay

	Males		Females	
CPI Scales	Visa (N = 23)	Naturalized (N = 20)	Visa (N = 22)	Naturalized (N = 21)
	M	M	M	M
Dominance	47.7	50.9	46.8	51.0
Capacity for Status	44.3	49.6	42.3	43.5
Sociability	45.9	49.0	41.2	47.7*
Social Presence	44.6	51.0*	44.5	49.8
Self-Acceptance	48.9	52.8	46.4	52.1
Sense of Well-being	39.1	46.5*	35.5	40.7
Responsibility	45.2	48.8	41.6	48.2**
Socialization	50.3	52.9	46.2	46.8
Self-Control	46.4	49.1	46.3	43.1
Tolerance	40.0	48.3**	40.1	44.9
Good Impression	47.3	49.6	44.6	42.1
Communality	45.3	52.5**	45.0	48.3
Achievement via Conformance	45.2	51.7**	43.5	46.7
Achievement via Independence	45.9	54.1*	47.2	51.1
Intellectual Efficiency	40.1	46.1	39.5	43.1
Psychological Mindedness	49.2	50.0	46.4	52.2*
Flexibility	44.6	51.0*	49.3	53.6
Femininity	55.7	55.1	50.0	58.6***

Table 1
Mean Scores of Naturalized and Visa Males and Females
on the California Psychological Inventory

*p < .10.
**p < .05.
***p < .01.

Area. They were all born in China, and the sample consisted of forty-three males and forty-three females. Of these Ss, twenty males and twenty-one females were naturalized American citizens or permanent residents eligible for citizenship. (Seven of these forty-one Ss fell into the latter; these seven have only recently been able to satisfy the residency requirement for citizenship and, presumably, plan to file for citizenship in the near future.) These forty-one Ss are referred to as the naturalized male and female groups in this study. Twenty-three males and twenty-two females were on student-visa status. The mean ages of these four groups of male and female Ss were 22.3, 21.2, 24.0, and 20.8 years, respectively. The naturalized Ss have lived in the United States for 11.5 mean years, and the visa Ss, 3.5 years. Most of the Ss were born on the China mainland (65 percent); the remainder came from Hong Kong (30 percent) and Taiwan (5 percent). Generally, the Chinese from the China mainland migrated before the establishment of the Communist government.

Procedure

Most of the Ss were obtained from psychology classes at San Francisco State College. Since the students are required to take two courses in psychology to meet the requirements of the college, the present sample represents a wide spectrum of curriculum majors. A few students at other colleges were also given the questionnaires. The questionnaires were filled out anonymously by Ss and returned by mail. Sixty-five percent of the questionnaires were returned. It is hoped that later studies will obtain a better rate of return than has been possible in this voluntary study.

All of the Ss were given a battery of questionnaires which included a Personal Data Form (Fong, 1965) and the California Psychological Inventory (CPI, Gough, 1957). The present report considered only the CPI; its relevance for cross-cultural research has been repeatedly demonstrated (e.g., Gough, 1960, 1966; Gough

and Sandu, 1964).

Results

The mean scores of the visa and naturalized males and females on the CPI scales are presented in Table 1. A two-way analysis of variance computed by the method of least squares for unequal cell frequencies (Winer, 1962) was performed on each scale with main effects of sex and citizen status. Results are presented in Table 2.

The effect of sex yielded significant differences on two scales, Socialization and Good Impression, with the males scoring higher on both.

The effect of citizen status (i.e., visa or naturalized) yielded significant differences on ten of the eighteen CPI scales. The naturalized Ss obtained higher scores than the visa Ss on all of them: Social Presence, Sense of Well-being, Responsibility, Tolerance, Communality, Achievement via Conformance, Achievement via Independence, Intellectual Efficiency, Flexibility, and Femininity. Since the last-named scale owed its significance entirely to the wide gap between the female groups (see Table 1), it is more accurate to speak of a yield of nine significant scales on the main effect of citizen status. The Femininity scale was the only one which showed a significant interaction between sex and citizen status. The naturalized females scored significantly higher on Femininity than the visa females.

Discussion

Males and Females

It was assumed that the female students would experience greater conflict with, and rebellion against, social norms and role expectations than the male students. This prediction is supported by the lower scores of females on Socialization and Good Impression, the two sex-discriminating scales of this study. Studies (e.g., Gough, 1965; Stein, Gough, and Sarbin, 1966) have shown that the Socialization scale deals basically with role-taking disposition and

| | | Citizen | | |
Scale	Sex (S)	Status (C)	S × C	Within
Social Presence				
MS	9.67	733.33	6.30	107.94
F	.10	6.79*	.06	
Responsibility				
MS	100.77	561.69	50.34	83.32
F	1.21	6.74*	.60	
Socialization				
MS	555.05	50.93	21.82	87.18
F	6.37*	.58	.25	
Tolerance				
MS	53.03	920.18	68.59	109.51
F	.48	8.40**	.63	
Sense of Well-being				
MS	470.77	841.79	26.01	149.71
F	3.15	5.62*	.17	
Good Impression				
MS	526.74	.23	122.95	75.04
F	7.02*	.00	1.64	
Communality				
MS	94.57	582.11	83.59	98.13
F	.96	5.93*	.85	
Achievement via Conformance				
MS	220.74	497.91	58.63	77.75
F	2.84	6.40*	.75	
Achievement via Independence				
MS	10.47	777.50	95.52	104.42
F	.10	7.45**	.92	
Intellectual Efficiency				
MS	63.34	499.26	30.11	107.95
F	.59	4.63*	.28	
Flexibility				
MS	296.42	601.17	23.37	121.49
F	2.44	4.95*	.19	
Femininity				
MS	35.15	342.51	460.11	85.33
F	.41	4.01*	5.39*	

Table 2
Analysis of Variance of CPI Scales

Note. —df = 1 for sex, citizen status, and S × C; df = 82 for within.
 *$p < .05$.
** $p < .01$.

relates to deviant or rule-breaking behavior. The low scores of the Chinese females on Good Impression indicate that they either reject or are less aware of the socially desirable response to enhance self-esteem in their social groups. The present view would, of course, presume that such scores reflect the same deliberate disavowal of cultural role demands that had been operating in their decision to attend college, and, possibly, to pursue a career.

Visa and Naturalized Status

The psychological consequences of the second variable, naturalization, have not, as far as the authors know, been reported before. Yet its effects seem to be large indeed. The naturalized Ss presented a picture of being more self-confident (higher Social Presence), freer from self-doubt and disillusionment (higher Sense of Well-being), more responsible and dependable (higher Responsibility), more accepting and tolerant of others (higher Tolerance), more flexible and adaptive in their thinking and social behavior (higher Flexibility), more productive in their intellectual functioning (higher Achievement via Conformance, higher Achievement via Independence, higher Intellectual Efficiency), and more in touch with the implicit and underlying values of the American scene (higher Communality). The visa Chinese, on the other hand, seemed to experience a degree of discomfort severe enough to disorder their functioning in these psychological and social areas.

Understandably, immigration status and length of American residence were confounded in this study. Whether length of residence, irrespective of citizenship (or eligibility), contributed to the higher CPI scores of the naturalized group can be gleaned from within-group correlations. For all of these nine significant CPI scales, correlations within the naturalized group were positive, but only significantly so on the Responsibility scale ($p < .10$); that is, those residing longer in the United States scored higher on this measure. It is reasonable to

suggest, therefore, that citizenship, or the prospect of citizenship, encourages a motivational state in which personal commitment to the new society is achieved by the full granting of its legal guarantees, relatively independent of the actual time of residence.

It is instructive to inspect the pattern of sex differences among the nine scales that showed a significant main effect for citizen status. (The Femininity scale is not considered here.) On eight of the nine scales, significant ts ($p < .10$) were obtained between the visa and naturalized groups within one or the other sex, but not within both sexes (Table 1). On seven of the eight scales, it was the difference between the male groups of visa and naturalized students which was significant; only on one scale did the female groups differ. Evidently, the contribution of the male groups to the main effect of citizen status outweighed that of the female groups. The sharper separation of the male groups may reflect the greater social disruption experienced by Chinese men on student-visa status. Being officially consigned to the limbo of "student-hood" while in America, without the legal right to plan a professional career here and with the considerably fewer employment opportunities in Free China, may constitute a blow to one's identity as a man, especially to those in their mid-twenties.

Femininity

The Femininity scale is of particular interest on two counts. First, its cross-cultural validity has been, perhaps, the best established of the CPI scales (Gough, 1966). Second, in this study, it is the only scale on which the Chinese males and females exceeded the American norms. This finding accurately mirrors the Chinese cultural emphasis on gentleness, modesty, patience, reserve, and social sensitivity. In the present study, it was the naturalized female students who scored highest and the visa female students who scored lowest, with the male groups falling in between. That the visa female students, in terms of the overall Chinese average, should be least feminine is not surprising in view of the unusual self-reliance and independence which the Chinese woman must show to make her way into higher education. Considered together with their low scores on Socialization and Good Impression, the visa females, as a special subgroup, would then appear to follow a style of the "masculine protest," so well known in Western characterology (cf., Yuntang's, 1935, protest against "those masculine women prize-winners at college"). But a surprisingly different style seems to characterize the naturalized females. Whereas their equally low scores on Socialization and Good Impression indicate a similar social estrangement, their high Femininity scores point to a compensatory compliance with feminine role demands. Since almost all live in America with both parents (twenty of the twenty-one girls, compared to seven of the twenty-two visa girls), parental influence is more assured, not merely for role modeling, but as a force to be appeased. We might say that the naturalized females are in an inescapable dilemma from which the visa females are, at least, spared: that of making — or pretending — peace between their educational ambitions in the permissive atmosphere of American coeducation and the anti-feminist values of Chinese parents with whom they continue to live in America.

This dilemma may diminish where older siblings have already helped to accommodate the family to Western values. The probable influence of older siblings on acquiring the feminine role is suggested by the diminishing Femininity mean scores of the naturalized female first-borns (65.5), second-borns (58.0), and later-borns (53.3). First-borns exceed the latter groups, $p < .05$. (For the visa females, all birth-order groups are essentially equivalent.) Interestingly, no similar birth-order differences for the naturalized females occur on the Socialization and Good Impression scales, where mean scores are essentially equivalent across birth order. We are perhaps left to conclude that the loyalty of naturalized first-borns to Old World

norms of femininity is more apparent than real, that is, more in the nature of role playing than an authentic acceptance of the Chinese status quo for women. It may also follow that these *Ss*' parents (their own citizenship status notwithstanding) are seen by their daughters as carriers of the ethnic culture who must be mollified. Perhaps, particularly toward sex roles, where parental attitudes are likely to have been settled for good and all, a display of obedience by the first offspring may both disguise and betray the alientation between the generations.

Chapter Note

1. This study is based on a paper presented at the Western Psychological Association Convention, San Francisco, 1967.

Harvey Peskin is also Research Associate, Institute of Human Development, University of California, Berkeley. Requests for reprints should be sent to Harvey Peskin, Department of Psychology, San Francisco State College, 1600 Holloway Avenue, San Francisco, California 94132.

References

DeVos, G. A., and Abbott, K. A., advisors. "The Chinese Family in San Francisco: A Preliminary Study." Group masters' thesis, University of California, Berkeley, 1966.

Fong, S. L. M. "Assimilation of Chinese in America: Changes in Orientation and Social Perception. *American Journal of Sociology* 71, 1965, 265-273.

Gough, H. G. *Manual for the California Psychological Inventory.* Palo Alto, Calif.: Consulting Psychologists Press, 1957.

_____. "Theory and Measurement of Socialization." *Journal of Consulting Psychology* 24, 1960, 23-30.

_____. "Cross-Cultural Validation of a Measure of Asocial Behavior." *Psychological*

Reports 17, 1965, 379-387.

____ . "A Cross-Cultural Analysis of the CPI Femininity Scale." *Journal of Consulting Psychology* 30, 1966, 136-141.

____ and Sandhu, H. S. "Validation of the CPI Socialization Scale in India." *Journal of Abnormal and Social Psychology* 68, 1964, 544-547.

Hsu, F. L. K. *Americans and Chinese.* London: Cresset, 1955.

Liu, K. C. *Americans and Chinese.* Cambridge, Mass.: Harvard University Press, 1963.

Stein, K. B.; Gough, H.G.; and Sarbin, T. R. "The Dimensionality of the CPI Socialization Scale and an Empirically Derived Typology among Delinquent Boys." *Multivariate Behavioral Research* 1, 1966, 197-208.

Winer, B. J. *Statistical Principles in Experimental Design.* New York: McGraw-Hill, 1962.

Wright, B. R. "Social Aspects of Change in the Chinese Family Pattern in Hong Kong." *Journal of Social Psychology* 63, 1964, 31-39.

Yuntang, L. *My Country and My People.* New York: Reynal & Hitchcock, 1935.

9. Selective Acculturation and the Dating Process: The Pattern of Chinese-Caucasian Inter-racial Dating

by Melford S. Weiss

The recent increase in Chinese-Caucasian dating may reflect a growing Chinese-American female preference for Caucasian courtship behavior. Chinese-American girls have internalized the dominant dating values of the Caucasian teenager to a greater extent than Chinese-American boys. Because many Chinese boys seem unable to master the American dating game, they often cannot meet the girls' expectations, prompting them to seek romance, companionship, and adventure in Caucasian arms.

Divergent expectations and/or dating behavior between Chinese-American boys and girls may be related to: (1) the pervasive influence of American racial stereotyping; (2) Chinese-American interpersonal relationships in American society; (3) sex-linked psychological profiles and socialization practices; and (4) the closed nature and efficient information exchange system in the Chinese community.

The initial expectation of this study[1] was that Chinese dating standards and patterns would be modernistic, reflecting the acculturation of Chinese into today's American youth culture. But, it was also expected that a sense of Chinese ethnic solidarity would produce a preference for dating within the Chinese group. Most Chinese males clearly expressed their preference for a Chinese dating partner. However, while almost all of the females admitted

they would prefer to marry a Chinese man, their descriptions of typical Chinese-American male dating behavior were not all complimentary. (For the purpose of this paper, Chinese-American refers to the first-generation, native-born American of Chinese descent.) The females continually compared Chinese and Caucasian counterparts and concluded that Chinese finesse at the dating game left much to be desired.

Dating attitudes are a product of the socialization process and have their roots in cultural institutions and ideologies. This paper is primarily directed at exploring the positive attitudes toward interracial Caucasian dating expressed by Chinese females. Because the informants in this study were all American-born Chinese youth, they are influenced by American social institutions.

This study suggests: (1) That the dating attitude of young Chinese-American males and females, influenced by their differential treatment by White American society, is both a consequence and result of continuous exposure to, and partial Chinese acceptance of, American racial stereotyping; (2) that the interracial dating success and failure of Chinese-Americans is linked to their involvement in American social life, and that males and females participate disproportionately in social activities; (3) that Chinese-American males and females demonstrate different psychological attitudes towards social-sexual situations, and that these sex-linked attitudes are related to both Chinese socialization patterns and acculturation and structural assimilation into American life; and (4) that the social structure of the Chinese community may inadvertantly encourage some interracial dating practices.

This paper is an initial attempt to explore these social-psychological factors responsible for divergent interracial dating patterns of Chinese-American males and females.

Methodology

This paper is based upon anthropological fieldwork in a West Coast Chinese-American community (1967-1968). Fieldwork methodology included individual and group in-depth interviews in both synchronic and diachronic perspective with Chinese-American boys and girls and their families, attendance and participation at Oriental and mixed dances, parties, organizational meetings, and other social events, as well as visiting Chinese-American homes and attending numerous Chinese community celebrations and dinners.

Supplementing traditional techniques of participant-observation, questionnaires were administered to 80 of the 400 Chinese students at a local junior college. Twenty-five Chinese-American students (thirteen females, twelve males) completing the questionnaire were subsequently interviewed about their dating attitudes and behavior.

Conclusions substantiated and/or suggested by this study are applicable to the teenagers and young adults (fourteen to twenty-one) presently living in the Chinese-American community in which this research was conducted. It may, however, have general applicability to other Chinese-American communities.

Background:
The Chinese Experience in America

The early Chinese communities in America (1850-1900) have previously been characterized by the dominance of traditional family and district associations in Chinese economic and political life, the acknowledged and unchallenged superiority of the male elders, the subservient position of women in the family, and the acceptance by the younger generation of parental controls in matters of courtship and mate selection (Kung, 1962; Lee, 1960).

By contrast, Chinese-American communities of the 1960s are intensely involved in the processes of urban sociocultural changes and acculturation and assimilation, both resulting in divergence from traditional practices. With the decentralization of the community and the dispersion of its members, the family associations are declining in importance, because they can no longer meet all the needs of contemporary community life (Willmott, 1964; Lee, 1949). Male elders are rapidly losing the ability to control inappropriate behavior of the younger generation — a generation more responsive to the nuances of American life than bonds of family and community (Lee, 1956). As women gain a more equal footing in the financial, recreational, and socializational practices of the family, the dominant position of the father is weakened (Barnett, 1958).

One of the more dramatic departures from traditional Chinese-American life is evidenced by Chinese-Caucasian dating patterns — patterns which emphasize Chinese youth's new-found independence from familial restrictions and increasing adherence to Western romantic demands, resulting in an eager attempt on the part of the Chinese-American female to embrace Caucasian courtship rituals and the concomitant social dictums that accompany them.

The General Patterning of Interracial Dating

The results of the questionnaire and interviews indicated that Chinese-American females have internalized the dominant dating values of the Caucasian teenager, have better adjusted to American social custom, and are better accepted by the Caucasian community as dating partners and potential mates than the young Chinese-American male. Consequently, Chinese-American girls expect to be treated like their Caucasian contemporaries. Many Chinese-American boys cannot meet these expectations, and, as a result, the girls may seek romance, companionship, and adventure in Caucasian arms.

Chinese-American males have experienced many successes in American society. They have proven themselves as scholars in our educational system, enterprising entrepreneurs in their business ventures, and professionals (Kwoh, 1947:113). Yet, in the area of interracial social relationships, dating and marriage, many Chinese-American males fail to exhibit the successes achieved by the female — and it is, specifically, in these interpersonal arenas that the future of assimilation of ethnic and racial minorities into American life will be determined (Gordon, 1964).

The Nature of Chinese Stereotypes

American society has historically been given to negative stereotypes of the Chinese male. In early years, male Chinese arrivals to America have been characterized as "bestial celestials," "Atheistic heathens," "opium smokers," "gamblers," and "gangsters" (Barth, 1964:129-156; Farwell, 1885:97-114). More recent Chinese character profiles include the evil and cunning Dr. Fu Manchu, the inscrutable Charlie Chan, and the agreeable, but puzzled and simple, proprietor of a hand-laundry shop (Sung, 1967). Although the Chinese male has also been popularly characterized as "clever, honest, industrious, and studious," "a paragon of family virtue," "respectfully obedient to his elders" (traits acceptable in business and family success), he is still identified as "shy," "introverted," "withdrawing," and "tongue-tied" (traits unacceptable to current ideas of romanticism) (Sung, 1967). Furthermore, the Occidental stage, screen, and television image of the "hero" and the "he-man," emphasizing virility

and sexual attraction — a prime factor in the courtship game — includes too few physical or cultural features of Oriental men. Chinese males are rarely mentioned as "heroic" and "adventuresome" and have never been popularized in American fiction as "dashing, impulsive lovers."

The Chinese female image, on the other hand, has been better accepted by the American public. "Suzie Wong" is portrayed as slim, sexy, and lovable in a tight cheong-sam. The "Oriental dishes" of Flower Drum Song and the well-publicized Miss Chinatown beauty pageants have particularly emphasized Chinese feminine beauty and charm. Chinese women have appeared in Playboy's centerfold and lend support to the exaggerated romantic tales of servicemen returning from Far Eastern duty ports. As a result, Chinese girls with Caucasian escorts receive few disparaging public stares, while Chinese men walking hand-in-hand with White women are often the subject of malicious gossip.

American stereotypes of "Chinese" — although based upon much fictitious characterization — accept the Chinese female as a satisfactory sexual and dating companion but reject the Chinese male in a similar category. Caucasian "social indices," reflecting an unfavorable Chinese male image, discourage the Chinese-American male from seeking dates with Caucasian girls. With little confidence as a romantic competitor, he is often unsuccessful with Chinese-American girls as well. Perhaps the most illustrative example of the Chinese-American female's acceptance of American sex-linked discrimination is the Chinese-American girl dining with her Caucasian date who just can't help staring at the Chinese boy and his White girl friend and wondering what in the world she sees in him.

Image and Identity:
The Chinese-American Male

Perhaps the most damaging indictment of Chinese-American male "dating ineptness" comes from the dating-age Chinese-American female. Girls who regularly date Caucasians can be quite vehement in their denunciation and disapproval of Chinese-American males as dating partners. But, even the foreign-born Chinese girls — who do not usually inter-date — also willingly support a demeaning courtship image of the Chinese-American male. Moreover, "Chinese inadequacies" and "failures" are contrasted with Caucasian "confidence" and "success" in similar situations. Chinese-American girls report that getting-to-know-you chatter with most Chinese-American boys is basically shallow and tends to revolve around common experiences as Chinese. Males are often considered to be egocentric and rarely to consider the girl as an equal partner in a common dating activity. Conversation is less likely to contain introspective elements. Questions relating to personal identity ("Who am I") and social meaning ("What is it all about") are usually excluded from Chinese-American male repertoire. The boys tend to joke about such matters ("You must be kidding") and to further ridicule the girl ("You're sick in the head").

Chinese-American dating activities are often limited to evening hours and to private or predominantly Chinese settings with the drive-in movie a favorite — leading one Chinese-American girl to sarcastically remark: "One more Chinese date this month and I'll have seen every drive-in movie in town." Chinese-American boys are often accused of behaving "childishly" at dances and parties, embarrassing their dates by not displaying "mature" and "sophisticated" mannerisms. Hurried, clumsy love-making attempts in parked cars do not meet the girls' romantic expectations, leading them to characterize Chinese-American boys as sexually inept. More often what they complain about is "lack of advances," but one Chinese-American girl reports: "It's easy to get pregnant with a Chinese boy; he never knows how to take precautions."

The aforementioned comments on Chinese-American male dating behavior are less the

observations of this researcher than the reporting of Chinese-American girls. Furthermore, current American dating ideology makes it fashionable to belittle and demean "traditional" role-type behavior. When presented with these "stories," Chinese-American males deny the more derogatory accusations, yet, basically, agree that they are more inhibited and less aggressive than Caucasian males, and admit to feeling uncomfortable, if not insecure, in racially mixed company and in predominantly Caucasian settings. Caucasian males, on the other hand, express more confidence in interracial dating, seem more familiar with dating procedures, and, in the absence of a shared "identity" with girls of Chinese descent, give the appearance of broadening their conversational horizons. When comparing Caucasian to Chinese-American males, the former are easily accorded more social and sexual maturity, and are often referred to as "suave," "cool," "sophisticated," "swinging," and "sexy" — adjectives rarely associated with Chinese-American males.

In order to elicit more definitive information about attitudes towards Caucasian and Chinese-American dating partners, Chinese-American females were asked to describe specifically their reasons for dating Chinese and Caucasian boys. Those who preferred to date Chinese-Americans constantly indicated "parental coercion," "Chinese and Caucasian community pressures," "respect for tradition," "the sharing of a common heritage with other Chinese," "race consciousness," and "the many problems associated with interracial marital unions." Responses for Caucasian dating preferences are of an entirely different nature: "Caucasians know better dating places," "more fun on dates," "more considerate," "sexy and good looking," "easy-going personality," and "they are the fun part of American culture."

These differing "preference typologies" for Chinese-American and for Caucasian dates suggest that the girls prefer the adventure, romance, and easy familiarity associated with Caucasian life, and, by accepting these "wants," have accepted many of the mores of "Americana." Although they may prefer Caucasian-style dates as best representative of the individuality and free expression of this society, the realities of family life and a future within this community channel their marital choice to a Chinese mate.

Thus, Chinese-American boys who demonstrate proficiency in the "Caucasian-style" dating game are in much demand as friends, dates, and, eventually, husbands. One Chinese-American girl neatly summarized her dating desires by posting on her dormitory door: "Wanted . . . a Non-Chinese American — of Chinese Descent."

The Chinese in America cannot help but be influenced by the nature of Caucasian stereotypes of Orientals. The reader should not be left with the impression that most Chinese-American males are either inept or inadequate. My contention is that Chinese-American females, born and reared in a predominantly Caucasian society and subject to the propagandizing influences of American mass media, either consciously or subconsciously accept many American racial stereotypes, and, furthermore, act upon the assumption that they have some validity. Thus, when a "Chinese date" turns out to be a disappointment, the Chinese male stereotype images are further reinforced.

Social Interaction and Dating Expectations

The results of the questionnaire indicated that Chinese-American college males usually carry a full-time course load (fifteen or more credits), demonstrate an intense commitment to their academic study program (predominantly science, math, and engineering), and spend many after-class hours at the school library. Many of these students hold part-time jobs in Chinese-owned grocery markets and restaurants as clerks, checkers, busboys, and waiters. Their on-the-job relationships with both Chinese and Caucasian clientele are subordinate and superficial.

Chinese-American female students, however, take fewer courses (twelve hours or less) in more non-academic subjects (cosmetology, home economics, typing), and spend less time in library confines than Chinese-American males. Most females are not employed after school, and those with part-time jobs are more likely to work for Caucasian employers. Chinese-American females spend many "leisure" hours in snack bars and on campus grounds in the company of their Chinese-American and Caucasian peers. The girls "tune in" to social conventions concerning heterosexual activities and quickly learn the expectations and frustrations of American teenage dating styles. Although Chinese-American extracurricular organizational life is largely spent with other Chinese-Americans, females are more likely to be escorted to Caucasian dances, invited to Caucasian parties, and attend predominantly Caucasian churches than are males.

Chinese-American males do participate in "Caucasian" school organizations, but these activities do not demand the same social sophistication as parties and dances. Chinese-American boys rarely join the predominantly Caucasian fraternities, while Chinese-American females are better represented in women's social associations. Females declare they are usually "at ease" in the company of Caucasian peers; males often indicate insecurity and anxiety in competitive interracial situations. The females consider themselves "more Americanized" than the males.

As Chinese-American females continue to participate in interracial activities, they learn the current fads and fashions associated with Caucasian courtship rituals and come to expect similar considerations. Chinese-American males, whose participation in the non-Chinese world is limited, are either unaware, or, more commonly, uncertain, of these "social graces." Since the males must take the initiative for arranging dates, Chinese-American males find themselves at a distinct dating disadvantage when compared with their Caucasian peers.

Our data suggest that the nature and degree of interracial social participation significantly affect dating expectations, and that Chinese-American females spend more time in "mixed" activities than Chinese-American males, thus hastening the females' incorporation into American social life.

Perhaps, a major factor affecting the dating attitudes of Chinese-American males and females is not so much the rate of acculturation but the sphere in which acculturation takes place. Chinese-American women become integrated primarily in the expressive sphere of interpersonal relationships, while Chinese-American men appear to be acculturated in the instrumental sphere of work (their dedication to their studies and part-time work suggests a real commitment to the American dream of social mobility). The strong motivation of Chinese-American men to achieve social status through educational means also suggests that the striving for occupational success takes precedence over, and may actually impair, their ability to "socialize" with other people.

Psychological Profiles and Sex-Related Differences

Abel and Hsu (1949:286) support differential sex-linked attitudes when reporting the responses for American-born Chinese males and females. Rorschach protocols suggest that Chinese-American females approach the American response pattern to a greater degree than do Chinese-American males. The males seem insecure about their sex roles, their acceptance in relation to Americans as people, and their relationship to girls in general. Although the females expressed adjustment difficulties, they marshaled their resources, faced their conflicts squarely, and handled sexual preoccupations more directly. Hsu further suggests that, because Chinese-American males are more responsible for carrying on the family name and following in their "ancestors'

footsteps," their exposure to Chinese and Western ideals often involves conflicting emotions. They are less sure of the roles they should or could play. In attempting to break away from tradition and better fit into the American patterns, they encounter many difficulties within both the Chinese and American communities. Their protocols suggest that many may be emotionally disturbed, since they show frequent anxiety signs, repressed feelings of rebellion, a dilemma in the sexual sphere, and the inability to work out sexual difficulties.

Chinese-American females have a less rigid role to maintain than their male counterparts. They are not as responsible for carrying on family "tradition" and are less subjected to parental pressures to conform. They, therefore, find it less challenging to adjust to contemporary American life. Male feelings of inadequacy are not complemented by female "adjustments" to acculturation. It takes but little imagination to project these suggested sex-role discrepancies directly into the dating situation.

Community Grapevine and Closed System

Most Chinese parents (native- and foreign-born) disapprove of interracial dating, yet certain features of social life in this Chinese-American community not only encourage Chinese-American females to date non-Chinese men, but even discourage casual and/or consistent dating within the Chinese-American group.

The Chinese are dispersed throughout the city, yet a "sense of community" is, nevertheless, consciously maintained in part by an efficient yet informal information exchange system, which unites the community by cutting across age, sex, and generational barriers. This Chinese "grapevine," strengthened by long-standing friendships and cross-cutting organizational and social activities, functions through the spreading of news and rumor to maintain a running commentary upon the activities of its younger members. "Grapevine" gossip exposes dating activities to "Chinese public view" by rapidly relaying dating stories to parents, relatives, dating partners, and potential mates.

While foreign-born Chinese parents consider "dating" a direct prelude to serious intentions, and see consecutive and/or consistent dates with one individual as swiftly leading to a future marital commitment, Chinese-American youth (particularly females) consider "dating" a pleasant end in itself. Thus, non-serious Chinese dating may lead to unwanted gossip. Caucasians more readily approve of casual courtship practices (particularly those of an interracial nature), and, because they are unable to directly contribute to Chinese gossip sessions, a "Caucasian date" may spare the girl a "double-pronged" feedback into the Chinese community, allowing the girl multiple and varied dating experiences without necessarily endangering her reputation. The grapevine functions most successfully with spicy and risqué episodes. Rebuffed and jealous Chinese-American males have been known to tell "tall tales" to enhance their social reputations — tales which add little to the girl's reputation, as scandal is appreciated neither by parents nor potential mates. In any event, Chinese-Chinese "heavy dates" rarely remain secret affairs. Although Caucasian males are also prone to ego-building "stories," because they are not plugged into the Chinese network their fictional and/or factual adventures are unlikely to reach Chinese ears.

Chinese parents opposed to interracial marriages may not seriously view a Caucasian escort as a possible choice, and are sometimes less concerned with multiple Caucasian outings than would be the case with a Chinese suitor. Chinese parents are concerned with all of their daughter's dating partners. However, Chinese dates are particularly scrutinized because Chinese males are, indeed, potential mates. A casual date with a Caucasian, although often disapproved of, is, in many cases, tolerated because he is not considered a potential marriage partner by the parents.

Two important structural features in this Chinese community are a relatively stable population for persons under twenty-five and the tendency for the Chinese to split into "foreign-born" and "native-born" social groups. Because the total community population is under 10,000, scattered throughout the city and further split into separate groups, eligible dates can be a considerable problem, particularly for American-born Chinese females who rarely date foreign-born Chinese boys. Moreover, close childhood and school ties continue with age-mates within groups, and friendship does not easily become romance. Thus, Chinese-Americans must frequently go outside the Chinese community in search of dating companions. Caucasians, whose life style already appeals to the Chinese-American female, are able to furnish an immediate identity and find it easy to meet "date-searching" Chinese-American girls. The Chinese-American male, finding it difficult to date Caucasian girls, remains frustrated.

Summary

The social and cultural orientations and sentiments of the Chinese in America are gradually shifting from the ethnic subculture to the larger American society. As Caucasian society continues to become a positive reference group, its norms and values begin to guide as well as modify the behavior and perspectives of the Chinese (Fong, 1965:271).

Yet, cultural and structural assimilation of the Chinese-American into White America have not always resulted in a similar acceptance of both Chinese-American males and females. Sex-linked American discriminatory practices have contributed to a male-negative/female-positive dichotomy. The effects of this "stereotyping" are further validated and reinforced by the Chinese-American female successes in interracial social activities and personality adjustment to American life. The social structure of the Chinese community, its restrictive nature, differential, sex-linked demands upon its youngsters also share in the responsibility for the continuance of the female's success in interracial dating.

Further Suggestions

Although the focus of this study is dating, with an obvious emphasis upon the cross-sex relationship, Chinese-American males still remain ill at ease with Caucasians of *both* sexes. The lack of successful interracial personal relationships in social activities carries over into adult lives, where the inability of the Chinese-American male to relate positively to mixed ethnic and racial social/sexual situations continues.

American sex-linked discriminatory practices and "poor" social interaction experiences combine to isolate the Chinese-American male from active participation in many community-wide organizational activities. When Chinese-American males do join in extra-Chinese city events, they often do so as members of all-Chinese groups rather than as individuals. Moreover, these activities are usually limited to business or "Chinese community" functions and rarely to specifically "social" events (Weiss, 1969).

Chapter Note

1. This paper was presented at the 67th Annual Meeting of the American Anthropological Association, November, 1968, Seattle, Washington. Melford S. Weiss, M.A., is Assistant Professor of Anthropology, Department of Anthropology, Sacramento State College. He is currently completing a doctorate degree [1970].

References

Abel, Theodora M., and Hsu, Francis L. K. "Some Aspects of Personality of Chinese as Revealed by the Rorschach Tests." *Research Exchange and Journal of Projective Techniques* XIII, 1959, 285-301.

Barnett, Milton L. "Some Cantonese-American Problems of Status Adjustment." *Phylon* XVIII, 1958, 420-427.

Barth, Gunther. *Bitter Strength: A History of the Chinese in the United States, 1850-1870.* Cambridge: Harvard University Press, 1964.

Farwell, Willard B. *The Chinese at Home and Abroad.* San Francisco: A. L. Bancroft and Company, 1885.

Fong, Stanley. "Assimilation of Chinese in America: Changes in Orientation and Social Perception." *American Journal of Sociology* LXIII(3), 1965, 265-273.

Gordon, Milton M. *Assimilation in American Life.* New York: Oxford University Press, 1964.

Kung, S. W. *Chinese in American Life: Some Aspects of Their History, Status, Problems, and Contributions.* Seattle: University of Washington Press, 1962.

Kwoh, Beulah Ong. "Occupational Status of the American-born Chinese College Graduate." Doctoral dissertation, University of Chicago, 1947.

Lee, Rose Hum. "The Decline of Chinatown in the United States." *American Journal of Sociology* LIV(5), 1949, 422-432.

——. "The Recent Immigrant Chinese Families of the San Francisco-Oakland Area." *Marriage and Family Living* 18, 1956, 14-24.

——. *The Chinese in the United States of America.* New York: Oxford University Press, 1960.

Sung, Betty Lee. *Mountain of Gold: The Story of the Chinese in America.* New York: The Macmillan Company, 1967.

Weiss, Melford S. "Conflict and Compromise: The Structuring of a Chinese Community in America." *Clearing House for Sociological Literature*, 1969,

CFSL No. 69-6.

Willmott, W. L. "Chinese Clan Associations in Vancouver." *Man* 49, 1964, 33-36.

10. Sex Temperament among Japanese-American College Students in Hawaii

by Gerald M. Meredith

Introduction

The differences between the two sexes is one of the important conditions upon which we have built the many varieties of human culture that give human beings dignity and stature (Reference 12). With the acculturation of Oriental minorities in America from the status of "emerged minority" to "converted minority" orientation (Ref. 11), there are corresponding changes in the definition of masculinity and femininity.

In traditional Japanese culture, good behavior for the sexes was defined primarily in terms of obedient, conforming, and responsible behavior. The prolongation of customs in acculturating Japanese groups, such as *Hina Matsuri* (Girls' Day, celebrated on March 3) and *Shobu no Sekku* or *Tango no Sekku* (Boys' Day, celebrated on May 5), reinforces differential sex-role behavior. For the female, particular stress has been placed on poise, grace, and control (symbolized by the peach blossom of *Hina Matsuri).* For the male, stress has been placed on manliness, determination, perseverance, and the will to overcome all obstacles in the path to success (symbolized by the flying carp of Boys' Day).

In the process of acculturation to American life, several areas of difference have been noted in the Japanese-American group. With respect to broad personality patterns, Meredith (Ref. 13, 14, 15) has found that third-generation Japanese-Americans (termed "Sansei") demonstrate a profile of introversion linked with heightened anxiety level. The group manifests greater deference and submissiveness (Ref. 3, 5, 7, 15), with a tendency for the Japanese-American female to express greater body-dissatisfaction than her Caucasian counterpart (Ref. 2). In terms of attitudes toward the marital role, the Japanese-American female has adopted an equalitarian orientation, while the Japanese-American male persists in a more tradition-directed orientation (Ref. 8).

The purpose of the present study was twofold: first, to compare the sex-role orientation of Japanese-American college students with the dominant group; and second, to compare the sex temperament of Japanese-Americans with Chinese-Americans, another Oriental group that is undergoing the process of acculturation.

Method

Ss of the investigation consisted of ninety-eight Japanese-American (twenty-nine male, sixty-nine female) and sixty-five Caucasian-American (thirty-one male, thirty-four female) undergraduate students enrolled in the introductory psychology course at the University of Hawaii. For comparative purposes, a sample of forty Chinese-American (twenty male, twenty female) were included, since they represent an Oriental minority in

95

Table 1
Part–Whole Properties of the M–F Temperament Scale

| | r_{xy} with M–F Total Score | | | Centroid Factor Loading[a] |
Variable	Males	Females	M + F	
M–F: Word association	.48*	.27*	.55*	.47
M–F: Information	.39*	.53*	.68*	.73
M–F: Emotional and ethical response	.67*	.79*	.81*	.65
M–F: Interests	.66*	.48*	.83*	.73
M–F: Personalities and opinions	.49*	.12	.40*	.32
Sex	N.A.	N.A.	.80*	.83
Ethnicity	.17	.37*	.26*	.32
Age	−.06	.13	.05	.08
Sample size	80	123	203	203

a M-F Total Score omitted from factor analysis.
* Significant at the .01 level.

Hawaii (approximately 6 percent of the population) that have shared many of the socialization experiences of the Japanese-American group. The mean age of the total group ($N = 203$) was 21.1 years, with slight variation of the ethnic groups around this value.

Sex temperament was measured with the Attitude-Interest Analysis Test, Form A (Ref. 16) — hereafter referred to simply as the M-F Test. The instrument was originally developed as a measure of "mental masculinity and femininity" and provides a quantitative estimate of the amount and direction of S's deviation from the mean of his or her sex group in interests, attitudes, and thought trends. A modified version of the test, using five of the original subscales, was employed: Word Association, Information, Emotional and Ethical Reponses, Interests, and Personalities and Opinions. Two subtests were omitted, Ink-Blot Association and Introvertive Response, because of low scale reliability (Ref. 16, 17) and the accumulated evidence concerning the introvertive pattern of Island ethnic groups (Ref. 3, 5, 7, 13, 14, 15). Each item of the subtests was scored +1 for a "masculine"

response and −1 for a "feminine" response; total sex temperament represented the algebraic sum of all positive and negative weights achieved on the 396 scored items of the M-F Test.

Results

Correlational Properties of the M-F Test

Initially, it was hypothesized that, if the M-F Test is measuring differential degrees of "masculinity" and "femininity," then there should be significant relationships between the subtests of the scale and Total Test performance. This should hold not only for the total sample, but also when the group is divided into male and female samples. The part-whole relationships between the five M-F scales and Total Score, expressed as Pearson rs, are presented in Table 1. In addition, three person variables were included: Age (in years), Sex (F = 0; M = 1), and Ethnicity (Oriental background = 0; Caucasian background = 1).

Inspection of Table 1 indicates that all the scales of the M-F for the entire sample correlated moderately well with Total M-F Score. The Sex variable correlated .80, which

Table 2
Comparison of Sex Temperament Scores

M–F Scale	Sex	Ethnic Group Means			t-test Comparison Between Means		
		Jap-Amer	Chin-Amer	Cauc-Amer	Jap-Amer/Cauc	Chin/Cauc	Jap-Amer/Chin
Word association	Male	− 8.62	− 6.40	− 4.19	2.22*	n.s.	n.s.
	Female	−13.72	−12.95	−14.41	n.s.	n.s.	n.s.
Sex difference	t	3.18**	3.42**	5.56**			
Information	Male	2.55	− 1.85	6.45	2.12*	3.39**	2.39*
	Female	−10.86	−10.65	− 4.97	3.68**	2.59*	n.s.
Sex difference	t	7.38**	3.08**	7.02**			
Emotional and ethical response	Male	27.69	33.25	34.29	n.s.	n.s.	n.s.
	Female	− 2.28	2.00	15.94	3.99**	2.13*	n.s.
Sex difference	t	7.55**	4.90**	3.53**			
Interests	Male	15.72	19.00	15.42	n.s.	n.s.	n.s.
	Female	−19.90	−22.70	−17.59	n.s.	n.s.	n.s.
Sex difference	t	10.26**	9.93**	8.99**			
Personalities and opinions	Male	− 2.69	− 1.20	− 2.77	n.s.	n.s.	n.s.
	Female	− 6.87	− 6.35	− 5.12	n.s.	n.s.	n.s.
Sex difference	t	3.30**	2.65*	n.s.			
Total score	Male	34.66	42.80	49.19	n.s.	n.s.	n.s.
	Female	−53.62	−50.65	−26.15	4.49**	3.02**	n.s.
Sex difference	t	13.32**	9.66**	9.75**			
Sample size		98	40	65			

* Significant at the .05 level.
** Significant at the .01 level.

suggested a high degree of relationship between sociological group membership and sex temperament. The significant and positive relationship between Ethnicity and Total M-F performance clearly indicated that cultural background influenced test behavior and served as a rationale for a more detailed analysis by the ethnic groups.

In addition, the intercorrelation matrix between the five scales of the M-F and the three person variables were factor analyzed and yielded a single "massive" centroid factor that accounted for most of the variance in the original R-matrix. The factor was clearly identified as a "sex orientation" component in performance on the M-F Test.

Ethnic Group Comparisons

The M-F means for each of the three ethnic groups are presented in Table 2, along with *t*-test comparisons for both sex differences and ethnicity differences. Inspection of the sex differences within ethnic groups on all component scores of the M-F Test demonstrates that seventeen of eighteen *t*-tests were statistically significant. Despite the age of the instrument, the M-F Test functioned well to differentiate the performance of male and female *S*s. Parenthetically, it should be noted that the mean Total Score for male *S*s was in the predicted positive direction, while the corresponding scores for female *S*s were in the negative direction. This did not hold for each of the subtests. On the Word Association and Personalities and Opinions subtests, there was a tendency for males to be displaced in the "feminine" direction, while on the Emotional and Ethical Response section there was displacement of the females in the "masculine" direction. Possibly, this was attributable to the selective nature of the sample, or to changes in the college population since the test was originally standardized.

With respect to ethnicity differences, the mean Total Score for Caucasian-American males is highest in the "masculine" direction, while the mean performance score for the Japanese-American males is lowest for "masculinity." The Chinese-American males occupy an intermediate position. However, the mean differences are not statistically significant and indicate that there is a good deal of common sharing of the masculine orientation by Oriental and Caucasian males. On two of the subtests, Word Association and Information, there is evidence of greater "femininity" for Japanese-American *S*s. On the latter subtest, the Chinese-American males score most "feminine" of the three male groups.

Regarding the female *S*s, the Japanese-American group score highest in the "feminine" direction, followed closely by the Chinese-American group. The Caucasian females are the least "feminine" of the three groups compared. The difference between the mean score of the Caucasians and each Oriental group is statistically significant. The difference between the two Oriental groups is not significant and suggests a good deal of sharing with respect to feminine orientation. The Information and Emotional and Ethical Response subtests appeared to account for the areas of difference between the Oriental and Caucasian *S*s.

Discussion

The results of the study support the earlier findings of Arkoff (Ref. 1) that, despite undeniable pressure and social change, Oriental females in Hawaii still demonstrate an essential core of qualities which appear to be classically feminine. The male *S*s have adopted an "exploitative" strategy, while the female *S*s — and especially the Japanese-Americans — have adopted an "accommodative" strategy (Ref. 4). In the case of the Japanese-Americans, the influences of early socialization experiences (Ref. 13) and maternal attitudes toward differential treatment of the sexes (Ref. 9) plays an important role in sustaining the "feminine mystique." The adolescent "youth culture" of the Islands reinforces a stereotype of a typical female (Ref. 13). Among Japanese-

American males, for example, there is a polarity formed between "Meiji-type" and "Haole-type" females. The "Meiji-type," taking its label from the Meiji Restoration, which covered the period 1868-1912 and marked the early immigration of Japanese to Hawaii, refers to the "traditional" — shy, obedient, impulse-bound — coquette of the Meiji Period. The "Haole-type," derived from the semi-derisive Hawaiian word for foreigner or outsider, is associated with the dominant, assertive, verbal Caucasian stereotype. In the *language of discourse*, there is recognition of changes in sex-linked behaviors within the Japanese-American group.

With respect to the Chinese-American, the picture is less clear (Ref. 6, 10, 11). There is some indication, however, that acculturating Chinese-American females are more dominant than their Japanese-American counterparts (Ref. 1, 5). Related to Japanese-American socialization procedures, Chinese-Americans are taught by their parents to live up to a role of detachment and self-control; this leads to a strong control over the expression of affective impulses. Therefore, it is not surprising to observe the similarity of performance by the two Oriental groups. Both groups appear high on the "accommodative" strategy dimension.

It is interesting to note that Oriental males have moved rapidly toward an American "masculine" orientation, despite a lag in certain traits of personality (Ref. 5, 14, 15). Definitions of masculinity and responsibility are related to "acting-out" behavior. The traditional Japanese and Chinese male role has controlled the impulsive "acting-out," which has been thought of as more characteristically American male behavior. With pressure toward acculturation (i.e., movement from "emerged-minority" to "converted-minority" status), both Japanese-American and Chinese-American males have adopted the "exploitative" strategy of American society.

Summary

With the rapid acculturation of Oriental minorities to American middle-class life, there are corresponding changes in culture-linked definitions of masculinity and femininity. The present study focused on the sex temperament of Japanese-American college students in Hawaii, and compared this group with Caucasians and students of Chinese ancestry. The Attitude-Interest Analysis (M-F) Test was administered to a sample of 203 Ss, and the results analyzed for sex and ethnicity differences. Few differences were found between the male groups, although Caucasians scored in the most "masculine" direction. With regard to the female comparisons, the Japanese-Americans scored highest in the "feminine" direction, followed closely by Chinese-Americans. The difference between the M-F scores of Caucasians and each Oriental group was statistically significant. The findings are discussed with reference to "exploitative" and "accommodative" sex-role strategies, and to the local distinction between "Meiji-type" and "Haole-type" females among the Japanese-Americans.

References

1. Arkoff, A. "Deference — East, West, Mid-Pacific: Observations Concerning Japanese, American, and Japanese-American Women." Paper presented on the symposium, "The Woman in the Japanese Family: A Cross-cultural View by Cross-cultural Psychologists," sponsored by the International Council of Psychologists, annual meeting, American Psychological Association, Los Angeles, September, 1964.

2. _____, and Weaver, H. B. "Body Image and Body Dissatisfaction in Japanese-Americans." *Journal of Social Psychology* 68, 1966, 323-330.

3. _____; Meredith, G. M.; and Iwahara, S. "Dominance-Deference Patterning in Motherland-Japanese, Japanese-American, and Caucasian-American

Students. *Journal of Social Psychology* 58, 1962, 61-66.

4. Bond, J. R., and Vinacke, W. E. "Coalitions in Mixed-Sex Triads." *Sociometry* 24, 1961, 61-75.

5. Fenz, W. D., and Arkoff, A. "Comparative Need Patterns of Five Ancestry Groups in Hawaii." *Journal of Social Psychology* 58, 1962, 67-89.

6. Fong, S. L. M. "Assimilation of Chinese in America: Changes in Orientation and Social Perception." *American Journal of Sociology* 71, 1965, 265-273.

7. Hutchinson, S.; Arkoff, A.; and Weaver, H. B. "Ethnic and Sex Factors in Classroom Responsiveness." Unpublished manuscript, University of Hawaii, Honolulu, Hawaii, 1967.

8. Kalish, R. A.; Maloney, M.; and Arkoff, A. "Cross-cultural Comparisons of College Students' Marital-Role Preferences. *Journal of Social Psychology* 68, 1966, 41-47.

9. Kitano, H. "Inter- and Intra-generational Differences in Maternal Attitudes Towards Child Rearing." *Journal of Social Psychology* 63, 1964, 215-220.

10. Klineberg, O. *Social Psychology*, p. 172. New York: Henry Holt, 1940.

11. Kwan, K. M. "Assimilation of Chinese in the United States: An Exploratory Study in California." Ph.D. dissertation, University of California, Berkeley, Calif., 1958.

12. Mead, M. *Male and Female: A Study of the Sexes in a Changing World.* New York: Dell, 1968.

13. Meredith, G. M. "Observations on the Acculturation of Sansei Japanese-Americans in Hawaii." *Psychologia* (Kyoto) 8, 1965, 41-49.

14. _____. "Amae and Acculturation Among Japanese-American College Students in Hawaii." *Journal of Social Psychology* 70, 1966, 171-180.

15. _____, and Meredith, C. G. W. "Acculturation and Personality Among Japanese-American College Students in Hawaii." *Journal of Social Psychology* 68, 1966, 175-182.

16. Terman, L. M., and Miles, C. C. *Sex and Personality: Studies in Masculinity and Femininity.* New York: McGraw-Hill, 1936.

17. _____. *Manual of Information and Directions for Use of Attitude-Interest Analysis (M-F) Test.* New York: McGraw-Hill, 1938.

Part Three: Personality

Introduction

Chinese and Japanese are often stereotyped as being passive, inhibited, obedient, introverted, and shy (Sue and Kitano, in press). To what extent do these characterizations reflect the personalities of Asian-Americans? From a study of Chinese, Japanese, Filipino, Hawaiian, and Caucasian college students, Fenz and Arkoff (1962) found some support for these stereotypes. In general, Asian-American males exhibited less need for dominance, aggressiveness, exhibitionism, autonomy, and heterosexuality. Asian females were more deferent, nurturant, and achievement oriented than their Caucasian counterparts. Meredith and Meredith (Chapter 11) suggest that both the family and peer group contribute to the personality of Sansei (third-generation Japanese). The investigators discuss the under-representation in leadership by Sansei males and the over-representation by females. Personality patterns appear to account for this difference.

Obviously, many factors shape personality. Sue and Sue (Chapter 12) discuss the influence of traditional Chinese values, Western values, and racism on the personality of Chinese. Several typologies are outlined. Some Chinese try to maintain traditional values; others reject Chinese ways and attempt to assimilate completely into White society; and, finally, many Chinese have joined with other Asian groups in becoming ethnically conscious and militant. The availability of these personality models often results in an identity conflict. In an interesting analysis of Jade Snow Wong, Chun-Hoon (Chapter 13) points out the conflicts experienced by many Asian-Americans in trying to develop an identity and to maintain some degree of self-determination. Similar conflicts are encountered by Filipino-Americans as indicated in the article by Cordova (Chapter 14).

The paper by Sue (Chapter 15) discusses the personality and vocational interests of Chinese and Japanese students. Although there are similarities between the two groups, he also notes important differences. On various personality measures, Japanese are more Westernized in their values than are Chinese. Various reasons are advanced for these differences. In contrast to previous papers in this section, Sata (Chapter 16) presents his subjective experiences as a Japanese-American. His analysis not only provides insight into his life, but also adds a personal touch to the Asian-American experience.

References

Fenz, W. D., and Arkoff, A. "Comparative Need Patterns of Five Ancestry Groups in Hawaii. *Journal of Social Psychology* 58, 1962, 67-89.

Sue, S. and Kitano, H. H. "Stereotypes as a Measure of Success." *Journal of Social Issues*, 1973, in press.

11. Acculturation and Personality among Japanese-American College Students in Hawaii

by Gerald M. Meredith and Connie G. W. Meredith

Problem

One of the major problems in behavior theory concerns the nature of the relationship between acculturation and personality structure (Reference 25). As viewed in this article, the process of acculturation is directed toward the ultimate assimilation of the ethnic individual into American society (Ref. 10); therefore, the psychological problem becomes one of specifying those mediating processes that relate culture change to personal organization. Ruesch (Ref. 30) has proposed the hypothesis that acculturation to "the American core culture" is a function of the number of the cues and the responses that an individual possesses in common with the dominant social group.

In support of the foregoing hypothesis, Caudill (Ref. 16) has interpreted the rapid assimilation of the Japanese-Americans in terms of the compatibility between the values of the Japanese culture and the value systems of the American middle class. However, Broom and Kitsuse (Ref. 10) point out numerous factors that create stress in inter-ethnic situations and provide for the prolonged survival of parallel ethnic institutions. Despite the direct continuity between the values of *Issei* (first-generation Japanese-Americans) and *Nisei* (second-generation Japanese-Americans), two recognizably different basic personality patterns emerge. DeVos (Ref. 17, 18) has viewed these differences between generation levels in terms

of the problem of achieving greater self-differentiation.

Hawaii, with its peoples of varied national and racial backgrounds and its geographical insularity, is a natural laboratory for acculturation research. Of Hawaii's ethnic groups, the Japanese constitute the largest segment (approximately one-third) of a population that has no majority group. While there has been sustained interest in Nisei (Ref. 1, 16, 17, 18, 21, 22), recent attention has shifted to the college-age offspring of the Nisei: the Sansei (third-generation) (Ref. 2, 3, 4, 5, 6, 19). The purpose of the present study was to determine the differences between Sansei college students and a comparable group of Caucasian-American students on a set of basic personality dimensions. (This research was supported in part through the Cooperative Research Program of Education, United States Department of Health, Education, and Welfare.)

Method

Ss of the investigation were sixty Caucasian-American (thirty male, thirty female) and seventy-five Sansei (third-generation Japanese-American) (twenty-six male, forty-nine female) undergraduate students enrolled in the introductory psychology course at the University of Hawaii. The mean ages of the Caucasian-American and Japanese-American males were 19.2 and 19.1 years, respectively, while the

		Japanese-American		Caucasian-American		
Symbol	Personality Factor	Mean	SD	Mean	SD	t
A	Schizothymia vs. Cyclothymia	7.6	2.70	9.6	2.97	2.64*
B	Low "g" vs. High "g"	8.7	1.94	8.5	1.98	0.38
C	Low Ego Strength vs. High Ego Strength	17.8	3.46	17.4	3.40	0.44
E	Submissiveness vs. Dominance	13.2	3.61	16.6	3.34	3.61**
F	Desurgency vs. Surgency	15.7	3.86	16.3	3.78	0.52
G	Low Super Ego Strength vs. High Super Ego Strength	12.0	2.52	10.2	3.40	2.27*
H	Threctia vs. Parmia	10.1	3.82	14.1	4.27	3.70**
I	Harria vs. Premsia	8.0	3.62	9.1	2.70	1.23
L	Inner Relaxation vs. Protension	9.7	3.48	8.8	3.75	0.96
M	Praxernia vs. Autia	9.4	3.37	11.4	3.30	2.24*
N	Naivete vs. Shrewdness	11.0	2.24	11.5	2.53	0.78
O	Confidence vs. Timidity	11.2	3.79	9.5	3.07	1.83
Q_1	Conservatism vs. Radicalism	10.1	3.25	10.4	3.75	0.32
Q_2	Group Dependence vs. Self-Sufficiency	9.5	3.11	10.4	3.30	1.05
Q_3	Low Integration vs. Self-Sentiment Control	9.3	2.97	8.8	2.76	0.65
Q_4	Low Ergic Tension vs. High Ergic Tension	13.0	4.24	11.7	4.22	1.15

Table 1
Comparison of Males

* $df = 54$, significant at the .05 level.

** $df = 54$, significant at the .01 level.

corresponding values for the female groups were 18.6 and 18.7 years, respectively. None of the age differences was found to be statistically significant. A basic set of source traits in the "personality sphere" was measured with the 16 P. F. (Personality Factor) Questionnaire, Form A (Ref. 14).

Results

First-Order Analysis

The results of the Japanese-American and Caucasian-American groups on the 16 P. F. are summarized with respect to the above problem. Initially, means and standard deviations were computed on each scale for each of the four subgroups (Japanese-American males, Japanese-American females, Caucasian-American Males, and Caucasian-American females). Because the sex variable is not of major concern to the present problem, t tests of significance were computed only between the personality scores of Japanese-American and Caucasian-American males and between Japanese-American and Caucasian-American females. Within the male comparisons, summarized in Table 1, five of the personality differences exceed the .05 level of significance.

Within the female comparisons, summarized in Table 2, four of the personality differences exceed the .05 level of significance. Only one dimension, Factor E (submissiveness vs. dominance), consistently differentiated Japanese-American and Caucasian-American Ss within both sex groups.

In terms of primary-trait description (Ref. 14), the Japanese-American males are more

Symbol	Personality Factor	Japanese-American		Caucasian-American		
		Mean	SD	Mean	SD	t
A	Schizothymia vs. Cyclothymia	9.1	2.97	10.2	2.88	1.64
B	Low "g" vs. High "g"	7.8	2.01	8.1	2.15	0.69
C	Low Ego Strength vs. High Ego Strength	15.0	3.87	16.8	3.71	2.15*
E	Submissiveness vs. Dominance	12.0	3.80	13.9	4.13	2.04*
F	Desurgency vs. Surgency	15.7	3.37	15.4	3.57	0.37
G	Low Super Ego Strength vs. High Super Ego Strength	12.5	2.69	12.8	2.76	0.47
H	Threctia vs. Parmia	11.8	4.24	13.4	5.02	1.46
I	Harria vs. Premsia	12.0	2.34	11.1	2.36	1.65
L	Inner Relaxation vs. Protension	9.5	2.99	7.7	3.23	2.47*
M	Praxernia vs. Autia	12.8	3.24	11.5	3.47	1.66
N	Naivete vs. Shrewdness	8.3	2.75	8.5	2.50	0.33
O	Confidence vs. Timidity	12.4	3.94	9.9	4.08	2.68**
Q_1	Conservatism vs. Radicalism	9.2	2.12	9.5	2.84	0.51
Q_2	Group Dependence vs. Self-Sufficiency	9.9	2.44	9.4	2.74	0.82
Q_3	Low Integration vs. Self-Sentiment Control	9.3	2.81	9.5	3.18	0.28
Q_4	Low Ergic Tension vs. High Ergic Tension	14.7	4.93	13.8	4.53	0.83

Table 2
Comparison of Females

* df = 77, significant at the .05 level.
** df = 77, significant at the .01 level.

reserved (A –), more humble (E –), more conscientious (G +), more shy (H –), and more regulated by external realities (M –) than are Caucasian-American males. Conversely, Caucasian-American males are more outgoing (A +), more assertive (E +), more expedient (G –), more venturesome (H +), and more imaginative (M +) than are Japanese-American males.

Japanese-American females are more affected by feeling (C –), more obedient (E –), more suspicious (L +), and more apprehensive (O +) than are Caucasian-American females. Conversely, Caucasian-American females are more emotionally stable (C +), more independent (E +), more trusting (L–), and more self-assured (O –) than are Japanese-American

females.

Second-Order Analysis

A higher order factor in the questionnaire domain is a source trait that contributes to the variance of several primary source traits and is broader in its influences (Ref. 29, 31). Recently, Gorsuch and Cattell (Ref. 23) factor analyzed the intercorrelations among the sixteen primary factors of the P. F. test and delineated a set of second-stratum source traits, the most salient ones being introversion-extroversion and anxiety. Standard weights for estimating S's endowment on these second-order factors were applied to transform S's sten scores on the primaries to sten scores on the derived secondaries (Ref. 14).

Table 3
Second-Order Personality Comparisons

Sex and second-order factor	Japanese-American		Caucasian-American		
	Mean	SD	Mean	SD	t
Males					
Introversion-Extroversion	4.8	1.99	7.5	1.73	5.35**
Anxiety	6.3	1.89	5.6	1.68	1.45
Females					
Introversion-Extroversion	5.2	2.02	6.0	2.24	1.66
Anxiety	6.5	2.19	5.4	2.20	2.32*

* Significant at the .05 level.
** Significant at the .01 level.

A comparison of the ethnic groups on the second-order introversion-extroversion and anxiety factors is presented in Table 3. Clearly, the Japanese-American males appear more introverted than do Caucasian-American males. The female groups did not differ on this higher order dimension.

The Japanese-American male appears to show "inhibition of external reactivity (in terms of past discouragement and present timidity) and greater attention to inner stimuli and ideas" (Ref. 13, p. 268). Caucasian-American males may best be described at this level of analysis as "socially outgoing, uninhibited persons, good at making contacts" (Ref. 14).

The second-order anxiety factor has been found to be the basis of clinical judgments of anxiety; therefore, it can be interpreted, in general, as clinical anxiety (Ref. 23). The factor score is essentially an index of the degree of dynamic integration of the total personality, under the Self-sentiment Q_3, utilizing Ego Strength C. Cattell and Scheier (Ref. 15) hypothesize that "poor integration permits anxiety through conflict (C −), through id pressure (Q_4), through Protension [L (paranoid maladjustment in relation to external realities)], and lack of control of fear impulses" (Ref. 15, p. 319). In comparing the present groups, the Japanese-American females scored significantly (but not dramatically) higher than the Caucasian-American females. The male groups did not differ on this higher order dimension.

Discussion

Aside from the early socialization patterns of the family, the adolescent peer group contributes substantially to the personality molding of Japanese-Americans in Hawaii (Ref. 9, 19, 27, 32). An important component of peer influence is a strong ingroup perception of being a "local" island resident, as opposed to being a "mainlander." Since many nonresidents are Caucasian (e.g., tourists, servicemen, and students), a social polarity of "local" versus "haole" (a semi-derisive Hawaiian term meaning "foreigner" but used synonomously for a Caucasian) is formed. A stereotype of a "local" is built and supported by the "youth culture" (Ref. 28) through symbols, such as clothing fads, hair styles, and the use of pidgin English speech patterns (Ref. 12, 26). The resultant swell-guy image of the adolescent male and the glamor-girl image of the adolescent female are Hawaii's own distinctive and Japanese-American counterpart of Talcott Parsons' youth roles (Ref. 28).

An important outcome of early socialization

experiences and peer influences is a lowering of leadership potential, particularly among the Sansei males. Bartos and Kalish (Ref. 7) found that (at the University of Hawaii) there appears to be an under-representation in leadership by Sansei males and greater-than-expected social participation and leadership by Sansei females. This finding is congruent with Kitano's observation of "social backwardness" among a mainland sample of acculturating Japanese-American males (Ref. 24) and supports Burma's commentary on the leadership "crisis" among this ethnic group (Ref. 11). Some have perceived a link here with the stress in (male-dominant) Japanese culture of individual needs in the face of group and family expectancy (Ref. 19). It is hypothesized that the introverted nature of the Sansei males sets the stage for diminished social participation and the "leadership crisis."

The traditional stereotype of a retiring and compliant Japanese female, as depicted by Benedict (Ref. 8), is difficult to find among Sansei females. Indeed, the evidence seems to indicate that females may be acculturating more rapidly or easily than males (Ref. 4, 5, 16, 18, 20, 24). While the present study reveals several first-order personality differences, there is a great deal of identification with the "core American culture" (especially indicated on the second-order introversion-extroversion factor). The heightened anxiety pattern is not unexpected, in view of the demands and expectations placed on the Sansei female. It is hypothesized that this elevation in anxiety is situationally induced and linked to the following: (a) parental stress on academic achievement, (b) dependency-independency conflicts within the Japanese-American family, (c) familial and peer pressures surrounding dating and sociology of jealousy"), and (d) social control exerted by the "youth culture." While it may be argued that Sansei males are subjected to similar pressures, it appears that the way anxiety is handled differs for each sex group, and this difference deserves further scrutiny.

Summary

The present study compared personality patterns of third-generation Japanese-American (Sansei) and Caucasian-American college students on the 16 P. F. Questionnaire. Analysis of the findings indicated five first-order personality differences among the males and four differences among the females. A second-order analysis indicated Japanese-American males higher on introversion, while Japanese-American females scored higher on anxiety. These findings were discussed with reference to a number of forces operative within the Hawaiian milieu.

References

1. Abe, S. K. "Nisei Personality Characteristics as Measured by the Edwards Personal Preference Schedule and Minnesota Multiphasic Personality Inventory." Doctoral dissertation, University of Utah, Salt Lake City, Utah, 1958.

2. Arkoff, A. "Need Patterns in Two Generations of Japanese-Americans in Hawaii." *Journal of Social Psychology* 50, 1959, 75-79.

3. ____; Meredith, G.; and Dong, J. "Attitudes of Japanese-American and Caucasian-American Students Toward Marriage Roles." *Journal of Social Psychology* 59, 1963, 11-15.

4. ____; Meredith, G.; and Iwahara, S. "Dominance-Deference Patterning in Motherland-Japanese, Japanese-American, and Caucasian-American Students." *Journal of Social Psychology* 58, 1962, 61-66.

5. ____; Meredith, G.; and Iwahara, S. "Male-Dominant and Equalitarian Attitudes in Japanese, Japanese-American, and Caucasian-American

Students." *Journal of Social Psychology* 64, 1964, 225-229.

6. ____ ; Meredith, G.; and Jones, R. "Urban-Rural Differences in Need Patterns of Third-Generation Japanese-Americans in Hawaii." *Journal of Social Psychology* 53, 1961, 21-23.

7. Bartos, O. J., and Kalish, R. A. "Sociological Correlates of Student Leadership in Hawaii." *Journal of Educational Sociology* 35, 1961, 65-72.

8. Benedict, R. *Chrysanthemum and the Sword.* Boston: Houghton Mifflin, 1946.

9. Bitner, H. M. "Ethnic Intergroup Differences in Personality, General Culture, Academic Ability, and Interests in a Geographically Restricted Area." Doctoral dissertation, Ohio State University, Columbus, Ohio, 1954.

10. Broom, L., and Kitsuse, J. I. "The Validation of Acculturation: A Condition of Ethnic Assimilation. *American Anthropology* 57, 1955, 44-48.

11. Burma, J. H. "Current Leadership Problems among Japanese-Americans." *Sociology & Social Research* 37, 1953, 157-163.

12. Carr, E. P. "The Fiftieth State: New Dimensions for Studies in Speech." *The Speech Teacher* November, 1961, 288.

13. Cattell, R. B. *Personality and Motivation Structure and Measurement.* New York: Harcourt, Brace, and World, 1957.

14. ____ , and Eber, H. W. *Handbook of the Sixteen Personality Factor Questionnaire.* Champaign, Ill.: Institute for Personality and Ability Testing, 1964.

15. ____ , and Scheier, I. H. *The Meaning and Measurement of Neuroticism and Anxiety.* New York: Ronald, 1961.

16. Caudill, W. "Japanese-American Person-ality and Acculturation." *Genet. Psychol. Monog.* 45, 1952, 3-102.

17. DeVos, G. "A Comparison of the Personality Differences in Two Generations of Japanese-Americans by Means of the Rorschach Test." *Nagoya J. Med. Sci.* 17, 1954, 153-265.

18. ____ . "A Quantitative Rorschach Assessment of Maladjustment and Rigidity in Acculturating Japanese-Americans." *Genet. Psychol. Monog.* 52, 1955, 51-87.

19. Fenz, W. D., and Arkoff, A. "Comparative Need Patterns of Five Ancestry Groups in Hawaii." *Journal of Social Psychology* 58, 1962, 67-89.

20. Fisher, S., and Cleveland, S. E. *Body Image and Personality.* Princeton, N.J.: D. Van Nostrand, 1958.

21. Fujita, B. "An Investigation of the Applicability of the Edwards Personal Preference Schedule to a Cultural Subgroup, the Nisei." Master's thesis, University of Washington, Seattle, 1956.

22. ____ . Applicability of the Edwards Personal Preference Schedule to Nisei." *Psychol. Rep.* 3, 1957, 518-519.

23. Gorsuch, R. L., and Cattell, R. B. "Second Strata Personality Factors Defined in the Questionnaire Medium by the 16 P. F. *J. Personal.* 1964.

24. Kitano, H. "Changing Achievement Patterns of the Japanese in the United States." *Journal of Social Psychology* 58, 1962, 257-264.

25. Kluckhohn, C. "Culture and Behavior." In G. Lindzey (ed.), *Handbook of Social Psychology* pp. 921-976. Cambridge, Mass.: Addison-Wesley, 1954.

26. Lind, A. W. "Communication: A Problem of Island Youth." *Soc. Process in Hawaii* 24, 1960, 44-45.

27. Linderfelt, R. M. "A Comparative Study of the Rorschach Protocols of Japanese and Caucasian College Students." Master's thesis, University of Hawaii, Honolulu, 1949.

28. Parsons, T. "Age and Sex in the Social Structure of the United States." In C. Kluckhohn and H. A. Murray (eds.), *Personality in Nature, Society and Culture* pp. 363-375. New York: Knopf, 1948.

29. Pawlik, K., and Cattell, R. B. "Third-Order Factors in Objective Personality Tests." *Brit. J. Psychol.* 55, 1964, 1-18.

30. Ruesch, J. "Social Technique, Social Status, and Social Change in Illness." In C. Kluckhohn and H. A. Murray (eds.), *Personality in Nature, Society and Culture* pp. 117-130. New York: Knopf, 1948.

31. Tsujioka, B., and Cattell, R. B. "A Cross-cultural Comparison of Second Stratum Questionnaire Factor Structures — Anxiety and Extroversion — in America and Japan." *Journal of Social Psychology* 65, 1965, 205-219.

32. Zald, M. N. "Family Patterns and 'Authoritarianism' Among Some Japanese-American Students." Master's thesis, University of Hawaii, 1955.

12. Chinese-American Personality and Mental Health

by Stanley Sue and Derald Wing Sue

In writing this article, we have tried to integrate personal observations, clinical impressions, and available research findings. Where clinical cases have been described of individuals in therapy, care has been taken to insure anonymity. Since there is a lack of research on Chinese-American personality and mental health, much of our discussion should be regarded as tentative rather than as the "final" word. Hopefully, this article will stimulate further thinking and raise issues.

The Development of Personality

Sometimes it seems as though a Chinese-American must possess great ego strength in order to survive the conflicts surrounding him. He must develop within the interplay of forces such as parental upbringing, the clash between Chinese and Western values, and racism. As a basis for developing a conceptual scheme of personality, let us briefly examine them.

The Traditional Chinese Family

Although generalizations of the "traditional" Chinese family do injustice to differences among families, we have decided to define the traditional family as having certain values and behavioral characteristics. A more extensive analysis can be found in studies by DeVos and Abbott[1] and Cattell.[2]

In the traditional family, ancestors and elders are viewed with great reverence. The primary family unit is strong and typically exerts great control over its members. Emphasis is placed on obtaining a good education, on being obedient to parents, and in giving the family a good name. "Bad" behavior on the part of a member (exhibiting antisocial or criminal behavior, disobedience, low achievement, or even psychopathology) brings shame on the entire family. In order to control members, parents use guilt-arousing techniques such as threatening to disown the person, verbally censuring the individual, or having the individual engage in activities that accentuate his feelings of guilt and shame. Many times, disappointed Chinese parents may say, "How could you do this to us?" or "After all we have sacrificed for you, you are still like this." An interesting example of the accentuation of shame is provided by Lowell Chun-Hoon[3] in his analysis of Jade Snow Wong. After Jade Snow Wong had stolen a piece of cloth from a visiting peddler, her father made her sit outside the house for a day with the item she stole. Thus, her wrongdoing was publicly displayed.

In addition, the Chinese learns strong patterns of self-control which have an effect on his personality. Fenz and Arkoff state that investigators have . . .

> stressed the strong family ties of Chinese families, as well as the traditional adherence of Chinese youths to parental mores. Chinese children are said to be taught by

their parents to live up to a role of detachment and self-control. This is said to be responsible for a lack of spontaneity and self-expression and for a strong control over affective impulses which is said to have become characteristic of the Chinese personality.[4]

In their study utilizing the Edwards Personal Preference Schedule, Fenz and Arkoff found that Chinese were generally more deferent and less autonomous, exhibitionistic, and heterosexual in interest than Caucasians. In a preliminary study of the Chinese community of San Francisco, DeVos and Abbott[5] attempted to conceptualize family life through interviews, a questionnaire, and a problem situation test. These investigators found that: (a) educational achievement is consistently valued above other types of achievement; (b) Chinese-Americans usually react passively to authority; (c) respect for elders is equated with respect for authority; (d) there is a strong sense of responsibility for relatives; (e) when a younger person fails to live up to the elders' expectations, self-blame is the result; and (f) proper methods of socializing the child are seen to exclude physical violence and punishment.

Western Influences

Against this family background, the Chinese-American also develops within the host culture. Peer group influences may begin to erode parental authority. He is constantly bombarded with Western values in the schools and in the mass media. These values reflect the attitudes, norms, emotional expressions, and other behaviors characteristic of the dominant society. It is inevitable that some changes will occur. For example, Fong[6] studied 336 Chinese college students by using three different instruments. He administered a personal data form to obtain background factors such as generational level, area of residence, citizenship status, etc. An assimilation-orientation inventory assessing social, cultural, and political attitudes was also employed. Finally, a stick-figures test was administered to demonstrate an individual's ability to perceive culturally determined modes of expression. Results indicated that, as the Chinese-American becomes increasingly exposed to the values and standards of the larger host culture, there is progressive inculcation of those norms. In fact, Chinese-Americans whose families had been in the United States for two or more generations were largely assimilated.

Racism

Finally, the Chinese-American also experiences direct and subtle forms of discrimination in his exposure to the host society. While it is beyond the scope of this paper to analyze racism, we note that racism can be individual and institutional. Individual racism involves a *person's* attitudes and behaviors toward the Chinese. He may believe that Chinese are "sneaky" or may try to prevent them from moving into his neighborhood. Interestingly, prejudice can also work in favor of the Chinese-American in specific situations. Teachers may believe that Chinese are intelligent and hard working and, thus, give them better grades. In the long run, side effects often develop. The individual may strive to maintain his hardworking image by being obedient and conforming. A Chinese who rebels against this stereotype faces the wrath of his teachers for violating *their* notions of a "good" Chinese.

Institutional racism refers to systematic discrimination in various institutions. For example, in the past, laws in some states prevented Chinese from marrying Caucasians; and current business practices may keep Chinese from attaining high executive positions in large corporations. Blacks have often been systematically denied admission to institutions of higher education because of failure to attain certain admission requirements. Although these requirements may be applied equally, they are insensitive to the factors behind the Blacks' inability to meet the standards. These forms of racism leave their mark on the personality of many ethnic minorities.

Figure 1

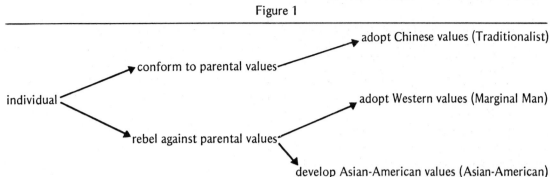

Personality: A Conceptual Scheme

Personality development can proceed in many ways. At this time, we are not prepared to present the possible factors determining which direction the individual ultimately takes. In order to examine some of the underlying dynamics and conflicts which many Chinese-Americans have, we will concentrate on only three typological characters. Figure 1 illustrates a conceptualization of the Traditionalist, the Marginal Man, and the Asian-American.

Traditionalist

The Traditionalist has strongly internalized Chinese values. There is an attempt to be a "good" son or daughter. Primary allegiance is to the family into which he was born. In fact, eventual obligations as father and husband may be secondary to his duty to parents. Self-worth and -esteem are defined by his ability to succeed in terms of high educational achievement, occupational status, etc. With success, he feels respectable in American society; he has brought honor to the family name and has accomplished this, all as a minority member. Gordon Allport, a social psychologist, noted that:

> People admire the cripple who has persevered and overcome his handicap. . . . Accordingly, some members of minority groups view their handicap as an obstacle to be surmounted by an extra spurt of effort.[7]

Thus, feelings of pride are felt because he has achieved despite adverse conditions. Allport also states that " . . . they may evoke abuse for being *too* industrious or clever."[8] This statement points to the limitations on achievement placed by the host society. The Chinese must work hard to achieve, but, if he works too hard and is too manipulating, he runs the risk of being stereotyped a "Chinese Jew."

We believe that the personal conflicts that the Traditionalist suffers come primarily from two sources. The first involves his attempts to be a good son. He must give his parents unquestioning obedience and must achieve well in order to maintain a good family name and to feel self-worth. However, if he feels that his parents are wrong or are demanding too much from him, what will he do? In these situations, his personal feelings are in conflict with parental expectations. His acquiescence to them means he must suppress or repress his indignation; his defiance of them brings on intense feelings of guilt and shame. Guilt feelings often emerge because his identity is defined within the family.

The Traditionalist feels responsible for his failure to obey parents or to achieve well. Since he has internalized values of respect for parents, he finds it difficult to blame them. On the other hand, he cannot blame the host society, since he has been taught by his parents that success is possible with hard work. He, alone, bears the responsibility for failure. The following is a description of a Chinese student seen by one of the authors for therapy.

The Case of John C.

John C. is a twenty-year-old junior student, majoring in electrical engineering. He is the oldest of five children, born and raised in San Francisco. The father is fifty-eight years old and has been a grocer for the past twenty years, and the mother is a housewife. The parents have always had high expectations for their eldest son and constantly transmitted these feelings to him. Ever since he could remember, John's parents had decided that he would go to college and become an engineer – a job they held in high esteem.

Throughout his early school years, John was an outstanding student and was constantly praised by his teachers. He was hard working and obedient and never gave his teachers any trouble. However, his parents seemed to take John's school successes for granted. In fact, they would always make statements such as "you can do better still."

John first came to the counseling center during the latter part of his junior year because of severe headaches and a vague assortment of bodily complaints. A medical checkup failed to reveal any organic malfunctioning, which led the psychologist to suspect a psycho-physiological reaction.

John exhibited a great deal of anxiety throughout the interviews. He seemed suspicious of the psychologist and found it difficult to talk about himself in a personal way. As the sessions progressed, it became evident that John felt a great deal of shame about having come to a therapist. John was concerned that his family not be told, since they would be disgraced.

Throughout the interviews, John appeared excessively concerned with failing his parents' expectations. Further exploration revealed significant sources of conflict. First, his grades were beginning to decline, and he felt that he was letting his parents down. Second, he had always harbored wishes about becoming an architect but felt this to be an unacceptable profession to his parents. Third, increasing familial demands were being placed on him to quickly graduate and obtain a job in order to help the family's financial situation. The parents frequently made statements such as, "Once you are out of school and making good money, it would be nice if you could help

your brothers and sisters through college." John's resentment of these imposed responsibilities was originally denied and repressed. When he was able to see clearly his anger and hostility towards his parents, many of his physical complaints vanished. However, with the recognition of his true feelings, he became extremely depressed and guilty. John could not see why he should be angry at his parents after all they had done for him.

The second source of conflict occurs because the Traditionalist must interact with the dominant society. Despite his attempt to confine his social life to the Chinese subculture, he is unable to fully isolate himself from members of the host society. Learned patterns of obedience and conformity are transferred to the interactions with them. Since role expectations in the Chinese family are well defined and structured, he may find it difficult to interact with Caucasians, who are often behaving under different expectations. Frequently, these expectations are diametrically opposed to one another. For example, Caucasian patterns of relating tend to stress assertive and spontaneous behaviors. The Chinese patterns of deference and reserve are at odds with these values. This causes the Traditionalist great discomfort in his interpersonal relations with Caucasians, who may view his behaviors negatively. In addition, individual forms of racism increase his level of anxiety and discomfort. He has not been taught how to respond aggressively to racism. He seeks to make the best of the circumstances without challenging the host society. Allport notes that the individual

> ... escapes being conspicuous, has no cause for fear, and quietly leads his life in two compartments: one (more active) among his own kind, one (more passive) in the outer world.[9]

As for institutional racism, the Traditionalist is often less aware or concerned, since he believes he can overcome obstacles if he works hard enough.

Marginal Man

Both the Marginal Man and the Asian-American cannot give unquestioning obedience to traditional parental values. The Marginal Man attempts to assimilate and acculturate into the majority society. Existing between the margin of two cultures, he suffers from an identity crisis. In attempts to resolve this conflict, the person may reject traditional Chinese ways by becoming over-Westernized. We believe that the Marginal Man finds his self-worth defined in terms of acceptance by Caucasians. For the Chinese male, the number of Caucasian friends he has and such things as his ability to speak without an accent are sources of pride. He may feel contemptuous of Chinese girls who are "short legged" and "flat chested" when compared to Caucasian girls.

Likewise, an anthropological field study conducted in a Chinese-American community by Weiss revealed that many Chinese-American females view their male counterparts as inhibited, passive, and lacking in sexual attractiveness. Data were obtained through attendance at social functions and by the administration of questionnaires. The investigator states:

> Perhaps the most damaging indictment of Chinese-American male "dating ineptness" comes from the dating-age, Chinese-American female. Girls who regularly date Caucasians can be quite vehement in their denunciation and disapproval of Chinese-American males as dating partners. But even the foreign-born Chinese girls — who do not usually inter-date — also support a demeaning court-ship image of the Chinese-American male. Moreover, "Chinese inadequacies" and "failures" are contrasted with Caucasian "confidence" and "success" in similar situations.[10]

Weiss feels that Chinese-American females are better accepted by American society than the Chinese-American male. Stereotyping of the Chinese-American male has been generally unfavorable as compared to the female. As a result, the highly Westernized female begins to expect her boy friends to behave boldly and aggressively. Because the Chinese male is perceived to lack these "desirable traits," many of the Chinese females begin to date outside their own race.

The Marginal Man is not without a great deal of conflict. Hostility and denial of his minority culture may cause him to turn his hostility inward and to develop a form of "racial self-hatred." An extreme form of self-hatred is demonstrated in the observations of Bruno Bettleheim as described by Gordon Allport:

> Studies of Nazi concentration camps show that identification with one's oppressors was a form of adjustment. . . . At first, prisoners tried to keep their self-respect intact, to feel inward contempt for their persecutors, to try by stealth and cunning to preserve their lives and their health. But, after two or three years of extreme suffering, many of them found that their efforts to please their guards led to a mental surrender. They imitated the guards, wore bits of their clothing (symbolic power), turned against new prisoners, became anti-Semites, and, in general, took over the dark mentality of the oppressor.[11]

Self-hatred can result in violence as well as in derogatory attitudes towards one's own group. It is our belief, however, that the Marginal Man has not resorted to widespread physical violence toward his own group because of subcultural values emphasizing restraint of disruptive feelings and because of underlying guilt feelings regarding violence to one's own group.

The Marginal Man's over-Westernized behavior is frequently in opposition to parental values and to Chinese culture and may arouse intense feelings of guilt. Again, Allport describes a similar process in the Jew:

> . . . the member who denies his allegiance suffers considerable conflict. He may feel like a traitor to his kind. A Jewish student confessed with remorse that, in order not to be known as Jewish, he would sometimes "insert in my conversation delicate witticisms pertaining to

Jewishness which, while not actually vicious, conveyed a total impression of gentile malice."[12]

Although the Marginal Man cannot disguise his appearance, he, too, may experience conflict and anxiety for telling jokes about Chinese or for contemptuously stating that other Chinese are old fashioned:

> Since he cannot escape his own group, he, thus, in a real sense hates himself. . . . To make matters worse, he may hate himself for feeling this way. He is badly torn. His divided mind may make for furtive and self-conscious behavior, for "nervousness," and a lasting sense of insecurity.[13]

Allport's observations point to the double conflict involved in self-hatred. First, the Marginal Man may hate himself for possessing "Chinese" characteristics. For example, he is frequently disgusted by his own physical characteristics such as shortness of height, round-flat nose, narrow eyes, and lack of a "manly" physique. Second, he may hate himself for hating himself! In the course of our work, we have observed many of these conflicts in Chinese-Americans. The following is the case of a student exhibiting problems typical of a Marginal Man.

The Case of Janet T.
Janet T. is a twenty-one-year-old senior, majoring in sociology. She was born and raised in Portland, Oregon, where she had limited contact with members of her own race. Her father, a second-generation Chinese-American, is a fifty-three-year-old doctor. Her mother, age forty-four, is a housewife. Janet is the second oldest of three children, has an older brother (currently in medical school) and a younger brother, age seventeen.

Janet came for therapy suffering from a severe depressive reaction manifested by feelings of worthlessness, by suicidal ideation, and by an inability to concentrate. She was unable to recognize the cause of her depression throughout the initial interviews. However, much light was shed on the problem when the therapist noticed an inordinate amount of hostility directed towards him. When inquiries were made about the hostility, it became apparent that Janet greatly resented being seen by a Chinese psychologist. Janet suspected that she had been assigned a Chinese therapist because of her own race. When confronted with this fact, Janet openly expressed scorn for "anything which reminds me of Chinese." Apparently, she felt very hostile towards Chinese customs and, especially, the Chinese male, whom she described as introverted, passive, and sexually unattractive.

Further exploration revealed a long-standing history of attempts to deny her Chinese ancestry by associating only with Caucasians. When in high school, Janet would frequently bring home White boy friends, which greatly upset her parents. It was as though she blamed her parents for being born a Chinese, and she used this method to hurt them.

During her college career, Janet became involved in two love affairs with Caucasians, both ending unsatisfactorily and abruptly. The last breakup occurred four months ago when the boy's parents threatened to cut off financial support for their son unless he ended the relationship. Apparently, objections arose because of Janet's race.

Although not completely conscious, Janet was having increasing difficulty with denial of her racial heritage. The breakup of her last torrid love affair made her realize that she was Chinese and not fully accepted by all segments of society. At first, she vehemently and bitterly denounced the Chinese for her present dilemma. Later, much of her hostility was turned inward against herself. Feeling alienated from her own subculture and not fully accepted by American society, she experienced an identity crisis. This resulted in feelings of worthlessness and depression. It was at this point that Janet came for therapy.

Finally, the Marginal Man must somehow handle instances of individual and institutional racism. For example, if he dates a Caucasian girl and is rejected by her parents, he faces conflict. He is not being accepted by individuals of the very group into which he aspires. In an attempt to resolve the conflict, the Marginal Man may overcompensate. He believes that rejection by the girl's parents is an isolated situation rather than a reflection of pervasive individual racism. Although he feels that it can happen again, the situation does not change his desire to assimilate. He may even double his efforts to date Caucasians, since they are now more symbolic of acceptance by the host society, i.e., the Caucasian girls are "forbidden fruits." The Marginal Man finds it difficult to admit widespread racism, since to do so would be to say that he aspires to join a racist society.

As in individual racism, the Marginal Man also minimizes or denies the impact of institutional racism. For example, he may believe that, if Chinese do not attain high executive positions, it is because they are too unassertive and reserved. His inability to be fully accepted by the host society is not so much a matter of personal failure or pervasive racial discrimination. He attributes blame to his own group for perpetuating Chinese values, which are maladaptive and which make the Chinese appear even more foreign and unacceptable to the host society.

Asian-American

Since he is in the process of self-definition, the Asian-American is much harder to define. Thus, we would like to pose some general impressions. Unlike the Traditionalist and the Marginal Man, who have found existing models, the Asian-American tries to formulate a new identity by integrating his past experiences with his present conditions. Unquestioning obedience to parents is too painful; racism is too pervasive to ignore; and pride in self is too underdeveloped. He also shares common patterns with the other two. For example, he associates with other Chinese without embarrassment as does the Traditionalist. And like the Marginal Man, he experiences some guilt for his unwillingness to fully accept the dictates of his parents. However, the Asian-American's defiance is less a rejection of Chinese ways than an attempt to preserve certain Chinese values in the formation of a new identity. He feels that complete obedience to traditional values limits his self-growth. Self-pride cannot be attained if his behaviors are completely determined by his parents or by society. Parental emphasis on high achievement is too materialistic for the Asian-American who is trying to find meaning and self-identity. In addition, his political and social awareness is more fully developed. He is more sensitive to the forces in society which have shaped his identity and have too often been left unchallenged. Problems such as poverty, unemployment, individual and institutional racism, and juvenile delinquency are of primary concern to him. More than anything, society is to blame for his present dilemma and must be changed. Emphasis is placed on raising group esteem and pride, for it is only through collective action that society's perception of the Asian-American can be efficiently altered.

The Asian-American's orientation also includes other Asian groups as a basis for identity. Allport believes that group cohesiveness is often due to a common-enemy hypothesis. For example, he states that:

> Threats drive them to seek protective unity within their common membership. The prevailing belief on the West Coast during World War II that "a Jap is a Jap" created a strong tie among Issei (foreign born) and Nisei (American born), although, before the persecution set in, these groups were frequently at odds with each other.[14]

The unity of Chinese-Americans with other groups (Japanese, Korean, Filipino, etc.), however, seems to be more than just a common reaction to racism or stereotypes. There appears to be a positive effort by the Asian-American to develop and form an identity which will enable him to reconcile viable aspects of his heritage with his present situation. The notions of "viable aspects" and of "present situation" are hard to define. The former probably includes pride in one's heritage, knowledge of one's culture, and unity with his group. The latter is the consideration of Chinese-Americans as a minority group and as Americans. The Asian-American must be assertive, questioning, and active in order to develop in his present environment.

The Asian-American also faces conflicts. Since he is attempting to find an identity with other Asian-Americans, the group is extremely important to him. Anyone who is perceived to threaten the Asian-American group is, in a real sense, threatening his identity. Thus, he may feel quite intolerant of the Traditionalist and, particularly, of the Marginal Man who wants to assimilate. Since he feels that many of the problems of minority groups are due to the host society, he must, somehow, reconcile this belief with the observations that there are "Uncle Toms" in his own racial group. That is, while he is contemptuous of the Marginal Man, he also believes that the Marginal Man is a product of the society.

In addition, the Asian-American may become extremely militant in his reaction to racism. While militancy may have valuable contributions in gaining civil rights, feelings of self-pride, and power, it may also make the Asian-American obsessively concerned with racism. He may become extremely sensitive and suspicious. Allport notes that this is not uncommon among Jews:

> One day in the late 30s, a recently arrived refugee couple went shopping in a village grocery store in New England. The husband ordered some oranges. "For juice?" inquired the clerk. "Did you hear that," the woman whispered to her husband, "for Jews? You see, it's beginning here, too."[15]

Finally, the Asian-American may experience a great deal of guilt and frustration in his relationship with his parents. His parents tend to view his disobedience, assertiveness, tendency towards long hair, and de-emphasis on academic achievement as signs that he is disrespectful to them and to traditional values. He finds it difficult to communicate that he is attempting to gain self-respect; that his parents have not failed in raising him; that he is, indeed, growing and achieving in his *own* way. Thus, the Asian-American may feel a real sense of loss. He is trying to help his people, many of whom do not understand his efforts. The following is a description of an Asian-American student seen for therapy.

The Case of Gale K.
Gale K. is a twenty-two-year-old, first-year graduate student in biochemistry. His father, once employed in an engineering firm, died recently from cancer. His fifty-two-year-old mother is currently employed at the San Francisco airport as a receptionist. Gale was born and raised in Oakland, California. He has three sisters, all of whom are married.

Much of Gale's early life was filled with conflict and antagonism between him and his parents. Like Janet T., Gale did not confine his social life exclusively to other Chinese-Americans. As he was the only son, his parents were fearful that they would lose their son should he marry a Caucasian. Five years earlier, their eldest daughter had married a Caucasian, which caused great turmoil in the family and the subsequent disowning of the daughter.

Throughout much of his life, Gale attempted to deny his racial identity because he felt shameful about being Chinese. However, within the last four years, a phenomenal change occurred in Gale. He actively participated in the Third World strike at the University and became involved in a number of community change committees. Gale recalls with great fondness the "esprit de corps" and contagion he experienced with other concerned Asians. His parents had been delighted about his reorientation towards certain Chinese values. They were especially happy to see him dating Asian girls and volunteering his time to help tutor educationally deprived children in Chinatown. However, they did not understand his activist thinking and outspoken behavior towards authority figures.

Gale came for therapy because he had not fully resolved guilt feelings concerning the recent death of his father. Several weeks prior to his father's death, Gale had a violent argument with him over his [Gale's] recent participation in a demonstration. When his father passed away, Gale felt a great deal of remorse. He had often wished that his father could have understood the Asian-American movement.

Throughout our sessions, Gale exhibited an understanding and awareness of economic, political, and social forces beyond that of the average student. He attributed the plight of Asian-Americans to the shortcomings of society. He was openly suspicious of therapy and confronted the therapist on two different issues. The first objection dealt with the use of tests in therapy. Gale felt them to be culturally biased and somewhat inapplicable to ethnic minorities. The second issue concerned the relationship of therapy to the status quo. Since therapy has, traditionally, been concerned with the adjustment of individuals to society, Gale questioned the validity of this concept. "Do you adjust people to a sick society?" Only after dealing with these issues was it possible for Gale and the therapist to focus on his feelings regarding the death of his father.

A final word should be said before we move on with our discussion. It has been our feeling that the Marginal Man comes in for therapy at a much higher rate than either the Traditionalist or the Asian-American. Our clinical impressions seem to indicate that, since psychotherapy is a White, middle-class activity, the three types are affected differentially. The Traditionalist does not understand therapy and feels great shame about admitting psychological problems; the Asian-American equates psychotherapy with the status quo and is openly suspicious of this type of activity; and the Marginal Man, in his attempts to assimilate, may view therapy more favorably than the other two. As a result, the Marginal Man would be more prone to utilize mental health facilities when he encounters

problems.

Limitations and Implications

At this point, we would like to note some limitations of our analysis. First, this conceptual scheme does not deal with important factors such as foreign- versus American-born Chinese, residence in versus residence outside of Chinatown, and length of residence in the U.S. In doing so, problems involving juvenile delinquency, poverty, educational and language difficulties, and peer group factors have been largely ignored. Second, individual differences and variations are submerged in this kind of analysis. For example, we know Traditionalists who are quite aware of the social and political forces surrounding them; we know of Marginal Men who function without much internal conflict and without "racial self-hatred," and we have seen parents of Asian-Americans who are as "Third World" as their sons and daughters. Third, sex differences within and between each character type have not been adequately handled. Finally, we have used many examples from Allport's analysis of Jews. Our purpose in presenting these examples is to illustrate some of the underlying processes and conflicts rather than to argue for the personality similarity between Chinese and Jews.

These typological characters have been carried to their logical extremes in an attempt to gain insight into some of the underlying dynamics and conflicts. Any typological analysis tends to limit the number of relevant variables it can handle. A tabular summary of the three types is given in Figure 2.

It is our impression that these polar types have been used in reality. Note the following terms: "F.O.B." or "typical Chinese" for the Traditionalist; "Banana" or "Uncle Tom" for the Marginal Man; and "radical" or "militant" for the Asian-American. These terms are often derogatory and demonstrate within-group divisions. Our position is that all three types can attain self-pride. This possibility has not

Figure 2

	Traditionalist	Marginal Man	Asian-American
Self worth defined by	Obedience to parents... Behaviors which bring honor to family...	Ability to acculturate into White society...	Ability to attain self-pride through defining a new identity...
Behavior which arouses guilt	Failure to live up to parental values...	Defiance of parental values...	Defiance of parental values...
Attribution of blame for one's lack of success	Self... White society...	Chinese values... Minimal blame on White society...	White society...
Handling of prejudice and discrimination	Deferring and minimizing effects...	Denying and minimizing effects...	Anger and militancy...

been recognized, since each type has defined pride and self-esteem from different reference points. The Traditionalist's failure to see how one can attain self-respect by not obeying parents is a result of defining pride and esteem within the family unit. The evaluation from his family is the critical factor. Evaluations from the host society, while being important, are secondary.

The Marginal Man's self-pride is determined by his relationship to the host society. He cannot see how one can attain pride by not assimilating. He views the Traditionalist as perpetuating outdated values. On the other hand, the Asian-American is seen to be "rocking the boat" by his militancy. The Marginal Man feels that both groups have difficulty in maintianing "real" pride, since the host society fails to accept them as well as it has accepted him.

Finally, the Asian-American's pride is in the reconciliation of past and present values. He may believe that the Traditionalist cannot have "real" pride, since the Traditionalist ignores racism and is unassertive. Between the Traditionalist and the Marginal Man, however, more of his wrath is directed to the Marginal Man,

who is perceived to be completely denying his cultural heritage.

We feel that, in all cases, there is a confusion between "self" and "pride." Self-pride, by definition, must involve the individual's own conception of pride. Although self-pride is often determined by one's environment, we do not feel that any of the typological characters have the "exclusive" definition of self-pride. It must be defined by the individual in his circumstance.

The real issue is the attainment of pride at what cost to one another. In this regard, the Traditionalist is the least threatening. With each succeeding generation, Chinese in America are becoming less "traditional." The possibility that immigrants can maintain traditional values is highly unlikely, since their number is relatively small. According to our conceptual scheme, the only viable alternatives for Chinese (Asians) in the U.S. are between the Marginal Man and the Asian-American.

To the extent that the Marginal Man feels "racial self-hatred" and contempt for Chinese, he demonstrates his willingness to gain self-pride at the expense of other Chinese. On the other hand, the Asian-American seeks pride by raising group esteem. As long as he rejects dogma and intolerance in his approach, he can do much to raise the esteem of Chinese-Americans and to give himself some choice in preserving aspects of his subculture. In terms of pride, each type can reconcile some of their differences, although social and political differences may always exist. We do not believe that assimilation necessarily involves hatred for self. The Marginal Man can try to assimilate without derogating the Chinese, once he feels secure in saying that he is a Chinese-American. Like the Marginal Man, the Asian-American is assimilating in many ways. Once the Asian-American's identity is firmly rooted, the "Banana" will be less threatening and less an object of scorn. Again, the issue is not assimilation versus separatism; it involves the striving for personal respect at the expense of disrespect for others.

Mental Health Problems

Thus far, our discussion has focused on the problems and conflicts of Chinese-Americans. Aspects of culture conflict and racism place, Chinese-Americans under greater emotional distress than members of the host society. When stress from these sources becomes too great, mental health problems are frequently the result. Although no direct statistics exist concerning the rate of mental illness, Tom[16] suggests that the rate is quite high in San Francisco Chinatown. He notes that there is an extremely low utilization rate of mental health facilities among the Chinese. Tom believes that cultural factors, such as (1) the manner of symptom formation (low acting out, such as inhibiting expression of strong impulses), (2) the traditional handling of difficulties within the family, and (3) fear of social stigma, contribute to the low visibility of mental illness. However, the suicide rate in San Francisco has historically been the highest in the nation. Chinatown has an even higher rate than the city. Since suicide indicates severe personal disorganization, Tom believes mental illness to be quite high among the Chinese.

In a comprehensive investigation performed by Sue and Kirk[17] at the University of California, Berkeley, the entire entering freshman class was surveyed and given various tests. Approximately 90 percent of the students completed at least one of the tests, which included the Omnibus Personality Inventory, the Strong Vocational Interest Blank, and the School and College Ability Test. Chinese-American Students (128 males and 108 females) were then identified and compared to all other students. Results indicated that Chinese-American students appeared more inhibited, conventional, and socially withdrawn. While they had higher quantitative ability scores, they demonstrated less verbal facility on the College Ability Test. A bilingual background could partially account for the latter result.

Furthermore, Chinese-Americans preferred concrete and practical approaches to life. This may reflect a dislike for uncertainty, ambiguity, and unpredictability. The Chinese males tended to avoid the social sciences, business contact occupations, and verbal-linguistic fields; they showed predominate interests in the physical and biological sciences. Chinese-American females were much more domestically oriented than other females. These results show intra-consistency. If Chinese are inhibited, socially withdrawn, and lower in verbal skills (but higher in quantitative abilities), then they, understandably, have interests in fields minimizing interpersonal interactions.

Recently, we[18] conducted a study of the students seen at the Student Health Psychiatric Clinic, University of California, Los Angeles. Preliminary results based on the Minnesota Multiphasic Personality Inventory (MMPI) and on clinical impressions indicate that Chinese (and Japanese) males exhibit more severe problems than non-Asians. Although test profiles for Asian and for non-Asian students were similarly patterned, the severity was clearly greater for Asian males. The combined test profiles for Chinese males also indicated problems involving blunted effect, dependency, inferiority feelings, ruminations, somatic complaints, and lack of social skills. The most common diagnosis for these problems is pseudoneurotic schizophrenic. Interestingly, Chinese females exhibited less disturbance than males, perhaps because 20 percent of the females applied for therapeutic abortions rather than for "purely" psychological problems.

Finally, Chinese males and females exhibited more somatic complaints and more familial discord on the MMPI. Somatic complaints are often the result of emotional conflicts. Perhaps the Chinese is reluctant to admit psychological problems, since there is much shame associated with these problems. Physical conditions are better recognized and more acceptable. As for family discord, it is apparent that most Chinese-Americans face not only a generation gap, but also a wide cultural gap from their parents.

Obviously, these findings can be quite disquieting. Not only do they point to the ills of Chinese mental health, but they can easily be used to maintain negative stereotypes of the Chinese. Furthermore, the findings have social and political implications far beyond the scope of this paper. For example, if the Chinese, as a group, exhibit maladaptive characteristics, then what will this mean in terms of their struggle to attain self-identity and pride through Chinese culture?

When viewed in its proper perspective, however, Chinese need not be ashamed nor embarrassed by seeing themselves as being reserved, emotionally inhibited, etc. These characteristics are highly valued and are a great part of traditional Chinese culture. Instead, concern should be addressed to the functional value of Chinese traits under the present circumstances. If the traits are no longer adaptive for attaining proclaimed goals, then they must be changed.

Our conclusion is not that Chinese-Americans have an extremely high rate of mental illness, as Tom suggests in his China-town sample. We do feel, however, that the mental health needs of Chinese are sufficient to warrant great concern, especially since few individuals have addressed themselves to these needs. Attempts to rationalize the results on the grounds that the research instruments are culturally biased are no longer adequate. They tend to deny the urgency of the problem and to undermine effective search for solutions.

The Inadequacy of Mental Health Care

If one accepts the notion that the mental health needs of Chinese-Americans are of great concern, then the problem is especially urgent since mental health care seems to be inadequate. Klein states that

> ... the individual facing any hazard is dependent on the resources that a particular community has to offer and is affected by the means of coping that the community either makes available to him or denies him.[19]

In this regard, the Chinese-Americans have not found appropriate facilities to handle their problems. They do not turn to professional mental health facilities. Furthermore, the results of our study[20] indicate that Chinese (and other Asian) students tend to under-utilize the psychiatric services at UCLA. While Asians represent 8.1 percent of the student body, they comprise only 3.9 percent of the clinic population.

Of course, one might argue that Chinese do not seek the clinic services because they have a low rate of behavioral problems. This possibility does not seem to have much support. Chinese and Japanese males seem to exhibit more severe problems than non-Asians. This finding points to the possibility that the most disturbed males come for therapy. Chinese experiencing milder problems merely avoid using clinic services. (An additional possibility — that Chinese have a low rate of mental illness but greater severity of problems among those affected — seems unlikely. We believe that mental health problems in groups follow a normal distribution.)

These ideas seem consistent with our belief that psychotherapy is essentially a White, middle-class activity. Therapy is not well understood by Chinese, and they frequently enter with much apprehension and suspicion. In addition, their lower verbal facility, greater inhibition, and low tolerance for ambiguity may make Chinese extremely uncomfortable in therapy. Psychotherapy is often geared for individuals who have high verbal functioning, high emotional expressiveness, and great tolerance for ambiguity.

Another barrier to the seeking of professional help is the Chinese-American's value judgment of psychological problems. He frequently equates such problems with shameful and disgraceful behaviors. To enlist the aid of mental health professionals would be to publicize the disgrace of the individual and his family. It is unfortunate that, unless a family member becomes overtly psychotic, he may not receive professional help.

Furthermore, professional help itself may be unresponsive to the needs of certain groups of Chinese-Americans. There is a critical shortage of bilingual therapists. More importantly, few attempts have been made to modify traditional therapeutic approaches to the cultural experiences of Chinese. Since Chinese may feel ashamed and suspicious in seeking help for emotional problems, the therapist may be able to establish more rapport by not making early demands for him to be open and expressive. Such demands can easily be interpreted by the Chinese as disrespect for his behavior. In addition, the Chinese may feel uncomfortable with a therapist who, initially, provides too little structure and too much ambiguity. The therapist may be more effective if he gives guidelines and takes an active part in the interaction.

Perhaps the most fruitful direction is in the area of community mental health. This involves the use of community resources in programs of primary prevention and of community intervention. Although we are not prepared to present an analysis of the problems involved in community organization, we would like to offer a few suggestions for programs. First, mental health professionals who work with ethnic minorities must be more aware of the fears, concerns, and aspirations of the people with whom they work. They should have an understanding and appreciation of minority group experiences. Second, the mental health needs of Chinese must be assessed through research. Community leaders, special organizations (social agencies and schools), and the community members must be made aware of these needs. Third, proposals for special programs can be offered. Such programs may involve the use of community personnel, briefly trained in counseling, to offer their services to Chinese. Other projects can focus on early detection and prevention of emotional problems such as in school children. Finally, continuing assessment of the effectiveness of these programs is necessary.

Chapter Notes

1. G. A. DeVos and K. Abbott, "The Chinese Family in San Francisco" (MSW dissertation, University of California, Berkeley, 1966).

2. S. Cattell, *Health, Welfare, and Social Organization in Chinatown, New York City* (report prepared for the Department of Public Affairs, 1962).

3. L. Chun-Hoon, "Jade Snow Wong and The Fate of Chinese-American Identity," *Amerasia Journal* 1, 1971, 52-63.

4. W. Fenz and A. Arkoff, "Comparative Need Patterns of Five Ancestry Groups in Hawaii," *Journal of Social Psychology* 58, 1962, p. 82.

5. DeVos and Abbott, *op. cit.*

6. S. L. M. Fong, "Assimilation of Chinese in America: Changes in Orientation and Social Perception," *American Journal of Sociology* 71, 1965, 265-273.

7. G. W. Allport, *The Nature of Prejudice* (Garden City, New York: Doubleday & Co., 1958), p. 152.

8. *Ibid.,* p. 153.

9. *Ibid.,* p. 143.

10. M. S. Weiss, "Inter-Racial Romance: The Chinese-Caucasian Dating Game" (paper presented at the Southwestern Anthropological Association, Las Vegas, Nevada, April, 1969), p. 3.

11. Allport, *op. cit.,* pp. 147-148.

12. *Ibid.,* p. 142.

13. *Ibid.,* p. 147.

14. *Ibid.,* p. 145.

15. *Ibid.,* p. 141.

16. S. Tom, "Mental Health in the Chinese Community of San Francisco" (paper found in Asian-American Studies Center, UCLA, 1968).

17. D. W. Sue and B. A. Kirk, "Psychological Characteristics of Chinese-American Students," *Journal of Counseling Psychology,* 1972.

18. S. Sue and D. W. Sue, "The Reflection of Culture Conflict in the Psychological Problems of Chinese-Americans" (parts of this paper presented at the First National Conference on Asian-American Studies, Los Angeles, California, April, 1971).

19. D. C. Klein, *Community Dynamics and Mental Health* (New York: John Wiley & Sons, 1968), p. 13.

20. Sue and Sue, *op. cit.*

13. Jade Snow Wong and the Fate of Chinese-American Identity

by Lowell Chun-Hoon

Perhaps the most important obstacle to the preservation of personal self-determination by Asians in America is the threat of cultural extinction. Because Asians in America comprise only one-half of one percent of the American population in total, it is, in theory, only a matter of time before Asian-American cultural identity disappears into what race relations expert Peter Rose adroitly terms "the cultural fondue." Immigration to the United States from Asia and the continuance of ethnic enclaves such as San Francisco and New York Chinatowns will retard the speed of this progress, but they, in themselves, can neither reverse its inevitability nor mitigate the psychological anxiety and confusion that, sometimes, is engendered by being a member of a minority race in America.

Assuming that the right to determine one's own lifestyle and culture is a basic and inherent human right and that not all Asians in America desire to become fully assimilated, it is both logical and necessary to define the essential elements of Asian-American cultures. Only with such definitions and a clear understanding of those forces working to preserve and subvert Asian-American cultures will it be possible for the individual Asian-American to evaluate the cultural alternatives available to him and to exercise his independent right to personal and cultural self-determination.

It is far beyond the scope of this essay to propose a complex theory about the relationship between minority and majority cultures in a given society. Rather, by examining the life of one Chinese-American, it is hoped that some of the principal elements of Chinese-American identity can be specified and that some of the forces affecting its future can be suggested.

Probably the best-known and most lucidly written autobiography for the study of Chinese-American identity is Jade Snow Wong's classic account of a Chinese girlhood, *Fifth Chinese Daughter*.[1] Published in 1950, it has enjoyed success as a best seller in America as well as being translated into Chinese, Japanese, Thai, German, Austrian, Urdu, Burmese, and Indonesian, under the auspices of the U.S. State Department.

Fifth Chinese Daughter is enlightening for a variety of reasons. It is an accurate and vivid account of growing up in San Francisco Chinatown during the 1920s, 1930s, and 1940s, an entertaining autobiography of a young woman, and the success story of an immigrant member of a minority race in America. Most significant in the present-day context, however, is the fact that *Fifth Chinese Daughter* is the story of an education in Chinese values, and the struggle of a Chinese-American to reconcile the conflicts between the values of a minority culture and the larger majority society. Rightly perceived, this unique book is a window not only into the past, but into the present and future as well. To understand it thoroughly is to begin to understand the forces at work shaping the fate of Chinese-American identity.

One of the principal unifying themes of *Fifth Chinese Daughter* is the concept of Chinese cultural authority and the series of confrontations between Jade Snow and her parents over the question of parental authority and filial piety. In American society, we have come to accept such confrontations as a natural and, indeed, necessary part of the maturation process. Children are expected and encouraged to become as independent as possible and are ultimately allowed, at least in theory, to choose their own role in life. In traditional Chinese society, this was, of course, not the case at all, and, in Jade Snow Wong's early childhood, the traditional Chinese ways are dominant. As a matter of fact, her first five years are spent in the entirely Chinese world of San Francisco Chinatown where "respect and order . . . were the key words of life." (p. 2) Jade Snow is so utterly conscious of parental authority and her place in the established family order that, throughout the book, she writes in the third person, never once referring to herself as "I" but rather as "small daughter Jade Snow." As she herself comments, ". . . in spite of her parents' love, she must always be careful to do the proper thing. Failure to do so brought immediate and drastic punishment." (p. 2)

A few examples that reflect the completeness of her subordination and the pervasiveness of parental control over her at this early age are worth noting. One day, when she was perhaps two or three years old, she knocked off Older Brother's hat as she passed him on the stairs. The result: "Father whipped her with a bundle of tied cane; then he withdrew permission for her to go with Oldest Sister to visit the city zoo." (p. 2-3) On another occasion, Jade Snow was spat upon by a neighbor's son. Mother, instead of offering sympathy, reproved her, "saying that she must have spit on her playmate first or he wouldn't have spit on her. She was

told to bring a clothes hanger, and in front of all the other women in the garment factory, Mother spanked her." (p. 3)

This particular type of punishment conforms neatly with Lucian Pye's observation in his book *The Spirit of Chinese Politics: A Study of the Authority Crisis in Political Development* that "the essence of Chinese discipline in the home is the ruthless use of shame."[2] Pye continues to explain that "children are socialized to obey a strict set of social conventions which they learn will bring parental and adult approbation, social clarity, and freedom from confusion." The child is, thus, "made to be hypersensitive to the judgments of others," Pye continues, "to look to the social situation for cues to guide his own actions, and to be cautious about initiatives and innovations. Here is the basis for the powerful mechanisms of conformity that dominate Chinese society. Whether they are reactionary traditionalists or revolutionary modernizers, the Chinese are, above all, conformists."[3]

It was, therefore, with perfect consistency to Chinese traditional teachings and culture that, when Jade Snow picked up and kept a bright piece of cloth that fell from the pack of a visiting peddler, her wrongdoing was publicly displayed. She was told to sit outside the Wong household all day, holding the piece of cloth, until the peddler returned, and, when people asked her politely why she was passing her time in so peculiar a fashion, she was to confess her crime time and time again in public expiation of her guilt.

Jade Snow's training in absolute filial piety was not eroded when she first began attending school with White children at the age of six. Here, there was no harsh spanking, but a surprising world of delightful games like "Farmer in the Dell," "Go Walking Round the Valley," and "London Bridge is Falling Down." When, one day, a bigger girl did dare to hit her without justification, she remembered her mother's warning, "Even if another should strike you, you must not strike him, for then your guilt would be as great as his." (p. 13) Not only does this, again, show us the role of authority in Jade Snow's life and in Chinese cultural identity, but it suggests the importance of controlling hostile and aggressive emotions. Pye again formulates this idea lucidly:

> What, in other cultures, has been the problem of controlling sexuality was replaced in some measure in the Confucian tradition by the problem of controlling all expectations of aggression. A host of Chinese behavior characteristics — ranging from their intense concern for form, ritual, and etiquette to their deep anxieties about social and situational ambiguity and uncertainty, their sensitivity to status issues, their acceptance of hierarchy, their dread of social confusion and political disorder, and their constant search for belonging, for identification groups, and for the security of success and power — all fit together in a common pattern and, in varying degrees, are related to the control of aggression.

Yet, school also introduces certain subtle contradictory forces which begin undermining her Chinese education and her commitment to filial piety. When she was hit by a stray baseball bat on the hand, she was comforted and embraced by Miss Mullohand, whom Jade Snow described as "the loveliest person Jade Snow had ever known." As she was held warmly to the bosom of this strange foreign teacher and comforted, she wondered at the difference between her parents' attitudes and her teacher's attitudes. Reasoned Jade Snow:

> When she was hurt, either inside or outside, it was much better not to let Mama or Daddy know at all, because they might criticize her for getting into such a situation in the first place." (p. 20)

At the same time Jade Snow entered fourth grade in an American school, she enrolled also in Chinese evening school. Here, she found discipline which reinforced what she had come to expect in her own home. Order was demanded, and transgressors were punished with the whip and public humiliation. One day,

Jade Snow herself was caught passing a note. To her surprise, and the astonishment of her peers, she spoke out in her own defense:

> Yes, I did pass a note, and for that, perhaps, I deserve to be stood out. But, I am no more guilty than the girl who passed it to me, and even less at fault are we than the girl who started it. If you whip me, you should also have here all the girls from my row, with their palms outstretched. And I won't hold out my hand until I see theirs held out also! ...
>
> "So, you dare question me?" the principal asked.
>
> I speak only for what is right, and I will always question wrong in the way my Daddy has taught me. I am willing to bring him here to submit this matter to his judgment. Until then, I hold out no hand. (p. 64)

The principal, who knew Jade Snow's father to be a strong financial backer of the school, let the matter drop. Jade Snow, however, did not. For, from this first public break with the traditional system of Chinese cultural authority springs an entire lifelong attempt to reconcile her personal quest for individual, independent identity, apart from the demands of collective, traditional Chinese authority. Simultaneously, it is important to notice that the terms of her resistance are an appeal to higher authority — the supremacy of what her father has taught her to what her teacher in Chinese school demands. In this instance, Jade Snow invokes the concept of parental authority and filial piety to defy her principal's authority.

A second breakdown in the traditional system of authority emerges when Jade Snow's father, worn from toiling long, hopeless hours during the depression, succumbs to illness and is hospitalized. Her mother, whom Jade Snow has come to regard as nearly God-like in her perfection and self-control, loses all restraints, crying at night in fear of her husband's death. Papa, however, eventually recovers from his illness. All this time, order and obedience to authority continue to be stressed in the Wong household, and Jade Snow does not protest the authority of her parents themselves. Her father still chides her scandalous lack of morality when she wears slippers into the living room instead of shoes, and when a friend of Jade Snow's comes to visit after being told to stay away, "Older Brother shot at her with a BB gun." (p. 92) But what was most important about this time in Jade Snow's life was the growth of the feeling that she had been wronged in not being allowed to choose her own friends. To herself she prayed:

> To make up for this neglect and prejudice, please help me to do my best in striving to [be] a person respected and honored by my family, when I grow up."
> (p. 93)

This prayer conforms nicely with Pye's observation:

> Anger and resentment towards superiors are supposed to make the individual work harder to achieve the objectively defined standards of behavior that can bring universal praise. One has to work out crises of anger by being a model of social propriety.

In vowing to bring honor to her family, Jade Snow is clearly submerging her hostility by striving to be a "model of social propriety."

At last, as Jade Snow graduates from high school, these problems in relating to cultural authority create problems in Jade Snow's relationship to parental authority and filial piety. She confronts her parents with the issue of the college education she is being denied because of her sex. Unable to receive any financial assistance from her parents for college, she insists, "I am a person, besides being a female! Don't the Chinese admit that women also have feelings and minds?" In its quest for stability and order in all relationships, Chinese society has decreed, in theory, that men will be superior to women, who are, therefore, not worth educating. Even in her confrontation with what, from her perspective, is clearly an arbitrary and unjustified disadvantage, Jade Snow's conditioning prevails, however. She turns — in the manner her Christian father has studiously taught her — to even higher authority, resolving to work and "leave it to God to take care of His share in bringing her college education to reality." What the earthly father denies, the Divine Father may yet fulfill.

In June of 1938, Jade Snow graduates from high school and begins college at an inexpensive junior college, which she can afford on her own earnings without parental support. At the junior college, her White sociology professor astounds her by arguing that parents ought not to expect unquestioning obedience from their children but respect the inherent rights of their offspring. The stage is set, thus, for her first overt confrontation with her parents. It comes about when they discover that she has been seeing a Chinese boy named Joe and instruct her not to go out. To which Jade Snow replies:

> That is something you should think more about now. Yet, I am too old to whip. I am too old to be treated as a child. I can now think for myself, and you and Mama should not demand unquestioning obedience from me. You should understand me. There was a time in America when parents raised children to make them work, but now the foreigners regard them as individuals with rights of their own. I have worked too, but now I am an individual, besides being your fifth daughter.

Astounded by his daughter's audacity, her father argues:

> What would happen to the order of this household if each of four children started to behave like individuals? Would we have one peaceful moment if your personal desires came before your duty? How could we maintain our self-respect if we, your parents, did not know where you were at night and with whom you were keeping company? (p. 128)

Her mother adds:

> Of course, we will not permit you to run the risk of corrupting your purity before marriage. (p. 129)

To which Jade Snow retorts:

> Oh, Mama! This is America, not China.

Don't you think I have any judgment? How can you think I would go out with just any man? Both of you should understand that I am growing up to be a woman in a society greatly different from the one you knew in China. You expect me to work my way through college — which would not have been possible in China. . . . Of course, independence is not safe. But safety isn't the only consideration. You must give me the freedom to find some answers for myself. (p. 129)

It is now clear that Jade Snow intends to assert her individual desires against the wishes of her parents and the traditional system of authority. Moreover, she bases her claim to independence not only on her own judgment and the implied trust her parents should have in her as a hard-working and bright child, but on her claim that "this is America, not China." As her exposure to the outside world has grown through school, working as a domestic, and junior college, she has increasingly allied herself with values of the dominant, White majority culture. Most importantly, she does so with a sense of righteousness and with a sense of pride. It is not a sense of rancor nor a feeling of recalcitrance which really prompts her assertion of independence. It is, rather, a feeling that what she is doing is the appropriate and right way to win success for herself and her family in American society.

Her father, the product of only one culture, can only reply in terms he knows. He tells her pointedly:

> You are shameless. Your skin is yellow. Your features are forever Chinese. We are content with proven ways. Do not try to force foreign ideas into my home. Go. You will one day tell us sorrowfully that you have been mistaken. (p. 130)

Still, in two years, Jade Snow graduates at the top of her class from junior college and proceeds to deliver the graduation address for her class. In her oration, she appears not to have betrayed her Chinese identity in quite so brazen a fashion as her father seems once to have thought:

The junior college has developed our initiative, fair play, and self-expression and has given us tools for thinking and analyzing. But it seems to me that the most effective application that American-Chinese can make of their education would be in China, which needs all the Chinese talent she can muster. (p. 134-135)

For the first time — now that her success is substantial — her parents symbolically acknowledge the existence of the world outside their home and its importance by inviting Jade Snow's teachers to dine with the family at a Chinese restaurant.

The rest of Jade Snow Wong's story, up to the age of twenty-four, where her autobiography ends, is merely icing on the cake. Jade Snow enrolls in Mills [College] on a scholarship, where she finds "Mills living . . . democratic living in the truest sense." (p. 157) At Mills, she becomes an informal teacher of Chinese culture to her classmates, an emissary to the White student body from Chinatown. Mills also solidifies her emergence into the wider American society by altering her patterns of thinking. No longer can she merely learn by rote memorization of facts and figures. Where once "she had never thought of the purpose of academic training as being anything else than that of disseminating superior information," she is now challenged in new and unexpected ways. When she tells her Mills instructor that she "learned a lot in junior college," he responds, "Sure, you learned a lot, but, now, I am trying to teach you to think!" (p. 162) This tiny episode is of great significance, because it truly marks Jade Snow's departure from a tradition-oriented Chinese style of thinking to a more Americanized style of thought, where the presumption exists that each individual is a potentially creative thinker. Historically, the tradition-oriented Chinese style of thinking is, of course, founded in the civil service examinations based on memorization of extensive portions of the Confucian classics. In contrast, an effort has been made in America to preserve the notion of the free individual and to deify his unique and irreplaceable qualities. Writes Jade Snow:

> She was being led gradually to reverse her lifelong practice, enforced by her parents, of keeping to herself what she thought. Her mind sprang from its tightly bound concern with facts, and the Chinese absolute order of things, to concern with the reasons behind the facts, their interpretations, and the imminence of continuous change. (p. 165)

Finally, she graduates with honors from Mills the next year, and her success, which has now clearly brought honor to the Wong family, is unquestionably established:

> For Jade Snow, the moment of triumph had come. She had proved that Mama could raise her children to be a credit to the Wongs. She had shown her father and mother that, without a penny from them, she could balance her own budget and graduate from college, not in debt, but with $100 of the original $174 still in the bank.
>
> But now, in her moment of triumph, she could find no sense of conquest or superiority. There was an overwhelming flood of happiness and release, and the great comfort that a supreme achievement secretly brings, but she could feel no resentment against the two who had no words of congratulation — Daddy, who wanted so much to record a picture of her and her college president, and Mama, working with tears of mingled joy and sadness in her eyes. (p. 181)

She seeks and obtains a job as a secretary in a shipyard with the War Production Board. In addition, she does research for her boss on the practicality of cold vaccines for the members of the shipyard and is highly praised for her meticulous work. Finally, she wins a national Congressional contest with an outstanding report on the cause of absenteeism, is hailed in all of the San Francisco papers, and returns home the pride of Chinatown itself.

Then, when illness hospitalizes her suddenly, the opportunity arises for her to see just how completely her parents, themselves, have been won over by her success. Daddy comes himself to feed her at the hospital and the entire family manifests a deep concern for her she never before realized possible. Once freed from her illness, they do, however, make one last attempt to recapture her by arranging a marriage. This, too, fails, however, when her parents discover, much to their embarrassment, that their daughter is taller by several inches than the partner they have found for her.

The war ends. During all the years since her graduation from college, Jade Snow has been gradually accumulating a great deal of expertise, fashioning pottery and slowly adding to the number of pieces in her collection. At last, she opens a small pottery shop by herself. While Chinese are, at first, skeptical of the ability of one tiny, twenty-three-year-old girl to run such an enterprise by herself, Jade Snow persists, and, as always, wins acceptance. The last paragraph of her autobiography seems to indicate the resolution of her conflicts with Chinese cultural authority:

> As for Jade Snow, she knew that she still had before her a hard upward climb, but, for the first time in her life, she felt contentment. She could stop searching for that niche that would be hers alone. She had found herself and struck her speed. And when she came home now, it was to see Mama and Daddy look up from their work, smile at her, and say, "It is good to have you home again!" (p. 246)

Although this is the end of Jade Snow Wong's autobiography, it is merely the beginning of our analysis of Chinese cultural identity and a consideration of Jade Snow's lifestyle as a strategy in responding to American society. The first thing we need to establish, in order to understand Jade Snow's first twenty-four years in perspective, is precisely how it reflects ongoing aspects of Chinese cultural identity. This will take a considerable digression now into the area of social scientific research on Chinese identity.

By far the most precise and intelligent

rendering of this problem has been articulated by Dr. Francis Hsu, Chairman of the Department of Anthropology at Northwestern University. In an article appearing in a symposium on *China in Crisis*, edited by Ping-Ti Ho and Tan Tsou, Dr. Hsu advances the theory that the four essential elements of Chinese kinship structure are authority, continuity, inclusiveness, and asexuality. These he contrasts with a definition of American culture, wherein he perceives the primary elements to be volition, discontinuity, exclusiveness, and sexuality.[6] To understand these specific factors, it is helpful to borrow on another distinction he draws between the two cultures in his book, *Americans and Chinese*, first published in 1953.[7] In this book, he notes that American society is governed by the "individual-centered" philosophy of life. Society exists to maximize the individual's potential. All men are endowed with inalienable rights to life, liberty, and the pursuit of happiness. In contrast, Dr. Hsu finds Chinese society built around the "situation-centered" philosophy of life. What is important is not the individual *per se*, but how he responds to a given situation in accordance with certain self-defined norms that are derived from China's Confucian heritage. One does not seek to gratify one's own desires, but to conform to a cultural code of ethics which, in turn, provides the individual with an ordered and meaningful existence.

From this perspective, it is easy to recognize how Dr. Hsu derives authority, continuity, inclusiveness, and asexuality as important factors in the Chinese kinship system and to the perpetuation of Chinese cultural identity. Authority is essential to control individuals and to see that they respond with the correct behavior, according to the dictates of the situation. An elaborate code of hierarchies which respects age and subordinates women is enforced. As Lucian Pye comments, authority is crucial in dealing with "the potentially destructive character of human emotions."[8]

Continuity is essential because, without continuity, the prevalence and persistence of the system of authority is jeopardized. To be able to respond to the dictates of the situation as one is supposed to requires that others, most specifically younger Chinese, continue to obey the established rules of order. Pye sees this manifested in the Chinese identification with historical greatness, the deification of the past, and the notion of "Chung-Kuo," the Middle Kingdom. On a practical day-to-day level, this is found in the practice of ancestor worship. To be sure, this is a somewhat ambiguous notion — to be Chinese is to worship what was Chinese. It is almost tautological. But, as Pye shrewdly notes, this has its advantages:

> The lack of strong attachments to specific institutions or articulated values has given the Chinese the capacity to accept a remarkable degree of change without compromising their identity and their feeling of association with greatness. This has been possible because, in spite of all references to civilization and culture, their sense of greatness has been rooted primarily in a profound, mystical, and self-conscious awareness of biological ties to their ancestors. The sense of identity is, thus, derived less from content of culture, which is always somewhat vague and ambiguous, and more from the fact of race, which is biologically ambiguous. The central place of ancestor worship and the compulsive desire for sons are both only surface manifestations of the deeper Chinese belief in the significance of their own beings as a part of immemorial history. The individual is subconsciously aware of a unique link with the past, and, thus, his very existence becomes the basis for an essentially mystical view of his unshakable roots in history. For other peoples, the self-conscious awareness of the existence of self can provoke questions about "Who am I?" "Why am I here?" and "What is the purpose of my existence?" For the Chinese, it is precisely the awareness of physical existence as Chinese that resolves all such questions.[9]

In a similar fashion, in the terms of Dr. Hsu's

kinship analysis, inclusiveness of vertical and horizontal kinship ties is necessary for the ongoing maintenance of the system and continuity. Asexuality is crucial to prevent the sporadic outbursts of passion that could destroy the order of the system in an orgy of self-indulgent anarchy. Sexuality finds its expression in individual gratification, which is always a threat to obeying the dictates of the situation.

American culture, by contrast, is centered on the individual and expresses sexuality more freely and openly. Instead of pure authority, it grants adults theoretical volition and freedom to act as they choose within certain broader social limitations. It is characterized by discontinuity to the extent that children are expected to leave home, once mature, whereas, in China, they would return home to dwell with their parents. Finally, it is characterized by exclusiveness, because autonomy is encouraged among individuals. Each individual is encouraged to express himself and his particular desires rather than simply to conform — at least up to a certain point.

Applying this analysis to *Fifth Chinese Daughter*, we can see, at once, that Jade Snow Wong represents a transition between the two polar and idealized expressions of the contrasting cultures as articulated by Hsu and Pye. Where her parents once sought to have complete authority over her life, including the right to name her spouse, decide whom she can go out with, determine how far she can advance educationally, and so on, we see Jade Snow, against all odds, exercising her own volition. We see her dating whom she pleases, putting herself through school, and even starting her own business, all in violation of traditional Chinese authority. Yet, it is instructive to recall that the need for authority has not been removed from her life. She constantly makes prayers to higher authority — to God — and always in the name of achieving success for the family. Though she breaks with the continuity of certain established traditions, she maintains their spirit in

alternative ways. The majority of her friends are Chinese, and the thought of marrying a White person never occurs to her. She, in fact, does respect her parents, although she does not always obey them. At Mills, she is a promoter of Chinese culture in the best sense of the word, and her Chineseness is, indeed, at the center of her life. While she does introduce a degree of discontinuity and volition into her life, she still remains in San Francisco to this very day, in her ceramics business, and enjoys returning to see her parents at home.

It is true that Jade Snow at various times violated explicitly formulated instructions from her parents — she did, in fact, sometimes violate their authority. Significantly, however, such violations usually involved attempts to suppress her rising in status, although this is not how her parents perceived their actions. What Jade Snow saw as personal freedom necessary for success, her parents saw as Americanization and the betrayal of Chinese ideals. Jade Snow violated her parents' wishes when she worked her way through junior college and Mills. She disobeyed their wishes, also, in choosing to open her own pottery shop instead of getting married to the young man who was brought to be her spouse. In these three instances, her parents apparently felt it in the best interests of preserving Chinese ways and Chinese continuity for her to return to her subordinate role as a woman. Each time, Jade Snow gambled on her own initiative and sagacity, and, each time, she won success, which, in turn, mollified her parents, who indirectly granted their forgiveness. This highlights the significance of Chinese cultural identity as a kind of collective identity, whether it be in the narrowest sense of one's immediate family or in the broader sense of identity as a member of the Chinese race. Anything which contributes to enhancing the strength and honor of the collective identity is eventually praised, although, because of the strong strain of situation-centered, tradition orientation, individual initiative that is too unusual and too deviant will, at first, be scorned. Thus, even though Jade Snow consistently defied her role as a woman in Chinese society, the success she brought to the larger community — in winning the Congressional prize for the study on absenteeism, her graduation with honors from junior college and from Mills, and the subsequent success of her pottery venture — exonerate her guilt in violating the tenets of authority, inclusiveness, and continuity. In a somewhat larger sense, it can, also, plausibly be argued that it is precisely her achievement and contribution to the collective identity that strengthen the Chinese community's overall authority, increase the probability of its continuity in American society, and encourage inclusiveness by allowing all of its members to vicariously identify with Jade Snow's success.

One could also suggest that the crux of Chinese identity is so rooted in obedience to authority that it simply follows that form of authority which appears strongest and most pervasive at a given time. In this sense, Chinese are truly situation-oriented conformists. Because Jade Snow's success depended upon the success of her acculturation, her acculturation was very successful.

Perhaps one reason for the focus on order and authority in Chinese culture, rather than pure individual achievement, is realistic acknowledgment that not all people can be creative and innovative. By not expressing a total allegiance to achievement, Chinese culture minimizes the stress for creative achievement, placing it instead on obedience and competence. In American culture, there always is a creative achiever in some fashion, whether it be manifested through physical courage beyond the ordinary or sheer inventiveness. Such a stress on achievement — and its concomitant linkage to the concept of American masculinity — places exceptionally high psychic demands on American males, which causes a certain amount of social discontinuity and anxiety when unfulfilled.

Jade Snow Wong represents the transition in Chinese-American identity from a purely Chinese emphasis upon rigid obedience to the proscribed Confucian individual and personal initiative, when it is successful in bringing honor to the larger Chinese-American community or a given Chinese-American family. Those values rewarded and deemed successful in American society may replace the pure hierarchies of filial piety and obedience in Confucian thought as the primary criterion for behavior. One might say this is a form of adopting American values of success, in the name of upholding the success of Chinese values.

In evaluating the transitional lifestyle evolved by Jade Snow Wong, we come to what appears to be fundamental contradictions. If the primary means for enhancing, honoring, and promoting Chinese cultural identity remain individual success in a culture which requires individual creativity and initiative, then the very values necessary for success and the temporary furtherance of Chinese-American identity simultaneously undermine the traditional Chinese identity rooted in obedience to Confucian authority. To state the problem in its most pessimistic perspective: Chinese identity, when transplanted from China, contains within itself the seeds of its own doom. For, instead of succeeding through obeying the dictates of Chinese cultural authority and restraining his individuality, the Chinese-American succeeds through his own individual initiative.

However, once the notion of individual initiative takes hold, it triggers a potentially irreversible and anarchistic process. If Chinese-American identity depends on the reverence of tradition and obedience to the persons and ways of previous Chinese generations, this reverence will inhibit success in America to the extent that it will inhibit creativity and self-assertion. There are people like Jade Snow Wong who can utilize their creativity and independence for the Chinese community and can remain both culturally Chinese and individually successful by American standards. They can say with pride and justification, as Miss Wong (now Mrs. Ong) did when interviewed by *Amerasia* in January, 1971, that "I can still move in my community and be accepted. I don't buy this 'I've climbed out of the ghetto' idea; I have never been ashamed of my background. I, personally, cherish Chinese culture and don't intend to become so Westernized that I can't go to my mother's house and listen to her stories of China."[10] Some persons may even be sufficiently committed to elements of Chinese culture — such as the intimate family system — to consciously limit their success in order to retain their Chinese identity. Miss Wong, for example, commented that "I have a career but my family comes first"[11] and has consciously kept herself from expanding her pottery business in order to devote time to her children and husband.

The question which faces us today, however, concerns the fate of Chinese-American identity in the generation that succeeds Miss Wong, a generation which may not share her remarkable ability to reconcile individual success with fidelity to her cultural identity and who automatically enter their lives one generation more Americanized than their parents. Particularly, apart from Chinatown in isolated suburbs and cities throughout the country, the process of education in American schools with American peers and the constant bombardment by television and other media continue the process of deculturization among young Chinese-Americans. It is, thus, one of the peculiar ironies of the Asian-American experience that, at any given time, it is the young and the unborn, those least knowledgeable about Chinese culture, who hold the greatest responsibility for its preservation. It is those who are least secure in themselves and who must still strive to forge their personhood in a turbulent and shifting society who must ultimately grapple with this dilemma.

Finally, it should be remembered that the constructs presented in this paper are idealized, synthetic abstractions with no tangible relationship to the actual world, except insofar as they are useful, conceptual tools with which to approach certain questions. Identity itself is something elusive and amorphous which constantly evolves, growing and dissipating. We speak of identity because we are concerned with the personal fulfillment of individual lives, which, to be truly satisfying, require a sense of unity and integration as well as a sense of variety and diversity, and which need a sense of continuity as well as an ability to change. Culture, ideally, should serve to help provide this unity and should contribute to the individual's sense of personal integrity and fulfillment.

The fact of being a minority people in American culture, however, introduces a degree of discontinuity and cultural schizophrenia which must either be suppressed or resolved. Since the demands for success in American culture and for obedience to Confucian norms in traditional Chinese culture require the assertion of individualism in the former and the restraint of individualism in the latter, this contradiction is particularly acute. However, it is precisely the collective willingness of Chinese-Americans to individually and collectively confront this ambiguity which will preserve the possibility of personal self-determination for Asians in America, by preserving the option to enter an Asian as well as an American culture. Paradoxically, Chinese-Americans must become assertive enough to achieve a sustained advocacy for their right not to become excessively and indulgently self-assertive. They must exhibit a certain clearly definable sense of independence from the rest of American society so that, within their own subculture, they can continue to fashion a lifestyle based on the recognition of human dependence and the need for difference instead of unbridled competition.

While the intricacies of Chinese and American identity presented in this paper may seem utterly irrelevant and unforgivably abstruse, one conclusion is inescapable: Unless Chinese-Americans choose to assert and retain their unique culture as Jade Snow Wong did, they will, by their inaction, destroy their right to be different and unique. If Chinese-Americans in particular, and Asian-Americans in general, do not choose to shape their own identities, those in the American majority will choose and decide an identity for them.

Chapter Notes

1. Jade Snow Wong, *Fifth Chinese Daughter* (New York: Harper & Row, 1950). All page numbers taken from *Fifth Chinese Daughter* appear in the text of this essay itself, following each particular quotation.

2. Lucian Pye, *The Spirit of Chinese Politics: A Study of the Authority Crisis in Political Development* (Cambridge, Mass.: M.I.T. Press, 1968), p. 95.

3. *Ibid.*, p. 96.

4. *Ibid.*, p. 33.

5. *Ibid.*, p. 105.

6. Francis L. K. Hsu, "Chinese Kinship and Chinese Behavior," in Ping-Ti Ho and Tang Tsou, *China in Crisis* (Chicago: The University of Chicago Press, 1968), pp. 579-608.

7. Francis L. K. Hsu, *Americans and Chinese, Two Ways of Life* (New York: Henry Schuman, 1953). Recently re-issued as *Americans and Chinese: Purpose and Fulfillment in Great Civilizations* with a new introduction by Henry Steele Commager (Garden City, New York: The Natural History Press, 1970).

8. Pye, *op. cit.*, p. xviii.

9. *Ibid.*, p. 55.

10. Interview with Jade Snow Wong held January 13, 1971, at Jade Snow Wong Ceramics, 408 Pacific Avenue, San Francisco, California.

11. *Ibid.*

14. The Filipino-American: There's Always an Identity Crisis

by Fred Cordova

Many Americans, not only Whites, do not know Filipinos and, surprisingly enough, it seems Filipinos do not know themselves, either.

There are two obvious reasons: institutional racism in White society and self-identity amnesia of the Brown man himself.

Yes, Brown. Contrary to popular misconceptions, the Filipino is not Oriental like his Japanese and Chinese brethren of the Yellow race, although the Filipino's ancestral land is a 7,000-plus archipelago in Southeast Asia called the Philippines — NOT the Philippine Islands, denoting the pre-republic American colonial era.

The Filipino is Malayan like the Indonesian and Malaysian. Contrary to another myth, he does speak fluent Spanish but, depending on his tribal source, communicates in Filipino through some 87 major dialects — a Malayan polyglot of Spanish, Sanskrit, Arabic, Chinese, and even English words. But the main language, both here and abroad, is English.

Publicly, statistically, and even visually, the Filipino is forever hidden as an integral American entity. He belongs to a minority within a minority.

For years, he fell under the statistical category of "Orientals and others." When the Japanese and Chinese elements had become more evident, the Filipino was relegated to "Indians and others." In a recent Office of State Superintendent of Public Instruction ethnic survey, the "orphan" Filipino lost even his "others" claim and was shuffled into the "with Spanish surnames" column.

The Filipino is a rare, beautiful human. If the 1970 census did not include him in its survey, he may have become sociologically extinct. As it is, a Filipino is readily mistaken for a Japanese, Chinese, Hawaiian and, at times, Indian or Mexican . . . to which may come the Filipino's (and America's) blessings.

The Filipino can relate to these ethnic groups, simply because of visual or cultural factors and/or marriage through his children. He can also relate to the Black because of skin color and similar tastes, as in music, and to the White because the Filipino, although Eastern physically and culturally, is Western by religion, education, and living habits.

"I've always grappled with identity crises," Val M. Laigo, 40, Seattle University assistant professor of art, said. "Once it was Malay-Filipino, then Spanish-Filipino, followed by American-Filipino. Lately, it's been Filipino-American.

"But, one fact remains constant: My parents, my children, and I all come from Adam and Eve. In the final summary, I suspect I'm Negrito-Malay-Indo-Chinese, Spanish-American-Japanese-Filipino-American... Human!"

Flamboyant, hospitable, accommodating, friendly, obtainable, the assimilated Filipino is outwardly all these to the White but generally not to his own and other dark-skinned brothers.

In the Pacific Northwest, the Filipinos' social commitment is, by all factual definitions, truly social as exemplified in the Filipino communities' endless rounds of banquets, dances, parties, and queen contests.

"Our parents have satisfied themselves in joining the silent majority," said another Filipino-American, Robert N. Santos, 36, member of the Seattle Human Rights Commission and president of the Catholic Interracial Council of Seattle.

"Purgatory was created for the do-nothing majority who would not stand up for any reason to question the problems of under-employment and understanding of minority people, especially our own. Our young Filipinos seem to be aware of only themselves and how pretty they look to others. They can look just as pretty marching in a grape boycott."

Anthony Ogilvie, Jr., 24, Blanchet High School social studies teacher, said:

"It is easy to understand why there is a strong feeling among most Filipinos of acceptance of, and/or resignation to, the particularly low level of their achievement in our society.

"Filipinos have just experienced 400 years of colonization under Spain and the United States. In this prostrate position, as in the case of the Blacks, Filipinos have been historically deprived and sterilized of any motivation to do better than their colonial benefactors. One only has to witness the low number of Filipinos going on to college and the even lower number in areas of prominence or excellence. It is obvious that we learned our role well."

Laigo, Santos, and Ogilvie represent a new breed of Filipino-Americans. They were reared in Seattle and fired with zeal to compete in a promising American society. There are all kinds of Filipinos with conflicting opinions among the estimated 9,000 in the Pacific Northwest and 6,000 in the Greater Seattle area, and not one either knows personally every other Filipino or associates socially with all of them.

"Pinoys," the common, in-crowd term for Filipinos, can be divided roughly into four main groups:

1. The "first generation" — permanent residents since the late 1920s and early '30s who have adopted the "American way of life" and retained the Philippine vernacular.

2. The "second generation" — the American-born children and their children's children, who neither have seen their ancestral land nor were taught to speak any Philippine dialect.

3. The early post-World War II arrivals — mostly war victims and veterans and their families, who brought forgotten Philippine amenities.

4. The newer immigrants — the majority young professionals, with a great number hoping to return to the Philippines.

Fractured as they are by tribal linguistics and attitudes, Philippine-born adults set themselves apart through memberships in some 35 divergent organizations in Seattle alone. There's a common "Pinoy" saying: "Get two 'Pinoys' together and there's a meeting." Hence come the in-fighting, irrelevance, and disunity in that great "Pinoy" sport of "leadership scramble."

Filipinos have no strong economic, political, or social base. There is a dearth of elected officials, practicing lawyers and physicians, business and industrial executives, and others to put muscle into key areas of American society.

Yet, in their supposed patience of waiting and hoping for some recognition from both sides of the White-Black confrontation, there is underfoot a movement of a "policy of self-containment," much like the Orientals of yesteryears. This means the "cultivating" of "super-Filipinos" — bright, industrious, well-behaved, docile, friendly, and academically qualified to compete successfully in jobs, education, and other equal opportunities.

"Among the Seattle Filipino professional groups," Mrs. Rosario DeGracia said, "nurses have contributed their share towards enhancing the image of the Filipino people."

The 39-year-old Seattle U. assistant professor of nursing added:

"Employed in various hospitals, Filipino nurses have received favorable comments both from employers and patients in regard to work efficiency, industry, and dedication."

Results have been slow in coming for these nurses and other professionals with admirable qualifications. But there is much concern for others who do not know how to jump into the American mainstream. They have to be pushed, and those pushing should be mostly White in the power structure.

Many Whites, and Browns, too, do not realize that non-White ethnic communities have doubts that Filipinos, along with their Asian brothers, really are discriminated against, simply because all have been described as being "once among the so-called persecuted minorities."

What must a minority group be subjected to before being considered "persecuted," one would ask.

Gene Navarro, 64, president of Local 37, International Longshoremen & Warehousemen's Union, said there were some 150,000 Filipinos in the continental United States before Filipino immigration was banned by law in 1934. The leader of the 2,500-member cannery workers' local remembered that the West Coast alone harbored 75,000, thanks to Hawaiian sugar planters and California growers and processors who turned to cheap Filipino labor after the Exclusion Act of 1924 had barred Chinese and Japanese.

Most Filipinos were recruited for as low as 15 cents an hour in the agricultural fields and $25 a month in Alaska canneries. They were non-citizens and could not qualify for citizenship under the law, Navarro pointed out. As aliens, Filipinos were forbidden to buy real estate and were barred from the professions and intermarriage with Whites.

"Because of all these discriminations — legal, social, and economic," Navarro, former

president of the Filipino Community of Seattle, Inc., said, "the California landscape was dotted with Filipino ghettos across the railroad tracks, where they were made prey by racists and vigilantes. But these immigrants fought back. In the early 1930s, they were among the first to form unions and mutual-aid societies, to forge fraternal and community organizations, and to raise wages and improve living conditions on the spot.

"Young Filipino students caught up with the times, too. In every university and college where they enrolled, they joined other forces of dissent to change the social, economic, and political system in the country."

Today, violence and civil disorder are distasteful to Filipino thinking. Yet labor strikes, pickets, demonstrations, and, sometimes, violence were the order of the day for Filipinos some 35 years ago. Militancy is not "the thing" for the Filipino "establishment" in 1970.

Yet their "established" status remains untenable, subject to unwarned, and frequently unwarranted, ostracization, coercion, intimidation, threats, and exploitation by White officialdom. These Filipinos may not be "oreos" or "bananas," as Blacks and other Asians depict their colleagues having dark skins outside and a White mentality inside. These Filipinos are "coconuts," vegetating with a ghetto mentality or forsaking their Brown brothers, who need their qualified help.

Thus, a renewed militancy against institutional racism is inevitable if "those who made it" do not make life relevant for those who did not.

"Unless the Filipino stops putting blind faith in the White man and makes the system work for him in the '70s, I am afraid we will continue to enjoy our third-class citizenship," said Michael A. Castillano, 31, On-the-Job Training Project field representative for the Seattle Urban League.

"Discrimination toward Filipinos does exist if we attempt to go outside our 'assigned roles' as envisaged by the 'establishment.' Witness our numbers in positions not commensurate with our educational background. We have almost resigned ourselves to this fate of accepting busboy and other menial jobs because of the influence from within and outside causing this peculiar circumstance.

"Color is the backbone of the racial bias in the United States. Because we are non-White, in addition to language difficulties of recent Filipino arrivals, full comprehension of the multifaceted discrimination becomes hard to grasp. The willingness of those ill-prepared or ignorant of the system to accept this discrimination should not be hidden under the guise of pride. This only allows institutionalized racism to fester."

Dreams of Filipino achievements and accomplishments rest mainly in the economic potential. Providing closed doors open to him and to other Asians, the moneyed Filipino can then dabble in politics, advisory boards, White social clubs, and other avenues where, through social intercourse, significant decisions are made which affect him as a citizen and resident.

Filipino self-identity is taking root in the form of folk dances and other public cultural offerings. Although limited in scope and sometimes talent, these minute contributions are making some impact of Filipino awareness among the Brown young and the predominantly White galleries.

The Rev. Manuel Ocana, 43, associate pastor of Seattle's Church of The Immaculate Conception, volunteered that "living in Seattle is a challenge."

"Our people are striving to improve more and more," he said. "The involvement of young Filipino-Americans in Seattle's problems and the support and encouragement of understanding parents and leaders are hopeful attempts to realize our Filipino-American dream — to revolutionize through talent and education."

The Catholic priest echoes the sentiments of Navarro, who said:

"These sacrifices and hard struggles paved the way for the younger generation and for those who came after World War II to carry on the struggle for a better way of life — devoid of exploitation by man of man."

Yet the Filipino "still shares the bottom of America's socio-economic totem pole with his brother, the American Indian," said Martin J. Sibonga, 44, publisher of The Filipino Forum, a 41-year-old Seattle monthly newspaper, which under his two-year direction has become the "spokesman for minority action."

"Like the native American," Sibonga said, "the Filipino has been stripped of his ethnic identity and heritage. Taught to be an American in a United States not yet ready to grant him all the civil rights which we must fight for today, he continues to search for peace from his dilemma.

"Some Filipinos remain passive and don't demonstrate for civil rights. But the Filipino has the potential. He has the right — the ultimate duty — to be an active, contributing citizen, not as a pseudo-White American but as an American of Filipino descent, ready, willing, and dedicated to enriching this demo-republic with his own unique identity, now becoming re-born."

There are no productive areas of negotiation today to effect quick and meaningful progress. That strategy, unfortunately, belongs in the past. It is now a time of confrontation, painful as it may be, to end the Filipino servitude in the social, economic, educational, political, professional, and legal American (not White) way of life.

The "rebellion of Tonto against the Lone Ranger" augurs the time when Kato ("the faithful Japanese-turned-Filipino-during-World-War-II houseboy-chauffeur") will demand a salary raise and all other fringe benefits from his White boss, the Green Hornet.

The human-rights parade so far is passing by the Filipinos. It takes more than a consistently award-winning drill team like that of the Filipino Youth Activities of Seattle to have Filipinos "get with it."

15. Ethnic Identity: The Impact of Two Cultures on the Psychological Development of Asians in America

by Derald Wing Sue

Among the many determinants of Asian-American identity, the cultural influences (values, norms, attitudes, and traditions) are of considerable importance. While social scientists agree that psychological development is not an isolated phenomenon apart from socio-cultural forces, most theories of personality are culturally exclusive. Furthermore, empirical studies tend not to deal adequately with the impact of cultural racism on the behavior of ethnic minorities. To understand the psychological development of Chinese- and Japanese-Americans, the cultural and historical forces of racism which serve to shape and define the Asian-American's identity must be examined.

Most studies which focus on the effects of culture on Asian-Americans tend to be highly compartmentalized. For example, one can find research investigating the relationship of culture to (a) personality characteristics (Abbott, 1970; Fong & Peskin, 1969; Meredith, 1966; Arkoff, Meredith & Iswahara, 1964; 1962; Fenz & Arkoff, 1962), (b) child-rearing practices (DeVos & Abbott, 1966; Kitano, 1964), (c) the manifestation of behavior disorders (Marsella, Kinzie, Gordon, 1971; Kitano, 1970; 1969a; Arkoff & Weaver, 1966; Sommers, 1960; Kimmich, 1960), (d) the ineffectiveness of traditional therapy (Sue & Sue, 1972a; 1971; Yamamoto, James & Palley, 1968), (e) acculturation (Matsumoto, Meredith & Masuda, 1970; Meade, 1970; Weiss, 1969; Fong, 1965;

Kitano, 1962; Arkoff, 1959), and (f) use of English (Meredith, 1964; Smith & Kasdon, 1961; Smith, 1957). Few attempts integrate these findings into a global description of how cultures influence the socio-psychological functioning of the "whole" person.

Cultural impact is clearly demonstrated in the study of Chinese- and Japanese-Americans, where remnants of Asian cultural values collide with European-American values. The historical meeting of these two cultures and their consequent interaction in a racist society have fundamental importance in understanding the personality characteristics, academic abilities, and vocational interests of Asians in America.

Asian Cultural Values

Although it is acknowledged that the Asian-American family structure and its subcultural values are in transition, they still retain their many values from the past. Because the primary family is generally the socializing agent for its offspring and because parents interpret appropriate and inappropriate behavior, a description of traditional Asian families will lead to greater understanding of their cultural values.

Chinese and Japanese family interaction patterns have been described as being similar by many social scientists (Sue & Sue, 1971; Abbott, 1970; Kitano, 1969a; 1969b; DeVos & Abbott, 1966; Kimmich, 1960). The Asian family is an ancient, complex institution, the fundamental unit of the culture. In China and Japan, it has long been more or less independent of political alliances; its form has survived political upheavals and invasions of foreigners.

The roles of family members are highly interdependent. Deviations from traditional norms governing behavior are suppressed to keep the family intact. Independent behavior which might upset the orderly functioning of the family is discouraged. The family structure is so arranged that conflicts within the family are minimized; each member has his own role to play which does not interfere with that of another. If a person has feelings which might disrupt family peace and harmony, he is expected to hide them. Restraint of potentially disruptive emotions is strongly emphasized in the development of the Asian character; the lack of outward signs of emotions has given rise to the prevalent opinion among Westerners that Asians are "inscrutable."

The Chinese and Japanese families are traditionally patriarchal with communication and authority flowing vertically from top to bottom. The father's behavior in relationship to other family members is generally dignified, authoritative, remote, and aloof. Sons are generally highly valued over daughters. The primary allegiance of the son is to the family, and obligations as a good father or husband are secondary. Asian women are expected to carry on the domestic duties, to marry, to become obedient helpers of their mothers-in-law, and to bear children, especially males.

The inculcation of guilt and shame are the principal techniques used to control the behavior of family members. Parents emphasize their children's obligation to the family. If a child acts independently (contrary to the wishes of his parents), he is told that he is selfish and inconsiderate and that he is not showing gratitude for all his parents have done for him. The behavior of individual members of an Asian family is expected to reflect credit on the whole family. Problems that arise among Asian-Americans such as failure in school, disobedience, juvenile delinquency, mental illness, etc., are sources of great shame. Such problems are generally kept hidden from public view and handled within the family. This fact may explain why there are low *official* rates of juvenile delinquency (Abbott & Abbott, 1969; Kitano, 1967) and low utilization of mental health facilities among Asians (Sue & Sue, 1972a; Kitano, 1969a; Yamamoto, James & Palley, 1968; Kimmich, 1960). On the other hand, outstanding achievement in some aspect of life (especially educational and occupational success) is a source of great pride for the entire family. Thus, each family member has much at stake in the behavior of others.

In summary, traditional Asian values emphasize reserve and formality in interpersonal relations, restraint and inhibition of strong feelings, obedience to authority, obligations to the family, high academic and occupational achievement, and use of shame and guilt to control behavior. These cultural values have a significant impact on the psychological characteristics of Asians in America.

Historical Experience: Cultural Racism

Kovel (1970) believes that White racism in America is no aberration but an ingredient of our culture which serves as a stabilizing influence and a source of gratification to Whites. In defining cultural racism, Jones (1972) states that it is "... the individual and institutional expression of the superiority of one race's cultural heritage over that of another race. Racism is appropriate to the extent that racial and cultural factors are highly correlated and are a systematic basis for inferior treatment." (p. 6) Any discussion concerning the effects of racism on the psychological characteristics of minorities is necessarily fraught with hazards. It is difficult to distinguish the relevant variables which affect the individual and to impute cause-effect relations. However, a historical analysis of Asians in America suggests that cultural racism has done great harm to this ethnic group.

Unknown to the general public, Asian-Americans have been the object of much prejudice and discrimination. Ironically, the American public is unaware that no higher walls of prejudice have been raised, historically, around any other ethnic minority than those around the Chinese and Japanese. Asians have generally attempted to function in the existing society without loud, strong, or public protest (Sue & Sue, 1972a).

The first Chinese immigrants came to the United States during the 1840s. Their immigration from China was encouraged by the social and economic unrest in China at that time and by overpopulation in certain provinces (DeVos & Abbott, 1966). During this period, there was a demand for Chinese to help build the transcontinental railroad. Because of the need for cheap labor, they were welcomed into the labor force (Daniels, 1971). However, a diminishing labor market and fear of the "yellow peril" made the Chinese immigrants no longer welcome. Their pronounced racial and cultural differences from the White majority made them conspicuous, and they served as scapegoats for the resentment of White workers. Although Daniels (1971) mainly discusses the economic aspect for the hostility expressed against the Chinese, he points out that the anti-Chinese movement soon developed into an ideology of White supremacy which was compatible with the mainstream of American racism. Chinese were seen as "subhuman" or "heathens," and their mode of living was seen as undesirable and detrimental to the well-being of America. Laws which were passed to harass the Chinese denied them the rights of citizenship, ownership of land, the right of marriage, etc. At the height of the anti-Chinese movement, when prejudice and discrimination against the Chinese flourished, many Chinese were assaulted and killed by mobs of Whites. This anti-Chinese sentiment culminated in the passing of the Federal Chinese Exclusion Act of 1882 which was the first exclusion act against any ethnic group. This racist immigration law,

justified by the alleged need to exclude masses of "cheap Chinese labor" from the United States, was not repealed until 1943 as a gesture of friendship toward China, an ally of the United States during World War II.

Likewise, the Japanese in America faced severe hostility and discrimination from White citizens. Japanese began immigrating to the United States during the 1890s when anti-Chinese sentiment was great. As a result, they shared in the pervasive anti-Oriental feeling. Originally brought in to fill the demand for cheap agricultural labor and coming from an agrarian background, many Japanese became engaged in these fields (Kitano, 1969b). Their fantastic success in the agricultural occupations, coupled with a racist climate, enraged many White citizens. Legislation similar to the anti-Chinese acts was passed against the Japanese, and individual-mob violence repeated itself. Such cries as "The Japs must go" were frequently echoed by the mass media and labor and political leaders. In response to hostility toward members of their race, both Chinese and Japanese formed their own communities to isolate and protect themselves from a threatening racist society.

Within this background of White racism, it became relatively easy for White society to accept the relocation of 110,000 Japanese-Americans into camps during World War II. Their pronounced racial and cultural characteristics were enough justification for the atrocious actions taken against the Japanese. The dangerous precedent created by American reaction to the Japanese is an ever-present threat that racial strains can again result in a repeat of history.

There can be no doubt that cultural racism has been practiced against the Chinese and Japanese. Many people would argue that, today, Asian-Americans face no such obstacles as their ancestors. The myth that Asians represent a "model minority" and are successful and functioning well in society is a popular belief often played up by the press

(Newsweek, 1971; U.S. News & World Report, 1966). The 1960 Census reveals that Chinese and Japanese, indeed, have higher incomes and lower unemployment rates than their *non-White* counterparts. A further analysis, however, reveals that Chinese and Japanese are lower in income and higher in unemployment rates than the *White* population. This disparity is even greater when one considers that, generally, Chinese and Japanese achieve higher educational levels than Whites. It can only be concluded that social and economic discrimination are still flagrantly practiced against Asian-Americans.

Thus far, the fact that cultural racism has and is being practiced against Asian minorities has been documented. Attention now will be focused on the psychological costs of culture conflict.

Culture Conflict

Jones (1972) believes that many forms of culture conflict are really manifestations of cultural racism. Although there is nothing inherently wrong in acculturation and assimilation, he believes that " . . . when it is forced by a powerful group on a less powerful one, it constitutes a restriction of choice; hence, it is no longer subject to the values of natural order." (p. 166)

When an ethnic minority becomes increasingly exposed to the values and standards of the dominant host culture, there is progressive inculcation of those norms. This has been found for both the Chinese (Abbott, 1970; Meade, 1970; Fong & Peskin, 1969; Fong, 1965) and Japanese (Matsumoto, Meredith & Masuda, 1970; Kitano, 1962; Arkoff, 1959). However, assimilation and acculturation are not always smooth transitions without their pitfalls. As they become Westernized, many Asian-Americans come to view Western personality characteristics as more admirable qualities than Asian characteristics. Constantly bombarded with what constitutes desirable traits by a society that has low

tolerance for differing life styles, many Asian males and females begin to find members of their own race undesirable social partners. For example, Weiss (1969) found many Chinese-American girls coming to expect the boys they date to behave boldly and aggressively in the traditional Western manner. They could be quite vehement in their denunciation of Asian-male traits. Unfortunately, hostility to a person's minority cultural background may cause Asians to turn their hostility inward. Such is the case when Japanese-American females express greater dissatisfaction with their body image than Caucasian females (Arkoff & Weaver, 1966). The individual may develop a kind of racial self-hatred that leads to lowered self-esteem and intense conflicts (Sue & Sue, 1971; Sommers, 1960). Among individuals of minority cultural background, we find many instances of culture conflict; the individual finds that he is heir to two different cultural traditions, and he may have difficulty in reconciling their effects on his own personality; he may find it difficult to decide to which culture he owes primary loyalty. Such a person has been called a Marginal Man. Because of his marginal status, he often experiences an identity crisis and feels isolated and alienated from both cultures.

In previous articles (Sue & Sue, 1972a; 1971), three different reactions to this stress were described. A person may remain allied to the values of his own culture; he may attempt to become over-Westernized and reject Asian ways; or he may attempt to integrate aspects of both cultures which he believes are functional to his own self-esteem and identity. The latter mode of adjustment is being advocated by the ethnically conscious Asians on many college campuses. In an attempt to raise group esteem and pride, Asian-Americans are actively exploring and challenging the forces in White society which have served to unfairly shape and define their identity (Sue & Sue, 1972b). No longer are they content to be a "banana," a derogatory term used to designate a person of

Asian descent who is "Yellow on the outside but White on the inside."

Psychological Characteristics of Chinese- and Japanese-American Students

The cultural background of both the Japanese and Chinese, the historical and continuing forces of White racism, and the cultural conflicts experienced in the United States have left their mark on the current life styles of Asian-Americans. Although it is difficult to impute a direct cause-effect relationship between these forces and the psychological characteristics of Asian-Americans, the following description, certainly, seems consistent with their past background. The remaining sections will focus upon the personality traits, academic abilities, and vocational interests of Chinese- and Japanese-American college students. Findings presented in these sections will rely heavily on research conducted at the University of California, Berkeley (Sue & Kirk, in press; forthcoming). Three tests consisting of the Omnibus Personality Inventory, the School and College Ability Tests, and the Strong Vocational Interest Blank were administered to an entire entering Freshman class. Chinese-American, Japanese-American, and all other students were compared to one another on these three instruments.

Personality Characteristics

The studies conducted at Berkeley reveal that Chinese- and Japanese-American college students tend to exhibit similar characteristics. This is not surprising in view of their similar cultural and historical backgrounds. Asian-Americans of both sexes tend to evaluate ideas on the basis of their immediate practical application and to avoid an abstract, reflective, theoretical orientation. Because of their practical and applied approach to life problems, they tend to be more intolerant of ambiguities and to feel much more comfortable in well-structured situations. Asian-Americans also

appear less autonomous and less independent from parental controls and authority figures. They are more obedient, conservative, conforming, and inhibited. In interpersonal relationships, they tend to be cautious in directly expressing their impulses and feelings. In comparison to Caucasian norms, both Chinese- and Japanese-American students appear more socially introverted and will more often withdraw from social contacts and responsibilities. Other investigators have found similar results for the Chinese (Abbott, 1970; Fong & Peskin, 1969; DeVos & Abbott, 1966) and Japanese (Meredith, 1966; Fenz & Arkoff, 1962; Arkoff, 1959).

Asian cultural values, emphasizing restraint of strong feelings, obedience, dependence upon the family, and formality in interpersonal relations, are being exhibited by these students. These values are in sharp contrast to Western emphasis on spontaneity, assertiveness, and informality. Because of socialization in well-defined roles, there is a tendency for Asian students to feel more comfortable in structured situations and to feel uncomfortable in ambiguous ones. As a result, they may tend to withdraw from social contacts with those outside their ethnic group or family. As discussed later, their minority status and sensitivity to actual and potential discrimination from White society may make them suspicious of people. It is possible, also, that their concrete and pragmatic approach was reinforced because it possessed social and economic survival value.

The socio-emotional adjustment characteristics of Asian-Americans also seem to reflect their cultural background and experiences as minorities in America. Meredith (1966), in testing Sansei students at the University of Hawaii, found them to be more tense, apprehensive, and suspicious than their Caucasian counterparts. A study by Fenz & Arkoff (1962) revealed that senior high school students of Chinese and Japanese ancestry possessed significantly higher needs for abasement. This trait indicates a need to feel guilty when things go wrong and to accept personal blame for failure. The Berkeley studies also support the fact that Asian-Americans seem to be experiencing more stress than their Caucasian controls. Both Chinese- and Japanese-American students exhibited attitudes and behaviors that characterize alienated persons. They were more likely to possess feelings of isolation, loneliness, and rejection. They also appeared more anxious, worried, and nervous.

Three factors seem to be operating in these findings. First, cultural elements are obviously affecting these tests. For example, Asian values emphasizing modesty and the tendency to accept blame (guilt and shame) would naturally elevate their abasement score. However, clinical observations and the consistency of personality measures revealing higher experienced stress point to real problems. Second, past and present discrimination and the isolation imposed by a racist society would affect feelings of loneliness, alienation, and anxiety. Last, the earlier discussion of culture conflict leading to a negative self-image could be a strong component of these findings.

Academic Abilities

Using the School and College Ability Tests, the Berkeley studies revealed that Chinese- and Japanese-Americans of both sexes scored significantly lower on the verbal section of the test than their control counterparts. In addition, Chinese-Americans of both sexes scored significantly higher on the quantitative section of the test. Although Japanese-American students tended to obtain higher quantitative scores, the differences were not significant.

Although the possibility of inherited racial characteristics cannot be eliminated, greater explanatory power seems to lie in a socio-cultural analysis. The Asian-American's lowered verbal performance probably reflects his bilingual background (Smith & Kasdon, 1961;

Smith, 1957). The nature of Asian society also stresses filial piety and unquestioning respect for authority. Limited communication patterns in the home (parent to child) and the isolation imposed by a dominant society (one that rewarded silence and inconspicuousness and punished outspoken behavior from minorities) greatly restricted verbal interaction (Watanabe, 1971). The higher quantitative scores may represent compensatory modes of expression. Quantitative activities also tend to be more concrete, impersonal, and structured. These attributes are highly attractive to Asian-Americans.

Vocational Interests

Most educators, pupil personnel workers, and counselors throughout the West and East Coasts have frequently remarked on the abundance of Asian students entering the physical sciences. Surveys undertaken at the University of California, Berkeley, (Chu, 1971; Takayama, 1971) reveal that approximately 75 percent of Chinese and 68 percent of Japanese males enter the physical sciences. Using the Strong Vocational Interest Blank, the Berkeley studies compared the interests of Chinese-Americans, Japanese-Americans, and all other students. Chinese-American men expressed more interest in the physical sciences (Mathematician, Physicist, Engineer, Chemist, etc.) than all other students. Although not statistically significant, Japanese-American men also tended to express more interest in these occupations. Males from both ethnic groups appeared more interested in occupations comprising the skilled-technical trades (Farmer, Aviator, Carpenter, Printer, Vocational-Agricultural Teacher, Forest Service Man, etc.) and less interested in sales (Sales Manager, Real Estate Salesman, Life Insurance Salesman) and the verbal-linguistic occupations (Advertising Man, Lawyer, Author-Journalist). Although Chinese-American males exhibited less interest in the social sciences, this was not true for the Japanese-American males. Generally, both groups expressed more interest in the business fields, especially the detail (Senior Certified Public Accountant, Accounting and Office Man) as opposed to the business contact vocations. They tended to be less interested in the aesthetic-cultural fields (Musician and Artist). Although they did not differ significantly in the biological sciences as a group, they did express more interest in the clinically applied ones (Dentist and Veterinarian).

The Asian-American females had a profile similar to their male counterparts. Both ethnic groups exhibited more interest in business occupations, applied-technical fields, biological and physical sciences and less interest in verbal-linguistic fields, social service, and aesthetic-cultural occupations. Although Chinese- and Japanese-American females tended to express more interest in the domestically oriented occupations (Housewife, Elementary Teacher, Office Worker, and Stenographer-Secretary), only the Chinese-American females scored significantly higher.

An analysis of the relationship between personality traits, academic abilities, and vocational interests for Asian-Americans reveals a logical consistency among all three variables. Greater interest in the physical sciences and lower interest in sales, social sciences, and verbal-linguistic fields are consistent with the Asian-American's higher quantitative and lower verbal skills. Furthermore, the people-contact professions call for some degree of forceful self-expression. These traits are antagonistic to the Asian-American's greater inhibition, reserve in interpersonal relations, and lower social extroversion. Physical sciences and skilled-technical trades, also, are characterized by more of a structured, impersonal, and concrete approach.

The Asian-American's restricted choice of vocations can be explained by two factors. First, early immigrants came from a strongly agricultural and peasant background. This is especially true of the Japanese who, according to the 1960 Census, were over-represented in agricultural fields. Second, early immigrants may have encouraged their sons and daughters into occupations with potentially greater social and economic survival value. Thus, their concern with evaluating choice of vocations on the basis of pragmatism was reinforced by a racist society. Agricultural fields, skilled-technical trades, and physical sciences can be perceived as possessing specific concrete skills that were functional in American society. Discrimination and prejudice were minimized in these occupations while people-contact professions were wrought with hazards of discrimination. Even though the Chinese and Japanese expressed more interest in the businesses, most of the fields were accounting and bookkeeping activities. Furthermore, business occupations which they have historically chosen tended to be within their ethnic community (import-export, family-owned businesses, restaurants, etc.) rather than within the larger society.

Differences Between Chinese- and Japanese-Americans

The discussion thus far has revealed many similarities between Chinese- and Japanese-American students. In light of their many common cultural values and experiences in America, this is not surprising. However, differences certainly exist. On all three measures (personality, abilities, and interests) administered at the University of California, Berkeley, Japanese-American students consistently fell into an intermediate position between the Chinese-American and the control students. In other words, Japanese-Americans are more similar to the controls than are the Chinese-Americans. This finding suggests two possibilities. It might be assumed that Japanese values are much more similar to European-American values than are those of the Chinese. An analysis of Japanese and Chinese cultural values would dictate against this as the sole interpretation. Additionally, the high rate of industrialization in Japan is a relatively recent phenomenon that may have minimal impact at this time. A more plausible explanation lies in the differential acculturation of both groups.

Arkoff, Meredith, & Iswahara (1962) conclude that Japanese-American females appear to be acculturating faster than their male counterparts. Weiss (1969) feels that Chinese females are much better accepted by American society than males. This leads to greater social contact with members of the host society and acculturation is fostered. If differential acculturation occurs between sexes of the same ethnic group, it might be possible that a similar phenomenon has and/or is affecting both the Chinese and Japanese. An answer to this question may lie in the historical past of both the Chinese and Japanese in America.

Prior to the outbreak of World War II, relations between Japan and the United States became noticeably strained. Many Japanese in America feared that their loyalty would be questioned. Fearing that war would break out between the two nations and bring retaliation against Japanese-Americans, many Japanese-American organizations such as the Japanese-American Citizens League emphasized the need to appear as American as possible. Pro-American proclamations were common, and offspring were encouraged to acculturate and identify themselves with the American people.

With the bombing of Pearl Harbor, war was declared on Japan and the relocation experience of 110,000 Japanese-Americans did much to foster acculturation (Umemoto, 1970; Kitano, 1969b). First, it broke up Japanese-American communities by uprooting their residents. Homes and properties of the Japanese were confiscated and lost. Even today, the Japanese communities (Japantowns) are not comparable to the cohesive Chinatowns in San Francisco and New York, which serve as visible symbols of ethnic identity for the Chinese. Second, the camp experience disrupted the traditional family structure and lines of authority. Elderly males no longer had a functional value as household heads. Control and discipline of children and women became noticeably

weakened under these circumstances. Third, many Japanese-Americans chose to migrate to the East Coast and Midwest rather than suffer the humiliation of internment. Even after the termination of the relocation centers, some Japanese-Americans chose not to return to the West Coast because of the strong anti-Japanese feeling there. Their greater physical dispersal increased contact with members of the host society and probably aided acculturation.

Conclusions

The psychological characteristics exhibited by Asian-Americans are related to their culture and the Asian-American's interaction with Western society. Any study of ethnic minorities in America must necessarily deal with the forces of racism inherent in American culture. Since there are no Asian-Americans untouched by racism in the United States to use as a control group, the relationship of racism to psychological development becomes a complex issue that cannot easily be resolved. If an attempt is made to use control groups in Taiwan, Hong Kong, or China, the problem becomes clouded by a whole complex of other social and cultural differences. For these reasons, the analyses presented in this article must be seen as somewhat tentative and speculative. Hopefully, further research will help clarify this issue.

References

Abbott, K. A. *Harmony and Individualism*, Taipei: Orient Cultural Press, 1970.

Abbott, K., and Abbott, E. "Juvenile Delinquency in San Francisco's Chinese-American Community." *Journal of Sociology* 4, 1968, 45-56.

Arkoff, A. "Need Patterns of Two Generations of Japanese-Americans in Hawaii." *Journal of Social Psychology* 50, 1959, 75-79.

_____; Meredith, G.; and Iswahara, S. "Dominance-Deference Patterning in

Motherland-Japanese, Japanese-American, and Caucasian-American Students." *Journal of Social Psychology* 58, 1962, 61-63.

_____; Meredith, G.; and Iswahara, S. "Male-Dominant and Equalitarian Attitudes in Japanese, Japanese-American, and Caucasian-American Students." *Journal of Social Psychology* 64, 1964, 225-229.

_____, and H. Weaver. "Body Image and Body Dissatisfaction in Japanese-Americans." *Journal of Social Psychology* 68, 1966, 323-330.

Chu, Robert. "Majors of Chinese and Japanese Students at the University of California, Berkeley, for the Past 20 Years." Project report, AS 150, Asian Studies Division, University of California, Berkeley, Winter, 1971.

Daniels, R. *Concentration Camps USA: Japanese-Americans and World War II.* New York: Holt, Rinehart, and Winston, Inc., 1971.

DeVos, G., and Abbott, K. "The Chinese Family in San Francisco." MSW dissertation, University of California, Berkeley, 1966.

Fenz, W., and Arkoff, A. "Comparative Need Patterns of Five Ancestry Groups in Hawaii." *Journal of Social Psychology* 58, 1962, 67-89.

Fong, S. L. M. "Assimilation of Chinese in America: Changes in Orientation and Social Perception." *American Journal of Sociology* 71, 1965, 265-273.

_____, and Peskin, H. "Sex-Role Strain and Personality Adjustment of China-born Students in America: A Pilot Study." *Journal of Abnormal Psychology* 74, 1969, 563-567.

Jones, J. M. *Prejudice and Racism.* Massachusetts: Addison-Wesley Publishing Company, 1972.

Kimmich, R. A. "Ethnic Aspects of Schizophrenia in Hawaii." *Psychiatry* 23, 1960, 97-102.

Kitano, H. H. L. "Changing Achievement Patterns of the Japanese in the United States." *Journal of Social Psychology* 58, 1962, 257-264.

_____. "Inter and Intra-Generational Differences in Maternal Attitudes Toward Child Rearing." *Journal of Social Psychology* 63, 1964, 215-220.

_____. "Japanese-American Crime and Delinquency." *Journal of Psychology* 66, 1967, 253-263.

_____. "Japanese-American Mental Illness." In S. C. Plog and R. B. Edgerton (eds.), *Changing Perspectives in Mental Illness.* New York: Holt, Rinehart, and Winston, 1969a.

_____. *Japanese-Americans: The Evolution of a Subculture.* New Jersey: Prentice-Hall, 1969b.

_____. "Mental Illness in Four Cultures." *Journal of Social Psychology* 80, 1970, 121-134.

Kovel, J. *White Racism: A Psychohistory.* New York: Vintage Books, 1971.

Marsella, A. J.; Kinzie, D.; and Gordon, P. "Depression Patterns among American College Students of Caucasian, Chinese, and Japanese Ancestry." Paper presented at the Conference on Culture and Mental Health in Asia and the Pacific. March, 1971.

Matsumoto, G. M.; Meredith, G.; and Masuda, M. "Ethnic Identification: Honolulu and Seattle Japanese-Americans." *Journal of Cross-Cultural Psychology* 1, 1970, 63-76.

Meade, R. D. "Leadership Studies of Chinese and Chinese-Americans." *Journal of Cross-Cultural Psychology* 1, 1970,

325-332.

Meredith, G. M. "Personality Correlates of Pidgin English Usage among Japanese-American College Students in Hawaii." *Japanese Psychological Research* 6, 1964.

____. "Amae and Acculturation among Japanese-American College Students in Hawaii. *Journal of Social Psychology* 70, 1966, 171-180.

Smith, M. E. "Progress in the Use of English after Twenty-Two Years by Children of Chinese Ancestry in Honolulu." *Journal of Genetic Psychology* 90, 1957, 255-258.

____, and Kasdon, L. M. "Progress in the Use of English after Twenty Years by Children of Filipino and Japanese Ancestry in Hawaii." *Journal of Genetic Psychology* 99, 1961, 129-138.

Sommers, V. S. "Identity Conflict and Acculturation Problems in Oriental-Americans." *American Journal of Orthopsychiatry* 30, 1960, 637-644.

Success Story: "Out-Whiting the Whites." *Newsweek*, June, 1971.

Success Story of One Minority Group in the U.S. *US News and World Report*, December, 1966.

Sue, D. W., and Sue, S. "Counseling Chinese-Americans." *Personnel and Guidance Journal* 50, 1972a, 637-644.

____, and Sue, S. "Ethnic Minorities: Resistance to Being Researched." *Professional Psychology* 2, 1972b, 11-17.

____, and Kirk, B. A. "Psychological Characteristics of Chinese-American College Students." *Journal of Counseling Psychology* in press [1972].

____, and Kirk, B. A. "Differential Characteristics of Japanese- and Chinese-American College Students." Research in progress at the University of California, Berkeley.

Sue, S., and Sue, D. W. "Chinese-American Personality and Mental Health." *Amerasia Journal* 1, 1971, 36-49.

Takayama, G. "Analysis of Data on Asian Students at UC Berkeley, 1971." Project report, AS 150, Asian Studies Division, University of California, Berkeley, Winter, 1971.

Unemoto, A. "Crisis in the Japanese-American Family." In *Asian Women*. Berkeley: 1971.

Watanabe, C. "A College Level Reading and Composition Program for Students of Asian Descent: Diagnosis and Design." Asian Studies Division, University of California, Berkeley, 1971.

Weiss, M. S. "Selective Acculturation and the Dating Process: The Patterning of Chinese-Caucasian Interracial Dating." *Journal of Marriage and the Family* 32, 1970.

Yamamoto, J.; James, Q. C.; and Palley, N. "Cultural Problems in Psychiatric Therapy." *General Archives of Psychiatry.* 19, 1968, 45-49.

16. Musings of a Hyphenated American

by Lindbergh S. Sata, M.D.

In recent months, there has been a proliferation of books on Japanese-Americans (References 1, 2, 4, 5). I have read these with a great deal of interest since I, myself, am Nisei (second-generation Japanese). In the process of reading historical accounts, I have relived various aspects of my youth and adolescence, unlocking doors to distant memories, hopes, friendships, and feelings. It has been necessary to engage in a dialogue with those long-forgotten memories which have lain dormant in the recesses of my innermost private self, and this has led me to write of my concern about, and aspirations for, a racial and cultural group to which I claim membership.

In the process of my reading, which has included both novels and documentaries, I have experienced a sense of incompleteness. Much of what has been written is like an accurate description of ships crossing the horizon, with little mention of the cargo manifest or the reason for the ships' being where they are, where they have come from, or where they are going. To help bring those distant ships of history into closer and sharper focus, I am writing now, both as a behavioral scientist and as a Nisei, of the past, present, and future of my people.

I'd like to begin with a brief examination of the Japanese-American heritage as it began with the immigration of the first Japanese to America. Interestingly enough, these fore-fathers were the culturally disadvantaged of their day, both in terms of the Japan they left and the land to which they turned. Japan had barely emerged from a primitive feudal system, ravaged by a hundred years of civil war, and was struggling for existence in a pre-industrial society. Moreover, these first immigrants were poorly educated and ill-prepared for, and unaccustomed to, Western cultures. It still seems unbelievable that viable roots were able to develop on what was to be such unwelcome soil. The blatant racism practiced against the Japanese immigrants, as documented in newspaper editorials, restrictive land laws, and anti-Oriental legislation regarding immigration, more than adequately substantiates the unfriendly climate which existed, particularly on the West Coast of the United States.

It should be objectively stated, also, that Japan was no more and no less racist in its belief systems and had, indeed, killed and purged Christians, segregated and mistreated aliens, and held to rigid adherence of a caste system, with the masses in statuses and roles only a cut above absolute servitude. Perhaps such human inequities existing in Japan contributed to the psychological substrata and provided sufficient resilience for these immigrants to withstand those early oppressive years in the United States.

Of particular interest to me is that history also documents that Issei (first-generation immigrant Japanese) were militant and organizationally competent. In the face of potential school segregation in California, Issei were able, through the Japanese consulate, to receive a hearing by the President of the United States, with subsequent presidential intervention in the State of California, abolishing segregational school practices for Orientals. Community resources were maximally utilized to form cohesive social action groups which included, for example, farm cooperatives, collective bargaining groups, Buddhist and Japanese Methodist churches, and Japanese language schools, all of which helped fill the economic, ethnic, and cultural needs of a people newly arrived in a strange and often hostile land.

One question which arises is why, in the face of historically documented accounts of organized resistance towards injustice and oppression (which, in the language of the 60s, is equated with militancy), were these attitudes so incompletely assimilated by the Nisei (second-generation Japanese-American)? I can recall what was said to me when, as a boy, I engaged in skirmishes with neighborhood Caucasian children. I was told, "If you have to fight, fight with dignity," or "Men shouldn't cry," or its equivalent, "Don't shame us by crying." I cannot, honestly, recall being encouraged to assume anything beyond a fatalistic stance in matters related to expectations for equality and human dignity. What was required was "ga-maan" (perseverance), and the lesson was usually closed with the statement, "Shi-ka-ta ga nai" (It can't be helped).

Could it be that the survival needs of the first-generation immigrants were of such high priority that my parents had to mince words in those brief communications, or did I and others like myself of my generation simply lack comprehension of what was actually being said? In reliving my history, I, at this point, have the same uncomfortable feeling which I experience on rare occasions, after attending a movie or play and feeling very much a part of it, only to

discover later that, somehow, I had completely missed the point of the underlying theme.

It occurs to me that communication, which is central to the understanding of ourselves as we relate to our past and to our future, is often fractured on both the inter- and intra-personal levels; and what is taken to be a dialogue between generations is often an alternate monologue. What the speaker says, what he thinks he says, and what the listener perceives are often three different things. Adding to these difficulties in communication, which are inherent in any language, are the following factors:

As stated earlier, the Issei, as an immigrant group, were poorly educated, averaging four years of formal education in Japan. Of equal importance were their origins from rural Japan which, in a nation undergoing social revolution, represented another generation of maturational delay, when contrasted to urban population centers from which such changes emanate. Then, too, the principal communication mode between Issei and Nisei was Japanese. Despite the existence of the Japanese language as the primary tool for communication at home, the degree to which the language was mastered by Nisei was hardly adequate beyond elementary communication. Among themselves, Nisei communicated in English. The time spent conversing with parents in the native tongue was far less than the time spent in American schools or among peer group members. Therefore, English was the principal mode of communication for Nisei.

As for myself, Japanese was my primary language until the third grade. The confusion I experienced, at the interface between the culture I knew and the school environment to which I was newly introduced, brings back painfully humorous incidences. I vividly recall an incident in the first grade when I tearfully presented my report card to my parents, upset over the fact that I had received four D's and two C's while my Nisei neighbor had bettered me with four C's and two D's. I recall the chastisement, both for crying and for having been scholastically overtaken by my neighbor, and the apprehension I experienced some weeks later when I discovered that my parents were equally ignorant of the outer world.

Without faulting my parents, I can see the difficulty they experienced in attempting to responsibly transmit their cultural belief systems to their children. Language was a major barrier, as was the lack of knowledgeable information on their adopted land. If one considers for a moment attempting to convey concepts such as "authenticity" or "integrity" to another English-speaking individual, the subtleties of concepts captured in a single word become apparent. Add to this the complicated nature of bilingual communication, and my family picture becomes complete.

Those early years with their incongruities can be appreciated in the context of a badly fragmented communication system. While being indoctrinated on protocol governing inter-personal and social conduct, I was sent, on those rare occasions when we could afford recreation, to the neighborhood movie, which, in reality, was burlesque. The fact that my parents did not know about burlesque never occurred to me, and I operated on the assumption that all movie theaters had dancing girls who did funny things with tassels attached to their breasts. Several years later, when I learned most movie theaters did not have dancing girls, I was ashamed, guilty, and somewhat relieved that I had not mentioned those earlier "movie" experiences, which surely would have led to physical punishment!

As previously stated, the Nisei were handi-capped in their reception of values, beliefs, and mores, since they lacked a sophisticated grasp of their parents' language and parents, in turn, often failed to realize that the finer points of their teachings were not understood. Since much of the information was presented as dogma, there was neither the opportunity to validate teachings experientially nor to engage in discussion in order to understand the teachings.

An illustration of my incomplete teaching and learning is that of judo, a sport tied to the Samurai tradition and a remnant of the feudal era of Japan. My father enrolled me in a judo class at the age of six, an activity I begrudgingly pursued for the next eight years. During the first several years, I dutifully practiced mastering form, precision of movement, diaphragmatic vocalizations, and physical toler-ance to pain caused by sitting for hours Indian fashion. Although I won only rarely, I learned to be graceful in being thrown to the mat and resigned to the obvious disappointment I caused my father. When I could muster suffi-cient courage to explain my obvious dislike for an activity that made me a frequent loser and my preference for the Boy Scouts or baseball, my father would respond with, "In my house, we only do one thing at a time, and you are doing judo." His statement left no room for discussion; and so I continued to master the form but lost touch with the essence of those teachings which might have enabled me to understand my body and to find the center of my body to successfully resist the physical assault of others.

While I continue to explore how I express myself through my body, I am simultaneously aware of the lack of spontaneity and the seeming unnaturalness of my body language. Although judo was cited as an example, kendo, karate, the tea ceremony, flower arranging, and the writing of prose are other examples of cultural pursuits placing emphasis on the mastery of the body in the performance of the arts. What to Westerners appears to be a diminution of body language cues, particularly of the upper torso and face, and the resultant stereotyping of the inscrutable Oriental is, in reality, a product of cultural teachings which underscore form, economy, concentration of body energy, and mastery of the body as a step towards self-knowledge. It is such disciplined practice that enables Zen masters to control alpha rhythm at will, or the judo master's capacity to center his body so as to passively resist being lifted by an individual twice his size, or to effortlessly topple the same opponent with a minimum of movement.

For a variety of reasons I do not fully understand, my incomplete teachings leave me with many outward similarities and little, if any, residue of the essence of such teachings. Like many of my generation, I evoke response from others on my inscrutability.

Although purely speculative, as I look at others of my ancestry, I am impressed with the acculturative process of adapting Eastern teachings to Western ways. Among Japanese males of my generation, there is an almost fanatical interest in golf and bowling, both of which require concentrated attention to form. I wonder if my friends also failed to learn the essence of those earlier teachings, since there are but a few professional quality bowlers and golfers, an illustration of form without substance.

However distorted were my teachings during the formative years, by early adolescence I had developed an idealized image of America and an appreciation of the rights and opportunities as a birthright in a democracy. With the announcement of Pearl Harbor, I shared with the rest of the nation my anger and disgust at the despicable actions of my parents' ancestral land. Living on the West Coast, I faithfully complied with the curfew placed upon us, as I thought it only American to observe its laws. Even with the announcement of planned evacuation, I continued to believe at the age of fourteen that we were being moved for our own protection, and that our participation would contribute to the overall war effort.

Several incidences occurred which cumulatively began eroding my idealized image of my native land. I began to discover that, with one single exception, those whom I cherished as my Caucasian friends hated me, blamed me, and ascribed to me those very characteristics which I had attributed to the "enemy" involved in the bombing of Pearl Harbor; namely, dishonorable, sneaky, treacherous, and barbaric. Following several beatings and countless incidences that were to continue for the next fifteen years, I retreated to the temporary security of the family unit. I shall never forget my utter disbelief and shock, when the day of evacuation finally arrived and we were being herded into a temporary compound, in seeing machine-gun emplacements facing inward and the sudden realization that, although we were "being protected," we were, indeed, considered the "enemy."

The "assembly center" in Portland, Oregon, and the "camp" in Minidoka, Idaho, were euphemistic descriptions of my home for the next three years. There I witnessed the erosion of the integrity of the family unit and the gradual undermining of the role of my father who never fully recovered, physically or psychologically. Most culturally meaningful activities were abandoned, English became the predominant mode for communicating, and peer influence predominated. The educational system was grossly inadequate; and, as a college preparatory student, I graduated with two years of vocational carpentry and vocational auto mechanics. In my more compassionate moments, I recognize that, for me, a war and three years in a concentration camp created a set of conditions facilitating my acculturation process; but I still have difficulty reconciling the tremendous cost and the realization that acculturation might have still occurred without such chaotic interruption of the lives of so many people.

As may be true with other minorities, my earlier quest for self-identity was best characterized by aimless wandering down many blind alleys and dead ends. A place in the sun for most tends to obscure the reality that for minorities that place may be in the shadows. Until that reality is reconciled, the quest for self-identity is punctuated with repeated disappointments and failures. Perhaps it is less an issue of a place in the sun as it is the process through which it takes place that deserves further attention.

My parents, being mindful of helping the family achieve an acceptable place in society, constantly reminded me of the need to co-exist with others unlike myself. Without conscious awareness, I began to function as a human chameleon, sensitive and adaptive to the response of others and only secondarily aware of those feelings within myself. More often than I care to remember, I have attempted to relate with others honestly and openly, only to discover that, when I least expected it, either my racialness would be denied, which is to deny an important aspect of my identity, or I would be reminded that, because of my racialness, I was less than equal.

Between those teachings at home and the encounters with the reality of the world outside the home, I and others like me have developed a life style I choose to describe as a form of cultural paranoia. In its most adaptive sense, it has enabled me to withstand both psychological and physical insult, when my cultural paranoia either insulated me in my own defensiveness or enabled me to diagnose potential situations that might lead to physical injury. In a maladaptive sense, it has constrained me and imprisoned me, and I have become my own jailer.

The hypervigilance characterizing cultural paranoia manifests itself in peculiar ways. The phenomenon is sufficiently common among Asian males that, in a survey conducted among Seattle prostitutes, Asian males are identified as being good dates, as they are polite and make little trouble, but are poor marks for robbery, as they never carry more money than necessary for conducting the transaction (Ref. 3).

A place in the shadows describes the marginality of Japanese-Americans in both the United States and Japan. To understand the statement, one needs to look beyond those social indices of success which Japanese-Americans have achieved, including high educational records and low unemployment, crime, and divorce rates. Without detracting from the many accomplishments derived in less than two generations, several examples of our marginality emerge.

Few, if any, Nisei have had successful acceptance in Japan and are referred to as foreigners. Inasmuch as our parental teachings reflected values practiced in Japan at the turn of the century, we continue to be out of step with modern-day Japan. Many Nisei have advanced economically with American institutions in Japan as facilitators but lack the sense of belonging except as foreigners in an unfamiliar land. It is as if they are re-enacting their earlier childhood experiences in a bilingual culture with a reversal of roles but, this time, with a recognition that to look and speak Japanese is not enough to be Japanese.

At the same time, our American ways are equally puzzling. We are avowed advocates of the democratic process and of participative government. Yet our voting turnout in local elections is miserably poor, while presidential elections bring most of us to the polls. It is almost as if we are unconcerned with issues that affect us directly on a local level and, when given the opportunity for free choice, have a greater investment in preserving the image of good citizenship than consistently practicing that principle. And, finally, though we have tasted the bitter fruits of prejudice, discrimination, and exclusion from the mainstream of American life and have been and still are intensely resentful of bigotry, hypocrisy and non-egalitarian practices, we are conspicuously absent in the civil rights movements of other minorities, and, unwittingly and pathetically, many of us have become bigots, hypocrites, and racists in the process.

As I look back, trying to understand myself and my people, it occurs to me that those whom we, as young people, perceived as being rather strange were probably persons who, for the most part, were more Japanese or more American than we. I think, particularly, of the children who achieved a comprehensive understanding of the teachings in our Japanese language school and who were thought to be strange and different. I think now that those youngsters appreciated what it was and how it was to be Japanese. I also recall those others who, by virtue of their actions, seemed unusual in a different way. The few who dared to question the constitutionality of the evacuation of the Japanese and risked imprisonment understood what it was to be American.

So it comes to me as a rude awakening, in the fourth decade of my life, that the "average Nisei" occupies a position of marginality, and those few whom we thought were deviant were, in fact, in the mainstream of the Japanese or the American culture. For these reasons, it seems justifiable that Nisei be identified as hyphenated Americans, a designation that continues to identify native-born Americans as being different and distinct as a racial and cultural ethnic group.

Given our past and emerging present, where will our future take us? We have glimpses of that future previewed in our growing children. I think, for the most part, they have turned out rather well; and I'm uncertain whether it's been because of us or in spite of us.

Several important barriers have been removed. Nisei and Sansei (third generation) communicate in a common language that enables reciprocal discussion and increases the possibility of mutual understanding. Belief systems are similar in both generations, although there may continue to be significant distortions in the respective perceptions of these belief systems. Finally, the basic referent group is the society at large which permits continuous revalidation for both Nisei and Sansei.

There appears to be a gradual emergence of a new breed of youth from the Japanese community. He does not suffer from the Enryo syndrome of constantly declining, as described by Kitano (Ref. 4). Both young men and women appear to be delayed products of the civil rights and youth movements, present themselves as Asians rather than Japanese-Americans, and have developed coalitions with the Chinese, Korean, Filipino, and Samoan communities. They have adopted the mannerisms of activist Blacks and Browns, have engaged in demonstrations, have been vocal on Asian issues, and have had a substantial impact on their elders. In a relatively short period of several years, Nisei parents have shifted from a critical and disapproving stance to a less conservative and more supportive role. The formation of the Governor's Commission on Asian Affairs in the State of Washington was the outgrowth of involved citizen participation by some of the very parents who were highly critical of social action strategems employed earlier by young people.

Although the social activist movement among Japanese-American youth constitutes approximately one percent of the Japanese population in Seattle, the numbers continue to grow as various organizational groups are formed. There is also increased evidence of Nisei and Sansei planning together and a feeling of mutuality of purpose for various community-directed projects. It was this process of collaborative planning which led to the first Asian Mental Health Conference in the United States, held in 1972 in San Francisco with representatives from throughout the United States.

Whenever there is an opportunity, I observe, listen, converse, and try to learn from Sansei. In varying degrees, I see fewer psychological constraints as compared with our generation, and there is a relative absence of the type of provincial thinking so characteristic of ghetto minorities. I both envy and shudder at their idealism, which seems to have limitless boundaries, and at their reckless courage, which is both untempered and untested. There is an emerging social conscience and a restlessness for changing basic societal inequities and outmoded institutions, and, in this regard, they are in the mainstream of young America. I also hear clearly their hopes for ways of strengthening their cultural and ethnic identity, not out of defensiveness but from a hunger to learn and from a sense of pride that they do have a Japanese heritage.

In my ruminations, I have been preoccupied with the acculturative processes involving myself and my people but have, perhaps subconsciously, avoided facing that issue squarely. Recognizing that acculturation may take place without assimilation, it seems to me that it is only the intermixing of races that will lead to a reduction of differential responses towards dissimilar racial groupings.

Even as Little Tokyos are abandoned in the search for middle-class neighborhoods and comforts, there is a lessened degree of subcultural community management and influence over social deviancy and delinquent behavior. The reduction of previously available community resources forces families to seek assistance from agencies and institutions with little prior experience in dealing with Japanese. Therefore, when it is stated that criminality, which ten years ago seemed inconsequential, is becoming a growing problem among Sansei and Yonsei (fourth generation), one is uncertain if such rates reflect an actual increase in criminal behavior or an indication of the gradual dissolution of social institutions no longer available to young people.

I am uncertain of the future but encouraged by what is evolving both from my children and my community. There is individuality, spontaneity, hope, and vitality among the young. They seem to be learning what we elders may have overlooked in our struggle for acceptance.

> By letting go,
> it all gets done.
> The world is won
> by those who
> let it go!
>
> But when you
> try and try,
> the world is
> then beyond
> the winning.
>
> Lao Tzu

References

1. Girdner, Audire, and Loftis, Anne. *The Great Betrayal.* London: Macmillan & Co., Collier-Macmillan, Ltd., 1969.

2. Hosokawa, Bill. *Nisei — The Quiet American.* New York: William Morrow and Company, Inc., 1969.

3. James, Jennifer. "Sweet Cream Ladies: An Introduction to Prostitute Taxonomy." *Western Canadian Journal of Anthropology* Spring, 1972, Edmonton, Alberta, Canada.

4. Kitano, Harry H. L. *Japanese-Americans: The Evolution of a Subculture.* Englewood Cliffs, N.J.: Prentice-Hall, Inc., 1969.

5. Zeller, William D. *An Educational Dream.* The American Press, 1969.

Part Four: Mental Health

Introduction

In the previous section on personality, several papers discussed the effects of Asian culture, Western values, and minority status on the individual. These factors also influence the expression of emotional and behavioral problems. In a comparison of Italian and Irish immigrants who were diagnosed as schizophrenic, Opler (1957) found that symptom patterns for the two groups differed widely according to cultural factors. Kitano (Chapter 17) and Abbott and Abbott (Chapter 18) studied juvenile delinquency among Japanese and Chinese, respectively. Both studies came to similar conclusions: rates of juvenile delinquency are difficult to assess accurately because of a "funneling effect"; Japanese and Chinese still exhibit low rates of delinquency. Kitano feels that the Japanese delinquent is essentially a marginal person, unable to identify with cultural institutions. In the case of Chinese, Abbott and Abbott found no differences in delinquent behaviors due to foreign versus American born and to area of residence in San Francisco. They noted, however, that aggressive crimes appeared to be increasing.

The rate of behavioral disorders among Asian-Americans is difficult to determine. On one hand, official statistics indicate that Chinese and Japanese have proportionately fewer admissions to psychiatric hospitals than Caucasians (Kitano, 1969). Minority group individuals, however, are reluctant to use psychotherapeutic services because of cultural variables and because the facilities are almost always insensitive to their ethnic sensitivities. Obviously, statistics on mental illness based upon the number of known psychiatric cases underestimate the number of individuals needing some kind of assistance. Alternative research strategies would be to (1) survey a "normal" sample, noting the frequency of behavioral problems, and (2) determine the severity of disorders among those who seek mental health services. The latter strategy assumes that, if the severity of problems among the relatively few Asian-Americans seeking services is greater than that among Caucasians, then it is possible that only the most severely disturbed are seen for treatment. Both research plans suggest that the rates for behavioral problems among Chinese and Japanese college students have been underestimated.

Kitano (Chapter 19) presents a comprehensive look at mental illness among Japanese-Americans. In his discussion, official statistics and impressionistic data are combined with a thoughtful analysis of culture, community, and family. One of the most ignored groups among Asian-Americans has been the Filipino. Duff and Arthur (Chapter 20) found that Filipinos in the U.S. Navy who were hospitalized for psychiatric reasons exhibited problems reflecting Filipino culture. The investigators, using a psychodynamic frame of reference, feel that therapists must understand the cultural factors in order to provide more effective treatment.

Most studies of the mental illness of Asian-Americans support the view that treatment procedures and facilities must respond to the needs and values of Asians. But how can mental health facilities provide better services for members of minority groups? Brown, Stein, Huang, and Harris (Chapter 21) give some valuable insights into this problem. Their study is important for several reasons. First, Chinese patients are found to be mainly an immigrant group with serious mental health problems. Second, the investigators offer concrete suggestions for the treatment of Chinese patients. Insight-oriented approaches were not very helpful; direct problem-solving techniques and medication were more effective. Third, recommendations are made for increased community participation.

References

Kitano, H. H. *Japanese-Americans: The Evolution of a Subculture.* Englewood Cliffs, N.J.: Prentice-Hall, 1969.

Opler, M. K. "Schizophrenia and Culture." *Scientific American* 197, 1957, 103-110.

17. Japanese-American Crime and Delinquency

by Harry H. L. Kitano

Introduction

In an era of rising rates of crime and delinquency, the Japanese population in the United States is remarkably atypical. Empirical data drawn from official sources show that their rates of crime are quite low, in spite of the fact that such negative environmental conditions as ghetto living, discrimination, and prejudice, often thought of as associated with criminal and delinquent behavior, have long been a part of the Japanese experience in the United States.

When we refer to low rates, the following figures are typical. Los Angeles County Probation figures (rates per 100,000) show that, in 1930, Japanese adult rates were 53, compared to 190 for the non-Japanese; in 1940, Japanese rates were 149, compared to 518 for the non-Japanese; in 1950, Japanese rates were 11, compared to 589 for the non-Japanese; and, in 1960, the Japanese rates were 67, compared to 793 for the non-Japanese. Juvenile figures from the same source show similar Japanese, non-Japanese differences; for example, in 1930, they were 300 to 1709; in 1940, they were 119 to 1069; in 1950, they were 180, compared to 1291; and, in 1960, they were 450 to 1481.

Official figures from FBI statistics on arrests (Reference 7) indicate that the Japanese are the lowest among all comparison groups, including the White, Negro, Chinese, and the Indian, for 1940, 1950, and 1960. Other research studies show the same differences (Ref. 1 and 6).

Although all official statistics on crime and delinquency are subject to what Cressey calls the "funneling effect" (Ref. 2) and all are open to biases in reporting, handling, arresting, sentencing, and the like, the consistency of the low Japanese position lends support to a generalization that they are a low official criminal and delinquent group.

The purpose of this paper is to offer possible explanations for this low delinquent culture by comparing delinquent and non-delinquent Japanese-Americans. (This study was supported by U.S. Public Health Grant NIMH, OM-476.)

Methodology

Sample

One of the difficulties in conducting research on Japanese crime and delinquency is the very small number of them who are held in official custody. Therefore, even if the study were designed otherwise, the research eventually would result in a small sample study. The number of adult Japanese currently in California prisons (less than 10) precluded any systematic analysis of this population; the number of Japanese in California Youth Authority Camps (again, less than 10) presented the same limitations.

The most available population was a group on probation from the Los Angeles County Probation Department (X=31) and from the

California Youth Authority (X=4). This group of Japanese-American male probationers comprised our delinquent population.

We used a matched-sample strategy, whereby a group of non-probationary Japanese, referred to as "normals," were chosen for comparison purposes. The normals were matched in terms of the same high school and, where possible, the same home room and the same grade as the delinquents. With the probationers who were already out of high school, we matched high school seniors. We selected thirty-seven Japanese normals to match closely the thirty-five delinquents. We were able to interview all thirty-seven normal adolescents and their parents; we were able to interview twenty-five delinquents and their parents. (From the probationer population, the author encountered four refusals; two who were never in after appointments were made; two who were not currently residing in the local area; and two who had been recommitted. Therefore our delinquent X=25.)

The sampling procedure controlled for ethnicity, age, sex (all males), and social class, since there were no significant differences between the groups on these variables.

Instrument

The basic instrument used for the study was a guided interview schedule. The interviews were conducted by six social workers of Japanese ancestry. Pretraining sessions and the interview schedule were aids to reliability. The average length of the interview was two hours. In most instances, the adolescent and his parent were interviewed in separate sessions.

A psychological test, the California Psychological Inventory (CPI), was also administered to the delinquent and the normal samples.

The results were analyzed in terms of chi square and Fisher's Exact Probability Test. All differences mentioned in the text are significant at the .05 level; all items in the tables reaching the same level of significance are in italics.

Results

The results are presented in terms of two hypotheses.

Hypothesis I

The Japanese delinquent and his family are different from Japanese normals.

a. *Structure of the home.* The overall general rate of divorced or separated homes in the Japanese population is small. U.S. census figures for 1960 show that broken homes make up only 1.3 percent of the Japanese population. This figure does not change by generation, since estimated divorce rates remain constant at 1.3 percent for successive generations.

There were no separated or divorced homes among the Japanese normals in the sample, while 32 percent of the Japanese delinquent homes of the sample were broken.

b. *Adolescent attitudes toward the home.* Attitudes of the normals and delinquents toward their homes are shown in Table 1. In the area of independence-dependence, the delinquents indicated a higher desire to leave home and to become independent than did the normals.

In the area of family relationships, *all* of the items were in the predicted direction. The normals consistently perceived their family in "good terms" — good relationships, reliance on verbal punishment, high obedience, and helpful parents.

The upward mobility of the normals is shown by the fact that 69 percent of them wished that their "fathers had a better job" as compared to 28 percent of the delinquents. This item could be interpreted in terms of possible home dissatisfaction among the normal sample.

Several overall generalizations can be inferred from the data. Both normals and delinquents generally agreed that they had good parents; that they received verbal discipline; that parents were helpful in

Table 1 **Attitudes Toward Home**			

	Percent "Yes" Response	
Variables	Normals N = 37	Delinquents N = 25
A. Independence-dependence		
1. *Want to leave home as soon as possible*	9	38
2. *Wish to become independent of home*	3	33
B. Family relationships		
1. *Good father*	97	76
2. Good mother	97	96
3. Good relationship with siblings	80	54
4. Compared to other parents, my parents get angry more often	14	40
5. Verbal discipline from father	81	40
6. Verbal discipline from mother	84	72
7. Obeys father most of the time	44	21
8. *Obeys mother most of the time*	41	13
9. Wishes parents would at least ask if they want cooperation	88	83
10. Parents helpful in money problems	100	92
11. Parents helpful in religious problems	40	28
12. Parents helpful in girl friend problems	47	45
13. Parents helpful in school problems	58	27
14. *Parents helpful in sex and growing-up problems*	69	20
15. Father available for discussion	26	36
16. Mother available for discussion	46	63
C. Desire for change		
1. *Wish father had a "better job"*	69	28

money problems; and that the best method of obtaining cooperation was *simply to ask* (although most parents told us that simple asking never really got much action!). It is also interesting to note that both samples generally agreed that they did not obey their parents most of the time; that parents were not helpful in religious or girl friend problems; and that father was usually unavailable for discussions.

| | Table 2 | |
| | Parental Responses | |

| | Percent "Yes" Response | |
| | Parents of Normals N = 37 | Parents of Delinquents N = 25 |
Variables		
A. Own upbringing		
1. Severity of own childhood	62	60
2. Abnormality of own childhood	27	57
B. Parent-son relationships		
1. *Bringing up son differently from own childhood*	43	84
2. Spend much time with son	36	11
3. Do things together with son	94	63
C. Parental agreement		
1. *Husband-wife agreement on handling son*	94	47
2. *Husband-wife agreement on family decisions*	92	33
D. Sanctions and effectiveness of sanctions, parent-child		
1. a. *Attempt to control smoking of son*	20	55
b. *Effectiveness of control*	79	11
2. a. Attempt to control drinking of son	14	21
b. Effectiveness of control	97	80
3. a. *Attempt to control hair style of son*	35	6
b. *Effectiveness of control*	95	53
4. a. Attempt to set control of time	9	16
b. Effectiveness of control	97	81
5. a. Attempt to know where son goes	3	16
b. *Effectiveness of control*	97	62
6. a. Attempt to communicate with son on problems	9	21
b. *Effectiveness of attempt*	100	60
E. Parent-son communication		
1. Son only discusses problems when in trouble or seldom	37	61
2. *Son enjoys parental discussions*	77	40
3. Son accepts parental advice	53	30
4. Son accepts punishment well	40	8
5. Have you struck your son recently?	61	53
6. Son usually avoids household chores	19	32
7. *Parent makes occupational choice for son*	69	20

	Percent "Yes" Response	
	Normals	Delinquents
Variables	N = 37	N = 25
Table 3 **Ethnic Interaction**		
A. Ethnic composition of clubs and organizations		
1. *Primarily Japanese*	100	75
B. Ethnicity of friends		
1. Primarily Japanese	60	16
C. Perceived parental preference of friends		
1. *Mostly Japanese*	94	53
D. Perceived parental preference of parental friends		
1. *Mostly Japanese*	94	53
E. Feelings about dating girls of specific ethnic backgrounds		
1. Japanese girls	92	100
2. Other Oriental girls	68	72
3. Caucasian girls	65	68
4. *Mexican girls*	27	68
5. Negro girls	8	36
F. Degree of participation in ethnic activities		
1. *General Japanese activities*	62	32
2. *Observance of Japanese customs at home*	39	0
3. *Preference for Japanese meals*	69	32
4. Occupational involvement with Japanese community	14	0
5. Family identification with Japanese community	29	5
6. Considers self more Japanese than American	19	24
G. Parental attitudes on interethnic dating		
1. Parents approve dating Japanese girls	97	92
2. Parents approve dating other Orientals	49	72
3. *Parents approve dating Caucasians*	43	76
4. Parents approve dating Mexicans	5	60
5. Parents approve dating Negroes	3	36

	Percent "Yes" Response	
	Normals	Delinquents
Variables	N = 37	N = 25

Table 4
The Neighborhood and School

Variables	Normals N = 37	Delinquents N = 25
A. Adolescents' attitudes towards neighborhood		
1. Same residence in last 5 years	86	79
2. Most friends in same neighborhood	58	48
3. *Visits other neighborhoods*	43	86
4. *Feels parents like neighborhood*	97	53
5. *Likes neighborhood*	100	78
B. Adolescents' attitudes towards school		
6. Likes school	86	16
7. *Grades in school above average or better*	97	68
8. *Study hard*	86	32
9. Friends' grades in school above average or better	92	72
10. *Been in trouble in school*	35	88
11. College plans after high school	95	79
12. *Friends plan to go to college after high school*	81	16
13. Participation in school extracurricular activities		
a. Athletics	78	72
b. Social dances, rallies, etc.	84	83
c. Social clubs	35	28
d. Special interest activities (drama, music)	16	28
e. Student government	16	8
f. Honor groups	35	16
g. Minor offices	51	24

c. *Responses between parents of normals and parents of delinquents.* Responses of the parents of the two samples are shown in Table 2. Generally, the parents of the delinquents answered in the more "unhappy" and "unhealthy" direction. For example, 84 percent of the parents of the delinquents felt that the unhappiness of their own upbringing led them to try to raise their own children differently; they spent less time with their children than did the parents of the normals; they disagreed with

Table 5
The Community and School

Variables	Percent "Yes" Response	
	Parents of Nonprobationers N = 37	Parents of Probationers N = 25
A. Parents' attitudes towards neighborhood		
1. *Like the neighborhood*	97	74
2. *Dislike specific things about neighborhood*	54	88
3. *Get along well with neighbors*	78	37
4. *Son gets along with neighbors*	84	52
5. *Son has had trouble getting along with others*	14	47
B. Perception of son's attitudes towards school		
6. *Son participates in school activities*	89	60
7. *Has time set aside for homework*	100	60
8. *Gets outside encouragement for extracurricular participation*	73	44
9. *Is satisfied with son's extracurricular activities*	73	23
10. Wants son to finish high school or better	92	78
11. *Can son go to college?*	94	53
12. *Does son cut school?*	9	74

their wives on the handling of their sons and on family decisions; and they tried, generally, to invoke sanctions on their children; but they were much less effective than were the parents of the normal sample.

There were areas of agreement between the parents of the two groups; for example, both samples agreed, generally, that their own upbringing was severe (overly strict Issei parents, poverty, lack of opportunity), and both groups were relaxed, generally, about permitting some freedom in drinking, about setting time limits on when to come home, and about keeping tabs on the whereabouts of their sons. The upbringing of girls, however, tended to be more strict than that of boys.

The parents of the normal sample did attempt to control the occupational choice of their children more than did the parents of the delinquent sample.

d. *Differences in ethnic interaction.* The normal adolescent sample was, generally, much more restrictive and ethnocentric than was the delinquent adolescent sample; for example, their clubs and their friends were primarily Japanese; they perceived that the friends of their parents were also mainly Japanese; they disapproved of dating Mexican and Negro girls; they participated in

Japanese activities, observed Japanese customs, and preferred Japanese meals. See Table 3.

Parental attitudes were also in the same direction. The normal parent sample preferred their sons to stay within their own group and disapproved of their sons' dating other Oriental [non-Japanese], Caucasian, Mexican, or Negro girls.

e. *Differences in perception toward the neighborhoods and the schools.* The delinquents were, generally, more dissatisfied with their neighborhoods and their schools (Table 4) than were the normals. They visited other areas; they felt that their parents disliked the neighborhood and they disliked the neighborhood more than did the normals. They also disliked school; their grades were poorer than those of the normals; they studied less; they were in more trouble; and few of their friends planned to go to college.

The parents of the delinquents also had similar perceptions (Table 5). They disliked their neighborhood, got along less well with their neighbors, and felt that their sons also got along less well in the neighborhood. They also perceived their sons as achieving poorly in school, as having less time set for homework, as receiving less encouragement for extracurricular participation (e.g., help from teachers, peers, and community people), and as possessing less of a chance to go to college. They also knew that their sons often cut school without a legitimate excuse.

A final question concerning an analysis of the future significantly differentiated the perceptions of the parents of the delinquent from those of the parents of the normal sample. Only 28 percent of the normals foresaw some major problems in the future for their sons as compared to 84 percent of the parents of the delinquents.

Hypothesis II

The personality of the Japanese delinquent is different from that of the Japanese normal.

The overall results of the California Psychological Inventory indicate that the scores of the Japanese delinquents were similar to the scores of the California delinquents (normative group on the CPI), and the scores of the normals were similar to those of the normative high school population (Ref. 3). (Arrangement was made with a private psychologist to administer the CPI. Each respondent was paid a small sum of money to take the test, and transportation was arranged. Therefore, the number of delinquents rose to thirty; the investigators stopped at thirty for the normals.)

Other interview items measuring self-concept of discrepancies in expectations and definitions of masculinity showed mixed results. The only items that significantly differentiated between the groups were (a) the answers that normals felt they were lucky and the delinquents that they were unlucky and (b) differences in describing self as a success.

Expectations and discrepancies were measured through the items "what I am," "what I wish I would be," and "what others think of me." There was close congruence among all these perceptions.

When asked to describe selves in terms of personality, 67 percent of the delinquents said "average," as compared to only 23 percent of the normals. When asked what it takes to be a man, 31 percent of the normals said "one is just born that way," a response which got *no* backing from the delinquents. This difference might be indicative of the male role in the Japanese system, which requires less validation in terms of "acting out" or proving oneself as compared to the American definition.

Discussion

The overall explanation of the differences between Japanese delinquents and non-delinquents relates to the concept of marginality. By marginality, we refer to both the sociological (e.g., individuals who do not belong to either the Japanese or the American middle-class society) and psychological (e.g., personality deviations).

The delinquents in the present study were the marginal population. They did not identify with their ethnic community; nor were they a part of their families, or their neighborhood, or the schools and other institutions. Their personality and self-perceptions also reflected this marginality. The broken home, high family conflict, minimal intercommunity interaction, and disturbed personality syndrome significantly differentiated the probationer from his non-probationer peer.

Clinical impressions provided further validation for this point of view. Our interviewers often mentioned the apparent "non-Japaneseness" of the delinquent sample — especially in terms of talking (e.g., high use of lower-class argot); of dress (e.g., sloppy, extreme forms of apparel); and of physical appearance (e.g., hair style and general physical impact). Their social participation patterns were typically with non-Japanese, lower-class populations. There is, of course, the question of whether the status of being a probationer has led to this marginality or whether this pattern was apparent before the probation role.

Basically, the marginal person does not identify with the major institutions of his culture and is, therefore, relatively immune to the social control influences of these forces. The problem is of identification, of socialization, of opportunities, and of reinforcement. Interestingly enough, the "marginal" population syndrome is also apparent among Japanese exhibiting other social-problem behavior (Ref. 4).

The important fact about the adaptation of the Japanese to life in the United States has been the ability of the ethnic system to provide a wide enough umbrella to control the development of a large "marginal group." There may be several reasons for this, including the essential congruence between American middle-class and Japanese styles of life. Therefore, initially, when interaction between the two

systems was limited, the Japanese culture played a major socializing role. At the current time, when the American system provides more ample opportunities than formerly, there is relative ease in moving over. It may be that other subcultures, less congruent with the American culture than is the Japanese subculture (e.g., possibly the Mexican-American), create special difficulties because integration into the ethnic or subgroup culture may mean a move away from the middle-class American culture and, therefore, eventual conflict when its members are faced with American institutions such as the public schools.

Although many of the role prescriptions of the Japanese culture are congruent with middle-class America as represented by institutions such as the public schools (e.g., values on hard work, conformity), an explanation of Japanese-American behavior must also stress the importance of its socializing and social control agents as represented by its intact and interdependent family and community. The ethnic school system, the ethnic economic and social welfare system, the ethnic voluntary and social opportunity systems all served as strong shapers and reinforcers of ethnic values (Ref. 5). It is, precisely, the development and maintenance of such a structure that, apparently, differentiate some of the more successful minority groups such as the Jews and the Japanese from the less successful minority groups such as the Mexicans and Negroes.

Marginality and deviant behavior may also arise from both the content and a conflict among norms. Some hypothesized Japanese-American norms that may help to explain low rates of delinquent behavior include their emphasis on conformity, on collective behavior as against individualism, on high dependence on the community and family, on a high tolerance for frustration, on a strong work and achievement orientation, on internalization rather than "acting out," on high savings and delayed gratification, on less conflict over the masculine role, on a high value towards education, and on low expectations for participation in the American system. The Japanese culture also emphasized obligation, duty, and responsibility; provided for equal emphasis on means as well as ends; and, in general, provided for norms that may be associated with low delinquency (Ref. 5).

Other possible explanations for the low rates of Japanese crime and delinquency may range from their immigration-emigration patterns, which have led to a highly selected population (Ref. 5), to a questioning of official criminal data that places undue emphasis on those who are caught.

It should also be emphasized that the "marginal" Japanese have many positive elements. They are less discriminatory (Ref. 3), less conforming, and they may, possibly, exhibit more creativity and uniqueness than the normals.

Summary

The research compared a group of Japanese delinquents and non-delinquents on a number of social-psychological variables. Significant differences between the groups were found on individual, family, neighborhood, and community variables in the predicted direction. The results were interpreted in terms of marginality. The ability of the Japanese culture to provide alternative opportunities for its membership as a control against a large marginal population was hypothesized as a major factor in the extremely low rates of Japanese crime and delinquency in the United States.

References

1. Beach, W. C. *Oriental Crime in California.* Stanford, Calif.: Stanford University Press, 1932.

2. Cressey, D. "Crime." In R. Merton and R. Nisbet (eds.), *Contemporary Social Problems* pp. 21-26. New York: Harcourt, Brace, & World, 1961.

3. Kitano, H. H. L. "Passive Discrimination: The Normal Person." *Journal of Social Psychology* 70, 1966, 23-31.

4. ____ . "Japanese-American Mental Illness." In S. Plog, R. Edgerton, and W. Beckwith (eds.), *Determinants of Mental Illness.* New York: Holt, Rinehart, & Winston, in preparation [1967].

5. ____ . *The Japanese-American.* Englewood Cliffs, N.J.: Prentice-Hall, in preparation [1967].

6. Misaki, H. K. *Delinquency of Japanese in California.* Vol. 1. Stanford University Series in Education-Psychology. Stanford, Calif.: Stanford University Press, 1933.

7. U.S., Department of Justice, Federal Bureau of Investigation. *Uniform Crime Reports for the United States.* Washington, D.C.: U.S. Government Printing Office, 1960.

18. Juvenile Delinquency in San Francisco's Chinese-American Community: 1961-1966

by Kenneth A. Abbott, M.S.W., and
Elizabeth Lee Abbott, M.A.

Juvenile delinquency in the Chinese-American community of San Francisco has exhibited three characteristics of note in the past few years. First, relative to delinquency among other cultural groups and even relative to the history of the Chinese-American community, when allowances are made for population increase, it has remained remarkably low. Second, there have been small but significant increases in the more aggressive offenses such as assault, robbery, and burglary between 1964 and 1966. It is this latter trend which recently may have caused alarm among the citizenry and has provoked public comment. Thus, while on the one hand, in view of the inevitable community turmoil occasioned by a rapidly increasing population and substantial immigration from Asia, the Chinese-American community can be proud of maintaining its relatively low rate of delinquency, on the other hand, there is justifiable reason for concern over even a small increase in delinquency, particularly since this increase is in the direction of more anti-social and/or violent offenses. Finally, offenses by Chinese-Americans tend to differ in kind from those committed by the general population in that they include a higher proportion of theft.

The following pages include several tables that show the distribution of offenses according to the type of offense committed, how it is handled, area of residence, birthplace, and the marital status of parents of the offenders. We have shown how these variables have changed or remained stable over the five-year period under study. The 1966 statistics for this report were gathered in the late summer and fall of 1967. Statistics for the first six months of 1967 were also collected, but are not included in the present report. While they showed a continuation of the same trends, they were not included since: (1) they did not show a dramatic departure from the 1966 figures, and (2) the six-month time period does not allow for seasonal fluctuations. Statistics for previous years were compiled by John Donner.[1] Statistics for 1966 and 1967 were compiled by Elizabeth Abbott. These efforts were made possible through the cooperation of the Youth Guidance Center and San Francisco Police Department.[2]

Because community feeling about delinquency is concerned with the total amount of delinquency, we want first to describe delinquency as a social process and the particular area of this process that our research has focused upon. Figure 1 delineates the formal aspects of the process that occur from the time a delinquent offense is committed until it is finally disposed of.

Obviously, our study cannot include figures on offenses not reported or when offenses have been reported but the delinquent has not been apprehended, although they are significant

Figure 1
Delinquency as a Formal Social Process

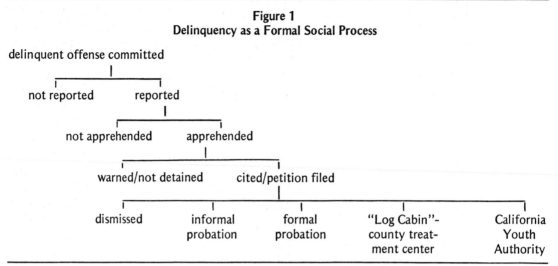

factors in the personal experience of community members. In instances when offenses are not reported to the police, even though they do not become statistics, they do add to community alarm about delinquency. When offenses are reported but the offenders are not apprehended, the facts of the offense may be hazy and, at best, are not verified. Thus, an offense alleged to a juvenile actually may have been committed by an adult. It is, also, quite possible for the account of a single delinquent act to grow and alter as it is passed from person to person, so that, eventually, it can be taken to be the account of two or more separate delinquent acts. There is no precise way of measuring the number of these offenses committed. Our discussions with law enforcement officials as well as with community leaders and workers do not lead us to feel that these unreported and unapprehended offenders constitute a more significant proportion of all offenders in the Chinese-American community than in other communities. As for those apprehended but only warned and not cited, statistics show that, in 1964, out of 225 Chinese-American juveniles who had contacts with the police, 67 were warned but not detained (29.8 percent), while in 1966, out of 253 juvenile contacts, 73 were warned but not detained

(28.9 percent).[3] These figures show that: (1) relative to the increase in the number of Chinese-American teenagers in the total population, the rate actually decreased; and (2) the ratio of warned but not detained remained relatively stable.

Statistics in this report refer to those youth who were apprehended, cited, and adjudicated in Juvenile Court. If they were not dismissed, they were placed on either formal or informal probation. Informal probation, now being less utilized, is an effort to continue a meaningful relationship with the delinquent youth for a few weeks or months without excessive formality. Formal probation is not only more formal but, generally, extends over a longer period of time.

The statistics utilized for this report were collected as part of the Chinese Family Life Study.[4] This is an intensive comparative study of the relationship between family functioning and cultural change with field offices in San Francisco and Taipei. Data have been collected in San Francisco and are now [1968] being collected in Taipei, while San Francisco data are being analyzed concurrently in both Berkeley and Taipei. While this short report reflects the authors' involvement in the Chinese Family Life Study, it cannot be considered a major report of project activities. We hope to publish results in the near future.

The number and change in official and unofficial probation cases of Chinese-Americans is shown below in Table 1.

By far, the greatest change indicated in this chart is that of unofficial cases between 1961 and 1964 when these cases almost tripled (185.7 percent). However, this category then dropped to an increase of only eleven cases between 1964 and 1966. This latter increase of only 9.1 percent can be easily accounted for by a corresponding increase in the Chinese-American population. Official probation cases increased by 7 (22.6 percent) and by eleven (28.9 percent) between 1961, 1964, and 1966. In view of the small totals involved, these increases are serious and cannot be attributed entirely to population increase. In part, this change in the Chinese-American community may be a reflection of the really substantial increase (21.7 percent) between 1965 and 1966 of petitions filed concerning delinquent acts committed by boys of all cultural groups and for all of San Francisco. It is interesting that the number of petitions filed increased by 21.7 percent while, at the same time, general referrals to the Probation Department increased by only 1 percent during the same period.[5] We could speculate that this change indicates a general increase in the seriousness of delinquent acts. That is to say, a larger percentage of

apprehended delinquents had committed offenses that required a petition to be filed than offenses requiring only being admonished. However, it also could mean that delinquents are being dealt with more formally and precisely. In any case, there was an increase in the city-wide rate that could be reflected in a similar increase among Chinese-Americans.

Table 2 relates the cause of the referral to the disposition of the case in 1961, 1964, and 1966. Here we see a clear increase of four robbery cases, twenty assault cases, eleven burglary cases, and thirteen auto theft cases — a total of forty-seven — between 1964 and 1966, although the total number of offenses increased by only twenty-two cases. This seems to be a clear indication that Chinese-American delinquents are committing offenses that are more serious and that this may be a major cause for the community alarm about delinquency. Both the verbal reports of residents of the community and a survey of the police records seem to indicate an increase in purse snatching which is categorized under petty theft but has a quite different emotional impact upon the community than less aggressive stealing. The classification system for Table 2 discounts a number of relatively minor offenses committed by the same delinquents, since only the most serious offense committed by any one person is counted. It seems that it is the quality of offenses that has changed rather than the

Table 1
Change in the Total Number of
Official and Unofficial Probation Cases
of Chinese-Americans in 1961, 1964, 1966

Year	Official		Unofficial		Total	
	N	% increase	N	% increase	N	% increase
1961	31		42		73	
1964	38	22.6	120	185.7	158	116.4
1966	49	28.9	131	9.1	180	13.9

Table 2

Numerical Changes in Delinquency Cases of
Chinese-Americans between 1961, 1964, and 1966
by Reason of Referral and Disposition

Reason for Referral	Total			Change Between			Official Cases			Change Between			Unofficial Cases			Change Between		
	1961	1964	1966	1961 and 1964	1964 and 1966	1961 and 1966	1961	1964	1966	1961 and 1964	1964 and 1966	1961 and 1966	1961	1964	1966	1961 and 1964	1964 and 1966	1961 and 1966
Robbery	0	1	5	+ 1	+ 4	+ 5	0	1	3	+1	+ 2	+ 3	0	0	2	0	+ 2	+ 2
Assault	5	4	24	– 1	+20	+19	4	3	4	–1	+ 1	0	1	1	20	0	+19	+19
Burglary	6	9	20	+ 3	+11	+14	4	7	8	+3	+ 1	+ 4	2	2	12	0	+10	+10
Theft (except auto)	31	76	70	+45	– 6	+39	9	4	8	–5	+ 4	– 2	22	72	62	+50	–10	+40
Auto theft	7	10	23	+ 3	+13	+16	7	9	14	+2	+ 5	+ 7	0	1	9	+ 1	+ 8	+ 9
Narcotics	0	0	1	0	0	– 1	0	0	0	0	0	0	0	0	1	0	+ 1	+ 1
Sex offenses	0	0	0	0	0	0	0	0	0	0	0	0	0	0	0	0	0	0
Other law violations	9	32	11	+23	–21	+ 2	1	7	3	+6	– 4	+ 2	8	25	8	+17	–17	0
Delinquent tendencies	15	26	26	+11	0	+11	6	7	9	+1	+ 2	+ 3	9	19	17	+10	– 2	+ 8
Total	73*	158*	180	+85	+22	+107	31	38	49	+7	+11	+18	42	120	131	+78	+11	+89

* Excludes one case in 1961 and two in 1964 for which intake disposition could not be determined.

quantity. City-wide figures for 1964 and 1966 also show a marked increase in auto theft (389-438) and burglary (244-355). However, assault cases decreased from 152 to 145, and robbery cases increased only from 63 to 67.[6] This means that Chinese-Americans not only committed an increased number of the more aggressive offenses of assault and burglary compared to their previous record, but they made this increase while the rest of the youth community of San Francisco was marking time.

There has been considerable speculation in the Chinese-American community about the percentages of delinquent offenses committed by American-born or foreign-born Chinese-Americans. This discussion has often been related to residence because of the general belief that more foreign-born live in or close to Chinatown. Analysis of this question is hindered by the absence of accurate, up-to-date census figures that delineate San Francisco's Chinese-American population by birth and current residence. The experience of the Chinese Family Life Study has established that both foreign-born and American-born youth live in all parts of the city, but that the percentages cannot be precisely defined. The fact is, San Francisco's Chinese-American population figures themselves can only be estimated. It is much more difficult to determine precisely where people reside. However, we believe this total population to be in excess of the official estimate of 42,900 for 1966.

Table 3 reflects probable population trends of Chinese-Americans. The percentage of all offenses committed by the foreign-born Chinese-Americans grew from 20 percent in 1961 to 28 percent in 1966 — an increase that is, quite likely, much less than the corresponding increase of foreign-born Chinese-Americans in the total population. Offenses committed by youth living in central Chinatown decreased from 27.1 percent in 1961 to 18.8 percent in 1964, reflecting the decrease in population in that area due to increased commercialization, conformity to apartment house code regulations, and increased opportunity to move away from Chinatown. This decrease in delinquent offenses by youth living in the central Chinatown area was followed by an increase of 4 percent between 1964 and 1966, probably a result of the impact of high immigration. This is verified by the doubling of delinquent offenses committed by the foreign-born living in central Chinatown. The influx of Chinese-Americans into North Beach and out of the Northeast District is documented by the dramatic increase (in quantity) between 1961 and 1964 of offenses in these two areas. While the percentage of all offenses committed by Chinese-American youth in these areas increased between 1961 and 1964, it either decreased or remained nearly the same between 1964 and 1966, again, probably, in relationship to general population distribution. In the first period (1961-64), the Chinese-American population surged out of the Northeast District; in the second (1964-66), the new immigrants flowed into Chinatown and North Beach.

In general, this analysis seems to reveal an equal susceptibility to juvenile delinquency by native- and foreign-born youth. The differences in figures represent the respective proportions of the population and change in these proportions. Furthermore, residence seems to have little relationship to the commission of offenses. The rate of offenses committed is in proportion to the number of Chinese-Americans living in an area.

Table 4 relates "reason for referral" to place of birth of the delinquent. The percentages at the bottom of this table refer not only to the percentage of total offenses committed, but also to the percentage of offenders, since we have related only *one* offense to one offender in this study. The remaining percentages are proportions of the total number of offenses in each category committed by either native-born or foreign-born Chinese-Americans. In all three years represented in the table, the majority of offenses are thefts (not including auto theft); and their respective proportions are directly

Table 3
Numerical and Percentage Distribution
of Delinquency Cases of Chinese-Americans
by Area of Residence and Birthplace — 1961, 1964, and 1966

Areas of Residence	Birthplace											
	1961				1964				1966			
	U.S. Born	For. Born	Total		U.S. Born	For. Born	Total		U.S. Born	For. Born	Total	
			N	% of total			N	% of total			N	% of total
North Beach	8	3	11	15.7	27	5	32	20.0	28	8	36	20.0
West of Chinatown	11	1	12	17.1	25	6	31	19.4	32	7	39	21.7
Chinatown	14	5	19	27.1	23	7	30	18.8	26	15	41	22.8
East and South of Chinatown	2	1	3	4.3	2	0	2	1.2	1	1	2	1.0
Outside of Northeast District	21	4	25	35.7	47	18	65	40.6	36	15	51	28.3
Out of town									6	5	11	6.1
Total N	56	14	70*	100.0	124	36	160	100.0	129	51	180	100.0
% of each year's total	80.0	20.0	100.0		77.5	22.5	100.0		72.0	28.0	100.0	

* Excludes 4 cases for which place of birth could not be determined.

Table 4
Numerical and Percentage Distribution
of Chinese-American Delinquency Cases
by Birthplace and Reason for Referral — 1961, 1964, 1966

Reason for Referral	1961					1964					1966				
	U.S. Born	% of total	For. Born	% of total	Total	U.S. Born	% of total	For. Born	% of total	Total	U.S. Born	% of total	For. Born	% of total	Total
Robbery	0	—	0	—	0	1	0.8	0	—	1	1	0.8	4	8.0	5
Assault	4	7.1	1	7.1	5	4	3.3	0	—	4	18	13.8	6	12.0	24
Burglary	6	10.7	0	—	6	7	5.7	2	5.7	9	12	9.2	7	14.0	19
Theft (except auto)	25	44.6	6	42.9	31	58	47.5	18	50.0	76	53	40.8	19	38.0	72
Auto theft	5	8.9	2	14.3	7	6	4.9	4	11.1	10	19	14.6	4	8.0	23
Other law violations	8	14.3	1	7.1	9	28	23.0	5	13.9	33	10	7.7	3	6.0	13
Delinquent tendencies	8	14.3	4	28.6	12	18	14.8	7	19.4	25	17	13.1	7	14.0	24
Total	56	100.0	14	100.0	70*	122	100.0	36	100.0	158*	130	100.0	50	100.0	180

* Excludes three cases in 1961 and two in 1964 for which birthplace could not be determined, as well as one case in 1961 and two in 1964 for which intake disposition could not be determined.

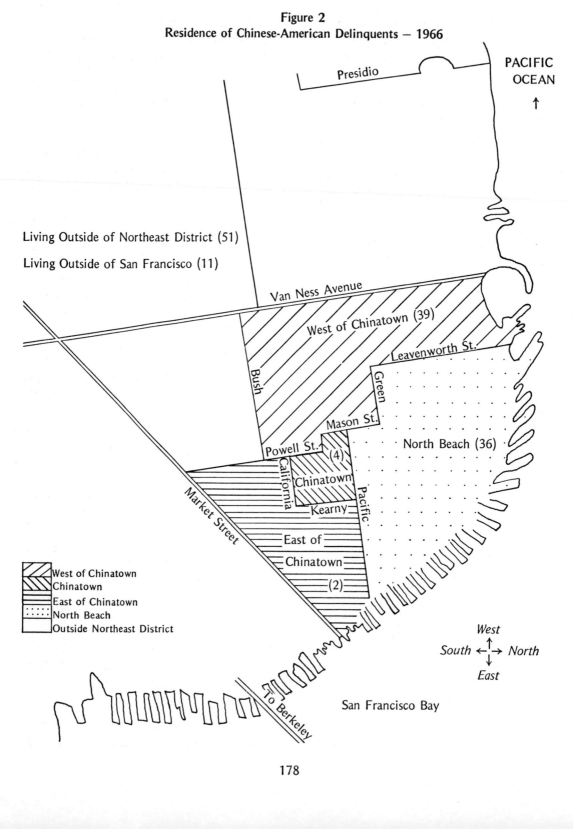

Figure 2
Residence of Chinese-American Delinquents — 1966

related to the ratio of foreign-born to native-born. Higher proportions of robbery, assault, and burglary all shift from one group to the other during the five years under study. Although the numbers are too small and the differences are too little for the results to be conclusive, the native-born have a slight tendency towards assault, theft, and auto theft, and the foreign-born towards robbery and burglary.

The above analysis establishes that there seem to be no dramatic differences between native-born and foreign-born that can be charged to cultural differences or to the Americanization process. However, there is a higher proportion of theft (except auto theft) among offenses committed by all Chinese-Americans than is true of the general delinquent population of San Francisco (15 percent of initial petitions on delinquent boys in San Francisco in 1966),[7] while their rate of auto theft is only half that of the general rate.

The final table shows the distribution of parental marital status by nativity for 1966.

There are no significant differences between native-born and foreign-born. However, the proportion of families with the parents living together is substantially higher for Chinese-American delinquents as a whole than it is for the general San Francisco population (54 percent of boys and 42 percent of girls who were living in two-parent homes at the time of initial court action in 1966).[8] It also appears that marital status of parents has little to do with the incidence of delinquency in this sample.

Our analysis has revealed that place of birth and place of residence within San Francisco of Chinese-American youth have little effect upon delinquency rates. At the same time, the statistics reported above have tended to establish three trends. The first is that major categories of delinquency among Chinese-Americans vary from those in the general community in that they have a higher proportion of theft and a smaller percentage of auto theft. The second is that delinquency among Chinese-Americans, although relatively low, is definitely increasing,

Table 5
Numerical and Percentage Distribution
of Delinquency Cases of Chinese-Americans
by Marital Status of Parents and Birthplace — 1966

| Marital Status of Parents | 1966 | | | | | |
| | U. S. Born | | Foreign Born | | Total | |
	N	%	N	%	N	%
Unmarried	—	—	—	—	—	—
Married, living together	101	78.7	37	72.5	138	76.7
Marriage intact, not living together	—	—	3	5.9	3	1.7
Separated	2	1.6	2	3.9	4	2.2
Divorced	11	8.7	1	2.0	12	6.7
Father or mother dead	15	11.8	7	13.7	22	12.2
Both parents dead	—	—	1	2.0	1	6
Unknown	—	—	—	—	—	—
Total	127	100.0	51	100.0	180	100.0

and, perhaps to a lesser degree, it is increasing in its rate. The third is that this increase is, primarily, in offenses of a more aggressive, anti-social nature.

We believe it is this third trend — this marked shift, shared by American-born and foreign-born alike, towards more aggressive offenses — as well as the quantitative increase (in numbers, not in the rate) that is responsible for the justifiable community concern about delinquency increase. Early impressions derived from our Chinese Family Life Study are in accordance with the preceding statistical analysis. Delinquency causation seems to us to be related primarily to family dynamics and psychological factors that are not determined by place of birth or by the residence and marital status of parents. These factors which pertain to the relationships between family members and to their psychosocial development will be analyzed in detail in our future reports.

Chapter Notes

1. John Donner, "Juvenile Delinquency and Dependency: A Statistical Study," *The Chinese Family in San Francisco*. A Master's in Social Welfare group thesis under the direction of George A. DeVos and Kenneth A. Abbott, University of California, Berkeley, 1966.

2. Appreciation is expressed to Mr. Elmer Gaechen, Chief Probation Officer, and to Mrs. Ann Billyard, Statistician of the Youth Guidance Center, and to Chief Thomas Cahill and Lt. Oesterloh of the San Francisco Police Department.

3. These figures were taken from Juvenile Court and police files. Some of the categories of "warned but not detained" contacts between police and youth relate to curfew (22), vehicle offenses (7), possible use of or sale of firecrackers (5), suspicion of theft or burglary (5), motorcycle offenses (4), trespassing (4), loitering, etc.

4. The Chinese Family Life Study is funded by the Institute of International Studies at the University of California (Berkeley). Its principal investigators are Dr. George DeVos of the Anthropology Department and Dr. Wolfram Eberhard of the Sociology Department. Mr. Abbott is the Project Head and Mrs. Abbott is the Fieldwork Coordinator.

5. San Francisco Juvenile Court Annual Report — 1966, Table 18.

6. San Francisco Juvenile Court Annual Report — 1966, Table 8.

7. San Francisco Juvenile Court Annual Report — 1966, Chart 6.

8. San Francisco Juvenile Court Annual Report — 1966, Table 12.

19. Japanese-American Mental Illness

by Harry H. L. Kitano

In earlier days, the phrase "immigrants from Asia" might have called to mind seething masses, cheap labor, and the inevitably inscrutable faces. Hopefully, the same phrase today is related to a more favorable, if not more realistic, image. We say hopefully because the Chinese and Japanese still remain relatively faceless and nameless populations, even to social scientists, and, as a consequence, they are often viewed as exceptions to generalizations of human behavior. For example, in a study just completed on Japanese crime and delinquency in the United States (Kitano, 1962),[1] reactions of professionals included such phrases as "Do they have any delinquency at all?" and "But how relevant are the findings to other groups?"

Reasons for these views are not too hard to find. The stereotype of an exotic culture and the mysterious East is difficult to discard when systematic knowledge about the Japanese is often lacking and when scientific data are scarce. Further, scholars of Japanese ancestry have been hesitant to pursue studies of their own ethnic group, and Japanese residential concentration in the western part of the United States has excluded them from on-going studies of European immigrants. But, perhaps most important, the Japanese do appear to be exceptions, especially to generalizations concerning "problem minorities." Poverty, discrimination, life in the ghetto, and non-white skin color are usually associated with such problem groups; and minorities often live up to this expectation by responding with high rates of crime, delinquency, and mental illness. It is believed, generally, that the Japanese (and, to a similar extent, the Chinese),[2] although saddled with handicaps such as discrimination and life in the ghetto, have somehow refused to respond to their negative environment with high rates of delinquency and mental illness. Therefore, the point of view that the Japanese are somehow different and perhaps not influenced in expected ways by environmental conditions is often reinforced.

Peculiarly, there has been little scientific interest in the Japanese-Americans until recently. As early as 1933, Hayner described the unique behavior of the Japanese. In studying crime in the Puget Sound area, Hayner noticed the high rates of crime in the ghetto area for all groups except for the Japanese, who had low rates. Up to the present time, this has remained an interesting, but unexplored, finding; and Petersen, in a current issue of the *New York Times* (January 6, 1966), has said:

> The Japanese-Americans, in short, ought to be a central focus of social studies. Their experience converts our best sociological generalizations into partial truths at best; this is a laboratory case of an exception to test a rule. Conceivably, in such a more intensive analysis, we might find a means of isolating some of the elements of this remarkable culture and

grafting it onto plants that manifestly need the pride, the persistence, and the success of our model minority.

Are the Japanese really so exceptional? An earlier study by the writer (Kitano, in progress [1969]) illustrates the extremely low rates of official crime and delinquency in the Japanese group. But the reasons behind the behavior do not appear to be so mysterious. A group with a strong family system, living in a cohesive community, with high values on achievement and conformity, and with overall styles of life congruent with the American middle class should be characterized by low rates of official crime and delinquency.

What do we know about Japanese-American mental illness? How prevalent is *ki-chi-gai* ("crazy") behavior in this population? Are there empirical hypotheses that may be explored to understand mentally ill behavior? The primary purpose of this chapter is to attempt to answer these questions.

Epidemiology

The true incidence of mental illness and mental health in any population is probably impossible to assess except in the most general manner. All mental health statistics have one thing in common — they represent data that are related to the "funneling effect." The funneling effect, as described by Cressey (1961) in criminological research, holds that the accuracy of criminal statistics is dependent upon distance from the bottom of the funnel. Therefore, in terms of official statistics, crimes known to the police are a more accurate index of incidence than statistics of those arrested. In turn, the arrest rate is a more efficient index than the conviction rate, which, in turn, is more accurate than imprisonment rates.

Although there are many differences between statistics on mental illness and crime, general rates of mental illness also can be related to the funneling effect. Therefore, a more accurate index of the true rates of mental illness can be determined from trained residents of a community who have intimate knowledge of its inhabitants, rather than from a random sample of a population drawn for diagnostic purposes. The random sample, in turn, probably is more accurate than statistics of those persons coming to a mental health facility; the diagnosis at a clinic is more relevant than statistics limited to persons accepted for treatment; and a consideration of the population under treatment is more efficient than an analysis of those patients residing in a mental hospital. There are interrelationships among the various levels, but the one most often used is the least efficient — the statistics on hospitalization. The error is similar to estimating the size of an iceberg by looking at the exposed portion.

The Bottom of the Iceberg—
The Top of the Funnel

It is difficult to hide in a Japanese community, even in a sprawling area such as Los Angeles. That is, it is difficult to hide from other Japanese; and the number of residents renders the ethnic interaction comparable to life in a small hamlet in Vermont. Common friends, common institutions, common interests, and common experiences provide fertile ground for communication and knowledge about each other. A further experience, probably unique among all ethnic groups, was the wartime evacuation and relocation which forced the majority of Japanese to live together under rather intimate conditions. Therefore, persons who have grown up in the Japanese community are in a strategic position to provide an assessment of mental health and mental illness.

Fortunately, there are a number of Japanese-American professionals who have grown up in the ethnic community and have acquired training in the mental health professions. We asked sixteen of them (two Ph.D. psychologists, four psychiatrists, and ten M.S.W. social workers) to complete a short check list concerning use and need of therapeutic resources by the Japanese in the United States. We followed up the check list with short interviews with selected respondents.

The Japanese have a convenient way of describing generations. The term Issei means first generation and refers to the immigrants from Japan, most of them arriving in the United States between 1900 and 1924. In general, Japanese currently over the age of sixty are probably Issei. The term Nisei means second generation and refers to the American-born children of the Issei immigrant. Their current estimated age range is thirty to sixty; their modal age lies in the forty to forty-five category. The term Sansei means third generation and refers to the American-born children of Nisei parents. They constitute the bulk of the adolescent and school-age population.

Mail responses to the check list were excellent. Of the sixteen contacts, fifteen responded within one week and are included in the coding. There was unanimous agreement (see Table 1) among the professionals that all three Japanese generations have seldom used the therapeutic resources of the larger community, including hospitalization. Most agreed that only the Issei used ethnic community services (that is, the social services provided by the Japanese community) at all.

Sharpest disagreement arose on Item 4, which refers to the need for therapy and mental health by Japanese generations. Sixty percent of the respondents indicated that all three of the Japanese generations were in need of services; the remaining proportion felt that the general mental health of the Japanese was quite good. There is, of course, a professional bias among mental health workers concerning the need for services for almost everybody. Nevertheless, it is interesting to note the discrepancy between "need" and "use" of services by the entire Japanese population.

Follow-up interviews were held with the professionals to gain more information about their perceptions of overall Japanese mental health. Most of them could recall very few signs of public "mentally ill behavior," either as they were growing up (including life in the wartime evacuation camps) or among their present ethnic acquaintances. However, all agreed upon the difficulty of assessing mental illness among a group where public "acting-out" behavior was kept under relatively formalized controls, and where the preferred modes of behavior encouraged formalism, politeness, and withdrawal.

However, the professionals who indicated a

		Have Used Therapeutic Resources of the Community	Have Used Therapeutic Resources of Ethnic Community	Have Needed but Not Used Therapeutic Resources
Table 1 Perceptions of Japanese Professionals Regarding Three Generations of Japanese and Mental Health				
Generation	Have Required Hospitalization			
Issei	No	No	A little	Yes
Nisei	No	No	No	Yes
Sansei	No	No	No	Yes
N = 15				

"need for therapy" among the Japanese referred, primarily, to current indications of conflict. The majority agreed that husband-wife roles and parent-child relationships were powerful sources of tension, but that the Japanese would not use professional services. As one psychiatrist commented:

> Every time I give a public lecture (usually sponsored by a church or service club) on family problems, sexual information, or child rearing, the place is packed, and they ask all kinds of questions. Some of the questions are remarkably naïve and others appear to indicate quite a bit of conflict, but I'm sure the questioners will never go for professional advice.

Others corroborate these perceptions — high interest and possible signs of problems regarding parent-child relationships, high attendance at public lectures — but report virtually no follow-up for further professional help.

The Middle View

Statistics from social agencies, often thought of as providing preventive and therapeutic services, constitute our second-level view. These agencies (family service, child guidance clinics) can be divided into two types — those representing the minority group (the ethnic agency) and those serving the larger community.

The number of Japanese using the professional services of the larger community is extremely small. We attempted to obtain a sample of Japanese using the Family Service Agency and Child Guidance Clinic in Los Angeles for a proposed study (Archer, Staugas, & Hoffman, 1962) and found that, even though more than 80,000 Japanese were eligible, theoretically, for these services, less than five cases could be counted in any single year. The writer worked for two years in a Child Guidance Clinic which served the San Francisco Public Schools, and, during this period, there were no referred cases involving children of Japanese ancestry. Therefore, the perceptions of Japanese professionals concerning the nonuse of larger community services by the ethnic group is strongly supported.

Closer to true incidence, however, are data gathered from agencies serving the Japanese community. For many Japanese, especially for those who are less acculturated, the facilities of the ethnic community are more acceptable resources. A family service agency, developed by the Japanese community in 1962, served an average of thirty active counseling cases per month during its more than two years of existence (Archer et al., 1962).

The most relevant source for analyzing mental health in the Japanese community on the agency level is the social service provided by the Japanese Chamber of Commerce of Los Angeles. An analysis of that caseload between the years 1962 and 1964 is presented in Table 2. Of the 604 cases, approximately 20 percent were classified "mentally ill." The majority of these cases were referred to county and state facilities.

Further analysis of the caseload shows an older male Issei population living on minimal income from lower status occupations and living in relatively isolated positions.

The most common diagnosis for mental illness was schizophrenia, and a typical case might be illustrated by the following story. Mr. H., owner of a small hotel in the "Little Tokyo" area of Los Angeles, begins to notice gradual deterioration of Mr. Watanabe (fictitious name). Mr. Watanabe had moved into the hotel with two other bachelor Issei — although information was difficult to obtain, all three had come from the same *ken* ("state") and had worked as fruit pickers the majority of their lives. Now they were too old to continue so they came to Los Angeles for retirement. The low rates at the hotel (average rent, $45 a month) and a communal kitchen helped to stretch the dollar. The nearby Japanese community and the recreation rooms at the Chamber of Commerce Building (*go, shogi, hana* — all Japanese games) filled up some space; but lack of money precluded gambling, once a favorite pastime. Savings were meager.

Table 2
Description of Caseload of Social Welfare Department,
Japanese Chamber of Commerce,
Los Angeles, 1962-1964

A. Generation	Percent[a]	B. Sex	Percent
Issei	83	Male	83
Nisei	7	Female	17
Sansei	10		
		D. Primary source of income	
C. Age		Public assistance	
55 or over	85	Social Security	85
25-54	9	Nonpublic assistance	15
Under 24	5		
E. Primary occupations		F. Marital status	
Farm laborer	42	Widower-widow	36
Cook	15	Single, never married	30
Housewife	15	Married couple	15
Gardener	10	Divorced, never legally	
Janitor	15	married	15
Unknown	2	Under-age	5

[a] $N = 604$. Rounding errors lead to totals of less than 100 percent in some instances.

With the death of his two friends last year, Mr. Watanabe withdrew further and further from the outside world. He soon failed to get up from bed — problems of going to the bathroom, of getting up to eat, and of cleanliness mounted. Eventually, Mr. H. contacted the Japanese social worker, who, in turn, brought Mr. Watanabe to the County Hospital. The diagnosis was schizophrenia, and Mr. Watanabe was sent to a state hospital. There were no known relatives here in the United States.

The same story, with minor variations, describes much of the "mentally ill" caseload. One variation includes an elderly widowed Issei living with his married children; high conflict and lack of communication finally lead to his moving out to a cheap hotel. Eventually, he experiences the loneliness, the absence of friends, the feeling that "no one cares," and similar symptoms (as had Mr. Watanabe); and, eventually, he is referred to the Japanese social worker.

Common behaviors indicating "mental illness" include "hearing voices" (of dead friends, in Japanese), emotional weeping, heightened irritability, loss of toilet control, and withdrawal.

The Top of the Iceberg —
The Bottom of the Funnel

The data on hospitalization represent the least complete reflection of incidence, but they present certain advantages. Hospitalization data are readily available and are quantifiable so

Table 3
Admissions of Patients by Ethnic Groups –
California State Hospitals for the Mentally Ill
1960-1965[a]

Year	Group (rates per 100,000[b])					
	Japanese	Caucasian	Mexican-American	Indian	Chinese	Negro
1960	40	150	40	150	70	190
1961	50	160	20	90	80	200
1962	50	170	30	140	90	210
1963	50	170	30	130	80	240
1964	60	170	40	170	90	250
1965	60	180	40	180	90	280

[a] Source: Adapted from *California State Department of Mental Hygiene*, Bureau of Biostatistics.

[b] Population base rates for each ethnic group are computed on 1960 population, United States Bureau of Census. Therefore, rates for the last several years are probably much lower for all groups.

that, instead of adjectives, precise ratios such as rates per 100,000 can be computed. Therefore, a comparison of hospitalization rates among Japanese in California, Hawaii, and Japan can be attempted, although such cross-cultural comparisons are quite deceptive. The problems of definition, diagnosis, availability of and access to the hospitals, and treatment objectives provide systematic differences which may invalidate all such comparisons.

The data on hospitalization are presented in terms of *admissions* and *hospitalization*. All statistics are computed in terms of rates per 100,000. Population figures by ethnic group are accurate for census years (for example, 1950, 1960); for in-between years, the closest census-year figure is used as the denominator. Therefore, we are dealing with gross statistics and gross estimates, which will preclude the use of more sophisticated statistical techniques.

California State Department of Mental Hygiene admission rates for various groups are shown in Table 3. Longitudinal comparisons within groups remain remarkably consistent, especially if we take population increases into account. Perhaps the only group with rising rates of admissions is the Negro (190 in 1960, 280 in 1965), although even this increase may be related to population changes.

The more interesting comparisons are between groups. The group with the lowest rate of mental hospital admissions is the Mexican-American, followed very closely by the Japanese. Standing somewhere in the middle are the Chinese admission rates, followed by a cluster of relatively high rates for the Indian, Caucasian, and Negro.

Admission rate comparisons among the Japanese, Chinese, and Caucasians in Hawaii are shown in Table 4. In general, admission rates are roughly similar for the Japanese in California and Hawaii, somewhat the same for the Chinese, and much lower for the Caucasians in Hawaii when compared to California.

Hospitalization. Although rates of hospitalization provide the least effective

	Table 4		
	Admissions, Hawaii State Hospital for Mentally Ill		
	by Selected Ethnic Group, 1955 and 1960[a]		
	Group (rates per 100,000)		
Year	*Japanese*	*Chinese*	*Caucasian*
1954-1955	90	81	141
1959-1960	88	63	99

[a] Source: Adapted from *Hawaii State Hospital Psychology Report*, Volume III, December 1964, Appendix 2.

method of measuring epidemiology, more complete data are usually available on hospital populations. For example, comparisons could be made on hospitalization rates among six prefectures in Japan (see Table 5), among six ethnic groups in California, covering a span of 14 years (see Table 6), and among four ethnic groups, using an age breakdown (see Table 7).

The six Japanese prefectures were chosen

Table 5
Rates of Hospitalization for Mental Illness
for Six Prefectures in Japan and Total, 1961[a]

Prefecture	Hospitalization Rate (per 100,000[b])
Hiroshima	117
Wakayama	122
Kumamoto	125
Fukuoka	153
Yamaguchi	115
Kagoshima	156
All Japan	130

[a] Source: Adapted from Masaaki Kato, *Annual Report on Mental Health*, 1962, National Institute of Mental Health, Japan, p. 12.

[b] Rates computed through population in prefecture.

because they most closely represent the *ken* background of the Japanese populations in the United States (exception: a large number of Japanese immigrants in Hawaii are from Okinawa). There is relative uniformity in hospitalization rates among the prefectures in Japan and the overall Japanese totals.

Hospitalization rates among various ethnic groups in California for 1950, 1960, and 1964 (Table 6) provide some interesting comparisons. The trend away from hospitalization in California mental institutions is seen in that all 1964 rates are lower than those for 1950. The Chinese hospitalization rates are the highest of all groups; the Mexican figures present a relatively low hospitalized population. However, the proportionate drop in hospitalization rates is very low for the Japanese and may indicate few alternative resources for a Japanese, once he gets to the stage of hospital referral.

Hospitalization rates of the Japanese in California are slightly higher than in Japan (Table 5), but these data are difficult to interpret.

Hospitalization rates computed on the basis of age distribution (Table 7) provide a firm generalization that the most vulnerable age for all population groups is the fifty-five-or-over age categories. The year chosen for comparison was 1962 (because of the availability of data); therefore, there is a slight discrepancy between Tables 6 and 7. There appear to be many more

Table 6
California Hospital Residents by Ethnic Group
for the Mentally Ill for Selected Years[a]

	Group (rates per 100,000[b])					
Year	Japanese	Caucasian	Mexican-American	Indian	Chinese	Negro
1950	216	300	188	356	535	364
1960	225	242	83	187	376	299
1964	198	213	74	174	361	296

[a] Source: Adapted from *California State Department of Mental Hygiene,* Bureau of Biostatistics.

[b] Rate for 1964 based on 1960 population.

Table 7
California Hospital Residents
by Age-Ethnic Group
for the Mentally Ill, 1962[a]

	Ages (rates per 100,000[b])		
Ethnic Group	12–24	25–54	55 Years or Over
White	60	214[c]	649
Negro	47	142	222
Chinese	34	126	285
Japanese	12	80	218

[a] Source: Adapted from *Statistical Report of the Department of Mental Hygiene,* State of California, June 30, 1962, Table 12, p. 28.

[b] Population base rates for age-sex from estimates of population on 1960 U.S. Census.

[c] Ratios were computed and are to be read as follows: 12,188 Whites of ages 25-54 in hospitals; estimated 5,698,000 Whites of ages 25-54 in California; rate of 214 per 100,000 of Whites, ages 25-54 in hospitals.

White hospitalized residents of fifty-five years or older than for the Chinese, the Negro, and the Japanese.

In general, the data support a firm generalization that the Japanese contribute a very small proportion to the hospitalized, mentally ill population. However, it also appears that, once he is hospitalized, he remains there longer. A hypothesis for further exploration includes possible differences in the severity of the illness for the Japanese, with the possibility that, since their rates are so low, only the most severely disturbed end up at the hospital, and, once there, they tend to remain.

Classification of Mental Illness

We have deliberately ignored some of the problems of definition, classification, and accessibility of mental health facilities in presenting the previous data. Terms such as mental health, mental illness, need of therapy, use of a social agency, admissions, and hospitalization are not consistent. Therefore, all generalizations are made with these limitations in mind.

An even more unreliable area is that of classification or diagnosis. What are some of the labels attached to Japanese, once they arrive at diagnostic centers? The training of the professional, his techniques, his tools, and his insight determine to a large extent the "label" attached to the patient. Generally, the most common diagnostic category for hospitalized Japanese populations, whether in California, Hawaii, or Japan, was schizophrenia.

Enright and Jaeckle (1961) compared symptoms between Japanese and Filipino mental patients in Hawaii. The hospitalized Filipino tended to express feelings freely and directly, with frequent motor responses, while the Japanese mental patient tended to be more inhibited and restrained, with ideational responses more frequent.

The other main difference was in the direction of behavior. The Filipino behaved outwardly, or alloplastically, so that attempts to resolve conflicts were through environmental manipulation and the expectation of changing the world. Conversely, the Japanese behaved inwardly, or autoplastically, so that attempts to resolve conflicts were through internalization or modification of one's own behavior, rather than through changing external conditions.

A preliminary analysis of hospitalized Japanese, as well as interviews with our Japanese professionals, corroborates the low degree of "acting-out" behavior among the Japanese mentally ill (as well as in the general ethnic population) and the high degree of withdrawal behavior.

1. At least as measured by official statistics, mental illness is not a major problem for the Japanese when compared to other groups.
2. The most vulnerable group for mental illness in the Japanese population is the single, old, lower-class male.
3. The rates of hospitalization, although subject to the most systematic biases, appear remarkably similar for the Japanese in Japan and in the United States.
4. The most common illness is schizophrenia, with withdrawal symptoms most common.

Explanations: Nontheoretical and Theoretical

Nontheoretical hypotheses refer to explanations for Japanese-American mental illness that deal with technical factors such as data gathering, definitions, and research design. Therefore, possible explanations of mental illness may be through biased statistics, distortions in recording, unreliable classifications, and other systematic "field" errors. All studies of "social problems" that are based in community settings (as opposed to the laboratory) are open to such criticisms, and the reliability and validity of our data can also be questioned.[3]

Our overall generalization that the Japanese are a *low group* in terms of official rates of mental illness appears to have validity because (1) there is consistency of data on all levels of the "funnel," (2) the data are consistent with independent observations about the Japanese, and (3) the data fit logically with what we know about the Japanese. A replication of our study, undoubtedly, will yield the same results.

With the limitations of the data in mind, we turned to two broad, theoretical hypotheses as possible explanations for the low rates of Japanese-American mental illness. The first hypothesis compares the Japanese with other ethnic groups in terms of overall stress. It is what we would term a "compare the scars" technique, which assumes that those groups with the highest rates of mental illness are those who have faced the highest degree of "stress." Although this hypothesis is not a particularly fruitful one from our point of view, it does provide an opportunity to present a short background of the difficulties faced by this immigrant group to the United States.

Past Attitudes Toward the Japanese

Several quotations from leading Californians provide a flavor of the anti-Japanese campaigns which occurred frequently in the early half of the century. For example, McClatchy (1921), publisher of the *Sacramento Bee*, in discussing the Japanese, wrote:

The Japanese cannot, may not, and will not provide desirable material for our citizenship. 1. The Japanese cannot assimilate and make good citizens because of their racial characteristics, heredity, and religion. 2. The Japanese may not assimilate and make good citizens because their government claims all Japanese, no matter where born, as its citizens. 3. The Japanese will not assimilate and make good citizens. In the mass, when opportunity [is] offered, and, even when born here, they have shown no disposition to do so.... There can be no effective assimilation of Japanese without intermarriage. It is, perhaps, not desirable for the good of either race that there should be intermarriage between Whites and Japanese.... They cannot be transmuted into good American citizens.

Or, in the words of Marshall De Motte (1921), chairman of the State Board of Control of California:

It is utterly unthinkable that America or an American state should be other than White. Kipling did not say "East is East" of the United States, but, if the star number 31 in Old Glory, California's star, [should become] yellow, West may become East. California has been loyal at all times to a flag that has honored her with a star of her own, so Californians, to a citizen, will see that the star of her glory shall not grow dim [nor] yellow.

And, finally, a citation from the Honorable James D. Phelan (1921), United States Senator from California:

Immigration and naturalization are domestic questions, and no people can come to the United States except upon our own terms. We must preserve the soil for the Caucasian race. The Japanese, by crowding out our population, produce disorder and Bolshevism among our own people, who properly look to our government to protect them against this destructive competition. California, by acting in time, before the evil becomes even greater, expects to prevent conflict.... We are willing to receive diplomats, scholars, and travelers from Japan on terms of equality, but we do not want her

laborers. We admire their industry and cleverness, but, for that very reason, being a masterful people, they are more dangerous. They are not content to work for wages as do the Chinese, who are excluded, but are always seeking control of the farm and of the crop....

The anti-Japanese feeling, which was most heavy in California, led to boycotts of Japanese-owned business, to anti-miscegenation laws, and to special discriminatory immigration and naturalization legislation. There was school segregation, restrictions on land ownership, and, generally, limited opportunity in the economic, political, and social spheres of the larger society. The "yellow peril" reached its peak with the 1942 wartime evacuation of all persons of Japanese ancestry, whether citizens or not, from the West Coast. If stress in the form of discrimination and limited opportunities is related in a simple, linear fashion to mental illness, we would expect to find large numbers of Japanese in mental institutions. It is obvious that a "compare the scars" approach is not an adequate explanation.

The second and more fruitful hypothesis conceptualizes stress in a more relative manner, so that a mere comparison of hardships faced by immigrant and ethnic groups is an insufficient explanation of behavior. From this perspective, the ability of an ethnic group to absorb stress and to provide alternative opportunities are important factors. Therefore, what may be considered heavy stress for one group might be handled without undue difficulty by another.

The ethnic community and family — their structure, their functions, their values, and their "culture" — are presented as the critical variables in understanding Japanese behavior. The strength of the culture was severely tested during the wartime evacuation of World War II, and the ability of the Japanese to rebound from this period may be cited as one example of the strength of the group.

The following areas will be analyzed: the

ethnic community and family, their definitions and attitudes toward mental illness, and the possible relationship of mental illness to other behavior.

Community Organization

There are several generalizations concerning the Japanese community that are related to conformity and mental illness. In the most general sense, the Japanese community provides an "alternative, legitimate opportunity structure"; that is, for most Japanese, an opportunity to satisfy economic, social, psychological, and political needs within the ethnic community, when such opportunities are restricted in the larger society. Churches; mutual aid societies; small business firms; newspaper and radio networks; recreational, educational, vocational, social, health, and welfare organizations — all are developed and maintained by the Japanese community (Miyamoto, 1939). The existence of these pluralistic structures (especially during the early days, when interaction with the American social system was much more limited) is probably a major factor in "absorbing" the stress of discrimination and prejudice.

The limited interaction between the Japanese community and the larger American system affected the use of larger societal institutions. One possible explanation for the low official rates of mental illness (and also of crime and delinquency) was the limited use of state and local facilities by the Japanese group. Instead, they "took care of their own." One positive consequence of the nonuse of public facilities was the avoidance of the institutionalization of a "mentally ill role," "public welfare role," or a "delinquent role." Therefore, the process of labeling, categorization, and reinforcement for developing and maintaining these dysfunctional roles was lacking in the Japanese system. An unfortunate consequence of some of our American health and welfare programming may be the reinforcement and subsequent continuance of certain dysfunctional role positions.

It is questionable whether the minority community could continue to handle its own problems if the number of "social problems" were large. Fortunately, a combination of its structure, its values, and its population kept problem behavior at a minimum. The population was a young one — the initial immigrant was a young male, in good health, vigorous, and highly motivated toward work. There was a low initial probability of major health and welfare problems occurring in this type of population.

The most important single control in terms of mental illness, however, is the direction of preferred behavior prescribed by the Japanese. In general, reactions to stress and to frustration are directed "inward" — the concept of *ga-man*," which refers to "handling of pain and frustration without any outward signs," is typically Japanese. Therefore, in interpersonal relationships, the Japanese, generally, do not bother others, preferring, instead, to internalize problems. He might "eat his own heart out" and yet exhibit few overt signs of disturbance.

One other important option for handling problem behavior by the ethnic community was the use of the mother country. Immigration-emigration statistics indicate that, from 1912 through 1941, the number of Japanese departing from the United States for Japan was larger than the number entering the country. There was also the "Kibei" custom, whereby an American-born child (Nisei) would be sent back to Japan to be reared by relatives in Japan. Although it is difficult to arrive at any precise figure, it is logical to assume that some families used both the Kibei system and the more permanent emigration to Japan as alternatives to handling problem behavior.

For example, one of our interviews in our study of crime (Kitano, in progress [1969]) is revealing:

> I remember two brothers (Nisei) who were hard to handle. They would get drunk . . . were always fighting, always in trouble, and were uncontrollable. Finally,

their father came to talk to my father and other Japanese families in the neighborhood.... All agreed that these boys would hurt the reputation of the other Japanese and provide poor models for the younger boys.... So, even though the brothers were already young adults and out of high school, they were sent back to Japan (1937). As far as I know, they never came back to the United States.

Several generalizations appear to be appropriate in describing the Japanese community:

1. The Japanese community is a cohesive, integrated body with many interdependent structures which play important roles in shaping desired behaviors. Desired behaviors include conformity and minimal "acting out."
2. The Japanese community provides a wide range of alternative opportunities (structural pluralism) that, in many instances, parallel the American system.
3. There is a strong group feeling which provides a "oneness," so that the behavior of one is a reflection on "all."

That the tightly knit ethnic community is a completely healthy development can be questioned. There is the risk of encapsulation, of a slowness of acculturation, of self-imposed isolation, restricted communication, and an overcontrol of adult supervision over the young.

Bradford Smith (1941) provides an apt summary of living in a Nihonmachi (Japanese town) before World War II:

> The Issei liked it. They had created it ... as a wall against prejudice and rejection, as a rebuilding of the life they had known at home, as a compensation for the return to Japan which they dreamed of.... Nihonmachi was home. Most of these enclaves were small enough so that the environment could be rigidly controlled.... They could be ... bound into the community by many of their accustomed institutions — the temple, the school, the neighborhood group. Etiquette, language, holidays — all were in the pattern of their upbringing....

> Those who failed to conform were soon brought about by the weapon of gossip, and ... economic sanctions could also be applied. (p. 232)

Although there have been changes as years have passed, the Japanese community, today, still retains many of the aspects of small town life described by Smith.

The Family

The Japanese family is an intact (1.6 percent divorce rate, which remains constant by generation), cohesive unit. It is structured vertically, with father as the authority and with relatively clearly defined roles for mother and sibs. It retains social control through techniques of interdependence (Japanese children remain dependent upon their family much longer than American middle-class children), shame, guilt, appeals to obligation, duty, and responsibility.

The Issei family was patterned to be self-sufficient; levels for help might include the extended family, then members of the same village or "mura," then the "ken" or state, then other Japanese. As a consequence, problems were handled by family, friends, neighbors — then the ethnic community. Outside "experts" played a minimal role in such a process.

This type of family interaction appears to be somewhat typical of lower-class immigrant groups, which helps, partially, to explain the low use of "professional" services by these populations.

The following generalizations can be made concerning the Japanese family:

1. The majority of Japanese families in the United States are intact. It is not unusual to find unmarried aunts and uncles as well as grandparents residing in the same household, even in urban areas.
2. Most families follow a vertical structure; that is, authority is primarily invested in the father and older males. Lines of social control and role functions are clearly defined. Duty and obligation are emphasized over love and motivation.

Family complementarity may be more easily achieved under this model than one based on love and affection.

3. There remains a long family dependence on the part of Japanese children. It is still rare for children to strike out on their own at an early age. Marriage is delayed.

4. Good children and good family members are defined, primarily, in terms of obedient, conforming, and responsible behavior.

5. Parental techniques for obtaining conformity and control appear, primarily, to be nonverbal. Observations of Japanese families indicate low verbosity but a high degree of effectiveness in obtaining social control.

6. Voluntary interfamily social patterns are largely within the extended family, the ethnic group, and the ethnic community. The relative homogeneity of interfamily and interethnic values strengthens social control functions.

7. The family is less apt to use outside "experts" and outside resources for the handling of social problems.

There have been changes by generations, but the Japanese family remains a tightly knit, cohesive group with a high degree of social control over its members.

Probably the most important role of the Japanese family in terms of mental illness is its protective function. The family name and the family identity might suffer if a member were mentally ill; therefore, most families would go to elaborate lengths to protect the public occurrence of such a catastrophe. Protection, in this sense, might include a high tolerance for "crazy behavior," a redefinition of family roles, and, finally, the use of external resources only if the effects of the deviant behavior caused major disruption in the family.

As a result of such ideas, Japanese families often view hospitalization as a final stage, with the point of view that, once an individual is hospitalized, he is out of their hands. The concept of "cure" and "treatment" has to be discussed carefully; otherwise, many Japanese families appear to be disinterested in their hospitalized member. This factor may be a further reason for the long hospitalization of Japanese patients.

Although we have discussed in general terms the community and the family, there are certain specific values and styles of life that may further help us understand Japanese behavior in the United States. We will present some of these changing values by Issei, Nisei, and Sansei.[4]

Ethnic Identity (Table 8)

Ethnic identity refers to the "degree of Japaneseness," as measured by self-perceptions, identification, and participation in ethnic activities. This variable was a powerful predictor of delinquent and nondelinquent behavior (Kitano, 1969) — Japanese with a higher degree of ethnic identification were less delinquent than those with a low degree of ethnic identity. A behavioral consequence of ethnic identity would be that, in America, one Japanese would be obligated to help another Japanese, even a total stranger, and that the success or failure of an individual Japanese would be a reflection on the entire group.

A knowledge of the degree of "Japaneseness" of an individual remains a powerful predictor of behavior today, even though the data show changes by generation. For example, predictions of marital choice, food habits, interaction with parents, attitudes toward education, and general styles of life might be comfortably made through knowledge of ethnic identity. On a higher level, the degree of an individual's identity (not necessarily ethnic) is believed to be highly important in understanding behavior.

Means-Ends (Table 8)

Traditional Japanese culture emphasizes both means (the process) and ends (the goals) as being of equal importance. Therefore, ethical behavior, or how one goes about a task, is as

	Issei N = 18	Nisei N = 37	Sansei N = 48	Caucasian N = 82
Table 8 **Generational Responses (in Percentages)** **to True-False Attitudinal Items**				
Items				
A. Ethnic identity				
1. Once a Japanese, always a Japanese (T)	78	63	47	
2. I always look forward to going to prefectural (or family picnics) (T)	62	50	17	
3. I would prefer attending an all-Japanese Church (T)	81	44	40	
4. I would prefer being treated by a Japanese doctor when sick (T)	69	50	26	
5. I prefer American movies to Japanese movies (F)	69	14	11	
B. Means-ends				
6. Even in a minor task, a person should put all his energies into it (T)	95	86	86	78
C. Masculinity and responsibility				
7. It is only right for a man to marry a girl if he has gotten her into trouble (T)	79	80	48	36
8. My definition of a real man is one who adequately supports his wife and family under all conditions (T)	81	82	63	35
D. Individual-group orientation				
9. A person who raises too many questions interferes with the progress of a group (T)	88	43	19	40
10. One can never let himself down without letting the family down at the same time (T)	89	79	59	46
E. Passivity				
11. If someone tries to push you around, there is very little that you can do about it (T)	39	29	12	6
12. I would not shout or fight in public, even when provoked (T)	70	69	55	51
F. Realistic expectations				
13. I think I will be a success once I acquire a nice home, a new car and many modern appliances (T)	50	32	8	6

valuable as the outcomes or end results. The changes from means toward ends are illustrated by our data (Table 8), although all groups tested still placed relatively high emphasis on the importance of means. The way of playing the game is considered as important as winning.

Masculinity and Responsibility (Table 8)

Definitions of masculinity and responsibility are related to "acting-out" behavior. It is believed that the American culture provides less clarity for a male role, which may often result in behavior that attempts to validate masculinity.[5] Conversely, the more secure Japanese male role may restrain the impulsive "acting out," which is thought of as more characteristically American. The inclusion of responsibility is, also, inherent in the Japanese definition of masculinity. The data indicate a trend by generation from the Japanese to the more American definition.

Individual-Group Orientation (Table 8)

Of special importance for group control and conformity are orientations and values emphasizing the individual and his relationship to the group. The American model of individualism, which is, perhaps, one key to American behavior, is relatively alien to the Japanese. For example, at the time of Issei immigration, the Japanese constitution made no reference to "individual rights," but, rather, to individual obligations and duties to the state and to the family.

Consequently, there is less of an egoistic orientation (self-needs, self-enhancement) and more of an "alter" perspective. For example, one technique for treating criminals in Japan is through self-reflection, which emphasizes one's own responsibility in the criminal act and its consequences to others. Treatment success, in these terms, comes about when the criminal perceives and acknowledges his lack of responsibility, his lack of respect for others.

The change from the Japanese perspective to a more American point of view is reflected by the data.

Passivity (Table 8)

Passivity is related to a fatalistic orientation, whereby an individual resigns himself to certain external conditions. It is related, also, to frustration tolerance — the Japanese phrase *shi-ka-ta-ga-nai* (usually accompanied by a shrug of the shoulders and meaning "it can't be helped" or "there's nothing you can do about it") illustrates this orientation. The wartime evacuation, business losses, natural disasters, and the like can all be covered by the phrase; and it is indicative of a style of life which counsels patience, tolerance, and repression. The changes in orientation from the Japanese to a more American perspective is illustrated by our data.

Realistic Expectations (Table 8)

Concepts such as frustration-aggression, anomie, and alienation are defined, usually, in terms of a discrepancy between expectations and reality. High expectations for success and blockage of legitimate opportunities for attaining goals provide background conditions for anomie, alienation, and illegitimate behavior (Cloward & Ohlin, 1961).

The Japanese, as a group, were an "under-expectancy" group — that is, aims for success were set so that goal attainment was not too difficult. A common practice was to settle for second best — rather than becoming a doctor, an individual might aim at a pharmacist level; rather than a Step III supervisory position, the Japanese-American might aim for Step I. The consequence is that many Japanese, even today, are overtrained for their level and, perhaps, even overproductive. Reaching for the stars is not a common practice, although changes by generation through acculturation are taking place. Probably, both overexpectancy and underexpectancy are, in the long run, dysfunctional perceptions.

Other general styles of life that proved compatible to life in the United States included high achievement (high education), high savings, and a "future" orientation. The general influence of certain Japanese Meiji period values, such as *shu-shin*, which emphasized duty, responsibility, and obligations, was, undoubtedly, quite important in shaping Japanese-American behavior.

Possibly, the most important point in presenting the values of the Japanese relates to their relatively fixed order, so that individual preferences are not given the same priority as within the American system. For example, the duties and obligations of the individual to the larger systems — the family, village, community, and nation — are relatively static, so that individual needs and preferences play a minor role in determining the significance of priorities.

One interesting facet of the Japanese styles of life emphasizing ritual, role-set, and formal behavior is the difficulty of separating normal and pathological behavior. A Japanese-American psychiatrist illustrates this point:

> Because of the relatively rigid, set ways for social interaction, it's often difficult to diagnose where the role-set ends and possible psychiatric symptomology begins. The person who reacts to extreme stress with a pattern of unemotional and ritualistic behavior may be relatively easy to diagnose psychiatrically in another culture, but for the Japanese (especially the Issei), it's really hard to figure one way or the other.

The choice of occupations is protective, also, for many Japanese. The stereotyped Japanese gardener is an example of an occupation in which the amount of social interaction can be held to a minimum and in which *ki-chi-gai*, or "crazy behavior," can be widely tolerated.

However, it is understandable that, when a Japanese is referred to a mental institution, his behavior is described, usually, as rigid and compulsive. Schizophrenia is the most common classification.

The overall result of a tight, cohesive family and community system, with certain socialization procedures and emphasis upon certain values and styles of life, is a group with high conformity and low rates of overtly deviant behavior. Personality data show the Sansei male as more reserved, more humble, more conscientious, more shy, and more regulated by external realities than are Caucasian-American males. Conversely, Caucasian-American males are more outgoing, more assertive, more expedient, more venturesome, and more imaginative than are Japanese-American males (G. Meredith and C. Meredith, 1966).

Sansei females are more affected by feeling, more obedient, more suspicious, and more apprehensive than their Caucasian peers. On the other hand, Caucasian-American females are more emotionally stable, more independent, more trusting, and more self-assured than their Japanese-American counterparts (G. Meredith and C. Meredith, 1966).

Problems of leadership (Burma, 1953), of social backwardness (Kitano, 1962), lack of creativity, and overconformity may be a high price to pay for "good behavior."

Japanese Attitudes Toward Mental Illness

There are several Japanese terms that describe mental illness. The word most commonly used by the Issei is *ki-chi-gai* ("crazy"); more professional and technical terms include *non-ro-seh* ("neurosis"), *sei-shin-byo* ("mental illness"), and *sei-shin-retsu-sho* ("schizophrenia").

Although there have been changes in both the conceptualization and treatment of the mentally ill in Japan (for example, introduction of group therapy, psychiatric social work, and psychiatric treatment), the main emphasis remains on physiological-neurological models. For example, on a recent trip to Japanese mental institutions, the writer noticed the widespread use of electro-shock therapy, of the measurement of GSR and ECG as more basic to the understanding and treatment of the mentally ill than interpersonal techniques.

General Japanese attitude toward the mentally ill, as well as other "gross deformities," has been that of fear, ostracism, and repression. The Issei brought to the United States many of these same attitudes, and the idea of a "hereditary taint" meant that families were hesitant to admit the existence of a *ki-chi-gai* person, since it might affect economic and social interaction (for example, chances for a job, for marriage).

The Lack of a "Mentally Ill Role"

A consequence of this perhaps unique combination of a young immigrant population, a strong family and community structure with its own resources, an emphasis on certain values and styles of life, a fear of and lack of sophistication regarding the origins and treatment of mental illness, and limited use of psychiatric facilities was the lack of a clearly defined "mentally ill role." Although everybody could act *ki-chi-gai* at one time or another, there was no process by which his behavior could be diagnosed, labeled, treated, and the changed behavior reinforced. The term "tolerance for mental illness" may not be an entirely appropriate one, since it connotes an understanding of the behavior in question — the tolerance is related more to the lack of "know-how," the form of the behavior, the lack of resources, and the lack of alternatives in handling the behavior.

For example, there is the case of an elderly Issei woman who died recently. During her lifetime, she was rather widely known for her eccentric behavior — talking to animals, communicating with spirits, and displaying extremely erratic behavior in conducting her business. She was a widow, left with the running of a small store; her absent-mindedness, her eccentric buying and spending habits, and her extreme emotionality would have meant immediate failure for most stores. Instead, her loyal employees protected her, gradually taking over and handling her as they would a child. There was no thought of sending her for any psychiatric treatment (who could talk to her in Japanese?), no thought of hospitalization, and a rather amused tolerance for her odd and eccentric ways. She, eventually, retired, made periodic, ritualistic visits to old friends, lived by herself on savings and social security, and, at the time of her death, had never been a statistic in any clinic or mental hospital.

The lack of a "mentally ill role" has both positive and negative consequences. It prevents an all-too-easy solution through quick hospitalization and the development of a "mentally ill role" as discussed by Szasz (1961), and it keeps the number of Japanese in mental hospitals extremely low.

However, it may hinder the use of appropriate resources (for example, clinics and "preventive services") when necessary and leaves the ethnic community relatively helpless when its members do exhibit persistent symptoms of mental illness.[6] The rather large proportion of the aged with psychiatric symptoms has never been fully faced by the Japanese in the United States. Hospitalization of this old Issei group in state institutions, where difficulties of language, dietary habits, and styles of life provide additional stress, is not a pleasant prospect. Belatedly, the ethnic community is planning a nursing home and a facility for the aged. Third-generation service groups are now showing an interest in the problems of its senior citizens.

Relationships among Mental Illness and Other Forms of Deviant Behavior

There are various ways of conceptualizing the relationship between mental illness and other forms of deviant behavior. For example, there is an oversimplified point of view that hypothesizes a homeostasis between internalization and "acting out," so that groups with low rates of mental illness are hypothesized as high in behavior such as delinquency, and vice versa. It is obvious that the Japanese in the United States does not fit into such a model — he is low in mental illness and low in crime and delinquency (Kitano, in progress [1969]). Conversely, the Mexican-American appears to provide a better fit — he is low in mental illness and high in delinquency. However, the reasons for this may be related to the type of data available on Mexican-American rates of mental illness.

Another point of view looks upon deviance as escape or release behavior, so that a certain amount is necessary for the health of any social system. From this perspective, one might hypothesize a monstrous blow-up for the Japanese, since his rates of mental illness, of crime, and of delinquency are so low. Further-more, although rates of suicide in Japan are high, Iga (in progress [1969]) indicates no such abnormality of the Japanese rate in the United States. The Japanese population minimizes acting-out behavior.

However, we hypothesize other forms of acceptable "release" behavior within this ethnic group to absorb stress. These would be, primarily, in the form of "somatization," that is, with psychosomatic symptoms and an over-concern with bodily functioning. Although there was no formal testing of this hypothesis, impressionistic evidence, as well as research on the Japanese, lends support to the validity of this point of view. The extremely widespread use of potent drugs, the overconcern with high blood pressure, the hot baths, the masseurs, the practice of acupuncture, the concern with the stomach and other internal organs are characteristically Japanese, whether in Japan or in the United States.

Our overall explanation concerning Japanese-American mental illness and its relationship to other forms of deviant behavior emphasizes the relativity of stress and the cushioning effects of the family and community. From this perspective, certain groups of Japanese are "marginal," and it is this population that is more vulnerable to stress. Those with a weak ethnic identity — those from broken or conflict-ridden homes — and those who have failed to integrate into either the Japanese or the larger social system will constitute the high-risk group in terms of mental illness, suicide, crime, and delinquency.

Our empirical data strongly support this position.

For example, Japanese delinquents (Kitano, in progress [1969]) could be differentiated from a matched group of nondelinquents on many variables, including broken homes, high conflict and lack of complementarity in the family life, less ethnic identity, and different values and styles of life. Our preliminary analysis of cases of suicides and of those hospitalized for mental illness[7] indicates surprising similarity.

A suicidal case is that of a thirty-five-year-old man from Japan who had minimal job security and minimal income. He was not a member of either the ethnic nor the majority community, and he had no close relatives or close friends. His suicidal act arose from an unhappy love affair with a Caucasian divorcée.

A case of mental illness is that of a forty-year-old female, married to a non-Japanese. She was rejected by both families and had a psychotic break after the death of her husband. The stress of adapting to widowhood, including the rearing by herself of several young children, was too much.

An analysis of Japanese-American hospitalized schizophrenics (Terashima, 1958) provides additional data. The lonely, isolated families and the lack of overall identity is common to the whole sample. The author, in describing one of the cases, says:

> The patient, the youngest of five siblings, was not only rejected and neglected by his father, who was domineering, irritable, and seriously alcoholic, but he was also isolated from friends in his childhood. The entire family was shut off from social relationships. . . . (p. 7)

We are confident that certain predictions can be made. We think it will be relatively easy to differentiate between "normal Japanese" and "abnormal Japanese" on a number of variables (most of these have been previously discussed). For example, we think that most clinicians analyzing interviews and case histories will be able to place samples into "normal" and "abnormal" categories with high accuracy. However, we predict, also, that there will be great difficulty in sorting the "abnormal" group into the correct dependent variables — suicide, mental illness, crime, and delinquency. The essential similarity of the case histories of the "abnormal" appears more than coincidental.

The interesting fact about the adaptation of the Japanese to life in the United States has been the ability of the ethnic system to provide a wide enough umbrella to control the development of a large "marginal group." There may be several reasons for this, including the essential congruence between American middle-class and Japanese styles of life. Therefore, initially, when interaction between the two systems was limited, the Japanese system played a major socializing role. At the current time, when the American system provides more ample opportunities, there is relative ease in moving over. It may be that other subcultures, less congruent to the American system (for example, possibly, the Mexican-American), create special difficulties because integration into the ethnic or subgroup culture may mean a move away from the American system and, therefore, eventual conflict when interacting with American institutions (the public school system, for example).

Overall, we have attempted to provide a broad picture of a subcultural group and mental illness. We have assumed that behavior that can be labeled as "mental illness" arises from diverse sources. It may have biochemical, physiological, or genetic origins; it may arise from situational or constant stress; it may involve peculiarities in the individual or in his upbringing and family environment. Rather than concentrate on the "causal," we have described what happens within the ethnic community when such behavior occurs. Therefore, from this perspective, the "form" of the behavior — how it affects others in terms of irritation and disturbance — is our important variable. The form ultimately affects the handling, the treatment, and the rates of mental illness.

In describing the Japanese system with its emphasis on a strong community and family, its values, its preferred modes of behavior, and its styles of life, we have presented a group in which mental illness rates are low. Given the same system for whatever group — White, Black, Red, or Yellow — we would expect the same low rates of mental illness. There appears to be little need to depend upon exotic or mysterious variables to explain the behavior of the Japanese in the United States.

The Future

There is a combination of factors that may be used for predictive purposes. Acculturation, changes in ethnicity and social class, the availability of trained mental health personnel (especially of the same ethnic background), and the nature of the population provide some clues for the future. It should be emphasized that, on certain objective criteria of "success" such as education and income, the Japanese group in California has achieved a remarkable level. In both education and income, the Japanese rank higher than all other identifiable ethnic groups as defined by the United States Census. Therefore, on social-class criteria, the Japanese are definitely upwardly mobile and will continue to be so; yet, there are certain values and styles of life which remain ethnic. Most important for mental illness are attitudes and feelings that more clearly reflect older "Japanese traditions" than they do the sentiments of a highly educated, middle-class population. The close family interaction model, with an emphasis on the extended family, friends, and neighbors for "assistance" on most matters, limits the use of "experts" or professionals. This is gradually changing, both from pressures within (breaking-up of the ghettos, the extended family system) and from pressures without (in this case, the most obvious being the large number of Japanese "professionals").

The pattern appears irreversible. The complexity of problems points to the need for the expert and the specialist. This means that the "wise old neighbor," whose main qualification might have been some knowledge of English (but who also provided a personalized service), or an older uncle, is no longer the most popular resource. The minimally trained Issei general practitioner, somewhat bumbling and with old-fashioned ideas about medicine, is being replaced by the young Nisei and Sansei specialist. A rising group of highly trained lawyers, social workers, psychologists, and psychiatrists is beginning to develop role positions modeled after appropriate middle- and upper-middle-class populations. The important part in this development is the training of ethnic personnel, so that they represent streams of acculturation arising from within the Japanese system rather than "experts" appointed from the outside by the American community. Therefore, hopefully, the changes in the Japanese social system will be through the incorporation of professionals in mutual interaction rather than a dictation and one-way flow. Unfortunately, experiences with professionals and experts have often been characterized by a one-way flow — the middle-class professional to the lower-class population. Phrases such as "imposing of values" and "taking clients where they are" are indications of this problem.

Finally, it is also of interest to note the changes in the handling of the mentally ill in the larger community. There have been swings to and from hospitalization, and the current American emphasis on "treatment in the home and the community" is congruent with the old Japanese-American way of handling mental illness, although the reasons may have been different. Ironically, the "cultural-lag" phenomenon may mean that the earlier American influence of diagnosis and treatment is just catching up — for example, there is a cry for more hospitals and hospital beds in Japan, and one proposed solution is to build "bigger

and better institutions." The need for more personnel — psychiatrists, psychologists, and social workers — employed in large institutions may very well be the next step across the sea.

For the Japanese in the United States, the older ways of treatment through the family, extended family, and community will soon give way to the use of professionals, of experts, and of institutions. As more experts are produced, more Japanese will use their services, and community concern will rise, since rates of mental illness will rise. Perhaps, in due course, through acculturation and the passage of time, the rate of Japanese mental illness will become, then, more nearly equal to that of the majority group in the United States.

Chapter Notes

1. This research was supported by NIMH Grant M-11112.

2. Although the Chinese and Japanese are completely different populations, census and other data often lump them together under the term Orientals. Such a category is useless for cross-cultural study.

3. We checked with one of the state hospitals to see how "ethnicity" is determined. There appears to be no systematic method of ascertaining the validity of the classification — in many instances, a clerk who helps fill out the initial form checks whether, in her judgment, a person is Japanese or Negro or Indian. Some become quite skilled at this; there is a check at later stages when other personnel have time to become acquainted with the patient.

4. The samples for comparison were drawn from available groups of Japanese in Los Angeles. The Caucasian group is a Psychology 1A class at UCLA. Test-retest reliability of the inventory was $r = .79$. Data are presented in percentage terms only.

5. A musician friend commented to us about the high quality of violin sections in Japan. It is not considered "feminine" for males to take up the violin; therefore, there are probably many more males playing the violin in

Japan than in the United States.

6. For example, one possible reason for the low rates of Mexican-American mental illness may be the nonuse of professional services. A medical doctor related to us that most Mexican-American children are, literally, "dying" by the time their parents bring them to the medical center.

7. A more comprehensive study under NIMH Grant OM-11112 is in progress [1969].

References

Archer, M.; Staugas, C.; and Hoffman, N. "A Descriptive Study of the Services and of Presenting Problems, Acculturation Levels and Social-Class Positions of a Japanese-American Social Agency." Master's thesis, School of Social Welfare, University of California at Los Angeles, 1962.

Arkoff, A. "Need Patterns in Two Generations of Japanese-Americans in Hawaii," *The Journal of Social Psychology* 50, 1959, 75-79.

Burma, J. "Current Leadership Problems among Japanese-Americans." *Sociology and Social Research* 37, 1953, 157-163.

Cloward, R., and Ohlin, L. *Delinquency and Opportunity.* Glencoe, Ill.: The Free Press, 1961.

Cressey, D. "Crime." In R. Merton and R. Nisbet (eds.), *Contemporary Social Problems,* pp. 21-26. New York: Harcourt, Brace and World, 1961.

De Motte, M. "California ... White or Yellow?" *The Annals* 93, 1921, 18-23.

Enright, J., and Jaeckle, W. R. "Ethnic Differences in Psychopathology." Paper presented at the Pacific Science Congress, Honolulu, Hawaii, August, 1961.

Hayner, N. S. "Delinquency Areas in Puget Sound Region." *American Journal of Sociology* 39, 1933, 314-328.

Iga, M., and Ohara, K. "An Interpretation of Durkheim's Concept of Anomie and Suicide Attempts of Japanese Youth." Manuscript (in progress [1969]), private copy.

Kitano, H. "Changing Achievement Patterns of the Japanese in the United States." *The Journal of Social Psychology* 58, 1962, 257-264.

Kitano, H. "Differential Child-Rearing Attitudes between First- and Second-Generation Japanese in the United States." *The Journal of Social Psychology* 53, 1961, 13-19.

Kitano, H. *Japanese-Americans: The Evaluation of a Subculture.* Englewood Cliffs, N.J.: Prentice-Hall, 1969.

McClatchy, V. "Japanese in the Melting Pot: Can They Assimilate and Make Good Citizens?" *The Annals* 93, 1921, 29-34.

Meredith, G., and Meredith, C. "Acculturation and Personality among Japanese-American College Students in Hawaii." *The Journal of Social Psychology* 68, 1966, 175-182.

Miyamoto, F. *Social Solidarity among the Japanese in Seattle.* Seattle, Wash.: University of Washington Publications in Social Science, vol. 11, no. 2. 1939, 57-130.

Phelan, J. "Why California Objects to the Japanese Invasion." *The Annals* 93, 1921, 16-17.

Rotter, J. *Social Learning and Clinical Psychology.* New York: Prentice-Hall, 1954.

Smith, B. *Americans from Japan.* Philadelphia: Lippincott, 1941.

Szasz, T. *The Myth of Mental Illness.* New York: Hoeber-Harper, 1961.

Terashima, S. "Cultural Aspects of Japanese-American Schizophrenic Patients." Manuscript, University of California at Los Angeles Medical Center, 1958.

20. Between Two Worlds: Filipinos in the U.S. Navy

*by Lt. Donald F. Duff, MC, USN, and
Cdr. Ransom J. Arthur, MC, USN*

Psychiatric illness among Filipinos in the U.S. Navy usually appears as a stereotyped clinical syndrome in which hypochondriasis and paranoia are prominent. The authors suggest that the distinctive Filipino child-rearing practices and certain cultural concepts related to feelings of obligation and shame are crucial in the determination of this clinical picture. A better understanding of the cultural factors in psychiatric symptomatology may help the therapist to establish a more effective relationship with such patients.[1]

Since antiquity, military forces have been an instrument of cultural diffusion and acculturation. Cultures have been spread by conquest; for example, Hellenism was spread by Alexander the Great, and British culture was brought to India, in part, by the armies of the East India Company and those of the Crown.

Less obvious, perhaps, is the process of partial accculturation within the military itself. The armies of Rome were filled with foreign levies who were, perforce, Romanized. The crews of the Royal Navy during the Napoleonic wars averaged more than 15 percent foreigners on board (Reference 15). At Trafalgar, Nelson's own flagship, *H.M.S. Victory*, had a mixed crew which included even Frenchmen!

Alas, we have no Xenophon or Boswell of the lower deck to tell us of the life and travails of these men. There may have been a kind of sameness to the Spartan military life that transcended cultural boundaries and which enabled these strangers to survive not only the hardships of the Navy but the cultural shock attendant upon service in a foreign fleet. Service of large groups of men in the armed forces of another country does not belong merely to past epochs. Even today, the British Army has regiments of Gurkha troops and the U.S. Navy has its Filipino enlisted men.

For many years before the independence of the Republic of the Philippines was achieved, Filipinos were serving honorably in our Navy. After independence, a treaty was negotiated between the two nations which enabled Filipino nationals to enlist in the U.S. Navy without loss of Philippine citizenship. As presently amended, the treaty allows up to 2,000 men a year to enlist for military and professional training in the rating of steward for periods of either four or six years (Ref. 1).

There is no lack of candidates. The 2,000 places are filled with men to whom a U.S. Navy career, in no matter how humble a capacity, represents a greater opportunity and reward than that offered them in their native rural barrios or villages, from which the Naval enlistees are largely drawn. These volunteers come, predominantly, from three of the eight major cultural-linguistic groups of the republic: the Tagalog, the Ilokono, and the Bisayan from the central portion of the archipelago. Many of the volunteers describe a life-long wish to join the U.S. Navy, particularly those from traditionally sea-going groups such as the Ilokono.

The volunteers must be between eighteen and thirty years of age, single, fluent in English, high school graduates, physically fit, and must have a score on a special intelligence test roughly equivalent to an I.Q. of ninety. Individuals with technical training, such as engineering, are discouraged from enlisting, because their skills are needed far more at home than they are by the American Navy. The applicants also must execute a certificate which states that they have no one dependent upon them for financial support. This question of dependency is of far greater significance in a society such as that of the Philippines, in which the extended family is of paramount importance; than in one such as ours, in which the nuclear family is the basic unit. In fact, throughout their careers, a large number of Filipino sailors do, indeed, send money back to their homes, even though no one there may be dependent upon them for support in a strict sense.

The process of acculturation begins in recruit training. The Filipino recruits are sent to the Naval training center in San Diego and undergo the standard recruit training. They are, in general, intermingled with the American recruits and treated in the same fashion. Although rarely are there all-Filipino companies in recruit training, usually the men are assigned so that there are about ten Filipinos in a recruit company of approximately eighty.

An attempt is made by the training command to maximize rapid acculturation. Although the strain of adaptation must be very great — for example, the necessity of adjusting to a totally new diet — the attrition rate among Filipinos in recruit training is very much lower than among United States citizens. Less than one percent of Filipinos are lost during recruit training, as opposed to an approximately eight percent attrition for all other recruits (Ref. 26). After graduation, they are trained for their particular Naval duties in the stewards' "A" or

basic school. After completion of this school, they enter the fleet.

The duties of a Naval steward include the preparation and service of officers' meals and the care of the officers' galley, wardroom, and living spaces, both afloat and ashore. The majority of men continue to serve in this capacity throughout their Naval careers; however, an increasing number are moving into other Naval occupational areas, particularly clerical ratings such as personnelman, yeoman, or disbursing clerk. In order to qualify for a change in rating or Naval occupation, the man must have served satisfactorily for some period as a steward and then, through study or an apprenticeship, have acquired the necessary skill to make the transition.

As stewards, the Filipinos in the Navy have daily contact with officers but, of course, the contacts are of the briefest, most circumscribed, and least intimate kind. At sea, the stewards' division lives and eats together. On liberty, there is usually little mixing with their American shipmates. However, those Filipinos who leave the steward's rating for other Naval jobs are in a different position. Of necessity, they achieve greater integration into the American Naval subculture.

As in any other group, mental illness appears in the Filipinos and is, sometimes, of sufficient severity to require hospitalization. It had long been axiomatic in Naval psychiatry that Filipino mental patients presented a stereotyped clinical syndrome in which hypochondriasis and paranoia were prominent. It was equally axiomatic that meaningful two-way communication between physician and patient did not appear to exist. The eager, young, middle-class, American psychiatrist and Naval officer, with a Weltanschauung shaped by the concepts of a Viennese genius, and the patient from another culture, which is a mixture of Occident and Orient, did not appear to get anywhere in their mutual task of healing the patient. However far the acculturation process might have gone — and, probably, it had gone only a very little distance — it had not extended to the patient's conceptualizing of uncomfortable sensations appearing to come from within the body, a feeling that malign forces are working against one, and the hearing of accusatory voices as all belonging to one disease entity, paranoid schizophrenia.

The present study grew out of the authors' distress at their inability to help these patients and even to talk with them in any way that seemed to make sense. Talking with paranoid patients, even those from one's own cultural and occupational group, is trying enough, but, occasionally, one feels that one has made a first step towards understanding. It was never our conviction prior to this study that we had made even this first step towards understanding with any of our Filipino patients. In the hope that from knowledge comes understanding, and with the wish to make a contribution to ethnopsychiatry, we embarked upon a study of the mental illnesses of Filipinos in the U.S. Navy.

Epidemiological and Clinical Study Methods and Findings

All admissions to Naval hospitals for Class V (nervous and mental) diseases of Filipino Navy men for the years 1956 to 1962 were scrutinized by analysis of data from the admission cards. In addition, the records of seventy-eight Filipino first admissions to the Neuropsychiatric Service of the U.S. Naval Hospital, Oakland, Calif., covering the eight-year period from January, 1956, through December, 1963, were analyzed. For purposes of comparison, equivalent data were obtained from the records of Negro patients in that hospital and, from admission cards, information on all hospitalized enlisted men for the entire Navy was catalogued.

Questionnaires regarding the patient's past life were mailed to the family in the Philippines, and follow-up data on certain patients were obtained from the authors' own clinical interviews with Filipino patients. Background material was gathered from interviews with Filipino officials and Filipino nonpatient informants, such as chief petty officers, who had had long and successful service in the Navy. Supplementary statistical information was obtained from the records of the states of California and Hawaii, as well as from the National Mental Hospital, Mandaluyong, Rizal, Republic of the Philippines. The pertinent demographic data are portrayed in Table 1.

It should be noted that the Filipino mental patients, as compared with Negro patients and with all enlisted patients, are significantly older, have had more schooling, and have had more active service time (differences are significant using χ^2 and t tests of significance). The clinical data are portrayed in Table 2. The striking findings are the very large number of Filipino patients who were psychotic as compared with other enlisted men and the similarly large number who displayed paranoid features. Admission data from Hawaii show a similar pattern of a high number of first admissions diagnosed as psychotic (89 percent) (Ref. 13, 27). Figures from the National Mental Hospital in Mandaluyong indicate that 1,009 out of 1,229 cases (90 percent) for calendar year 1962 were diagnosed as psychotic, largely schizophrenic (Ref. 24).

In summary, we find that the Filipino sailor hospitalized for a mental disorder tends to be older and has had more active-duty time but no higher rank than other Naval patients of different ethnic groups. Psychosis, most commonly paranoid schizophrenia, is the predominant syndrome, with character and behavior disorder diagnoses lagging far behind in number. A clinical case summary which illustrates the cardinal features presented by the modal patient follows.

Case Summary

B. R. was a twenty-seven-year-old, married, Malayan Filipino, nonrated Navy steward with eight years of active duty. On admission, he was noted to be suspicious and taciturn. He described

Table 1
Distributions of Demographic Variables for
Three Navy Ethnic Groups Hospitalized for Mental Disorders

Variable	Filipinos*		Negroes**		Other Enlisted Navy Personnel***	
	Number	Percent	Number	Percent	Number	Percent
Pay Grade						
E-1	4	5	22	8	566	10
E-2	8	10	48	18	1523	28
E-3	31	40	102	38	1564	28
E-4	17	22	39	15	682	12
E-5	12	15	37	14	540	10
E-6	6	8	16	6	367	7
E-7	0	0	4	1	251	5
E-8	0	0	0	0	17	0
Total	78		268		5510	
Age						
17-19	3	4	64	24	2330	42
20-21	5	6	42	16	1074	19
22-23	5	6	34	13	571	10
24-25	8	10	24	9	285	5
26-27	11	14	24	9	188	3
28-29	18	23	14	5	140	3
30-33	11	14	25	9	298	5
34-40	14	18	34	13	472	9
Above 40	3	4	7	3	152	3
Total	78		268		5510	
Years of Service						
0-1	15	19	77	29	2169	40
2	8	10	28	10	863	16
3-5	21	27	44	16	948	17
6-8	9	12	44	16	435	8
9-11	3	4	21	8	225	4
12-15	13	17	21	8	303	6
16-19	9	12	28	10	399	7
20-25	0	0	5	2	127	2
Total	78		268		5469	

*Filipino male enlisted personnel who were hospitalized for mental illness in the U.S. Naval Hospital, Oakland, California, during an eight-year period (1956-1963).

**All Negro male enlisted Navy personnel hospitalized for mental illness during 1961.

***All male enlisted Navy personnel (less Negroes and Malayans) who were hospitalized for mental illness during 1961.

Table 2
Diagnostic Distributions of Three Ethnic Groups
of Navy Enlisted Personnel
Hospitalized for Mental Disorders

Diagnostic Category	Filipinos*		Negroes**		Other Enlisted Navy Personnel***	
	Number	Percent	Number	Percent	Number	Percent
Psychosis	58	74	51	19	453	8
Psychoneurosis	5	6	63	24	1028	19
Character or behavior disorder	11	14	127	47	3621	66
Transient personality disorder	4	5	27	10	408	7
Total	78		268		5510	

*Filipino male enlisted personnel who were hospitalized for mental illness in the U.S. Naval Hospital, Oakland, California, during an eight-year period (1956-1963).

**All Negro male enlisted Navy personnel who were hospitalized for mental illness during 1961.

***All male enlisted Navy personnel (less Negroes and Malayans) who were hospitalized for mental illness during 1961.

persecutory delusions and auditory hallucinations telling him that he had syphilis and that he would soon be executed by a "firing squad." He was oriented in all spheres and without evidence of organic brain disease. Memory was intact. Mood and affect were severely blunted.

Longitudinal history revealed that the patient was born and reared in a rural area of the Philippine Islands. He was the second of six children. He completed high school with above-average grades and went on to one and one-half years of college but left because of financial difficulties. When he was unable to find satisfactory employment, he joined the U.S. Navy. On completion of basic training, he attended steward school and continued in that Naval occupation without advancement. He was married, two years prior to hospitalization, to a Filipino nurse, who continued her employment in a hospital in the Philippine Islands. Throughout his Navy career, he had sent the majority of his income back to the Philippine Islands to help support his parents and younger siblings. Following one month of hospi-

talization, during which he rapidly improved, he was returned to limited duty but experienced an exacerbation of his psychosis after five months and was rehospitalized for another two months prior to transfer to the Veterans Administration Hospital in Manila.

Cultural Contributions to Symptom Formation

How does one explain the striking uniformity of the clinical picture presented by male Filipino psychiatric patients in the U.S. Navy and, indeed, elsewhere? A genetic interpretation seems implausible to explain why patients from different families and different islands show so uniform a syndrome. Of course, it is commonly thought that people such as refugees, living in an alien culture, may have a high incidence of paranoid diseases. But this factor does not seem to be directly applicable here, as the reported incidence of paranoid diseases in Filipino patients in the Philippine Republic itself is, also, exceptionally high (Ref. 24).

It is well known to behavioral scientists that the culture of a people shapes the limits of personality possibilities and, to some unknown degree, manifestations of mental disorders (Ref. 2, 18). A glimpse into the Filipino culture might well offer clues as to why the mental illness of Filipino Navy men appears to be so uniform.

All of the literature on the peoples and culture of the Philippine Islands emphasizes two central points: (1) it is family centered, emphasizing family loyalty and support, with the interests of the indicidual secondary to those of the family; and (2) it is a shame culture (Ref. 2, 3, 6, 7, 8, 9, 10, 11, 12, 19, 20, 21, 25, 28).

The basis for these conclusions is readily apparent in the child-rearing practices of the barrio (rural) Filipinos, the population from which the vast majority of Navy recruits are drawn. These are outlined below under the developmental milestones of infancy, weaning, preschool, and school age.

Infancy. Infancy among the Filipinos is marked by indulgence, constant attention, and few, if any, demands on the child. This takes the form of complete demand feeding, the infant's never being allowed to cry but always being fed or picked up and comforted. Under such conditions, the child is rarely able to explore the environment. Erikson spoke of the interplay of autonomy with shame and doubt in this connection (Ref. 5). An exception to the indulgence is a common form of "play" between the infant and mother, whereby she, verbally or gesturally, threatens to remove some loved object.

Weaning and preschool. Weaning is traditionally accomplished at approximately three years and is sudden and irrevocable. Not uncommonly, this is accompanied by the birth of another child. Usually, the mother absents herself from the home for a day or two and, on her return, the child is removed from her bed for the first time. The child's complaints are met with teasing and shaming. If there is no new

infant to nurse, the mother will dissuade the child further by smearing the breast with burnt manure or some peppery substance.

For the preschool child, there is an increase in responsibility and demands for obedience. These he learns from his older siblings and adults by teasing and laughter at his failures. The expression of anger, however, is strongly discouraged, as is any initiative in responsibility. This serves to teach the lesson of reliance on others for all but essentials. At this stage, another "game" appears. This involves shaming of the child by any strange adult visiting the home after the mother begins the dialogue with the announcement that the child is naughty. The shaming is continued until the child is reduced to tears, whereupon the mother soothes and comforts him.

School age. With school, the horizons are widened, as are the responsibilities and the modes of discipline. At home, responsibility increases to include care of younger siblings, with the important reward of justifiable punishment of one's charges. Here, too, spankings give way to ridicule and any boldness is looked on as bad. All this leads, in the school, to a striving for adequacy as opposed to excellence. "To excel is to shame one's friends." Free time is spent with the peer group, whose power over its members is enforced by ridicule, shaming, and teasing.

A further appreciation of this culture is attained by an understanding of two important concepts: *utang na loob* and *hiya.* The former, freely translated, means "debt of prime obligation." However, its full meaning embodies much more to include an important system of reciprocal obligations and behavioral expectations which governs the lives of Filipinos. This system of reciprocal obligations is based on unsolicited gifts, of service rather than goods. While utilized to extend the sphere of the security held within the bilateral family setting, it is within the elementary family unit of mother, father, and child that *utang na loob* manifests its greatest strength and deepest obligation. Life

207

is an unsolicited gift and, thus, the basis of a debt which cannot be repaid.

Hiya, means "shame." This can run the continuum from mild embarassement in social situations to the gravity of either failure to recognize or refusal to repay *utang na loob*. Of significance here is the fact that an individual's actions, or nonattainment of expected goals, reflect shame on the entire bilateral family, with intensity related to degree of kinship. The individual is burdened with the gravest obligation to repay a debt that one can never repay. The failure to do so brings deep shame.

Discussion

It is to be anticipated that such important elements of the culture as *hiya* and *utang na loob* would influence not only normal behavior but also the clinical manifestations of mental illness, whatever its underlying primary cause. In this connection, the etiology of schizophrenia is still to be determined. The disorder seems to be ubiquitous, recognizable in all epochs and in all parts of the world (Ref. 14, 16). Its prevalence, as opposed to that of neuroses, say, is also roughly the same in many areas studied (Ref. 17).

However, the precise symptomalogy characteristic of one ethnic group of schizophrenics versus another often differs. That is, a group of Japanese schizophrenics differs from a group of Filipino schizophrenics in the differential prevalence of certain manifestations, such as type of delusions, violent behavior, accompanying depression, and apathy, although both groups share the primary Bleulerian features of autism, associative disturbance, inappropriate affect, and ambivalence (Ref. 4). Opler has shown the same phenomenon to be true of Irish-American versus Italian-American schizophrenics (Ref. 22). There is no reason to believe that whatever single or multiple factors may give rise to schizophrenic illness are absent or different in Filipinos than in any other group.

If it is impossible to state the cause of a schizophrenic illness, it is often equally difficult to clearly fix the event which precipitates its onset. And, indeed, it has proven impossible for us to find, in most of the cases studied, any event or series of events which seemed to mark the onset of mental illness in the Filipino sailors.

Even with full recognition of the barriers to understanding the etiology and onset of any mental disorder, the authors are bold enough to offer some speculations as to how a given cultural inheritance, an alien military environment, and an individual who carries a high potential for the development of a psychosis, all might interact to produce a stereotyped clinical syndrome.

The Filipino in the Navy is faced with acculturation problems while doing servile work and maintaining close ties to home, with all the implications of responsibility based on *utang na loob*. Some incident or life crisis, such as the arrival of a new and tyrannical chief petty officer, perhaps, some physical illness such as influenza, might prevent the individual from fulfilling his obligations. This failure to meet obligations and to attain his goals might give rise to feelings of inadequacy, impotence, and *hiya*, or shame, accompanied by anxiety.

Piers (Ref. 23), in delineating his classical distinction between shame and guilt, makes the following points which may be germane here:

1. Shame arises out of a tension between the ego and the ego ideal, not between the ego and superego as in guilt.

2. Whereas, guilt is generated whenever a boundary (set by the superego) is touched or transgressed, shame occurs when a goal (presented by the ego ideal) is not being reached. It, thus, indicates a real "shortcoming."

3. The unconscious, irrational threat implied in shame anxiety is abandonment and not mutilation (castration) as in guilt.

The anxiety accompanying shame over one's inadequacy or failure to fulfill one's necessary responsibilities is a tension that must be dealt with by the individual. A culture which discourages open expressions of anger and boldness as well as individual initiative makes an active attempt at mastery difficult. Activity, regardless of degree or quality, may lead to a transgression of the superego, which will be followed by guilt, a need for punishment, depression, and further anxiety. The patient's upbringing, as noted above, predisposes the Filipino to a passively attempted solution to the problem of shame, inadequacy, and mounting anxiety. The patient may use a classic, passive method of handling feelings of inadequacy, namely, somatic complaint or hypochondriasis.

Moreover, diffuse bodily complaints are a common and accepted manifestation of an excusable illness within the culture. What we would regard as somatization accompanying a mental disorder — for example, vague pains, numbness, shaking, and tingling in body parts such as the arm and hand, without evidence of any possible organic lesion to account for these symptoms — the Filipino might regard as a single disease, *sui generis*, with a known etiology and a specific therapy. Indeed, there is such a disease concept, called in the Philippines *pasma sa ugat*, a chronic disorder marked by vague pain, numbness, perhaps weakness, etc., treated by the *arbulario* (native herb doctor) with poultices of garli, oil, and herbs.

Somatization, a socially acceptable means of expressing the patient's illness, may facilitate further regression. In his contact with Naval physicians, the patient may be told that he has no organic basis for his complaints, that he is not really sick. The effect of this intelligence upon the patient, who knows better, is a deepening of feelings of shame, inadequacy, and anxiety. Projection, that universal human mechanism of relieving just such feelings, is increasingly called into play to get the blame for failure off oneself and onto others.

If any of these speculations has validity, therapeutic intervention might be considered to interrupt the cycle of inadequacy, shame, guilt, anxiety, regression, and projection. The intervention would be based on understanding of the patient's cultural and social, as well as personal, needs. This has been attempted, with some success, by the senior author, and an account of the therapeutic measures employed will appear in a further communication. Recently, we appear to have been able to have meaningful encounters with our Filipino patients, a limited success not attained in the past. The dawn of understanding may be brightening the horizon.

Summary

The U.S. Navy contains within its ranks a large group of Filipino nationals, who work primarily as officers' stewards. In spite of vigorous attempts to acculturate these sailors, most continue to maintain close ties with the Philippines and to live within their own cultural framework. When psychiatric disease is diagnosed in members of this group, the disorder typically noted is a paranoid illness, usually schizophrenia, accompanied, and, indeed, often preceded, by hypochondriacal complaints. The child-rearing practices of the Filipino culture, which emphasize passivity and the discouragement of outward expressions of aggression, and the key cultural concepts of *utang na loob*, or debt of prime obligation, and *hiya*, or shame, are thought to be crucial in shaping the clinical picture encountered.

Chapter Note

1. Paper read at the Western divisional meeting of the American Psychiatric Association, Honolulu, Hawaii, September 1, 1965. Lt. Duff is with the Neuropsychiatric Service, U.S. Naval Hospital, San Diego, Calif., and Cdr. Arthur is Officer in Charge, U.S. Navy Medical Neuropsychiatric Research Unit, San Diego, Calif. 92152. This work was supported by Department of the Navy Research Work Unit Grant MF022.01.03-9002 from the Bureau of Medicine and Surgery. The opinions or assertions contained in this paper are those of the authors and are not to be construed as official or as

necessarily reflecting the views of the Department of the Navy.

References

1. U.S. Department of the Navy, Bureau of Naval Personnel, BUPERS Instruction 1130.9A. Washington, D.C.: August 3, 1963.

2. Eaton, T. W., and Weil, R. J. *Culture and Mental Disorders.* Glencoe, Ill.: The Free Press, 1955.

3. Eggan, F., ed. *Human Relations Area Files: Area Handbook on the Philippines,* vols. I and II. Chicago: University of Chicago, for Human Relations Area Files, Inc., 1956.

4. Enright, J. B., and Haeckle, W. R. "Psychiatric Symptoms and Diagnosis in Two Subcultures." *Int. J. Soc. Psychiat.* 9:12-17, 1963.

5. Erikson, E. *Childhood and Society.* New York: W. W. Norton, 1963.

6. Fox, R. B. "Filipino Family and Kinship," in Eggan, F., ed. *Human Relations Area Files: Area Handbook on the Philippines,* vol. I, chapter 8. Chicago: University of Chicago, for Human Relations Area Files, Inc., 1956.

7. _____ . "Prehistoric Foundations of Contemporary Filipino Culture and Society." *Comment* first quarter, 1958.

8. _____ . "The Study of Filipino Society and Its Significance to Programs of Economic and Social Development," in *Philippine Areas Study Handbook.* Hilo, Hawaii: Peace Corps Training Center for Southeast Asia, 1964.

9. Guthrie, G. M. *Filipino Child and Philippine Society.* Manila: Philippine Normal College Press, 1961.

10. Hollnsteiner, M. R. "Reciprocity in the Lowland Philippines." *Philippine Studies* 9:387-413, 1961.

11. Isidro, A. *Philippine Social Life and Youth.* Manila: McCullough Printing Co., 1963.

12. Kant, C. *"Utang Na Loob:* A System of Contractual Obligation Among Tagalogs." Report of Field Work 1956-1958 Under Philippine Studies Program. Chicago: University of Chicago Department of Anthropology, 1956.

13. Kimmich, R. A. "Ethnic Aspects of Schizophrenia in Hawaii." *Psychiatry* 23:97-102, 1960.

14. Leighton, A. H.; Lambo, T. A.; Hughes, C. C.; Leighton, D. C.; Murphy, J. M.; and Macklin, D. B. *Psychiatric Disorder Among the Yoruba.* Ithaca, N.Y.: Cornell University Press, 1963.

15. Lewis, M. *A Social History of the Navy, 1793-1815.* London: George Allen & Unwin, 1960.

16. Lin, T. "A Study of the Incidence of Mental Disorder in Chinese and Other Cultures." *Psychiatry* 16:313-336, 1953.

17. Lin, T. S., and Standley, C. C. "The Scope of Epidemiology in Psychiatry." *WHO Public Health Papers* No. 16. Geneva: World Health Organization, 1962.

18. Linton, R. *The Cultural Background of Personality.* New York: Appleton-Century, 1945.

19. Lynch, F. "The Conjugal Bond: Where the Philippines Changes." Address given at plenary session, First National Conference on Filipino Family Life, Manila, December, 1957.

20. _____ . "Philippine Values II: Social Acceptance." *Philippine Studies* 10:82-99, 1962.

21. _____ . "The Less Entangled Civil Servant," in *Philippine Areas Study Handbook.* Hilo, Hawaii: Peace Corps Training

Center for Southeast Asia, 1964.

22. Opler, M. K. "An Italian and Irish Contrast of the Schizophrenias — U.S.A.," in Opler, M. K., ed., *Cultural Differences in Mental Disorders*. New York: Macmillan Co., 1959.

23. Piers, G., and Singer, M. B. *Shame and Guilt*. Springfield, Ill.: Charles C. Thomas, 1953.

24. Republic of the Philippines, Department of Health, National Mental Hospital, Mandaluyong, Rizal. *Classification of Cases for 1962.*

25. Stoodley, B. H. "Some Aspects of Tagalog Family Structure." *Amer. Anthropologist* 59:236-249, 1957.

26. U.S. Naval Training Center, San Diego, California, Recruit Evaluation Unit. Personal communication, June, 1964.

27. Wedge, B., and Age, S. "Racial Incidence of Mental Disease in Hawaii." *Hawaii Med. J.* 8:337-338, 1949.

28. Yabes, L. Y. *In Larger Freedom: Studies in Philippine Life, Thought, and Institutions*. Quezon City, P. I.: University of the Philippines, 1961.

21. Mental Illness and the Role of Mental Health Facilities in Chinatown

by Timothy R. Brown, Ph.D.; Kenneth M. Stein, Ph.D.; Katherine Huang, MWS; and Darrel E. Harris

Introduction

The history, characteristics, and problems of the Chinese in Los Angeles share similarities to those of Chinese persons throughout the United States. Discussions of these aspects for other Chinese in the United States (Kung, 1962; Barth, 1964; Sung, 1967) have applicability to Los Angeles. There are, however, some differences in development and some concerns particular to Los Angeles (Bingham, 1942; Chen, 1970). Therefore, although it may well be that the findings of this paper are generalizable to other areas, caution must be used in applying our conclusions more widely than to the Chinese of Los Angeles County and, specifically, to the population of Chinatown.

There have been Chinatown areas in Los Angeles since the early 1870s (Bingham, 1942). Unlike most other major American cities, however, there has not been just one Chinatown, but two or, sometimes, three. Moreover, the locations have moved several times, only becoming established in the present location in 1938. Currently, Chinatown is situated in the northern part of the downtown section of Los Angeles. Even now, it is possible to designate three separate "Chinatowns" in this area; each has a different history and economic structure. Yet, all three lie within a few blocks of one another, and, with the expansion of population and growth in the last decade, they have coalesced into one community.

Chinatowns have functioned, primarily, to offer a place of security for Chinese immigrants and to provide a focal point for their cultural identity. To this day, much of the population in the Los Angeles Chinatown consists of persons born outside the United States. In order to make clear the distinction between the two Chinese populations in Los Angeles, the term "Chinese-Americans" shall be used to refer to the immigrant groups and the term "American-Chinese" to persons born and raised in the United States of Chinese ancestry. Traditionally, the Los Angeles Chinatown has been the point of entry into the United States for many Chinese-Americans. Some, after they have adjusted to life in the United States, move out and diffuse into Los Angeles at large. Others stay, some because they prefer living among other Chinese-Americans even though they are adjusted to life in this country, and some because they have not adjusted. The latter do not learn English, nor alter their life patterns. For them, Chinatown is the only place to live. For the most part, the American-Chinese, the children of the immigrants, leave Chinatown either when their parents do or upon reaching adulthood.

The changes in immigration laws have greatly affected the number and characteristics of Chinese-Americans who have come to live in Chinatown. Beginning with the Chinese Restrictions Act of 1882 and culminating in the Quota

Act of 1924, increasingly restrictive limitations were placed on Chinese immigration to the United States. By the 1930s, legal immigration was reduced to a few hundred each year. Numerous Chinese-Americans, especially men, were cut off from their families in China. Consequently, a significant social problem in Chinatown today is the alone and isolated, elderly person, the last of so-called sojourners, or early Chinese-American immigrants. Since 1943, there has been a succession of legislative actions which have eased the immigration restrictions against Chinese, resulting in a marked increase in the number of Chinese-Americans. However, these modifications stressed a selective admittance policy. Priorities were given to persons with skills or advanced education. Some of these persons settled in Chinatown but many did not. In 1965, there was a major alteration in immigration laws. No longer is there so great an emphasis on skills. It is now possible for persons to enter the United States simply with the sponsorship of an immediate relative.

The effect of the 1965 changes in immigration laws on the Los Angeles Chinatown community has been dramatic. The 1970 Census reveals that the Chinese population of Chinatown has more than doubled since 1960. Recent immigrants have included small children, the elderly, and the infirm. More often than not, these new immigrants speak little or no English and have few skills with which to acquire jobs to support their large families. Neither the existing job market nor the available housing in Chinatown have been able to meet the increased demand. Unemployment and underemployment are widespread. Families live in substandard housing or tolerate overcrowded living arrangements in order to remain close to Chinatown, where there is some familiarity with their environment. In order to support their family, both parents work long hours; the young and the elderly are left alone.

The problems of the Chinese population living in the Los Angeles Chinatown community reflect this community's history and development. Chen (1970), in a recent article discussing the problems of the Chinese community of Los Angeles, listed three major subpopulations of residents who are in need of help: senior citizens, new immigrants, and youth. The immigrant experience of the Chinese-American is a pivotal factor in the problems of each of these three subpopulations.

In light of these problems and other problems of persons residing in the Los Angeles Chinatown needing mental health services, there are many questions which are of concern for Resthaven, the community mental health center for downtown Los Angeles, including Chinatown. What are the characteristics of the persons who make use of mental health services? Particularly, are they more typically Chinese-Americans or American-Chinese? What is the nature of their psychiatric disturbances? Are there differences in psychiatric symptoms and problems between Chinese patients and others? Are there indications about what might be better treatment strategies and approaches for Chinese patients? What type of community mental health effort would be beneficial for the Chinatown area?

The remainder of this paper shall be addressed to developing tentative answers to these questions, through data specifically collected for this purpose and the observations and judgments of mental health staff who have worked in the Los Angeles Chinatown community.[1] The remaining discussion is divided into three sections. The first section describes a research study which compared a sample of Chinese in-patients to a matched sample of Caucasian in-patients for the purpose of characterizing and differentiating the types of severe mental health problems of the Chinese. The second section contains the clinical impressions and insights of a Chinese mental health professional concerning Chinese-Americans treated in Resthaven's out-patient clinic. Finally, the third section develops a rationale for applying a modified community mental health model to the problems of Chinese-Americans and concludes with a proposed community-based program for the Los Angeles Chinatown community.

I. A Study of Chinese In-patients

The previous discussion described the background and some of the problems of the Chinese population living in the Chinatown community. In the present section, the more severe mental health problems of the Chinese, i.e., those that have required psychiatric hospitalization, are characterized. A sample of Chinese in-patients, their demography and psychiatric symptomatology are described and compared to a matched sample of Caucasian in-patients.

Method and Procedure

Subjects The case files of twenty-three persons of Chinese origin or ancestry who had been in-patients at Resthaven since its designation as a community mental health center were obtained from its medical records. These records had been filed in sequence according to date of admission. A matched comparison group was selected by removing for each Chinese case the case file of the nearest non-Spanish surname Caucasian (Anglo) of the same sex, age (± five years), approximate financial status (estimated from the source and type of payment for treatment), and legal status at admission (i.e., voluntary or involuntary).

Data Collection Each case file (twenty-three Chinese and twenty-three Caucasian) was read, and information was abstracted about the demographic characteristics of the patient, his background, and adjustment before his first admission to Resthaven, his treatment while at Resthaven, and his status at discharge. Moreover, ratings were made of twelve dimensions or syndromes of psychotic behavior by two clinically trained research staff members (Lorr and Vestre, 1968; Lorr, Klett and McNair, 1962). These empirically derived dimensions of psychotic and severely neurotic behavior were

selected primarily because they had been used in cross-cultural research and had been confirmed both in Western and non-Western cultures (Lorr and Klett, 1969). They are usually scored by someone who has interviewed the patient or by hospital personnel after observing the patient for several days. In this study, however, they were made after the raters had carefully read the psychiatric intake summary, the social history obtained by a social worker from family and/or friends of the patient, and the nursing activity and psychiatric progress notes for the first ten days after admission. The two raters read the case files and made their ratings independently. Each rater gave a score on a four-point continuum for each of the twelve dimensions for each of forty cases.

Results

Description of the Chinese Subjects These subjects were culturally Chinese. Nineteen, or 83 percent, of the Chinese subjects were born in China. The median length of time in the United States for these patients before admission was sixteen years, with a range from one-and-a-half to sixty-two years. Fourteen, or 61 percent, of the Chinese sample came to the United States when they were eighteen years of age or older. Moreover, one of the four Chinese patients who was born in the United States had lived in China during most of his childhood. In addition, the English language abilities of these Chinese patients indicated that they were culturally Chinese. Their case records were examined for mentions of English language ability. For two patients this was impossible to ascertain. However, ten, or nearly half of the remaining cases, were found to have had only limited ability to understand or be understood in English, and six of these ten had no, or very minimal, English language abilities.

Other important descriptive aspects of Chinese subjects were sex, age, and occupation. Sixteen, or 70 percent, of the Chinese subjects were men. In a six-month sample of all in-patient admissions regardless of race, only 40 percent were found to be men. This difference in sex representation between the Chinese sample and a general in-patient population sample was statistically significant ($X^2 = 7.54$ p $< .01$). The Chinese, also, may be slightly older when admitted. The mean age of the Chinese was 39.0; whereas, the mean age for all admissions for the six-month period was 34.7; however, this difference failed to reach statistical significance. The occupations tended to be ones which do not depend upon high levels of formal education. Five were unskilled workers (e.g., stockboy, waiter); four, skilled workers or craftsmen (e.g., tailor, butcher); three owned small businesses (two restaurants and a grocery store). Three were students and only one was a highly trained professional, a civil engineer. All seven women were housewives, although one worked part time in a sewing factory.

In summary, the most striking characteristic of the Chinese patient sample is that these patients were Chinese-Americans, not American-Chinese. The great majority were born in China, and most of them came to the United States when they were adults. Consequently, about half of the sample had difficulty speaking and/or understanding English. The Chinese patients were, also, more typically men, and they tended to be slightly older when compared to a sample of all admissions. The occupations tended to be ones which do not require a great deal of formal education or knowledge of life in the United States. Thus, this sample of Chinese patients appears to be culturally similar to the population of the Los Angeles Chinatown.

Comparison of the Chinese and Caucasian Sample Prior to Admission   Table 1 lists the sixteen variables about the patients' demographic characteristics, the backgrounds, and their adjustment prior to their first admission to Resthaven. Tests of significance (X^2 and students t) reveal only a few differences between the groups on these variables. Several appeared to indicate differences but, for samples of this size, failed to reach significance.

Although thirteen of the Chinese patients resided in the central section of Los Angeles, the area around the hospital, and only seven of the Caucasians did, it could not be concluded that the Chinese tended to reside more frequently in this area.

The greatest difference between the two groups was foreign birth. Nineteen of the Chinese were foreign born and four native, whereas, for the Caucasians, it was exactly the opposite, with four foreign and nineteen native born. This, clearly, illustrates that, based on these samples, severe Chinese mental health problems tended to be those of immigrants, and this is not, typically, true of Caucasian patients.

The mean number of years of education for the Chinese was 9.9, which is less than the other patients' 12.0 years. However, this difference, again, is not statistically significant.

The next four items, which refer to family situation, do not differentiate the Chinese patients from the Caucasians. There were no significant differences in marital status, the number of patients living with their family, family size, or the number of patients living alone. While not significantly different, all four items were in the direction of greater family ties for the Chinese. No Chinese were divorced or separated, whereas three Caucasians were divorced and two separated. Twenty of the Chinese were living with their families when they were admitted, as were eighteen of the Caucasians. The mean family size for the Chinese and Caucasians was 3.75 and 3.0, respectively. Four Caucasians lived alone and only two Chinese did so. These data show that both groups of patients tended to have strong family ties. The majority of patients admitted to Resthaven are persons who are acutely disturbed and/or seen as likely to benefit from relatively brief in-patient treatment. Such persons have not broken their family connections, nor have family members become worn out from dealing with a chronic problem and, consequently, rejected the patient.

Items 8 through 11 refer to the stresses

		X^2	t	Direction of
	df	Value	Value	Chinese Scores
1. Central Los Angeles residence	1	2.21		
2. Foreign birth	1	17.04**		foreign birth
3. Education	40		1.62	
4. Marital status	3	6.16		
5. Live with family	1	0.61		
6. Family size	41		1.49	
7. Live alone	1	0.77		
8. Family discord	2	6.13*		more discord
9. Separation or loss	1	0.14		
10. Employed	1	1.42		
11. Employment stress	1	2.47		
12. Prior psychiatric hospitalization	1	0.00		
13. Number of prior psychiatric hospitalizations	1	0.35		
14. Time between onset and Resthaven admission	3	3.29		
15. Time between first difficulty and first Resthaven admission	4	1.20		
16. Level of community adjustment	5	2.21		

Table 1
Demographic and Background Variables

*$p < .05$
**$p < .01$

operating on the patient prior to admission. The one significant stress factor was that there was more interpersonal discord in the families of the Chinese patients prior to the patient's admission than in Caucasian families. Seven of the Chinese patients had no interpersonal stress in their families, twelve had some stress, and four had much stress. Twelve of the Caucasian patients had no family stress, four had some stress, and seven had much stress. Caution must be used in interpreting this finding. First, this is a judgment made from material in a case

record, and, second, it is impossible to separate the cause from the effect, i.e., did the discord cause the patient's illness or vice versa.

The trend of the two employment items is for more employment difficulties for the Chinese. Fifteen of the Chinese were unemployed; whereas, eleven of the Caucasians had no jobs. For men only, nine Chinese were unemployed and seven employed; whereas, for the Caucasians, it was four and twelve, respectively. However, these differences were not significant. The case files were also read, and it was

---

Table 2
Twelve Psychotic Syndromes

1. *Excitement* (EXC): The syndrome represents a tendency to be noisy, overtalkative, high in mood, and aggressively overactive.

2. *Hostile Belligerence* (HOS): Hostile and obscene language, belligerence, and a tendency towards combativeness define this syndrome.

3. *Paranoid Projection* (PAR): The syndrome is characterized by suspicion, resistiveness, complaints concerning care and treatment, and ready annoyance at imagined slights.

4. *Anxious Depression* (ANX): An anxious, bewildered depression is defined in this pattern. Depressive Mood is a correlated pattern.

5. *Retardation* (RTD): Movement, speech, and response are slowed, sometimes to the point of apathy and stupor, in this syndrome.

6. *Seclusiveness* (SEC): The dimension measures degree of interpersonal interaction. High scores represent seclusiveness or withdrawal from contact.

7. *Care Needed* (CAR): The pattern is evidenced by an inability or unwillingness to care for oneself. Low scores may be regarded as a measure of competence.

8. *Psychotic Disorganization* (PSY): The syndrome is defined by motor disturbances (bizarre postures and movements) and indicators of conceptual disorganization. The pattern is probably central to schizophrenic withdrawal.

9. *Grandiosity* (GRN): A delusional grandiosity is briefly characterized in this syndrome.

10. *Perceptual Distortion* (PCP): Hallucinatory experiences usually associated with paranoid tendencies are represented in this syndrome.

11. *Depressive Mood* (DPR): The syndrome is characterized by self-reports of dejection, hopelessness, and failure.

12. *Disorientation* (DIS): This is a functional disorientation due, perhaps, to self-preoccupation with inner fantasies, conflicts, or hallucinatory experiences.

(Taken from Lore & Vestre, 1968.)

---

specifically noted if there was mention of an employment problem (e.g., difficulties on the job, unhappiness over being unemployed). Ten of the Chinese had mentions of employment stress and thirteen had not; whereas, only five Caucasians had mention in their file and eighteen had none. For men only, nine of the Chinese had mention of employment stress and seven did not; only five of the Caucasians had this stress and eleven did not have it. Neither of these comparisons significantly differentiated the two groups.

Items 12 through 16 were of particular concern, because they were intended to assess an hypothesis of a Chinese staff member who had treated many Chinese in-patients, including eleven of the Chinese subjects in this study. It was his feeling that Chinese patients are less familiar with mental health resources and would be maintained by the family longer before being admitted to a mental health facility, even though the patients were disturbed. Therefore, these items attempt to assess the degree to which mental health facilities were used before admission, the length of time between the onset of the symptoms and admission, and the chronicity of the problem.

The comparison of the Chinese and Caucasian samples revealed no significant differences on any of the five variables. Nor were the trends in the predicted direction; exactly the same number (ten) of the patients in both

		Table 3			
		ANOVA Summary Table			
Source	*SS*	*df*	*MS*	*F*	*F crit.*
Btw S	179.28	39			
A (ethnicity)	39.1	1	39.1	10.59	p < .01
S/A	140.18	38	3.69		
Within S	1225.92	440			
B (syndromes)	395.08	11	35.92	*19.31*	p < .01
AB	54.67	11	4.97	*2.67*	p < .01
B/A	776.17	418	1.86		

samples had been hospitalized previously, the number of prior admissions was nearly the same, the modal length of time prior to admission was between one to six months for both, twelve of the Chinese and eleven of the Caucasians had never had difficulties as severe as those that preceded admission, and the distribution of levels of community adjustment were highly similar. Thus, the direct comparison of the samples does not support the hypothesis of the Chinese lack of knowledge and greater reluctance to utilize mental health facilities.

Admitting Psychiatric Symptoms A picture of admitting symptomology was obtained by ratings made after reading materials describing the patient's status at admission and the following ten days. Descriptions of the twelve dimensions or syndromes of psychiatric behavior on which the ratings were made are found in Table 2 (taken from Lorr and Vestre, 1968).

Three of the Chinese patients were placed on sleep therapy, receiving very high levels of medication for the first few days after admission. It was not felt that comparable ratings could be made for these persons. Therefore, admitting psychiatric ratings were not made for these subjects or for their matched controls, leaving a total of forty S's (twenty Chinese and twenty Caucasians).

The inter-rater reliability was very high, ranging from a low of .80 for disorganization to a high of 1.00 for perceptual distortion. The mean inter-rater reliability coefficient across the twelve dimensions was .88.

Figure 1 displays the mean scores for the two groups on each of twelve syndromes. The profiles of both groups appear somewhat similar. The Chinese subjects, however, do tend to be more elevated on most of the dimensions.

An analysis of variance comparing the Chinese and Caucasian subjects (summary table shown in Table 3) reveals that there is a highly significant overall difference between the two groups. The bulk of this difference could be accounted for by the nearly across-the-board higher level of disturbance of the Chinese patients. Moreover, there is a significant interaction effect. A possible interpretation of the latter is that there is some difference in the profile or pattern of scores for the two groups. Reported in Table 4 are the tests of simple main effects for the twelve syndromes between the Chinese and Caucasian subjects. Four of the dimensions — retardation, seclusiveness, care needed, and psychotic disorganization — are significantly different between the two groups. On all four, the Chinese subjects demonstrated higher levels of disturbance. If the high scores on these four syndromes are interpreted as a

FIGURE 1

$\overline{X}$ Ratings: Ethnicity (Chinese and Caucasians) by Psychotic Syndrome

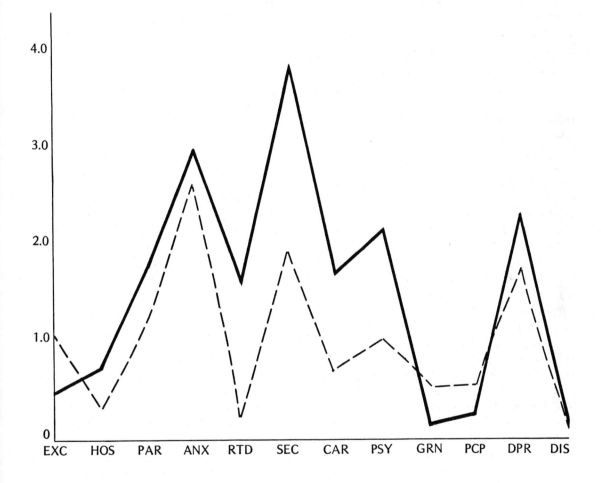

Chinese ▬▬▬▬
Caucasians ▬ ▬ ▬ ▬ ▬

	$SS_{a\ at\ b_i}$	$MS_{a\ at\ b_i}$	F	
		Table 4 Simple Effects of A (ethnicity) at b_i		
at b_1 (Excitement)	.03	.03	*.01*	
at b_2 (Hostile Belligerence)	2.3	2.3	*1.06*	
at b_3 (Paranoid Projection)	6.4	6.4	*2.96*	
at b_4 (Anxious Depression)	1.6	1.6	*.74*	
at b_5 (Retardation)	21.03	21.03	* *9.74*	$p < .01$
at b_6 (Seclusiveness)	34.23	34.23	**15.85*	$p < .001$
at b_7 (Care Needed)	10.1	10.1	* *4.67*	$p < .05$
at b_8 (Psychotic Disorganization)	13.23	13.23	* *6.13*	$p < .025$
at b_9 (Grandiosity)	1.23	1.23	*.57*	
at b_{10} (Perceptual Distortion)	.91	.91	*.42*	
at b_{11} (Depressive Mood)	3.23	3.23	*1.49*	
at b_{12} (Disorganization)	.10	.10	*.05*	

pattern, then the symptom profile of passive schizophrenic withdrawal would appear to be more typical for Chinese patients than Caucasians. In summary, the Chinese patients, when admitted, tended to be more disturbed than the Caucasian patients when measured across all twelve syndromes and, particularly, highly disturbed in the areas of retardation, seclusiveness, care needed, and psychotic disorganization.

Treatment and Discharge Table 5 reports the significance between the two groups on the five treatment and discharge variables.

The classifications by psychiatric diagnosis were compared. First, the diagnoses were categorized into psychotic, neurotic, and personality disorders, and, second, categorized as schizophrenic, depression (including both neurotic and psychotic depression), and all others. Sixteen of the Chinese were diagnosed psychotic, six as neurotic, and one as a personality disorder; whereas, for the Caucasians, it

was fourteen psychotic, seven neurotic, and two personality disorders. There was no significant difference between the groups. For the second breakdown, thirteen Chinese were classified as schizophrenic, eight depressed, and two other. For the Caucasians, it was nine schizophrenic, eleven depressed, and three other. Again, these differences were not found to be significant.

The mean length of stay for the Chinese was 33.6 days, with a range from 3 to 161 days; whereas, for the Caucasians, the mean was 37.3 days, with a range from 4 to 99 days. Neither the mean difference nor the difference in the variance of the distributions ($t = .04$, $p > .45$; $F = 1.62$, $p > .10$) was statistically significant.

The last three items could be used as indices of success of treatment. Discharge status has four categories: Maximum hospital benefit (MHB), against medical advice (AMA), eloped, and transferred. The majority of both groups were discharged MHB. Sixteen of the Chinese

Table 5
Treatment and Discharge Variables

	df	X^2 Value	t Value	Direction of Chinese Scores
1. Psychiatric diagnoses				
a. psychotic–neurotic personality	2	0.54		
b. schizophrenia–depression–other	2	1.40		
2. Length of hospital stay	44		0.04	
3. Discharge status	1	0.94		
4. Condition on discharge	1	2.70		
5. Return to Resthaven	1	0.00		

were MHB, one AMA, two eloped, and four were transferred; whereas, for the Caucasians, eighteen were MHB, none AMA, two eloped, two transferred, and the status of one patient was unknown. Categorizing the MHB classification as successful and all others as unsuccessful, there was no significant difference. Condition at discharge is a judgment, made by each attending psychiatrist, of the benefit of the hospitalization for each patient. Seventeen of the Chinese were judged to be treated and improved, and six were judged treated and unimproved; whereas, twenty-two of the Caucasians were judged to be treated and improved and only one was judged to be treated and unimproved. A Chi square analysis found this difference to be significant at the .05 level, but, when adjusted for continuity, it failed to reach significance. Exactly the same number (six) of the patients in both groups returned to Resthaven for additional in-patient treatment.

In summary, there were no significant differences in any of these variables. There does, however, appear to be a trend for more of the Chinese to be more frequently judged to be unimproved after treatment. There are two likely explanations of this trend. It might be, simply, that Chinese tended not to benefit from the treatment as greatly as the Caucasians did.

On the other hand, the Chinese were more disturbed and, therefore, may not have been as amenable to treatment.

Discussion

Caution should be used in interpreting findings from a case file study such as this. There are at least two levels of observation and recording between the subject's actual behavior and what is reported. First, there is the staff member who observed the patient directly and recorded his observation in the file; and, second, there is the rater who read the file and recorded the data for this report. There is the likely possibility that at least some information may be incompletely or selectively recorded in spite of the attempts at objectivity by the recorders. However, many of their data, such as the demographic items and length of stay, are beyond such distortion. Moreover, inaccurate information would be equally likely for either the Chinese or Caucasian subjects. Such random error would not bias the findings.

There do remain possible biasing effects, however. There is the possibility that some of the more apparent psychotic behavior was due to misunderstanding of the Chinese patients because of the culture differences and/or language barrier. Nearly half of the Chinese were found to have some difficulty speaking or understanding English, indicating their cultural difference from the Caucasians. The impact of this effect is lessened somewhat when it is noted that eleven of the Chinese patients were treated by a bicultural and bilingual Chinese psychiatrist, and, when perhaps two thirds of the patients were in the hospital, there was at least one Chinese-speaking staff member. Consequently, in the case files of the Chinese patients, there are, frequently, written notes by Chinese staff describing such aspects as thought disorder, hallucinations, etc. And, finally, in all other cases where there was a language problem, an interpreter was used, at least for the social history and initial psychiatric examination.

There is another possible biasing effect. For example, in the file of one Chinese patient there were several mentions, during his first few days, of his isolation and seclusiveness, remaining in his room for all but the scheduled activities of the milieu program. After a few days, however, another Chinese patient was admitted, after which there are mentions of the close relationship and interaction between these two patients, and by them together with other patients, and no further mentions of any seclusiveness. Thus, while the behavior of the patient may be accurately recorded during his entire stay, caution must be used in inferring what this behavior means. Was the patient's seclusiveness during his first few days aspects of psychotic behavior or, more likely, the result of the imposed isolation of being the only Chinese patient in an overwhelmingly non-Chinese setting? There remains, then, the possibility that some of the more disturbed behavior demonstrated by the Chinese patients is the result of such cultural isolation. However, since some of the psychiatric dimensions, such as retardation and care needed, refer to reasonably clear, interpretable behaviors, they should be less affected by such bias, and it is, therefore, not likely that all the increased psychiatric disturbance can be accounted for by this effect.

Given these limitations of the study, the two major findings remain supportable: (1) the severe mental health problems in the Chinatown area tend to be those of Chinese immigrants, and (2) the Chinese in-patients are, typically, more psychiatrically disturbed when admitted than Caucasian in-patients. In addition, the data suggest that Chinese in-patients are more frequently men, experience a higher level of family discord, tend to have more difficulties with employment and employment stress, and tend to be more frequently judged to be unimproved after treatment than Caucasian in-patients.

The data indicating a more pronounced psychiatric disturbance for Chinese in-patients than for Caucasians are similar to the finding of Sue and Sue (1971b). A comparison on the Minnesota Multiphasic Personality Inventory (MMPH) of American-Chinese male students and other male students who sought psychiatric services at a university clinic revealed that the Chinese tended to have more elevated profiles, indicating greater disturbance. The finding of greater disturbance for males who seek mental health services appears to be applicable to both Chinese immigrants and Americans of Chinese descent.

The suggested pattern of passive schizophrenic withdrawal for Chinese patients is supported, also, by evidence from other studies. Sue and Kirk (1972) reported that, based on data from personality and vocational tests, American-Chinese college students appear more inhibited, conventional, and socially withdrawn. If it is assumed that mental illness is an exacerbation of normal functioning, then, when the level of incapacitation has become severe, passive schizophrenic withdrawal might be a typical pattern for Chinese. Scofield and Sun (1960), using personality measures, found a group of Chinese immigrant college students to be more withdrawn, more shy, more emotionally insecure, more introverted, more sensitive, more suspicious, more cold and aloof than American college students. They predicted that

Chinese would tend more toward being schizothymic than Americans.

The hypothesis that the Chinese are unfamiliar with, and/or reluctant to use, mental health facilities was not supported in a comparison of the psychiatric histories of the Chinese and Caucasian samples. Of the data available from this study, this psychiatric history information is, probably, the most direct test of this hypothesis. However, this is in conflict with the conclusions drawn by Jew and Brody (1967), Tom (1968), and Sue and Sue (1971a) that Chinese underutilize mental health services in spite of psychiatric problems as great or greater than those of other groups. A comparison of Chinese patients in treatment at Resthaven finds, also, that they are seeking services at less than half the rate which would be expected from their population in downtown Los Angeles.

Although not supported by the direct test of this hypothesis in this study, some of the other data, such as the findings of higher levels of disturbance for the Chinese patients and the predominance of men, suggest that this hypothesis is worthy of further investigation. It may be that psychiatric hospitalization services are used by the Chinese only when the individual is very disturbed and when he is a man. In view of the findings of this study, the typical Chinese in-patient admission could be characterized as a male immigrant who, when he becomes severely disturbed, frequently is unable to work and, consequently, places a great deal of stress on the family. Under this pressure, the individual is brought by the family to a psychiatric hospital. If the person is a woman or a child on whom the family is not economically dependent, or a man who is not disturbed severely enough to encounter employment problems, it would be less likely that psychiatric hospitalization would be used. This model assumes that psychiatric hospitalization tends to be used by Chinese immigrant families when they are driven by necessity such as the severe incapacitation of the head of the household. In other instances, mental health problems would tend to be handled in other ways.

The two major findings of this study, also, have treatment implications. First, since the great majority of Chinese patients were immigrants, many of whom had English language problems, the need for a Chinese cultural influence in the in-patient treatment is apparent. Bicultural and bilingual Chinese staff are indicated. Not only could they converse with the patient in his natural language, but they could also differentiate between culturally determined and truly disturbed behavior. Moreover, they are, also, more likely to be seen by the patients as persons they can trust and in whom they can have more confidence of being understood.

Another way in which a cultural influence can be made is to encourage the family members to continue close contact with the patient. Visiting hours can be expanded and other rules which hinder patient-family contact can be eased. For example, Resthaven has encouraged the families of Chinese patients to bring in food and for the family, including the patient, to continue having meals together. Another way to increase Chinese cultural influence is to have more Chinese patients. The Chinese community underutilizes the in-patient service at Resthaven, even in spite of an effort which, for a period of time, removed all economic restraints. Other efforts should be made to increase the acceptance by the Chinese community of in-patient treatment for psychotic and other severely disturbed persons.

The second finding, the higher level of psychiatric disturbance, also points out the need for increased out-reach efforts to get patients to treatment sooner and for a preventative community mental health program. Such a program is discussed later in this paper.

II. Clinical Impressions of Chinese Out-patients

The discussion in this section draws, primarily, upon the experience of one of the authors, a bicultural and bilingual Chinese psychiatric social worker, with twenty Chinese patients who received service in Resthaven's out-patient clinic during 1971. However, the impressions recorded here also are based upon prior treatment efforts of this clinician and reflect her discussions with other psychiatrically trained Chinese mental health professionals, drawing upon their experience both at Resthaven and in other clinics and private practice situations in the Los Angeles Chinatown community.

Description of Chinese Out-patients

In one major regard, the Chinese out-patients closely resembled the in-patients described previously; they were, overwhelmingly, Chinese-Americans. Seventeen of the twenty out-patients were born in China or Hong Kong. Moreover, they, typically, spoke very little English.

The Chinese out-patients differed, however, from their in-patient counterparts on several other important dimensions. Whereas, 70 percent of the in-patients were men, the great majority of the out-patients, sixteen of twenty, were women. Although we did not have sufficient comparable data about the income of the out-patients to permit an exact comparison with the in-patients, the out-patients, as a group, appeared to have achieved a markedly lower income level. Nearly all of the out-patients were referred to our Center because they could not afford private fees. Furthermore, the out-patients seemed to be less well educated than the in-patient sample; only two of the twenty had any education beyond the equivalent of American high school. Finally, the out-patients were less severely disturbed as a group than were the Chinese in-patients. None of them were diagnosed to be psychotic. Typically, they complained of symptoms of anxiety and depression, particularly agitation, sleeplessness, and loss of appetite.

The symptomatic complaints were related to circumstances which were remarkably consistent for nearly all of these Chinese immigrant women. Frequently newly married prior to immigration, they had come to the United States expecting a dramatic change in their life style. They had imagined that in America their husbands would achieve a measure of wealth and prosperity. In fact, however, their husbands were able to provide only a marginal income. Most of the women had children shortly after their arrival and were forced, then, by the family's meager earnings, to take sewing into their homes or to work in sewing factories to supplement their incomes. Consequently, they found themselves working long hours, perceiving themselves as having insufficient time to devote to their children and family, and continuing to live in modest circumstances with little likelihood of change in the future.

Characteristically, they had no history of prior psychiatric disorder. The onset of the symptoms precipitating the treatment referral occurred within six to ten years after immigration, except for two patients who had been in this country more than twenty years. The referrals originated from family physicians or social service workers in local Asian agencies. They were, usually, presenting themselves for mental health services for the first time and at a time which was relatively early in the evolution of their emotional disorder.

Treatment Concerns and Recommendations

Attitudes Toward Mental and Emotional Problems   The Chinese out-patients were not "psychologically minded." They did not recognize a connection between previous events, and the emotions associated with those experiences, and their current circumstances and symptoms of emotional disorder. Symptoms were attributed to present situations. Considering the difficult circumstances under which many of these immigrants existed, there may have been considerable validity to their assessment of the derivation of their presenting symptoms.

However, the reliance of the out-patients upon explanations based solely on direct causality of immediate stressors, coupled with anxiety about mental health treatment, raised major barriers to giving them needed services. For example, several of the out-patients terminated treatment after two or three appointments, after explaining that they did not want to be identified as patients of a mental hospital. They expressed concern about becoming known within their community as having a mental illness. Because of such concerns, it is recommended that the focus and manner of treatment be altered to be in concert with perceptions of Chinese-American patients.

Problem-Solving Therapy and a Bicultural Therapist As one might expect, the Chinese out-patients were not responsive to insight-oriented interpretations. Treatment was seen by the patients to be most helpful when it focused on the presenting complaints and generated practical and immediate measures with which to deal with the perceived causes of their difficulties. Therefore, attempts to help these patients gain insight were limited to assisting them to see the immediate situation more realistically. A bilingual and bicultural Chinese therapist familiar with the local community was of great importance. The extremely limited English language capability of the Chinese-American out-patients made a bilingual therapist an absolute necessity. Moreover, since more than one dialect is spoken in Chinatown, the therapist had to have a multi-dialect capability. The therapist's bicultural familiarity was equally important to her language abilities. Her familiarity with the life style in China and Hong Kong permitted her to assist the patients to put their current circumstances into realistic perspective. She was able to discuss the discrepancy between the patients' expectations and their current situation. Furthermore, she was able to perceive the distortions that had been imposed on these discrepancies and communicate these to the patient.

Typically, it was found that, although the present circumstances in Chinatown were severe, the environmental factors were better than in China or Hong Kong. The cause of most of the patients' emotional problems and complaints was that they had little hope for a better future, mostly in terms of financial achievements, complicated by their experiences of cultural isolation and alienation which they were neither aware of nor willing to accept. Many of the patients had been forced to obtain employment outside the home, mostly in sewing factories, for minimal wages, in order to supplement their husbands' limited incomes. A few had the additional stress of trying to raise children in a strange land while having little time to devote to them. Whatever the specific circumstances, the greatest disappointment was that life was an ever-lasting struggle for bare survival with no tenable hope of improvement, contradicting what they had hoped and dreamed of before coming to the "land of golden opportunity."

Beyond clarifying the basic origin of the patients' difficulties, the focus was on assisting them to improve their current situations. The therapist was direct, participating with the patients in solving their problems. For example, it was pointed out that there were limited but increasing opportunities for change available through new community resources in Chinatown (English-as-a-second-language classes, employment and occupational training programs). With her familiarity with these programs, the therapist was, in some instances, able to make a referral which could alter the patient's current circumstances. Others were encouraged and motivated to seek social outlets such as community church groups and family associations in order to minimize their feeling of isolation.

Medication One form of specific and direct assistance that was particularly well received by the Chinese out-patients was the prescribing of medications. The medications often led to relatively prompt symptomatic relief. Furthermore, the prescribing of medications seemed to be a more familiar and acceptable form of treatment. It is of interest to note that the Chinese patients were unable to take medications in the same dosages that are typical for other clinic patients. Consistently, the dosages had to be reduced by one-half. A full dose would cause the patients to complain of feeling drugged. We can only speculate about the extent to which this is the result of differing physical tolerances to the chemicals or culturally determined psychological reactions to taking medications.

Irregular and Brief Treatment The Chinese out-patients were not inclined to recognize or to accept the structure of a "50-minute hour," or a once-weekly, scheduled appointment, both of which typify out-patient psychiatric clinic operations. Interviews often extended as long as two hours. Patients would often come in to the clinic unannounced and without an appointment or would come very early or very late for scheduled interviews. Moreover, the Chinese out-patients continued in active treatment only until a reasonable homeostasis had been restored. Treatment usually lasted no longer than six or eight interviews, after which patients would return for review of their medications or drop out altogether.

Individual Treatment Our experience suggests that Chinese-Americans seeking out-patient treatment are best treated in a one-to-one relationship rather than in a group. The vastness of China allowed for the development of many distinct dialects, each of which is quite different. Although it is possible, perhaps, to find a mental health professional fluent in several dialects, a group could not be conducted in several dialects simultaneously.

The close-knit quality of Chinatown is an even more important reason to avoid group modalities of treatment. The Chinese are eager to keep all of their difficulties within their immediate family. We have already pointed out the social pressure the immigrants fear from being identified as mentally ill. Discussion of emotional or interpersonal problems would be made almost impossible in a group situation. Finally, group modalities are doomed to improbable success, given the immigrants' focus

on restoration of homeostasis, and the quick termination of the verbal counseling situation, plus their disregard for regular appointments.

Chinese In-patient and Out-patient Differences The striking difference in the sexes of patients seeking in-patient and out-patient services (i.e., almost entirely men for in-patient and almost entirely women for out-patient) requires some discussion. One possible reason for the large percentage of women out-patients is that the therapist herself was a woman and might have been seen by the patient as a person similar to themselves and, consequently, more approachable. Moreover, the therapist had been involved, for several years, with the elementary school in Chinatown and had become known to mothers and professionals in the area. The women out-patients sought treatment, also, relatively early in the evolution of their disorder. This, too, is in contrast to the male in-patients, who, typically, were not actively seeking treatment themselves. It is possible that Chinese women will actively seek out some help to alleviate their emotional distress; whereas, Chinese men characteristically will not. In this instance, with the availability of a mental health professional, psychiatric services were utilized. If this mental health professional had not been available, then, it is likely that a herbologist, a medical general practitioner, or some other resource would have been sought and some treatment received that produced some symptomatic relief. For men, on the other hand, as was discussed in the previous section, treatment, typically, will be utilized only when the problem is very severe and incapacitates the head of the household. An additional factor may be that the woman's role as a secondary financial provider permits her more freedom to seek help; whereas, any time her husband spent away from work obtaining help would result in too great a financial loss. These explanations seem best to fit the data in this study. There are, of course, other possible ones.

In summary, it is indicated that out-patient

psychiatric treatment consisting of a combination of short-term, problem-centered, individual therapy, plus medication supervision, is most suitable for Chinese-American patients. In addition, a bilingual and bicultural Chinese therapist familiar with the local community is of crucial importance for the success of such treatment.

III. Community Mental Health Programs for Chinatown

The empirical and clinical observations presented in the previous sections of this paper suggest that innovative models of intervention must be developed for the Chinese-American immigrant. The American-Chinese who has been culturally assimilated may be treated adequately within the treatment modalities and service networks developed to serve the mainstream of Americans. The culturally unassimilated Chinese-American, on the other hand, does not readily enter these service networks, and, even if he enters, the treatment modalities offered him are oftentimes inappropriate.

One model of programming which seems particularly suited to the needs of Chinese-Americans, as Sue and Sue (1971) have previously suggested, is the community mental health model coordinated by a local community mental health center. Community mental health centers are established to serve a fixed geographic area. Because of the concentration of immigrant Chinese within relatively small areas or Chinatowns, it is likely that the entirety of that subcommunity would be contained within a single community mental health center's area of responsibility. One advantage of this is that it serves to focus more clearly, both for the community and the center, the shared responsibility for the residents of Chinatown.

There are several principles of operation common to all community mental health centers which also appear to be appropriate when considering comprehensive mental health services for the Chinese-American community.

In order to develop the rationale for applying a community mental health model, each of these principles will be discussed briefly below, followed by a description of a model program which exemplifies these principles as applied to the needs of Chinese-Americans living in the Los Angeles Chinatown community.

Modified Treatment Models Each community mental health center is charged to develop services particularly suited to the residents of its area of primary geographic responsibility. Treatment is to take place within the local community rather than in far-removed institutions such as the state hospital system. When a patient is hospitalized, the patient's usual roles within his family and community are severely disrupted. The effects of such isolation were discussed in Section I. Community mental health centers strive for alternatives to full hospitalization. When in-patient treatment cannot be avoided, centers attempt to minimize the length of the hospitalization and return the patient to the community as quickly as possible.

Local treatment of major mental illness and fast resumption of primary family and community roles are particularly important among Chinese-Americans. When the patient is hospitalized close to the family residence, they [the family] can maintain contact with the patient throughout the hospital phase of treatment. At the time of discharge, the patient may agree more readily to continued after-care services if he and his family are already familiar with the treatment facilities and staff.

The efficacy of problem-solving approaches with practical and limited goals when treating Chinese-Americans was previously discussed. Many community mental health centers have emphasized short-term, crisis-oriented, out-patient services in order to avoid more debilitating disorders, to serve more residents of their area, or to suit those patients who are less psychologically minded. Short-term, problem-solving treatment models are appropriate for Chinese-Americans for all of these reasons. In addition, these treatment techniques can be imparted more readily to paraprofessionals, and mental health manpower is a crucial problem when planning programs for Chinese immigrants.

Paraprofessionals and Mental Health Manpower There is a widely recognized shortage of professionally trained personnel to meet the existing demands for services in the mental health fields. This shortage of mental health professionals is even more acute among ethnic minorities. Furthermore, for the Chinese-American, there is little hope in sight for the appearance or training of bicultural and bilingual professionals (Koran, 1972). In Los Angeles, there is only one bilingual Chinese-American psychiatrist. American-Chinese who have been assimilated into the mainstream of American life and enter the mental health professions often share neither culture nor language with the Chinese immigrant.

In response to this manpower shortage, and, in addition, in recognition of the desirability of having staff who are familiar with the experience of their service population, community mental health centers have advocated the development of new mental health paraprofessionals and have stressed the recruitment and training of individuals from their indigenous population. These paraprofessionals can be trained to perform both the direct services described above and the preventive activities which follow, and their development and employment is particularly suited to the Chinese-American population, where language and cultural sensitivity are critical.

Programs of Primary Prevention Probably the most significantly unique feature of a community mental health model has been the emphasis on programs of prevention of mental illness. Preventive programs assume that mental health is more than the absence of mental illness. The preventive programs attempt to isolate and to strengthen behaviors and attitudes which constitute or contribute to positive emotional functioning and also, through

prompt treatment when needed, to prevent a full-blown psychiatric disorder from developing. Mental health programs are developed for both individuals and larger systems, e.g., neighborhoods, Head Start and child-care centers, senior citizen residences, etc.

Rationale for a Chinatown Community Mental Health Program

The flood of Chinese immigration to the United States which began in the 1960s shows no signs of ebbing in the foreseeable future. Neither the mainstream of the American economy nor the far less well-endowed Chinese business community can hope to absorb these new immigrants without considerable hardship. Similarly, the social service and health-delivery systems which have evolved gradually over the last fifty years to serve Chinatown are already overwhelmed by the influx of new residents. In the face of these circumstances, programs of prevention are a necessity rather than a luxury. If the health and social service needs are not anticipated and minimized, the available resources will prove hopelessly inadequate.

Because Chinese immigrants settled in a geographically distinct area, a network of services has grown up around them. Schools, health services, businesses, employment offices, immigration services, housing facilities, and entertainment activities exist in and around Chinatown. Many of the health and social service agencies have been able to recruit and train bilingual and bicultural employees. These bicultural employees constitute one primary vehicle through which a community mental health center can implement programs of primary prevention.

Each of these agency employees has access to immigrants in need of a particular service. Each also has expertise in a particular area — education, housing, employment, legal services, medicine, etc. Through programs of consultation, the mental health professional can impart to these professionals in other disciplines a better understanding of the mental health implications of their functions. With a greater knowledge of the symptoms of emotional stress and malfunctioning, the agency professionals can identify and refer persons in need of counseling services. Moreover, because of their access to, and acceptance by, the immigrants, they can not only refer individuals for mental health services but, also, have an educational impact on them.

For this reason, the mental health professional may attempt to promote coordination among the many agencies providing services to the Chinatown community. By promoting discussion and the exchange of information among agency personnel, interagency referrals are facilitated for multi-problem immigrant families. Furthermore, cooperative programs can be developed whereby two or more agencies can share their individual resources to accomplish their primary objectives. Recent Chinese-American immigrants have been slow to adjust to new and unfamiliar customs. They have avoided available educational, health, mental health, and welfare services in favor of traditional customs and folkways. Interagency community organization and consultation are effective methods of intervening and altering these attitudes and patterns of behavior.

Chinatown Health Team

The formation is proposed of a Chinatown Health Team which emphasizes the use of paraprofessionals, early identification and referral (case-finding), and direct efforts at education of the recent immigrants in areas which will assist in the process of acculturation and positive emotional functioning. The sponsor of this Chinatown Health Team would be a Community Council which would be composed of the business, civic, and religious leaders in the Chinatown community and of representatives from the various public and private agencies and organizations which serve the Chinatown area. The local community mental health center would contribute the needed initial community development and organization to unite the

groups behind this effort.[2]

Through the combined efforts of the bilingual Chinese professionals employed by the agencies and organizations participating in the Community Council, a small cadre of community workers would be recruited and trained from the indigenous Chinese-American population. The activities of these community workers would be coordinated by an experienced psychiatric social worker on the staff of the local community mental health center who would be supervised by the combined bicultural professionals contributing to this project. The community workers would perform casefinding, information and referral, case-aid, and educational functions in support of all of the agencies and organizations contributing professional staff time. The community workers would engage in home visits, allowing the professionals to deliver their more specialized skills to the immigrant families who are referred to the agencies' out-stations.

The community workers would make their initial contacts in the community through that subset of the Chinese immigrants who have managed to establish contact with one or another of the agencies supporting this project. Eventually, the project would accept direct referrals. These referrals should come from families of new immigrants who were, themselves, helped or knew of someone who was put into contact with help through the project. Referrals would be accepted, also, from local physicians and herbologists and from the churches ministering to the immigrant Chinese.

The community workers would be trained to take maximum advantage of the trust that the school teacher, minister, family member, or agency professional has already established with the new immigrant. This trust should be the vehicle through which the community worker would gain entry to the family home. The worker would be trained to go beyond the focus of the original referral to explore other possible areas of difficulty. Through a brief series of home visits, the worker would assist the family in identifying areas of need, interpret the services available relative to those needs, and elicit and correct common misconceptions about the problems or services. The community worker's involvement with an individual family would extend through the establishment of contact between the family and the appropriate resources.

In addition to the information and education imparted to individual families through the series of home visits, the community workers would conduct discussions and classes whenever opportunities would arise. Discussions would center on issues of understanding American customs and culture and the availability of resources. Furthermore, the community workers could distribute pamphlets and flyers printed in Chinese and describing the services of the individual agencies.

The community workers would be available, also, to the participating agencies for limited case-aid services. If a family or an individual should terminate services prematurely or if a problem should arise, the community worker who facilitated the initial referral would be available to make further contact with the family.

In summary, this model program would provide the Chinese-Americans living in the Los Angeles Chinatown community with the coordinated services of a health team augmented by the use of trained paraprofessional Chinese-Americans who are familiar with their customs, their language, and their problems. This Chinatown Health Team would facilitate the Chinese-American's entrance and experience in the service networks which he, presently, does not utilize and, in addition, provide him with preventive programs. Finally, such a program should accentuate, to the individual agencies the need to provide treatment modalities modified to meet the needs and expectations of the Chinese-American.

Chapter Notes

1. The authors are mental health professionals at Resthaven, a Community Mental Health Center in Los Angeles, California.

2. Such a health team has been initiated in the Los Angeles Chinatown, supported by a grant from the California State Department of Mental Hygiene to Resthaven Community Mental Health Center.

References

Barth, G. *Bitter Strength*. Cambridge: Harvard University Press, 1964.

Bingham, E. R. "The Sage of the Los Angeles Chinese." Master's thesis, Occidental College, 1942.

Chen, P. N. "The Chinese Community in Los Angeles." *Social Casework* 51, 1970, 591-598.

Jew, C. C., and Brody, S. A. "Mental Illness among the Chinese I. Hospitalization Notes over the Past Century." *Comprehensive Psychiatry* 8, 1967, 129-134.

Koran, L. M. "Psychiatry in Mainland China: History and Recent Status." *American Journal of Psychiatry* 128, 1972, 84-92.

Kung, S. W. *Chinese in American Life*. Seattle: University of Washington Press, 1962.

Lorr, M., and Klett, C. J. "Cross-cultural Comparison of Psychotic Syndromes." *Journal of Abnormal Psychology* 74, 1969, 531-543.

_____ ; Klett, C. J.; and McNair, D. M. *Syndromes of Psychosis*. Oxford: Pergamon Press, 1962.

_____ , Vestre, N. D. *Psychotic In-patient Profile*. Manual. Los Angeles: Western Psychological Services, 1968.

Scofield, R. W., and Sun, C. W. "A Comparative Study of the Differential Effect upon Personality of Chinese and American Child-Training Practices." *Journal of Social Psychology* 52, 1960, 221-24.

Sue, D. W., and Kirk, B. A. "Psychological

Characteristics of Chinese-American Students." *Journal of Counseling Psychology* 6, 1972, 471-478.

Sue, S., and Sue, D. W. "The Reflection of Culture Conflict in the Psychological Problems of Chinese-Americans." Paper presented at the first National Conference on Asian-American Studies, Los Angeles, 1971a.

_____ , and Sue, D. W. "Chinese-American Personality and Mental Health." *Amerasia Journal* 1, 1971b, 36-49.

Sung, B. L. *Mountain of Gold.* New York: Macmillan Co., 1967.

Tom, S. "Mental Health in the Chinese Community of San Francisco." Paper found in the Asian-American Studies Center, University of California, Los Angeles, 1968.

Part Five: Contemporary Issues

Introduction

Many important and unresolved issues face Asian-Americans. In this final section, we deal with several of these issues. One of the most invisible groups among Asians has been the elderly. Kalish and Yuen (Chapter 22) discuss the history and immigration of Chinese-, Japanese-, and Filipino-Americans. The authors point to the tremendous need to conduct research on the interaction patterns, role of dependency, response to chronic discrimination, changing kinship patterns, and value systems among the aged. Elderly Asians seem to be a particularly powerless group, and major problems, such as poverty, unemployment, loneliness, ill health, and frequent residential displacement by new construction, are quite common. The paper by Fujitomi and Wong (Chapter 23) analyzes the experiences of another often-ignored group — the Asian females. Traditionally, Chinese and Japanese families have considered the female inferior to the male. As a result, many girls accept their second-class status and exhibit low aspirations. This pattern continues throughout their lives and is strongly reinforced by males of all races. The Women's Liberation Movement has facilitated the re-examination of the position of Asian females, both as females and as members of a racial minority. Fujitomi and Wong note that, even among Asian youths, females are still considered inferior.

The article by Weiss (Chapter 24) attempts to dispel the stereotype that Chinatown inhabitants represent a homogeneous group. To the contrary, many factions within the Chinese community compete for political power and representation. Weiss identifies two major groups in the community. Some Chinese identify with traditional associations and conduct social and political affairs in a traditional "Chinese" manner. Others are aligned with values emphasizing both an American and Chinese orientation. Many youths are joining other Asians in order to create a new identity different from the first two groups. Weiss feels that the diversity within Chinese communities has facilitated the development of these alternative organizations. In general, most Asian communities suffer from a multiplicity of difficulties. Poverty, inadequate housing, and psychological stress are major problems. Sue (Chapter 25) discusses the innovative community programs designed to help Asian-Americans. These self-help programs include tutorial services, community organization, control of schools, and the use of paraprofessionals.

Endo's article (Chapter 26) analyzes another contemporary issue — the role of Asian-American Studies Programs at colleges and universities. Emphasis on Asian culture and the Asian-American experience is a recent phenomenon. As a result, the future direction for Asian-American programs is unclear. Currently, some programs have emphasized the history of Asian-Americans, personality and identity, community intervention, or research. Endo favors the research approach. The final paper, by Wagner (Chapter 27), analyzes Filipinos as a "minority within a minority."

22. Americans of East Asian Ancestry: Aging and the Aged

by Richard A. Kalish, Ph.D., and
Samuel Y. Yuen, MSW

[Editor's Note. In addition to the difficulties of conducting research in the area of minority groups noted in these papers, there are other difficulties, such as use of the terminology and even spelling. For example, grammatical rules and past usage indicate the use of hyphens, as in Asian-American. Many minority group members, however, object to the hyphen. The author of this paper preferred not to use the hyphen. However, the editor has inserted the hyphen to provide consistency with the other papers; and Black and White have been capitalized.]

Background

Those Americans who trace their national origins to East Asian countries are united by the accident of geography. Their countries of origin are in the same part of the world; they followed each other in successive immigration waves to the United States and Canada and filled similar job slots upon arrival; they settled, initially, on the West Coast and in Hawaii; and the vast majority of their people remain in that portion of North America today. As the result of these historical events, perhaps intensified by their relatively high social visibility as non-Europeans, they are often categorized as one group. Building upon this happenstance, many socially and politically active persons of these ethnic groups are attempting to build a pan-Asian consciousness.

Asian immigrants to the United States are racially distinct from other Americans; they are the products of high civilizations very different from those of the Occident; and most of these persons have come to the United States lacking skills of great value to an industrial society — they came as laborers and farmers. As a result, their history in this country has been, generally, one of struggle. They have suffered from racial discrimination; they have encountered major linguistic and cultural barriers to assimilation; and they have held low occupational status. Most of the elderly are immigrants and have very little education in this country, although many are literate in their native languages. As a result of these factors, their personal and occupational histories have been controlled by a culture that they did not understand and that they felt unable to influence. Research and services involving elderly Asian-Americans must be understood in this context.

Although, for purposes of this paper, we are going to consider the three largest nationality groupings from East Asia, we wish to be explicit that these are very much separate people in their traditions, their languages, their religions, and — most certainly — in their histories in the United States. They do, of course, share certain characteristics. Until recently, Japanese, Chinese, and Koreans all used an ideographic, rather than a phonetic, writing system invented in China; however, the diversity of native East Asian languages exceeds the diversity of European languages, and the linguistic picture is complicated by centuries of European contact and occupation. Although East Asian religion is vastly different from that of the United States (overwhelmingly non-Protestant), various forms of Buddhism are dominant in Japan; the Chinese tend to be Confucian; the Filipinos are largely Catholic and Muslim. We have not even included Koreans, Tibetans, Mongolians, and other East Asian groups in our discussion, because they are not separately counted by the U.S. Census, their numbers are, apparently, few; and we were unable to fund sufficient substantive, or even speculative, materials on them. However, once in the United States, their common designation by the term "Asian" and their common encounter with discrimination may produce, for many individuals, an ethnic experience similar enough to call forth a shared pride in the achievements of all Asian peoples and a shared anger at their neglect in the United States.

A paper of this nature runs into an additional difficulty: that of overassuming homogeneity within ethnic groups. Americans of East Asian ancestry include Chinese from the rice-rich plains of the south, the barren hills of the north, and the great commercial and cultural capitals of China. Japanese came from the Ryukyus, Hokkaido, and everywhere in between; Filipinos, from Manila and the relatively undeveloped areas of the southern islands.

One more complicating element requires comment. Until 1965, the correlation between age and generation among Asian-Americans was substantial and, of course, negative. Thus, the first-generation Japanese (Issei) were consistently older than the second generation (Nisei) which, in turn, was older than the third generation (Sansei); students and war brides were among the many exceptions, but the relationship was reasonably consistent. By 1970, however, the picture had changed. The new

immigration laws, set forth in the early 1960s, permitted relatively large numbers of immigrants from these Asian countries; most of these were (or, at least, were supposed to be) relatives of those already American citizens. Some were old, but many were middle-aged. Filipinos and Chinese came in large numbers (again, these figures must be considered in reference to the minuscule immigration quotas of past decades); those entering from Japan were not so numerous. Thus, the straight-line function between age and generation ceased to exist; today, the grandfather might well have been born and reared in San Francisco's Chinatown, while the middle-aged nephew has just arrived from Hong Kong, to which he had migrated during the "land reforms" of the People's Republic.

The complexities described above hold true for many behavioral scientific discussions. While important to note in an explicit fashion, they do not destroy the integrity of research, theory, or speculation regarding these persons. In essence, the purposes of this paper are twofold: first, to assess the state of knowledge about the lives of elderly people of East Asian ancestry now living in the United States, with particular focus upon those from Japan, China, and the Philippines; and, second, to suggest avenues for research with these groups.

The Need for Research

As this volume amply demonstrates, professionals and planners working with the aged are faced with two very distinct, but equally severe, problems: first, many of the elderly have general needs which are obvious and critical; they need the means to purchase goods and services; they need the opportunity and the setting to be with others with whom they share values and traditions; they need access to supportive services provided by knowledgeable persons who speak their language, literally and figuratively; they need the support of persons who understand the mores and customs of their reference groups; and they need whatever little they receive from their society to be given with a sense of respect for their dignity. Second, the urgent task of compiling, systematizing, and disseminating the vast body of data required to cope with the vastly heterogeneous, specific needs of the elderly has scarcely begun.

Extensive formal research and informal observation on elderly Asian-Americans on the part of the authors indicate that both these problems apply to this group no less than to any other. The common assumptions that Asian-Americans "take care of their own," or "respect their elderly," or "rarely become social problems" are gross oversimplifications with very limited applicability.

Attempts to solve the twin problems of intervention and research must, ultimately, compete for funds; and, since elderly individuals *know* what many of their own specific needs are, from their point of view research carries a comparatively low priority. The authors of this paper agree with the elderly that, if they had the money and power to pay for needed services, the market place would provide the research necessary to develop those services — and the services themselves. If, by the reallocation of research funds to public services, the needs of the elderly could be met, adequately and appropriately, it would be a mistake to demand research. However, this is not the case. If all government funds now spent on research involving elderly Asian-Americans were directed to services, the impact would hardly be felt by those persons. In addition, elimination of research would reduce, substantially, possibilities of more effective use of funds for future programs. Also, it is not merely use of funds that is important but also improvement of human interactions through improvement of human understanding, and research is, often, helpful in this regard. In the following discussion, we assign first priority to research that involves maximizing the effectiveness of existing funds and programs, pointing the way to appropriate new kinds of services, and improving life satisfaction through improved understanding.

Review of Relevant Literature

Sources of Material

Our presentation is based upon several sources. These include (a) printed sources, e.g., government documents (especially census materials), published books and papers, and, in exceptional circumstances, unpublished theses and other unpublished materials; (b) the personal research, observations, and professional experiences of the authors and their informants.

For census data, we have had to rely mostly on reports from the 1960 United States Census and on those of various state agencies. Since 1960, however, there has been a sharp increase in the number of immigrants arriving in the continental United States from China and the Philippines, caused by changes in the immigration law. Data regarding death rates, incomes, and places of residence of these people are not readily accessible to us and may, in fact, be nonexistent. It is very likely that many elderly Asians are not counted by the Census. For example, the official records show 47,000 Chinese in San Francisco in 1969 [San Francisco Chinese Community, 1969 (SFCC)], but unofficial estimates of well-informed observers run as high as 80,000 — a sizable difference. Dr. Isao Fujimoto, a sociologist at the University of California, Davis, reports that there are many neglected enclaves of poor elderly Asians in rural California (personal communication). These elderly are apt to be underrepresented in the Census and in state and local surveys because they are among the most mistrustful of government agents, suffer the greatest language handicaps, and, often, are poorly informed regarding worldy matters — nor are they likely to come forward in response to propaganda efforts by government authorities to encourage the recalcitrant to register for the Census.

Published books and articles are sparse in this area. In an attempt to add to those materials with which we were already familiar, we sent letters to forty scholars, primarily Asian-Americans themselves, to elicit additional sources; this led only to a handful of published studies. In a further attempt to seek out published works, we submitted a complete draft of this paper to an additional group of knowledgeable persons, and, although we were able to incorporate some of their suggestions, this did not lead to additional articles or books.

It will quickly become evident in the following pages that an unusual amount of source material reflects California in general and San Francisco in particular. To some degree, this has occurred because both authors reside in the Bay Area. Equally instrumental in this circumstance is the fact that, excluding Hawaii, the majority of Asian-Americans in the United States reside in California, and some of the best sources of data in the country are located in the San Francisco area.

Statistical Descriptive Data

Chinese-Americans

The Chinese began arriving in the United States in the 1850s, mainly as coolie labor. The Chinese population reached a high tide in 1890, then began to decline to a low in the 1930s. This decline resulted from two factors: one, a period of rigorous exclusion of Chinese immigrants, and, two, the return to China of many earlier immigrants. During the late 1930s, the Sino-Japanese war sharply reduced the flow of re-emigration to China, and, following the war, the exclusion of Chinese from the United States was gradually eased.

Although most Chinese immigrants settled on the West Coast, there has been a steady trickle to cities east of the Rockies. In spite of large fluctuations in the Chinese-American population, the percentage who are aged does not seem to have changed much since 1910 (Schmid, Nobbe, and Mitchell, 1968). This is probably due to the cutoff of young immigrants, the low rate of population growth from births until 1940, and the tendency for the middle-aged to return to China.

The 1960 Census lists 12,415 Chinese-Americans over 65. (Data include Alaska and Hawaii.) This is 6.88% of the total Chinese population. The sex ratio of the elderly is heavily skewed in the direction of males, and the skewing increases with age, so that there are, approximately, three men for every woman over 65 — a fact which reflects the pre-World War II immigration pattern. Twenty-seven percent of the elderly Chinese-Americans live with a spouse (U.S. Census, 1960), compared to 43 percent for the general population of elderly.

During the late 1950s and early 1960s, about 200 Chinese over 60 immigrated to the United States each year (Sung, 1967). Beginning with the Immigration and Nationality Act of 1965, which became fully effective in 1968, there has been a sharp upturn in Chinese immigration; and the number of elderly entering per year has been around 500 since 1965, about 3 percent of total immigration [United States Immigration and Naturalization Service, various dates (USIN)]. The number of Chinese-Americans over 65 in 1970, therefore, must be somewhere around 15,000.

About 95 percent of this small population live in cities. San Francisco alone had an elderly Chinese-American population of approximately 10,000 in 1969 (SFCC, 1969), some two-thirds of the nation's total, and Chinese communities of significant size also exist in Boston, Chicago, Honolulu, Los Angeles, New York, Oakland, Philadelphia, Portland, San Antonio, and Seattle.

The median annual income reported for the total Chinese-American elderly group in 1959 was $1,281; however, 21.6 percent reported no income (U.S. Census, 1960) . (Because these data are over a decade old, they should be interpreted with considerable caution.) In spite of this apparently wretched economic picture, only one in ten elderly Chinese-Americans in San Francisco received Old Age Assistance benefits in 1969 (SFCC, 1969). There are no reliable data on sources of livelihood for these people. Most of them receive small Social

Security benefits, but many were self-employed or worked at menial jobs that provided no Social Security coverage. Support from family, neighbors, and friends is an unknown quantity, but observations of a large number of families in San Francisco indicate that there has been a serious erosion of Chinese patterns of kinship and community in the urban United States, so that even old folks who are lucky enough to have children can, by no means, count on them for help.

All of the above are further complicated by the fact that about 90 percent of San Francisco's elderly Chinese are immigrants from abroad, and nearly all of them have difficulty with the English language (SFCC, 1969).

Japanese-Americans

Significant Japanese immigration to the United States began in 1880. Like the Chinese, the Japanese who came first were mostly young, unskilled males, and, like the Chinese, most planned to return to their homeland after a few years. However, with the exception of a few years in the 1929s and 1940s, the Japanese population of the United States increased steadily; this increase may conceal the large turnover during the 1910s and 1920s (Ichihashi, 1932). Unlike the Chinese, the sex ratio began to shift around 1908, and, by 1930, most immigrants had established families. Prior to World War II, when the Japanese-Americans were evacuated from the West Coast, more than 80 percent lived in the Pacific Seaboard states, and the population, as a whole, was about evenly divided between urban and rural areas. As a result of their wartime internment and relocation, the percentage living in the West Coast states dropped to about 70 percent, and the number living in cities rose to 71 percent (Lyman, n.d.).

The 1960 Census reported 29,235 Japanese-Americans over 65 in the United States, including Alaska and Hawaii, comprising 6.03 percent of total Japanese-American population. The sex ratio is, approximately, four men for every three women, again reflecting the pattern of previous immigration. The sex ratio is presently shifting toward female preponderance, since Japanese-American men tended to marry women of a much younger age, and since the Japanese-American women, like their Occidental counterparts, live considerably longer than men. Perhaps, the 1970 Census will show a one-to-one ratio. The proportion of elderly living with a spouse is 38 percent.

The immigration from Japan since the last Census has been only about a tenth that of the Chinese, and less than 2 percent have been over sixty, so the increase in this age group due to immigration cannot be more than a few hundred (U.S. Census, 1960; USIN, various dates).

The reported median annual income of elderly Japanese-Americans in 1959 was $1,163 — lower than that of either the Chinese- or Filipino-Americans. (Because these data are over a decade old, they should be interpreted with considerable caution.) Twenty-one percent reported no income. In spite of these figures, it is our impression that the majority of the elderly are adequately cared for by their relatives, or are able to live on savings. Kanagawa (1955) reports that less than 1 percent of Japanese over sixty-five in Honolulu in January of that year were receiving Old Age Assistance. This figure takes on added significance if there is truth to the observation that Japanese immigrants, typically, acculturated faster than the Chinese. We would expect elderly Japanese-Americans to be better aware of their rights as welfare recipients. Most elderly Japanese-American men speak at least broken English, but there are many women who speak only Japanese.

Health statistics indicate that the elderly of this group are surprisingly healthy and long-lived. A study done in Hawaii in 1958-1959 showed sick days for Japanese-Americans over 65 to be less than one-third of the national average and less than half of the average for Hawaii (Bennett, Tokuyama, and Bruyere,

1963). Psychiatric hospitalization rates are low for all age groups of Japanese-Americans; but, like Chinese-Americans, once hospitalized, Japanese-Americans tend to remain longer than Caucasians (Kitano, 1968).

Filipino-Americans

Of the three ethnic groups covered in this report, least is known about the Filipino-Americans. Prior to 1920, there were probably not more than 5,000 Filipinos in the continental United States. After that, there was free migration between the Philippines and the United States; and it is now difficult to reconstruct the immigration picture. By 1930, there were some 45,200 Filipinos in the United States; and, about the same time, immigration virtually ceased, due to the Depression. During the years 1935 to 1945, an immigration quota of 50 a year was imposed (Burma, 1954). Some 40 percent of the country's 106,426 Filipinos in 1960 had appeared on the scene since 1950. The immigration rate has continued to rise [in the 1960s], so that there may be twice that number today. So far, this immigration has been overwhelmingly young. Prior to the war, it was also overwhelmingly male. Although the Filipino-American population was about half rural and half urban in 1950, by 1960 it was about two-thirds urban; and this trend appears to be continuing. Informed sources estimate a stable increase in the Filipino-American population of San Francisco alone of about 3,000 per year since 1964.

According to the 1960 Census, there were 6,546 Filipino-Americans over sixty-five in the United States (3.61 percent of the total population), of whom nearly 85 percent were male. The fact that 29.3 percent of the elderly were living with spouses in 1960 reflects the high rate of interracial marriage for Filipino-American men. This may also reflect the fact that many were prohibited from marrying by anti-miscegenation laws until 1948 — giving marriages less time to terminate in death or separation than is the case for other groups.

Since 1965, only 561 Filipinos over sixty years of age have legally entered the United States; and, today, the total number of elderly is, probably around 7,300.

Most of these live in Honolulu, Los Angeles, New York, Seattle, Portland, San Francisco, and in rural California (especially around Stockton). Language is a serious problem for the elderly, many of whom were born and raised in the Philippines and speak, with fluency, only Spanish, Tagalog, or Ilocano. Although many of the elderly sought American educations in their youth, most were unable to survive as students; and their education level is, generally, low (Burma, 1954). The California Department of Mental Hygiene (DMH) reports a disproportionately large number of Filipino men in state mental hospitals (DMH, various dates), but we are aware of no studies showing age at admission or seeking an explanation of this statistic.

Current Research

Published material specifically on elderly Asian-Americans is extremely scanty. The existing material is scattered throughout historical, social, literary, and biographical writings. It is often dated and repetitive, and it is, usually, difficult to interpret sociologically. Rather than review these fragments individually, we have elected to summarize their contents in a general way and to append a bibliography of the more useful works. Data also are being collected and analyzed in a few research projects, and these projects are briefly described.

Chinese-Americans

China has been described as a "gerontocracy" because of the position of the elderly in the family and the general veneration of the aged in the Chinese world view. Ideally, old age is a time when one presides, both literally and symbolically, over a large group of co-resident kin. One of the greatest misfortunes a Chinese can suffer is to fail to produce sons who will care for him in old age and in the afterlife. The aged are regarded not only with respect but also with profound affection.

Although this ideal was, probably, not often lived up to, there is plenty of ethnographic description of pre-Communist China showing that the aged did command considerable power in the family (Freedman, 1958; Gamble, 1963; Hsu, 1948; Yang, 1945). Sources on elderly Chinese-Americans point uniformly to the marked breakdown of these traditions in the United States. In this respect, there is some contrast between the Chinese-Americans and the Japanese-Americans. The main reason for this difference seems to have been the greater degree of overt discrimination against the Chinese immigrant. Although both groups were the victims of many discriminatory laws and a great deal of extra-legal persecution, the Chinese bore the brunt of this. When they arrived in California, the West was less "civilized" than when the Japanese came, some 30 years later. Mob violence often characterized interracial relations, and the foreigners, usually, were blamed for it. To make matters worse, the Chinese were a conspicuously large minority in the sparsely settled Pacific region of the United States. In 1880, there were about 87,000 Chinese in this region, compared with about 87 Japanese (Lyman, n.d.). The imagined threat of inundation by Chinese hordes stimulated a frenzy of anti-Chinese feeling in the Pacific states. This, in turn, resulted in laws which prohibited Chinese immigrants from — among other things — bringing wives or families to the United States or marrying other races. This produced the sex ratio which has plagued Chinese communities throughout the country ever since. In most areas with large Chinese-American populations, there are groups of single males who have been derailed, as it were, from the normal cycle of life. They have missed the normal payoff for a life of hard work and self-sacrifice: an honored position in a family.

By contrast, the Japanese came later, in smaller numbers, and from a nation which was to be reckoned with as a military and industrial power. Until the third decade of this century, Japanese immigration was regarded much more benignly. Although the "Gentlemen's Agreement" between Japan and the United States in 1907 required self-imposed limits on Japanese passport issues, women and skilled men were allowed to immigrate in sizable numbers until the Alien Exclusion Act of 1924. About a third of the Japanese who legally entered the United States during this period were women and children (Ichihashi, 1932).

The Chinese pattern of immigration speeded the breakdown of many native patterns of community organization and social control. This was true, especially, in urban areas, with the result that children no longer are required by their community to take responsibility for their aged parents. The American emphasis on material success, the functional autonomy of the nuclear family in an urban-industrial milieu, and economic discrimination often create pressures upon the children of Chinese immigrants to disregard their elderly parents. Many succumb to these pressures.

It is interesting to note that the Chinese-Americans had an unusually high rate of narcotics addiction prior to 1960 and that single male "sojourners" — men who intended to return to China and had formed few ties of either a personal or an ideological variety in this country — appeared to be the most susceptible to addiction. Bell and Lau (1966) found that there were, apparently, many elderly bachelors who never got into trouble with the law but who, eventually, wound up in public health hospitals, seeking help for their drug problems.

We are aware of only a single current research project which focuses, specifically, on elderly Chinese-Americans. This is centered at Self-Help for the Elderly (SHE), an organization devoted to coping with the problems of senior citizens in San Francisco's Chinatown. Through contacts with clients, SHE is collecting information on the financial, housing, health, and recreational problems of the elderly, and it is an excellent source of information.

The Community Mental Health Services office of the San Francisco Health Department is, currently, conducting a detailed study of hospital admissions which will yield more detailed data on age, ethnicity, and mental illness than that currently available from state and local agencies. The Bureau of Biostatistics of the California Department of Mental Hygiene has data on all state mental hospitals that also could be used to study all Asian-American groups.

Japanese-Americans

There are a few studies of the Japanese in America that contain some data on the history of the immigrant generation, most of whom are now over sixty-five. There was a greater tendency among Japanese immigrants than among other Asian groups, in the early decades of this century, to establish families on American soil. Although we do not know what percentage of the immigrant generation married, Caudill (1952) reports that 69.5 percent of the 181 Issei interviewed in Chicago in 1950 were living with children. The familism of the Japanese immigrant has had a profound influence on the current status of the elderly Japanese-Americans in at least four ways. First, because their American children developed strong ties to their country of birth, many immigrant parents gave up their original intention of returning to Japan. They became more interested in American culture, if only to protect themselves and their children from its influences; however, in the process, they became more acculturated than other Asian groups. Second, some of the fluency of the American-born children in the idioms of this culture rubbed off on the immigrant parents. Third, Japanese family patterns, including a sense of responsibility for aged and dependent family members, had a chance to take hold in the subculture, and, today, many of the elderly enjoy at least economic security provided by their children. Fourth, the second and third generations in America have been well educated

and, on the whole, economically successful. This has given the elderly a deep sense of pride in their accomplishments, has improved their lives materially, and has helped to compensate for the discrimination they suffered when young.

Upon arrival in the United States, the first-generation Japanese-Americans (Issei), generally found work in agriculture and small business. They were often self-employed, if not initially, then within a few years after settling (Kitano, 1968). Even today, many of these now-elderly men work in nurseries and as contract gardeners. To provide in-group cohesiveness, for both practical and psychological reasons, these Issei established the Japanese Association (a protective league) and, often, retained close ties with others of their region ("ken") in Japan (Miyamoto, 1939).

Prior to World War II, the immigrant generation exerted powerful control over their offspring; the War radically changed that. When the Japanese were forcibly removed from their homes on the West Coast and interned in relocation centers, the power of the immigrant generation was severely curtailed. Many immigrants lost their means of livelihood and, with it, the economic basis of their authority. In addition, the immigrants were barred from citizenship, and their citizen children found themselves carrying much of the legal responsibility for their crisis-stricken communities.

One might hypothesize that the wartime relocation merely accelerated a change that would have come from other factors. In Japan, the role of the parent is well-defined and receives substantial community support; this was particularly true at the time the Issei left Japan. In the United States, the relationship of child to parent is more a function of internalized values than community pressures. As acculturation occurred, the Issei parents lost their power to control their children by community pressure and had not sufficiently socialized these children into filial respect through internalized values. Thus, social, economic, and psychological factors conspired to affect the elderly Issei.

From an Anglo point of view, the second-generation children (Nisei) appeared loyal to, and supportive of, their parents; from the viewpoint of these parents, such loyalty and support, often, were uncertain. We know of no research reports that explore the effects of these factors upon the elderly Japanese-Americans.

Currently underway are several research projects which will provide much new information on the elderly Japanese-Americans. Drs. Warren Winkelstein and S. Leonard Syme of the School of Public Health at the University of California, Berkeley, are conducting an epidemiological study of heart disease and acculturation. Approximately 3,500 Japanese-American males, aged thirty to sixty-nine, are included in this study. This should yield important data on health and health-related behavior. The Japanese-American History Project at UCLA has collected detailed interviews from 1,047 Japanese immigrants and from 62 percent of their living children, as well. (The project was under the administrative direction of Mr. Joe Grant Masaoka until his untimely death in June, 1970. Principal investigator is Dr. Gene N. Levine.) Although not based on a random sample of elderly Japanese-Americans, the study will yield much information on acculturation, family life, attitudes, and social problems of this group. These data were being collected prior to 1967 and are now being analyzed.

Drs. Richard Kalish and David Reynolds of the School of Public Health at UCLA are currently studying death and bereavement among Japanese-Americans as part of a cross-cultural and cross-generational study. Results, based upon both community survey and participant-observer methods, were to be available in 1972. Drs. Margaret Clark and Chris Kiefer of Langley-Porter Neuropsychiatric Institute are conducting a cross-cultural study in San Francisco of aging and intergenerational relations among Anglos, Japanese-Americans, and Mexican-Americans. This study combines an ethnographic description of the minority communities with intensive interviews in three-generation families. The interviews focus on perceptions of aging and the elderly, and on intergenerational relations. Preliminary results were to be available in late 1971.

Filipino-Americans

There are no published studies of the elderly Filipino in America. This may be due partly to their small number and partly to their migratory patterns which prevented the founding of stable communities. Many of their principal occupations — such as domestic service, seamanship, and seasonal agricultural labor — have been among the least conducive to community life. A fair number of Filipino-Americans managed to find spouses, often marrying non-Filipino women.

The unusually large number of Filipino-American men in psychiatric hospitals (DMH, various dates) might be an indication of the stress experienced by those whose social environment is predictable only in the sense that it is consistently nonsupportive.

Directions for Future Research

Previously, we referred to the need for research in the interests of more effective and humane social policy. Here, we would like to clarify the relationship between research and policy, as applied specifically to Asian-American elderly. We will divide our remarks into three rather crude and overlapping categories for purposes of discussion.

Theory Building

An adage, widely accepted by scientists, is that there is nothing more practical than a good theory. Granting that the statement is a mere tautology, or bit of literary cleverness, until the concepts are defined, good theoretical research on older Asian-Americans can be made to serve humanistic purposes. For example, does disengagement theory apply to these populations? Do Erikson's developmental stages help us understand Asian-American elderly? Do Kluckhohn's dominant value orientations clarify interethnic and intergenerational conflicts? Which theory of suicide is best in explaining the suicide rates and related behavior of older Asian-Americans?

On the other hand, we also feel strongly that services are very much needed for a large proportion of Asian-American elderly, and we dislike having to pit research against services, even though the funds allocated to research might not make much dent in the need for services. Therefore, we encourage behavioral scientists to turn their creative efforts to conducting theoretical research in the field, in such a fashion that this research might be part of a program evaluation or might lead to the introduction of a new program.

Thus, it appears obvious that behavior modification theory could be tested upon these populations in the context of improving self-esteem or esteem for the subject's ethnic identity group. In evaluating theories of suicide, can some community intervention be introduced that might, in the long run, reduce suicide and other self-destructive behavior? The investigator of disengagement theory should, in any event, determine the conditions under which disengagement is adjustive and the conditions under which it is maladjustive for these groups; then, by using appropriate modes of communication, this information can be fed back into the community to help appropriate practitioners.

The tendency of theoreticians to leave the terms "practical" and "good theory" undefined, or to acquiesce to definitions supplied by research funding agencies, has not engendered trust for their profession among research subjects, especially those in ethnic communities. Subjects are no longer so docile in the face of the researcher, and older Asian-Americans are, in some instances, being exhorted to be noncooperative with researchers who do not offer some form of *quid pro quo.*

We do not have any particular preference as to which theories are tested in the Asian-American communities; our concern is that a major effort be made to tie these studies to an ongoing service, to use them to provide a service or to establish the base for a possible future service.

Improving Understanding

Some research is geared neither toward theory building nor program evaluation, although it may be tangentially involved with either or both. Rather, it attempts to produce an improved understanding of individuals or groups. Attitude surveys and other forms of testing may be included in this classification, e.g., a study comparing religious values and practices of various groups of older Asian-Americans, or a longitudinal investigation of personality changes that occur beyond age sixty.

In many instances, the utility value of such studies is obvious. Religious leaders in the ethnic communities may find it very helpful to gain an understanding of how the elderly feel about religious and theological issues; such information can easily help improve church-related programs for the older person, can help ministers and pastoral counselors relate to their old parishioners on a personal basis, and may well produce increased interest in the elderly on the part of the clergy. At the same time, such a study might have major theoretical implications in terms of, for example, the relationship between cultural assimilation and value change or the relationship between religious identification, church affiliation, and disengagement.

At the risk of slighting important topics for the Asian-American elderly, we would recommend that the following be pursued:

1. *The interaction between age and generation.* As mentioned earlier in this paper, the correlation between age and generation is not as high as it was a few years ago, at least among the Chinese and the Filipino. Thus, not all elderly Chinese are first generation; not all young Chinese are native-born Americans. In order better to

serve the Chinese-American elderly, we should gain some insights into those needs, expectations, feelings, and so forth that differentiate the elderly first-generation Chinese-American from the elderly native-born Chinese-American and from the middle-aged first-generation Chinese-American. We may, then, be able to learn which characteristics are, primarily, a function of having been born and reared in China prior to immigrating to the United States, and which characteristics result, primarily, from being elderly in a Chinese-American community. Such a study would add to theorizing on assimilation and acculturation and would, simultaneously, provide clues for the provision of services for Chinese-Americans today; equally important, it would be very helpful in planning ahead as today's middle-aged Chinese-Americans become older. An additional outcome of such research would be added insights into intergenerational differences and similarities and how these relationships relate to age-by-generation breakdowns.

2. *The role of dependency.* The parental cultures of these people are perceived as instilling intense pride in independence. Although dependency upon family members in old age is characteristic of traditional Japanese and Chinese culture, it is unacceptable to many of the elderly themselves, unless legitimized by the proper attitudes on the part of the young. According to the observations of the authors and of many knowledgeable persons, old Asian-Americans will, often, suffer extreme physical hardship rather than "lose face" by asking for help from impersonal institutions, an act they perceive as requesting charity. Research is needed to determine whether these feelings are actually more intense and more common in older Asian-Americans than in other populations; to learn how these

feelings interfere with or abet their general well-being and self-esteem; to evaluate whether some services are so important for health and personal satisfaction that some intervention might be introduced to make the dependency role more palatable; and to evaluate these interventions in terms not only of alleviating the immediate problem but of doing so without adversely affecting individual self-esteem.

Another aspect of dependency is the various kinds of dependency that the elderly have upon family members, especially siblings and children. We perceive the ideals of the general American culture as being extremely ambivalent in this regard, but the ideals of traditional Asian society as being fairly explicit in establishing the responsibility of the children. What, then, takes place in a setting when initial expectations, developed during early periods of socialization, conflict with contemporary norms? How do the elderly cope with these changes? How do their middle-aged children deal with them?

3. *Response to chronic victimization from discrimination.* The elderly Asian-American who has lived much of his life in the United States has been, in varying degrees, discriminated against (and, occasionally, discriminated "for," i.e., has received favorable treatment) over an extended period of time. He is often perceived, by the general community, as "being used to hardship," "accepting suffering philosophically," and "taking care of his own." These stereotypes, regardless of their validity, serve to alleviate the conscience of the general community. They may, also, work against the provision of adequate services for those elderly Asian-Americans who are in need. We need to investigate the degree to which these stereotypes have a kernel of

truth (the authors do *not* advocate a direct attitude survey for such a study) and and those coping mechanisms utilized by these persons in their dealing with discrimination. How effective have these personal, social, and community coping mechanisms been? How has self-esteem been affected by the discrimination and to what extent, if any, has this impact been reduced by coping strategies? What can be learned to help others, both old and non-old, to make use of the most effective mechanisms in their adult development? And, of course, what can be done to help reduce discrimination?

4. *Changing kinship patterns.* We are so accustomed to hearing that Asian-Americans "take care of their own" that it is difficult to believe some of the claims that there is a breakdown in traditional kinship patterns to the detriment of the older persons. Yet, one of the authors has learned of increasing interest in social gerontology on the part of aging Nisei who fear that their Sansei children will not provide them with the care they have given (they feel) to their Issei parents; other observations fortify this view. We should address ourselves to the ways in which kinship patterns are changing, the impact this has upon the older Asian-American, the bases for the changes, and what interventions might be instituted. This last, it must be emphasized, is a very complex, and even dangerous, matter, since an intervention to aid the elderly might have deleterious effect upon other family interactions, upon family finances, upon Asians' beliefs that they are being pressured into adhering to norms established by non-Asian persons, and so forth.

5. *Out-group contacts.* Very little is known about the kinds and frequency of contact between older Asian-Americans and those not of the Asian communities. It would be helpful to learn the nature of such social contacts, the circumstances under which they occur, the perceptions of each of the participants, and the long-range outcome. Is the elderly Asian-American an "invisible man?" Is he politically ineffectual, both within his ethnic community and outside it?

6. *Value systems.* Differences between the ways of life of elderly Asian-Americans and those of the majority of Americans, undoubtedly, create conflicts. Frequently, well-intentioned attempts to help only exacerbate the situation. Thus, a non-Asian welfare worker is likely to respond negatively to the discovery that her elderly client is buying rare medicinal herbs or is giving gifts to his friends; a program to provide food for the Asian-American elderly should be cognizant of Asian-American food preferences. By learning more about what the various groups of Asian-Americans enjoy, expect, desire, need, feel, value, and do, those providing services — and those providing simple friendship — are better armed to accomplish their tasks.

7. *Epidemiology.* Good medical and social epidemiological data would be very helpful. Who are the older Asian-Americans and where do they live? What kinds of chronic disease do they have (and how do they develop)? What is the incidence of crime, disability, social isolation, attempted suicide, mental illness (and what is the response of their ethnic community to their participation in these roles)?

We have attempted, in this section, to relate each of our topics for discussion to the provision of improved services. We wish to go one step further: such studies should be conducted either under the direct supervision of a qualified member of the ethnic group involved or through close and on-going consultation with such persons. Nor should a project director assume that, because he, himself, is a member of one Asian-American ethnic group, he, therefore, understands the cultural history and values of other groups. Any community is a composite of dynamic forces; a person living outside that community is often not able to gauge correctly the direction of those forces. Perhaps we should add that the person living within the community is also in need of consultation with someone qualified on the topic, whose self-esteem is not deeply invested in the community being considered.

Evaluation Research

Throughout this paper, we have focused upon services and programs. We feel that meaningful program evaluation is extremely useful; we also feel that inadequately conceptualized or inadequately conducted program research is worse than useless. Although this latter statement should be self-evident, we are concerned when we see much evaluation research being superficial and unrelated to the actual goals of the project.

Some programs, we feel, do not require evaluation as to their being needed, at least not behavioral science evaluation. We believe that older Asian-Americans are entitled to a good, nutritious, tasty meal a day, if they so wish; it might be a good idea to learn whether their health improves as a result, but we think that sufficient evidence exists that such nutrition will be helpful and that there will be many positive secondary effects of such a program. We have similar feelings about better housing: we are not concerned about proving that better housing improves health, adds to longevity, or betters social relationships. If older Asian-Americans wish the imporved housing, we will accept this, knowing how inadequate much present housing is.

On the other hand, we would like to see planning research accompany both such programs: the kind of food, the method of distribution, the social environment for eating, and so forth should be based upon sound information, not the whim of the service agency, even though it is run by members of that ethnic group. Similarly, we assume that a senior citizen housing program will receive adequate planning, and we recognize that such planning must be based, in part, upon behavioral scientific research.

Programs and services need research during the planning stages, during the initial implementation period, and throughout their lifetime. This does not require an expensive and elaborate program, nor does it mean that every recreation program, foster grandparent program, rent subsidy program, or personal counseling program must be researched. Since the Asian-American life style and value system differ from others of similar age and social class, it is important that services to these persons be studied in the context of an Asian-American community. If a prototype program is effectively studied, its imitators may not need researching.

In some instances, evaluation does not require behavioral research. An effective program director who remains attuned to all elements that he is trying to service and who keeps communication channels open can make necessary alterations in his program. Sometimes, a simple questionnaire or a brainstorming session with representative participants will provide most needed information.

We are not advocating the elimination of research; we are advocating the elimination of redundant studies, of counting heads when the purpose is to change behavior, of research in the cause of verifying the need to maintain a program that actually requires extensive change or, possibly, elimination.

Obviously, program research must be discussed with reference to particular programs. We will, therefore, outline several kinds of programs that we feel are very much needed and that should be carefully researched with Asian-American elderly.

1. For reasons outlined previously, Asian-Americans have less visibility and less power in obtaining services than members

of larger and more politically aggressive groups. A prime example of this is the Manilatown Information Center, the only free social service agency specifically serving the 40,000-plus Filipino-American community in San Francisco. On a small ($10,000) annual grant from the Economic Opportunity Council, plus a trickle of private contributions, they cannot even pay their utility bill and, as a result, have operated for months without electricity. Evaluation research could probe optimum fund-raising methods, ways in which the Filipino-Americans could, themselves, provide voluntary services, community organization approaches that would increase community power, and so forth.

2. Elderly Asian-Americans are frequently displaced by new construction, and relocation efforts are frequently ineffective in obtaining housing that permits continuation of social relationships, community involvement, and so forth. How can an effective relocation program be instituted? What are the important variables in relocation effectiveness? Or to consider another vantage point, can urban renewal programs be altered to avoid the dislocation of the older Asian-American?

3. The elderly Asian-American, especially if he is first generation, may find the services of a bilingual person useful, and the possibility of using volunteers, especially students, for such a program should be explored. Evaluation of this kind of program would not be unduly difficult. It might consist of nothing more than asking the older persons whether they liked the service. If a sufficient number indicate that they do, the program should be retained. However, subsequent research might investigate whether it was the bilingualism or the human relationship that led to the satisfaction.

4. Older persons are being used as paid and volunteer workers in providing services for other older persons. We suggest that such programs be instituted within each of the Asian-American communities and between each Asian-American community and non-Asian communities. Research into community organization and on intergroup relations would be most useful in this regard.

5. Practitioners have long complained that research is published in jargon that is unintelligible and in journals that are unavailable. Members of the minority communities have begun to complain most vociferously that the benefits of research are rarely passed on to them. To these complaints, the research investigator notes that practitioners do not read what he has written, even when it does appear without jargon and in publications easily available through college libraries or by joining appropriate professional organizations. He comments, further, that he has developed skills in research, but not in use of the media which might be required for the ethnic community to learn the results which affect them directly. It seems evident that a program should be established that will provide the missing communication links. Such a program, effectively evaluated and altered accordingly, might well be the most utilitarian in this paper.

Final Comments

Regardless of the nature of the research we undertake, we must be continually alert to predictions as to what the Asian-American elderly will be like in ten, twenty, and thirty years. Epidemiological and other statistical data will be useful, but other forms of social and technological forecasting will be necessary. While serving the needs of today's older person, we must be considering the needs of tomorrow's.

In essence, then, we recognize that the older

Asian-American, like most other elderly, lacks adequate services; we recognize, also, a lack of adequate research data that, through theories or simple human understanding, point to ways in which the Asian-American elderly differ from other elderly and ways in which the various Asian-Americans differ from each other.

In dealing with these concerns, we strongly recommend that, whenever possible, research that is not directly for the evaluation of programs be conducted in a setting that involves real services for real people, or else that the research investigator take it upon himself to communicate his results and the social utility of these results to social policy-makers and practitioners, and to the ethnic communities most directly affected by his work.

The authors wish to express their indebtedness and appreciation to the many people who donated their time so generously in the preparation of this report. With many thanks to Christie Kiefer of the Langley-Porter Institute, University of California, San Francisco Medical Center, for participating extensively in the research upon which parts of this article are based. Sr. Joaquin Legaspi, Srita. Jovina Navarro, and "Bullet" of the San Francisco Manilatown Information Center were most helpful with the Filipino data. Dr. Stanford Tom, Sophie Wong, and Ken Abbott provided valuable help on the Chinese. Innumerable people in the Japanese-American communities in San Francisco, Los Angeles, and Seattle have helped with the data on the Japanese; specifically consulted for this report were Dr. Isao Fujimoto of the University of California, Davis, and Alex Yamato of UC, Berkeley.

References Cited

Bell, J. C., and Lau, M. P. "The Chinese Narcotic Addict in the United States." *Social Forces* 45, 1966, 68-72.

Bennett, C. G.; Tokuyama, G. H.; and Bruyere, R. P. "Health of Japanese-Americans in Hawaii." *Public Health Reports* USPHS, 1963, pp. 753-762.

Burma, J. H. *Spanish-Speaking Groups in the United States.* Durham, N.C.: Duke University Press, 1954.

Caudill, W. A. "Japanese-American Personality and Acculturation." *Genetic Psychology Monographs* 45, 1952.

Freedman, M. B. *Lineage Organization in Southeastern China.* London: University of London, Athlone Press, 1958.

Gamble, S. P. *North China's Villages.* Berkeley: University of California, 1963.

Hsu, F. L. K. *Under the Ancestor's Shadow: Chinese Culture and Personality.* New York: Columbia University Press, 1948.

Ichihashi, Y. *The Japanese in the United States.* Stanford, Calif.: Stanford University Press, 1932.

Kanagawa, W. Y. "A Study of Old Age Assistance Recipients of Japanese Ancestry under the Honolulu County Department of Public Welfare, Territory of Hawaii, January 1955." Master's thesis, University of Hawaii, 1955.

Kitano, H. H. L. *Japanese-Americans: The Evolution of a Subculture.* Englewood Cliffs, N.J.: Prentice-Hall, 1968.

Lyman, S. M. "Social Demography of the Chinese and Japanese in the United States of America. University of Nevada, n.d. (mimeo).

Miyamoto, S. F. "Social Solidarity among the Japanese in Seattle." *University of Washington Publications in the Social Sciences* 11, 1939, 57-130.

San Francisco Chinese Community Citizens' Survey and Fact-Finding Committee. *Report* (abridged ed.), San Francisco: H. J. Carle & Sons, 1969.

Schmid, C. F.; Nobbe, C. E.; and Mitchell, A. E. *Non-White Races, State of Washington.*

Olympia: Washington State Planning & Community Affairs Agency, 1968.

Sung, B. L. *Mountain of Gold: The Story of the Chinese in America.* New York: Macmillan, 1967.

Yang, M. C. *Taitou: A Chinese Village.* New York: Columbia University Press, 1945.

Additional References

Bessent, T. E. "An Aging Issei Anticipates Rejection." In G. Seward (ed.), *Clinical Studies in Culture Conflict.* New York: Ronald Press, 1958.

Kitagawa, D. *Issei and Nisei: The Internment Years.* New York: Seabury Press, 1967.

Lee, R. H. *The Chinese in the United States of America.* Hong Kong: Hong Kong University Press, 1960.

Lowe, P. *Father and the Glorious Descendant.* Boston: Little, Brown, 1943.

Sone, M. *Nisei Daughter.* Boston: Atlantic Monthly Press, 1953.

23. The New Asian-American Woman

by Irene Fujitomi and Diane Wong

The women's struggle is the liberation of MEN. As women shed their roles, so goes the "masculine image," the "masculine ego," the "masculine hang-up." A man won't have to be tall, dark, strong, aggressive, competitive, rugged, or independent, any more than a woman has to be small, delicate, passive, artistic, or dependent. The old order will be destroyed for the creation of a new, emancipated order. Men will be free to create humanistic relationships from natural interactions. New relationships and new roles. New frontiers, new freedoms, new directions. Power to the sisters.
(Yamamoto, *Gidra*, Jan. 1971, p. 13)

Reserved, quiet, shy, and humble — are they really virtues of the Asian woman? Those are the characteristics people typically apply to her. Impressed by the Asian woman's femininity, which is rooted in the traditions of the past and is being perpetuated by the mass media in the present, all Asian sisters are being stereotyped by people who have never met them and by Asian brothers who will not accept them if they do not fit their "nice Asian girl" stereotype.

Since the image of the passive, demure Asian woman is pervasive, the struggle for a positive self-identity is difficult. Within the Asian community, the family supports the development of the male's personality and aspirations, while the sister is discouraged from forming any sense of high self-esteem and individuality. Her worth is measured by the "good" husband she catches by being the epitome of Asian feminity. According to modeling theory, both the male and female child learn to adopt the sex roles practiced by their parents. In Asian families, roles are well defined; the father is the decision-maker and the mother is the compliant wife. Thus, Asian sisters soon come to perceive their roles as inferior to all men.

The Asian woman's struggle is a third-world struggle and is, therefore, distinctively different from the White woman's liberation movement. The Asian woman is a minority individual, and, within her own family, she is delegated a lower status than the male; for these reasons, she is doubly oppressed. As the larger society continues to repress the Asian males, the Asian males find it necessary to oppress their own females. In order to redeem dignity in his male-ness, the Asian man exerts his masculinity by keeping his woman in her place. Traditionally, the subordinate role of the Asian woman was an acceptable custom; today, anything but the traditional role is a threat to the Asian male.

Like the Black women, in their struggle for liberation, Asian sisters, first, would like to see their Asian brothers succeed in the larger society. But, in the process of the struggle for racial equality, Asian women are working to discover new potentials. Many are concerned with discarding old images and developing their own positive self-identities . . . and becoming human beings.

Compared to the status of the Asian woman fifty years ago, the position of the Asian woman of today has improved. She is able, now, to marry the man she loves, to hold skilled and professional jobs, and is allowed by the family to attend college. Although this improvement is desirable, it often hides the immense problems still faced by the Asian female.

The Traditional Asian Woman

To understand the status of the Asian-American woman, it is not enough to merely analyze the present condition. It is necessary to examine the attitudes and values which existed in Asia and were later brought to the United States by the immigrants. These attitudes and values affected the status of the woman as an inhabitant of the homeland, as an immigrant, and as a resident of the United States.

Being a woman in traditional Asia was considered undesirable. Confucianism, while establishing a stable government and providing the society with a strong set of moral virtues, committed a great injustice to the Asian woman. Prior to the widespread dissemination of, and adherence to, the teachings of Confucius, the position of Asian women was markedly higher: they were scholars, warriors, leaders, and respected members of communities (Faust, 1926). But the emergence of his teachings as the principles of social relationships for all of Asia ensured for women several centuries of status inferiority and imposed incapability.

At birth, the status of the female child was already lower than that of the male child. Because of the patrilineal, patrilocal, and patriarchal principles guiding the Asian society, the birth of a boy was a particularly joyous event. Through the boy, the parents could be assured that the family name and the memory of ancestors would continue to be worshiped in the afterworld (Burkhardt, 1960). The birth of a daughter, on the other hand, was a liability to the family: she neither carried on the family name nor worshiped her natal ancestors (Fei, 1962; Sung, 1967). Her lower status, often, made her a victim of negligent care, especially in her early years of life (Yang, 1959), or led to her being disposed of in times of family hardship (Loomis, 1969).

Sexual discrimination in early childhood, though limited, did exist. In Japan, if the baby was a male, on the 31st day after his birth he was taken to the shrine to be blessed; if the baby was a female, the mother took her to the shrine on the 33rd day. A Chinese father, if asked about his children, usually mentioned only his male children unless he had only daughters, in which case he then, reluctantly, discussed them (Burkhardt, 1960).

The first major source of discrimination was education. Women seldom enjoyed the advantages of formal education, as this was usually reserved for the sons (Burkhardt, 1960). Instead, their schooling consisted almost entirely of learning household chores as taught by their female relatives (Burkhardt, 1960; Fried, 1953). The women were not only denied formal education, but were discouraged from developing abilities or talents which might have been useful for a career outside the home.

In all situations, the young girl learned to respond submissively. This prepared her for married life (Burkhardt, 1960). A woman had no say in the marriage arrangement; it was all planned by the families concerned (Faust, 1926). The love and happiness of the bride and groom were not among the salient factors considered in the marriage contract. Rather, the marriage was arranged with these classical purposes in mind (Yang, 1959):

a. perpetuating the patrilineal line
b. maintaining the performance of ancestral sacrifice
c. obtaining a daughter-in-law to serve and help the parents
d. establishing a growing family with potential to earn money to increase the

family's security.

The marriage symbolized the death of the female's relationship with her natal family. She visited them only rarely, on festival days (Sung, 1967). From her home, she was deeply thrust into an unknown environment; she had to assume intimate terms with almost total strangers (Fei, 1962). In arguments between the wife and the parents-in-law, the husband was expected to ally himself with his parents (Yang, 1959). As a mere possession of the husband's family, the Asian woman was expected to cater to the demands of all the family members and to attend to the menial household duties.

This particular period of a woman's life has been described as "the most personally humiliating and emotionally disturbing stage of a woman's life . . ." (Yang, 1959).

Since the most crucial factor of a marriage was the birth of a male progeny, barrenness was deemed more than sufficient cause for the dissolution of the marriage. In addition to barrenness, the husband had six other classical reasons for divorcing his wife, among which were filial impiety, jealousy, and talkativeness (Burkhardt, 1960; Faust, 1926). The husband could, and, to the extent that it ensured continuance of the family name, was expected to, remarry. The most common type of remarriage — concubinage — had no institutional guarantee for the wife's security or the permanency of her position in the family (Yang, 1959).

The wife, on the other hand, had no right to ask for a divorce (Fei, 1962). The factors which discouraged the wife from dissolving the marriage were that she had no property rights or other means of support, and she could remarry only under severe social sanctions (Yang, 1959). If the husband should die, the wife's supreme act of faith was to take her own life. Should she choose not to die, she, generally, remained with her in-laws as long as they could afford to take care of her. Her husband's death had no effect upon her obligations as a dutiful daughter-in-law. If a widow remarried,

she was considered no better than a concubine (Yang, 1959).

Although a man was socially allowed to take additional wives or otherwise to indulge in promiscuous behavior, a woman was not (Sung, 1967). According to Kaibara, a famous Confucian scholar of Japan's middle ages, a woman was required to obey men, who had the absolute right to rule her. Sexually, she was to be pure and chaste, while no restrictions were placed on the men (Faust, 1926). This great stress placed on the woman's chastity and the corresponding laxity in its application to the man fostered not only highly inequitable social norms and values concerning divorce, widowhood, and remarriage, but also led to other dehumanizing customs. For example, at the wedding, the Japanese bride was given a short dagger. If her chastity was ever placed in doubt, she was expected to commit suicide. This act was considered the greatest and only credible proof of her faithfulness. Male jealousy led to other peculiar practices which further reinforced the principle of male superiority and female inferiority. Wives wore their long hair in a marumage, which is a plain, round chignon worn on the back of the head. Furthermore, the prettier wives were required to blacken their teeth with a certain chemical (Faust, 1926). Therefore, with the marumage and the black teeth, the married woman was not only an unattractive sight but was a walking symbol of her faceless inhumanness!

The life of the female was difficult, more so in many ways than the life of the male (Loomis, 1969). The following passage illustrates the lot of the traditional Asian woman:

> . . . a girl began her working age earlier than a boy. At the age of about eight, she started with light household duties such as watching the younger children and fetching light objects; she also worked along with her mother in the fields at light work. Her duties at home and in the fields increased until she was married at sixteen or seventeen to another family, where her arduous domestic and produc-

tion tasks continued until she reached her fifties, when they tapered off to lighter tasks. The woman's burden was so heavy that she, generally, looked older than her age (Yang, 1959, p. 22).

The woman worked in both the home and the field and was a servant to her husband, father, and brothers. It was in old age that she could look forward to rest, and then only when her in-laws and her husband had passed away (Yang, 1959).

It is no great wonder, then, that a woman's life was considered a punishment for a previous life of evil and wanton disregard of a virtuous life.

Immigrant Chinese Women

Beginning in the 1850s, there was a large influx of Chinese coming into the United States. While some came to find political and religious freedom, most of the Chinese immigrated to America in hopes of earning enough money to make up for financial losses incurred during the natural catastrophes of flood and famine and the political disasters of unrest and rebellion. The discovery of gold attracted the Chinese to California and increased their hopes of making money to support their families back in China.

In the mass movement of Chinese, there were very few women involved. Constrained by cultural attitudes and beliefs, the woman was not to leave her husband's family home for any reason. If the parents-in-law passed away while the husband was gone, she was expected to attend to their proper burial and mourning rites (Lyman, 1971; Tow, 1923). Most Chinese husbands did not intend to reside permanently in the United States but planned to return to China (Jung, 1971; Lyman, 1971). Therefore, as sojourners, they had no need nor desire to transplant their entire families and ancestral hearths to America (Lowe, 1943).

Exacerbation of this culturally based practice came in 1882 in a series of legislative acts. It started with the passage of the Chinese

Exclusion Act of 1882, which was approved by a United States Federal Court ruling in 1884 (Lyman, 1971; Sung, 1967). The act prohibited the entry of Chinese women who were not the wives of classes of Chinese exempt from the Exclusion Act, e.g., merchants, students, teachers. The majority of the Chinese immigrants were affected by this act because they came as laborers and workers. Therefore, the wives were forbidden to enter the United States even though the husbands were willing to break the traditional Chinese custom that the women stay in the homeland.

The combination of Chinese tradition and American law had destructive consequences. In China, many wives had, virtually, no husbands, since thousands of miles of ocean separated them. Again, because of cultural norms, wives could not easily obtain a divorce and remarry and, thus, were compelled to endure a "mutilated marriage" (Sung, 1967). They did have a family life — that is, they were able to interact with the husband's family, who took care of them.

Though this condition was serious, the distressing problem was the severe scarcity of Chinese women in the United States, which is only now being ameliorated (Sung, 1967). Lyman (1971) believes that, had the Chinese been allowed to intermarry with White women, the shortage of women could have been mitigated. But, as it was, there were several obstacles to this possible course of action:

> The mutual peculiarities of dress, language, habits, customs, and diets, not to mention the physical distinctiveness of both racial identities, kept the Chinese and Americans apart. In addition, both Americans and Chinese have tended to enclose themselves in mutually exclusive associations, thus reducing the amount of personal contact to a minimum and severely restricting the possibility for romantic attachments to rise. (Lyman, 1971, p. 29)

Commencing in 1860, several states passed laws which reinforced this racial segregation and declared marriages of interracial mixture as acts of miscegenation (Lyman, 1971).

An inevitable consequence of the highly disproportionate number of Chinese men to Chinese women in the United States and of the inaccessibility of other women was the establishment and growth of prostitution, which was designed to satisfy the sexual needs of the single or married Chinese male in America.

The women prostitutes were obtained through various, often devious, methods. Many were lured to America by false promises of marriage to a Chinese sojourner; some were captured by pirates who sold them into slavery; and still others were kidnapped from their homes, both in China and America (Dillon, 1962; Loomis, 1969; Lyman, 1971). All who had survived the trans-Pacific journey and who eventually landed on the shores of America were sold to brothel owners or were placed under contract with them to pay for their passage.

The lives of these women were tragic and difficult. A few managed to escape from the brothels and seek asylum in missions which were attempting to eradicate this business. Still others were able to marry single Chinese men or become concubines of already married men whose wives were in China. Of those who managed to escape, many were returned to their owners on charges that they had not fully paid their passage loan, or that they had stolen articles of clothing and jewelry (Dillon, 1962; Louie, 1971; Lyman, 1971). Even the protectors of the law — the police, lawyers, and judges — were, often, aligned with the brothel owners and, therefore, ordered the capture and return of the prostitutes (Dillon, 1962). Women who became concubines had no legal rights and could be forsaken at any time by their husbands. The majority of the Chinese women who were unable to escape from their owners were convinced into accepting their lot as the best available to them in America.

The Chinese women of the United States in the late 1800s and early 1900s were severely oppressed, reduced to mere slaves and sexual commodities. The principles associated with female inferiority which were prevalent in traditional China were carried over by the immigrants.

Immigrant Japanese Women

The story of the immigrant Japanese woman has long been overshadowed by the Issei man's history. In examining her side of the human drama, we shall raise the questions usually asked of men. What influenced her decision to come to America? How did she adjust to the stark realities of the hostile and foreign land? More particularly, how did she live through the poverty, the social rejection by the larger society, and the legal injustice? In the following sequence, a glimpse of the Issei woman's struggle will be presented.

The immigration data for Japanese females indicate a pattern which was initially similar to that of Chinese female immigration. In the early period of Japanese immigration (1880s-1890s), very few women came to the United States. The 1900 Census revealed that, out of the total Japanese population of 24,326, only 985 were women (Gee, 1971). The female-male sex ratio was, thus, 1:24 (Gee, 1971). At the turn of the century, the immigration pattern for Chinese and Japanese women deviated. The years from 1900 to 1920 marked the great immigration period for Issei women. By 1920, when the United States passed legislation to curtail further Japanese immigration, the population of Japanese women had risen to 22,193 out of a total Japanese population of 111,010 (Gee, 1971).

The Japanese immigrant population in America changed from that of temporary male immigrants to one of permanent family residents. It was facilitated by the traditional custom of omimai-kekkon. As was previously discussed, marriage was strictly a family matter. Marriage was a partnership rather than an intimate relationship developing from love.

Thus, the heads of the bride and groom's families exercised complete control over mate selection. Investigation into the prospective spouse's family tree and economic and political background was customary. Through the services of a "go-between," marital contracts were arranged between the families. Marriages became legal when the wife's name was officially registered in the husband's koseki — a family register. Since the consolidation of marriage did not require the presence of both parties, it was possible for hundreds of Issei men in America to take brides. Pictures of the prospective spouses were exchanged for approval, while all the formalities were handled by the "go-between." Thus, for the single Issei men, the custom of omimai-kekkon extended across the sea to provide them with "picture brides" who were selected by the family, according to the sacred tradition.

Prospects for the brides' future life in America varied. In the case of one woman, her mother convinced her that the streets in America were paved with gold. Expecting a life of prosperity, the dream of this young bride was shattered as she discovered that the streets were not made of gold but stone, and her new house in America was a mere shack, worse than the poorest shacks in Japan.

> ... I discovered that our house was a house in name only, a shack where hunters had lived, located in the middle of a field. There was only one room with beds placed in three corners. My husband was living here with a younger boy and older person . . . thus, a makeshift curtain had to be made by stretching a rope across the room and hanging clothes from it. The shack had been fashioned out of boards and leaked. There were no eaves to drain the rain. Sometimes, we passed the night with raincoats over our beds. It was unsuitable for us newlyweds, to say the least! (Gee, 1971, p. 12).

Generally, the "picture brides" came from large farming families. Their mundane lives as country girls accounted for the enthusiasm and hopeful dreams they held of the "New World."

Young, spirited, and naïve, the Japanese picture brides were overcome by exaggerated glamour stories told to them in letters by their anxious grooms. Occasionally, Japanese males who had made a small fortune in America returned home in their Western garb to show off their success. Reinforced by such displays, many of the picture brides looked toward American as the "promised land."

There were husbands at the other extreme who were truthful with their brides. According to another picture bride, her husband warned her that, if she were coming to America with great expectations, she would be disappointed. He emphasized that, should she accept his proposal of marriage, she had to come prepared to see things through without giving up. With this understanding and forewarning of hardships ahead, the bride made this resolution:

> Aboard the ship, on the way from Koe to Yokohama, gazing upon the rising majestic Mount Fuji in a cloudless sky, I made a vow. For a woman who was going to a strange society and relying upon an unknown husband whom she had married through photographs, my heart had to be as beautiful as Mount Fuji. I resolved that the heart of a Japanese woman had to be sublime, like, like that soaring, majestic figure, eternally constant through wind and rain, heat and cold. Thereafter, I never forgot that resolution on the ship, enabling me to overcome sadness and suffering. (Gee, 1971, p. 11)

When the brides arrived in America, picture matching was not an easy task. To the disappointment of both wives and husbands, the "go-between" often gave them pictures which were either dated or false. Last minute exchanges, and even refusals, were probably made.

For the Issei brides, there was neither time nor money for a honeymoon. Almost immediately, they were put to work alongside their husbands. The need for money and the constant deprivation required the women to work laboriously in the fields and factories. Besides her regular housekeeping chores and child caring, a wife of a dry cleaning operator recalls having to put in overtime regularly.

> I started at 5:00 p.m. to prepare supper for five to six people, and then I began my evening work. The difficult ironing remained. Women's blouses, in those days, were made from silk or lace, with collars, and long sleeves and lots of frills. I could only finish two in one hour, ironing them with great care. Hence, I worked, usually, until 12:00 Midnight or 1:00 a.m. But it was not just me . . . all who worked in the laundry business did the same thing. (Gee, 1971, p. 14)

Child bearing followed in accordance with the custom of ancestor worship. Emphasis was placed not only on bearing male offspring to continue the family line, but on having many children. Families of farmers, typically, were large, because more family members meant more working hands. With the passage of the 1924 Immigration Act, which barred Japanese immigration, family size increased with the intention of guaranteeing a viable future for the Japanese-American community.

The greatest hardship which the Issei woman endured was childbirth. In rural areas, doctors were not readily available. Those who were available were either too expensive for the family to afford, or the doctors would refuse to treat Japanese women. Thus, two alternatives were left: to perform childbirth by herself or to employ the services of a midwife. Post-natal recuperation was a luxury in most households. Since wives were economic units crucial to the family incomes, they often worked until the day of childbirth and were working within three days afterwards.

Child rearing was strictly a woman's chore. Despite the fact that the Issei woman worked as hard as her husband in the fields, she, alone, had to bear the responsibility of raising her children properly according to the Meiji tradition. Her role as a good wife was to sacrifice and be dutiful to her husband first, her children second, and herself last. One woman reveals . . .

My husband was a Meiji man. He did not

think of helping in the house or with the children. No matter how busy I may have been, he never changed the baby's diapers. Though it may not be right to say this ourselves, we Issei pioneer women from Japan worked solely for our husbands. At mealtime, whenever there was not enough food, we served a lot to our husbands and took very little for ourselves. (Gee, 1971, p. 15)

The persistence of Issei women in the face of obstacles helped to carry the family through the pre-war and war eras. When anti-Japanese feelings were intense and the humiliating cries of "damn Jap" were hurled at the Japanese males, the females made sure their husbands found comfort and reassurance of their male identity as the powerful and honorable "papa-sans." With deep understanding and quiet fortitude, the Issei women suffered and survived.

Duty and obligation continued to guide the Nisei woman's behavior and lifestyle. As a young girl, she was raised to become a respectful wife and good mother to her sons. Getting a college education was not important, so only a minority of the Nisei women have college degrees. Today, the Nisei women, typically, hold occupations as factory workers, waitresses, secretaries, nurses, and teachers. The major concern of the Nisei women is their families. Like the Issei family, the Nisei family is vertically structured. The husband is the decision maker, the head of the household. Family size is decreasing to an average of two children per family (Kitano, 1960). Mothers continue to live vicariously through their children, encouraging all of them, regardless of sex, to pursue, at least, a college degree. In order to help their children through school, the Nisei women will sacrifice their own luxuries to provide the children with the opportunities denied themselves.

Divorce rates are low among the Nisei. When the Nisei married, it was usually between friends of long acquaintance, either through personal or family contacts. Nisei men married

Nisei women. Interracial marriages were rare, primarily because the Issei families absolutely forbade such marriages, and the United States Government's anti-miscegenation laws had deemed them illegal.

Current Trends

Interestingly, the attitudes of Japanese females are becoming less "traditional." A study on attitudes of Japanese-American and Caucasian-American students toward marriage roles was conducted by Arkoff, Meredith, and Dong (1963). The Jacobson Scale was used to measure male-dominant and equalitarian attitudes toward marriage.

Results of the questionnaire indicated that Japanese-American males were more male-dominant in their attitudes regarding husband-wife marriage roles. Japanese-American females, Caucasian-American females, and Caucasian-American males were found to agree in their attitudes about marital roles' being equalitarian. The study suggests that Japanese-American women, today, are "American" in their conception of marriage roles and family living, while the Japanese-American males still believe in the classical, male-dominant "Japanese" marriage.

Omimai (or arranged) marriages are relics of the past. Dating among young Asians follows an acculturative pattern, where early and steady dating has become a common practice. Marrying for love based on mutual interests and compatability has replaced the marriage for convenience. As the third generation of Chinese- and Japanese-Americans becomes more assimilated, interracial dating and rates of interracial marriages are expected to increase.

Recently, Tinker (1972) completed a survey of the marriage records of Japanese-Americans in Fresno, California. He found that, within the past decade, the marriage pattern of the Japanese-Americans was significantly changing; the rate of intermarriage was increasing sharply. Up until 1948, California had prohibited marriages between Asian and Caucasian-Americans. In 1959, over ten years after the law had been repealed, fewer than three out of every ten Japanese-American marriages were interracial (Barnett, 1963; Burma, 1963). In 1972, Tinker reported that 56 percent of all Japanese-American marriages in Fresno were interracial. Because the rate of intermarriage is a reliable indicator of the permeability of ethnic boundaries, implications of Tinker's study are controversial.

An examination of intermarriage rates reveals two distinct patterns. One pattern is the tendency for marriage to respect religious differences between the couple concerned. Another observation, based on Black-White marriage studies (Barnett, 1963; Burma, 1963; Merton, 1941) and those of Jews and gentiles (Sklare, 1967), has shown that men of a racial, religious, and ethnic minority "outmarry" at higher rates than minority women. Tinker's study, however, suggests that the religiously and racially distinct Japanese-American women were outmarrying at a slightly higher rate than the Japanese-American male. Barnett (1963) found that, between 1956 and 1959, in California, almost twice as many Japanese-American females (494) as males (256) intermarried with Caucasian-Americans. In the case of the Chinese-Americans, 196 females, as compared to 172 males, intermarried with Caucasian-Americans.

To imply that the Asian woman's increased rate of outmarriage is a function of her sudden preference for a Caucasian-American mate is oversimplification. Stereotypes of Asian males and females have differential implications, with the male's still being portrayed as short and unmasculine, while the image of the Asian woman is improving in the eyes of Caucasian-Americans. Although many Asian sisters consider the tiny, exotic geisha, or china doll, an equally dehumanizing stereotype, this stereotype, at least, is considered favorable enough to make the Asian woman an eligible candidate for marriage to the American male.

The dating of Caucasian-American males by

Asian females did not impose as great a threat to the White community as did the dating of Caucasian-American females by Asian males:

> I have a Japanese man friend who was once beat up by some White boys for being on the street with a White girl. Actually, it was an unusual situation in the first place, since many White women won't go out with Asian men because "they aren't attracted to them." So, where Asian men are restricted to Asian women, Asian women are free, more or less, to go out with White men. As a result, some Asian men will resent the Asian women who take advantage of that freedom, and we Asian women don't know how to feel. (Masaoka, 1971, p. 58)

Differential acceptance of minority group members, based on sex, creates numerous problems. It creates jealousy and serves to divide the males and females of a minority group. Friction is generated by arguing over whose stereotype is better than the other's. Although females are better accepted by the dominant culture, inferiority and self-hatred may develop on the part of those Asian women who want to resemble the long-legged, fair-skinned American cover girl. Men are equally vulnerable to the dictates of the American values of sexual attractiveness, as this quote, by an Asian male, conveys:

> I, at first, was strongly critical of the physical appearance of the Japanese. The men were, by White standards, short and skinny; the females, plain and thick-legged. Those females who seemed beautiful to me were precisely the ones who most closely resembled Caucasians. (Okimoto, 1971, p. 7)

Asian Women as Leaders

The Asian-American woman bears the burden of a double onus: she must be an Asian-American and a female. In striving for success and positions of leadership, the female must work harder than the male in proving her capabilities. For most women, their idea of "femininity" — being supportive followers — prevents them from seeking power over other men and women. The Asian-American woman is taught from birth that she is inferior in quality to her male counterpart; inferior in ability, intelligence, perception, and emotional stability. "Brainwashed" through mass media stereotyping and interactions with family and friends, she concludes that, to be feminine and desirable, she must be passive, submissive, and contented with married life (Cade, 1970).

These oppressive conceptions of the "ideal" Asian-American female are being seriously questioned. Young Asian-American women are now beginning to reassess their goals and self-perceptions. Encouraged by the rise in ethnic-group and sexual pride, Asian-American women are entering positions of higher status and leadership.

The Asian woman faces complex obstacles in her endeavors to become a leader. Being a minority group member and an American, she must successfully integrate two cultures (Burma, 1953); often, much of her energy is dissipated in this struggle. Many of her own people may be against her for the following reasons:

a. to be effective, she must be aggressive and assertive, but this is contrary to the Asian values of passivity and submission (Benedict, 1946; Burma, 1953);

b. in being effective, she, often, becomes highly visible and public, which is contrary to traditional Asian values of modesty and moderation (Benedict, 1946; Burma, 1953).

Burma has observed that many Japanese-Americans are overly concerned with doing the "proper thing." The Asian-American leader, in an effort to respect this concern, falls into a tendency to retard innovative and aggressive actions, and to minimize the leadership often needed to mobilize the community. Asians have been characterized as strong individuals but weak groups (Burma, 1953; Chang, 1934). Chang described Chinese-Americans as individuals who are extremely capable, but who are, collectively, "very much like a heap of loose sand" (Chang, 1934). Consequently, in order to be an effective community leader, the Asian-American female, first, must organize individuals to work as a group.

In rejecting her traditional role, the new Asian-American woman is vulnerable to pain and frustration. The role of her leadership is still vague and in the process of evolution. Her position has been described as a "limbo" state of being (Loomis, 1969). She has no clearly defined role or precedence, and, so, people do not know how to react to her, and, correspondingly, she has difficulty relating to them (Lundberg, 1968). By attempting to expand her life space to include personal feelings, individuality, and creativity, she risks being labeled and treated as "unfeminine" or "castrating" (Horner, 1969). Needing and wanting to be herself conflicts with being a "good" traditional Asian woman. This conflict becomes a source of anxiety which the new Asian-American woman must learn to overcome.

The labeling is done by various groups, sexists and racists, and even by those in the Asian-American movement. Many of the females in the movement, who are so acutely attuned to racial prejudice, have amicably accepted or have not become cognizant of the inferior status ascribed to them. They reject the notion of sexual prejudice and ignore the Asian-American woman who espouses the need to end both racism and sexism. The movement males consider the new Asian-American woman a threat to their masculinity. While advocating freedom from racial oppression, many of the movement males are unable to see that, in relegating their Asian-American sisters to clerical, social, and cleaning-up roles, they are oppressing part of their own group.

It must be remembered that it is not the Asian-American woman who has deprived the Asian-American male of his self-determination, for she, too, has been denied power over her own life. Beal (1970) writes that oppression proceeds without the consent of the minority woman; it is fallacious to believe that, for the man to be strong, the woman must be weak. Thus, all Asian-Americans must work together to attain that measure of freedom from racism and sexism to which they have a right.

Conclusion

The authors have tried to present an evolutionary picture of the Asian woman's development as a real and interesting person, as opposed to a flat, subordinate character behind a man. The silent struggle of the traditional and immigrant woman, which has been neglected, has now received some degree of tribute. In order to assess the direction which Asian-American women, today, are taking, it is important to reflect upon the past. There is, in the Asian women of the past, a source of pride which Asian sisters can share. Although the status of women has greatly improved since the time of Confucious, Asian-American women are still struggling to overcome their inferiority complex which has been perpetuated by traditional thinking.

In the discussion of Asian-American women as leaders, the most crucial fear that not only Asian women but all women must overcome is the fear of being unsexed by success (Horner, 1969). Too many women are afraid to strive for positions of leadership because they are afraid of losing their femininity. In turn, men are trapped, also, in this sexist game, where failure to succeed is equated with immasculinity. Therefore, it is necessary for both men and women to reassess their role hang-ups and to work together in improving the human community.

Once Asian-American women have stopped denying themselves the chance to grow, to discover all the qualities with which they have been endowed, then, and only then, will they be born again to live as total human beings.

References

Arkoff, A.; Meredith, G.; and Dong, J. "Attitudes of Japanese-American and

Caucasian-American Students toward Marriage Roles. *Journal of Social Psychology* 59, 1963, 11-15.

Barnett, L. D. "Interracial Marriage in Los Angeles, 1948-1959." *Social Forces* 25, 1963, 424-427.

Beal, F. "Double Jeopardy: to be Black and Female." In T. Cade (ed.), *The Black Woman.* New York: Signet, 1970.

Benedict, R. *The Chrysanthemum and the Sword.* Boston: Houghton Mifflin, 1946.

Burkhardt, V. R. *Chinese Creeds and Customs.* Vol. 3. Hong Kong: South China Morning Post, 1960.

Burma, J. H. "Current Leadership Problems among Japanese-Americans." *Sociological and Social Research* 18, 1934, 541-553.

_____. "Interethnic Marriage in Los Angeles, 1948-1959." *Social Forces* 42, 1963, 156-165.

Cade, T. (ed.) *The Black Woman.* New York: Signet, 1970.

Dillon, R. *The Hatchet Men: The Study of the Tong Wars in San Francisco Chinatown.* New York: Coward McCann, 1962.

Faust, A. K. *New Japanese Womanhood.* New York: George H. Doran Co., 1926.

Fei, H. T. *Peasant Life in China: A Field Study of Country Life in the Yangtze Valley.* London: Routledge & Kegan Paul, 1962.

Fried, M. H. *Fabric of Chinese Society: A Study of the Social Life of a Chinese Country Seat.* New York: Praeger, 1953.

Gee, E. "Issei: The First Women." In *Asian Women.* Berkeley: University of California, 1971.

Gidra. Los Angeles ethnic newspaper, Jan. 1971, Apr. 1972, May 1972.

Horner, M. "A Bright Woman is Caught in a Double Bind." *Psychology Today*, Nov. 1969, 36-38.

Jung, B. "Chinese Immigrant Women." In *Asian Women.* Berkeley: University of California, 1971.

Kitano, H. L. *Japanese-Americans: The Evolution of a Subculture.* Englewood Cliffs, N.J.: Prentice-Hall, 1969.

Loomis, A. W. "Chinese Women in California." *Overland Monthly* II, Apr. 1969, 343-351.

Louie, G. "Forgotten Women." In *Asian Women.* Berkeley: University of California, 1971.

Lowe, P. *Father and Glorious Descendant.* Boston: Little, Brown, and Co., 1943.

Lundberg, G.; Schrag, D.; Larsen, O.; and Larsen, P. *Sociology.* New York: Harper and Row, 1968.

Lyman, S. M. *The Asian in the West.* Reno: Western Studies Center, University of Nevada, 1971.

Masaoka, J. "I Forgot my Eyes were Black." In *Asian Women.* Berkeley: University of California, 1971.

Merton, R. K. "Intermarriage and Social Structure: Fact and Theory." *Psychiatry* IV, 1946, 361-374.

Okimoto, D. *American in Disguise.* New York: John Weatherhill, 1971.

Skalre, B. L. "Intermarriage and the Jewish Future." In M. Barron (ed.), *Minorities in a Changing World.* New York: Alfred A. Knopf, 1967.

Sung, B. L. *Mountain of Gold.* New York: Macmillan, 1967.

Tachiki, A.; Wong, E.; Odo, F.; and Wong, B. (eds.) *Roots: An Asian-American Reader.* Los Angeles: Continental

Graphics, 1971.

Tinker, J. N. "Intermarriage and Ethnic Boundaries: The Japanese-American Case." Paper presented at the meeting of the Pacific Sociological Association, Portland, Ore., Apr. 1972.

Tow, J. S. *The Real Chinese in America.* New York: Academy Press, 1923.

Yamamoto, M. "Male Perspective." In *Gidra.* Los Angeles, Jan. 1971.

Yang, C. K. *A Chinese Family in the Communist Revolution.* Boston: Massachusetts Institute of Technology Press, 1959.

_____. *A Chinese Village in Early Communist Transition.* Boston: Massachusetts Institute of Technology Press, 1959.

24. Division and Unity: Social Process in a Chinese-American Community

by Melford S. Weiss, Ph.D.

Introduction

The Chinese-American community is, often, publicly visualized as a maze of narrow streets, filled with small shops displaying novelty wares and exotic foods, advertised by painted signs in cryptographic characters. It is a mystical, magical, Oriental wonderland.

The "Chinaman" associated with this distinctly foreign enclave is pictured shuffling through the streets, in nondescript clothing, intent upon some inscrutable rendezvous. Tied to his traditional beliefs, he celebrates his holidays with parades and feasts and faithfully submits to the demands of his elders and the dictates of his "clan" or "tong." While his actions may not always be understood, they are accepted because "after all, he's an Oriental."

These stereotypes are disturbing to members of the Chinese and academic community, particularly because they are largely based upon erroneous supposition rather than social fact. In time, these narrow characterizations will pass into history and be recognized for the ethnocentric amorphisms they are. Yet, these cultural stereotypes are, also, responsible for structural distortions in the interpretation of Chinese community life. The cultural biases are slowly disappearing, but their implications still remain to cloud the understanding of Chinese community social structure.

The purpose of this paper is twofold: first, to explore some of the structural biases associated with the "Chinatown syndrome" — those social and structural referents used to characterize the Chinese community; secondly, to propose an alternative framework more realistically suited to contemporary Chinese-American community organization.

The Myth of Geographic Restriction

The Chinese community stereotype is supported, to some extent, by the large urban Chinatowns of San Francisco (Dare, 1959), New York (Heyer, 1953; Barnett, 1952), and, to a lesser extent, Los Angeles (Chen, 1952). However, these "Chinatowns" are far from representative of the Chinese community, even for these metropolitan centers. Chinatown may remain a bounded cultural enclave, but it is, often, neither the geographic nor population center for all Chinese in any city. In 1960, only 23.6 percent of the Chinese living in New York City made their homes in Chinatown (Yuan, 1966: 323). Moreover, Chinatowns throughout the United States are rapidly decreasing and losing their Chinese residents as the Chinese continue to migrate to more desirable suburban and city areas (Lee, 1949, 431-32). For example, Sacramento's Chinese population is so dispersed throughout the city that its members must *commute* to Chinese community centers and to Family Association headquarters (Weiss, 1971). Furthermore, those Chinese residing within Chinatown's confines tend to come from specific social and cultural categories and are by no means a representative cross-section of Chinese urbanites (Yuan, 1966, 325; Lee, 1948). Thus, the Chinatown ghetto is only a part of the larger Chinese community. Each may have its own organizational framework, its unique character, and its special problems.

The Myth of Homogeneity

Although the Chinese in America can be distinguished by age, sex, and generation and fall into a multitude of distinct sociological categories, the mystique of Chinese homogeneity still prevails. It is assumed, often, that all Chinese speak a common language, honor the same institutions, worship common deities and act as a corporate body in pursuing common goals. Chinese immigrants in both the historical past and recent present not only come from different social, linguistic, and territorial backgrounds (Chen, 1940; Hambro, 1955), but have been continually subject to changing patterns of social life, both in their other overseas communities and in America. The Chinese have been forced to adjust their traditional organizational patterns to new experiences. This accommodation, often, involves rearrangements in social organizations, resulting in a syncretic blending of "Chinese" and "American" prerogatives, where traditionally oriented associations exist side by side with more modern groups (Lyman, 1968, 53). Males and females participate disproportionally in association life and the social arrangements of Chinese youth may remain peculiarly their own.

Furthermore, many Chinese residents of every city are second- and third-generation Americans, whose cultural heritage is more American than it is Chinese. The members of this native-born population are rapidly replacing their immigrant forefathers, constantly reassessing their ethnic identity in White America, and reshaping community structure to better answer the problems of contemporary American living (Barnett, 1958; Smith, 1925).

Homogeneity is relevant to neither cultural nor structural categories.

Traditional Stability and Communal Consensus

The appearance of stability and consensus within the Chinese community is misleading because it obscures the ongoing competition for political power and community representation between divergent Chinese factions (Grafstein, 1968, 22-24; Lyman, 1968, 64).

Internal conflict is a basic ingredient of contemporary Chinese community organization in America rather than an inconsequential and temporary break in the fabric of Chinese unity. The supposition that all Chinese are represented adequately by their traditional associations is false, as it characterizes community organization as a simple, hierarchical structure, with the more traditional organizations occupying its upper ranks, and wielding the legitimate and final authority for the entire community. Hierarchy and segmentation (Crissman, 1967, 191-193) may be a Chinese organizational factor. However, not all groups submit to a single political system, nor do they share a common ideology.

The images of homogeneity, traditional stability, and communal consensus underscore the dramatic social and economic changes of the post-World War II years and misrepresent the character of the current Chinese experience in America. Therefore, I would like to present a descriptive analysis of Chinese organization life, based upon heterogeneity, conflict, and acculturation.

Classificatory Scheme

Sociological variables, such as age, generation, sex, occupation, education, and residence, are commonly used to create meaningful social categories. These interdependent variables are applicable to current Chinese community structure. But, because they, rarely, create mutually exclusive categories, they may lead to confusion rather than clarification. A more inclusive classificatory scheme is needed to complement the aforementioned indicators of social distinction. Moreover, it is appropriate to utilize similar concepts which are currently being applied to other racial and ethnic minority studies (Goldstein and Goldscheider, 1968; Kitano, 1969; Glazer and Moynihan, 1963; Gordon, 1964).

I now would like to propose that the internal structure of the Chinese community, as represented by its members' associational identities, clearly follows divisions created by acculturation, and that the Chinese community is split, significantly, along these lines into Traditionist and Modernist groups[1] (Sung, 1967; Kung, 1962; Lee, 1960). A word of caution is necessary. The assignation of all Chinese to either of these two basic categories cannot take into consideration all the complexities pertinent to group identification. These typologies explain neither overlapping memberships nor individual and organizational choices in all situations. Nevertheless, this distinction is currently supported by social and anthropological literature and, frequently, is verbalized and recognized by the Chinese members of the community. Moreover, these typologies emphasize the cultural determinents of group identification and cross out other social categories, making these types useful for gross social distinctions.

Traditionists and Modernists

Traditionists include those Chinese, regardless of age, residence, or generation, who adhere to the values, attitudes, sentiments, and themes reminiscent of Chinese society. Although they now live in America, they are oriented more toward a "sojourner" life style (Siu, 1952). Often referred to as Chinese-Americans, they tend to perpetuate Oriental stereotypes. When Chinese and American values clash, they prefer a Chinese solution. Their identification with their Chinese heritage carries over into multiple activities, and, most important for this paper, guides their choice of organizational affiliation.

Modernists, on the other hand, include citizens of Chinese descent now residing in America, who, consciously and conspicuously, pursue an American life style and who willingly embrace their American heritage. When faced with decision, they, frequently, opt for an American solution. Their organizational life is strongly influenced by their modern perspectives.[2] However, not all Chinese in America, although they may share either Traditionist or Modernist sentiments, wish to become identified with Chinese institutions. These Chinese, rarely, become active participants in Chinese community life. They may either exclude themselves from formal organizational affiliation or join predominantly non-Chinese groups (Sung, 1967).

Our discussion of community structure will be limited to persons who actively identify, through associational membership, with their Chinese heritage and ancestry. While Modernists may prefer American material goods and intellectual styles, they, nevertheless, consider themselves to be Chinese and feel more comfortable among Americans of Chinese descent than among Caucasians. Active participants are those members who either take part in the decision-making process or who attend most of the organization's major functions.[3]

Chinese community organization is based upon adult groupings. However, the same divisions are often reflected in youth associations[4] (Chen, 1945).

The Chinese Experience in America

Early Chinese arrivals to America lived in Chinatowns, communities whose interrelated social elements combined to provide an atmosphere of organizational interdependency, assuring protection and security for its members. While new immigrants overpopulated these Chinese centers, because they, too, came from the "old country,"[5] ideological conflict was minimal. The elder statesmen continued their domination of organizational and community life (Wu, 1928; Reynolds, 1935). Time does not permit a detailed, diachronic analysis of all the social and structural changes from the 1850s to the present day. Social changes in community structure were gradual and limited, at least until the turn of the 20th century. Change increased, somewhat, during the 20s and 30s, becoming rapid and extensive in the 50s and 60s. Multiple revisions in social, familial, economic, and political life, in both Chinese and American society, created organizational chaos as new problems continued to demand new solutions (Barnett, 1958; Lee, 1949, 1956). As the Chinese participated more and more in the larger society surrounding their Chinese enclaves — ghettos which were rapidly losing their Chinese residents because of population movement into formerly restricted areas — two concurrent social changes occurred. First, the institutional foundations of ghetto life began to crumble. The increased participation in American economic life, confusing, yet liberating (Abel and Hsu, 1949), demanded a new Chinese identity (Fong, 1965). But the ability of the Traditionist associations to successfully solve the problems arising from involvement in American society decreased (Willmott, 1964). Many community leaders understood neither the nature of these social forces nor the dilemmas they were creating. Secondly, many Modernists, having achieved status in the Caucasian community by Caucasian standards (Kwoh, 1947), could not achieve the same recognition within the Traditionist Chinese organizations. Their Chinese language inadequacies, as well as their relative youthfulness, excluded them from full participation in the Traditionist power structure. Thus, to assure themselves of their Chinese identity as well as their American accomplishments, and to allow themselves an outlet for their social and political ambitions, they created their own organizations (Lee, 1960).

The following discussion of Chinese community structure is based upon field work (1967-1969) in an urban Chinese-American community. While the description of organiza-tional life is specific for this community, the analysis and descriptions have applicability to other Chinese communities.

The Traditionist Associations

Today's Traditionist associations are concerned, basically, with the preservation and continuation of the Chinese heritage. Their organizational activities reflect this primary concern. They support the Chinese language school and the weekly showing of Sunday after-noon and evening Chinese language movies, provide for the social and recreational needs of their senior citizens, and sponsor events stressing the history of their Chinese identity, with dinners and festive occasions. Many of their active leaders are foreign born and, primarily, Chinese speaking. They may have little formal education in either English or Chinese. Leaders are chosen by a quasi-democratic process which assures their self-perpetuation in controlling positions. Their meetings, conducted in the Cantonese language, are irregularly scheduled and organized in a style in which the subtleties and nuances of decision making, often obscure to Caucasian understanding, remain traditionally Chinese. They continue their attempt to speak for the entire Chinese community, although their function as a representative body is rapidly declining. Their involvement in extra-Chinese affairs is often limited to events emphasizing Chinese history and customs. When they must deal directly with the Caucasian superstructure, they are formal and polite and interact, primarily, as representatives of their organizations, rather than informally, on an individual basis.

The Modernist Associations

Modernist organizations are primarily concerned with establishing and maintaining both an American and a Chinese identity. Their events are ordered around their members' social and recreational needs, which emphasize their American self-image. Leaders are democratically elected and, often, are persons who have achieved success in the Caucasian economic structure. Their regularly scheduled meetings are conducted in English, in an informal and casual manner, with serious business occasionally interspersed with jovial remarks. Ceremonial observances, when practiced, are often directed at American symbols. While many of their major functions reflect a Chinese heritage, this identity is transmitted via modern American idiom. Caucasians may be invited to their major events and members of the group deal directly with their Caucasian counterparts on an informal social basis.

Conflict and Confrontation

Both groups tend to be exclusive, although some overlapping memberships do occur. Membership as an active participant in Traditionist associations demands a speaking knowledge of Cantonese, while Modernist organizations require competency only in English. Those speaking only Chinese are limited to Traditionist groups. Bilingual persons may join either or both groups, although native-born Americans have never held the presidential office in the Traditionist associations. Ideological conflict concerning the aims and methods of the organization are minimal within Modernist groups, since a common belief system, that is, an agreement with group goals, is usually a prerequisite for membership. However, intra-organizational conflict in Traditionist groups is increasing, particularly where the associations are being invaded by younger men, who possess the necessary qualifications for admission yet have accepted many American ideas. These new members express their dissatisfaction with old-fashioned custom and prerogative. They, often, are accused by their elders of being disrespectful. These young men are impatient. Because they have been accepted as successful members of the greater society, they are unwilling to play subservient roles in their organizational life. Their anger and resentment produce conflict, because the activities of Traditionist

groups are still controlled by Chinese elders.

As a consequence of divergent goals and means, sincere cooperative ventures at the inter-organizational level are few and far between. While some major events are sponsored, ostensibly, by the "entire Chinese community," joint organizational cooperation is, usually, a one-sided affair. Nevertheless, such effort is presented to the non-Chinese public as a united community endeavor. The distribution and allocation of funds for active participation in, and attitude towards, such "community events" rarely demonstrate pan-Chinese solidarity. Although these two groups vie for prestige in socially distinct areas, they, nevertheless, must compete for members, monies, and, most important, recognition for their efforts in both the Chinese and Caucasian communities. As a result of this "competition," conflicts of interest frequently occur.

There is, presently, a new and still emergent grouping among Chinese youths of high school and college age. Members of this current generation of Chinese — the "Asian-Americans" — are concerned, also, with their heritage and identity, as Americans and as Orientals. They receive little support from elder community leaders (Traditionists) and only a passive acceptance from most Modernists, who often do not understand their goals nor their association with more militant "Black" and "Brown" "brothers." Unlike their elders in both groups, they are creating a new image in a pan-Asian sodality. Their emphasis is upon Asians rather than upon Chinese, and their programs call for social action and consequent change. Through ethnic studies, community programs, and other means, they are reassessing their Oriental heritage and, in the process, re-examining old and new Oriental stereotypes, attitudes, and experiences that their parents and grandparents prefer to forget.

Traditionists rely heavily upon recruiting active members from newly arrived immigrants. Yet, recent additions to America, unlike their predecessors, may come complete with their families and are less dependent upon traditional associations for economic and social security. Many Hong Kong immigrants in this community are "Westernized" and enter directly into American occupational life. While some of the leaders want younger recruits to staff their depleted ranks, they, often, do not know how to communicate with them. And, while some youth wish to participate in Chinese associations, there are no youth-oriented programs to attract them.

The Modernists have been more successful and are able to attract willing recruits, primarily business and professional men. Recruitment may, however, become a future problem as many Modernists increasingly view all-Chinese social service clubs as detrimental to their full participation in American life and prefer to join predominantly Caucasian organizations.

Many Chinese youths have given up Chinese exclusiveness in favor of their new "Asian" identity and have successfully assimilated with other Oriental groups. Although some of their leaders embrace their Black and Brown brothers, most of them are suspicious of many Negro and Mexican-American activities. This recent rekindling of "Asian-togetherness," presently, is not conducive to assimilation within Caucasian America.

Division and Unity

With the Chinese community split into divergent adult groups, neither of which are attentive nor particularly sympathetic to the demands of Chinese youth, these social divisions could harden and become formalized factions. Yet, this is precisely what has NOT happened. Many antagonisms are muted and differences are, if only temporarily, reconciled. Nor would it be proper to assume that intra-community conflicts always lead to social disorganization. Conflict between diverse segments can act, also, as a unifying factor for the Chinese community. As Coser (1956, 137) states:

Conflict creates links between contenders. It creates and modifies common norms necessary for the readjustment of the relationship, makes possible a reassessment of relative power, and, thus, serves as a balancing mechanism which helps to maintain and consolidate groups.

Moreover, social conflict always denotes social interaction. Conflict acts to define group boundaries, thus contributing to the reaffirmation and the identity of the group, so that the group may maintain its boundaries against the surrounding social world.

There are, also, forces which act to integrate the Chinese, forces which crosscut diverse organizational identities, emphasize what is common to all groups, and maintain a holistic and united community.

First, all Chinese in this community and in America share a historical legacy. They are the recipients of a continuous cultural tradition which separates them from all other Americans, including those of non-Chinese, Asian ancestry. Traditionists attempt to perpetuate and maintain the ceremonial and commemorative aspects of their heritage, and their organizational system remains based upon Chinese structural antecedents. They are Chinese first and Americans second. Modernists have a dual cultural identity — American and Chinese. Many of their attitudes, as well as their organizational format, are more American than Chinese. Yet, in their overall orientation, they evidence a strong identification with their Chinese identity, reinforcing the influences that tend to maintain a voluntarily segregated community. Asian-Americans, too, are proud of being Chinese. Though they may represent themselves to outsiders as Asians, within their own ranks they self-consciously recognize ethnic differences. This Chinese identity, a powerful factor in social cohesiveness, is strengthened by a history that predates the history of Western man. Modernists and activists may use different phraseology to express links with their Chinese past and may

269

choose to publicize their ancestry by emphasizing different aspects of that heritage. Yet pride — pride in ancestors and their accomplishments, pride in history and culture — is common to, and shared by, Traditionists, Modernists, and activists alike.

Regardless of their differences, all Chinese are united by a sense of "family." This familistic spirit, a cultural product of a Confucian ethos, has been strengthened by the more objective realities of Chinese life in America. Early Chinese immigrants, strangers in a strange land, stayed close to their kinsmen and relatives, often living in the same quarters or in adjoining houses. Families, often, operated shops and restaurants as a unit, drawing upon their members for labor and financing, and living above, or in back of, the family enterprise. Today, the family remains a basic unit of Chinese-American life. Moreover, the special feelings reserved for close kin, often, are extended to both maternal and paternal relatives and include some remotely related affinities. Close family friends are accorded, often, the amenities and, sometimes, the nomenclature, of kinsmen.

Most families celebrate both Chinese (Ch'ing Ming, Moon Festival, New Year's) and American (Thanksgiving, Easter, Christmas) holidays with family dinners. Chinese delicacies, like bird's nest soup, often share the table with turkeys and roasts. At these frequent gatherings, ideological differences are temporarily put aside as Traditionist grandparents, Modernist parents, and their children enjoy feasting and fellowship. As they retell old tales and relive precious moments from the past, they are bound together in the "spirit of family unity."

A Chinese communication network, also, is consciously maintained by an informal, yet efficient, information exchange system which unites the community by cutting across age, sex, generation, and culture boundaries. This Chinese grapevine, strengthened by long-standing school ties and business friendships, functions, through the spreading of news and rumor, to maintain a running commentary upon the activities of the Chinese. Stories and gossip about Chinese people and Chinese events travel from mother to daughter, to boy friend, to peer group, to relatives, and back again. Thus, the effect of Chinese geographic dispersion is minimized and a "community spirit" remains.

Thus far, I have refrained from discussing those individuals who belong to, and participate in, both Traditionist and Modernist organizations. Though small in number, probably no more than 5 percent, these individuals, often, are respected spokesmen of their associations. These men, often, have achieved monetary success within the Caucasian economic structure yet still wish to maintain a position in the Chinese community. By actively participating in both Traditionist and Modernist groups, they are aware of the plans and prevailing attitudes of both kinds of organizations and, often, by functioning as intermediaries, can prevent conflict situations from arising.

Finally, perhaps the most important key to a common Chinese identity must be sought outside the community itself — for, in the parlance of the Occidental, "all Chinese are alike." Stereotyped images of the "Chinamen," serving in a menial and inferior capacity, still remain rooted within Caucasian thought. Thus, attempts to move toward the dominant American groups are either rebuffed or only partially satisfied. Racial and cultural barriers continually prevent the Chinese from full membership in American society, throwing them back among their own people. Thus, out-group hostility often fosters in-group cohesiveness.

As long as structural assimilation — the large-scale entry of the Chinese into Caucasian cliques and clubs — remains a myth for most Chinese, and as long as Chinese are distinguished, categorically, from other Americans, the Chinese community will find it advantageous to act as a cohesive unit.

Fission and Fusion

Underlying the realities of Chinese community life is a process of fission and fusion. There are times when internal divisions can split the community into hostile factions. Yet, at other times, the community acts as a cohesive unit, often with a single spokesman. Both division and union are situational. Whenever there is a need to raise funds, or sponsor a pan-community Chinese cultural event, or present a unified front against the dominant society, they will find it advantageous to combine their resources. Should they ever wish to make their small numbers a significant political force, or should they ever feel overtly threatened by discrimination or prejudice, they may be expected to act as a single unit. At other times, when threats from outside forces appear to be minimal, or when divergent philosophies cannot be reconciled, the community will fragment, and each segment will pursue separate goals.

I believe that this ability to coalesce and to fragment, to shift identity and reference group, to join in, or withdraw from, a common effort is beneficial to the Chinese minority, because it enables them to maintain their ethnic identity and to participate, to varying degrees, in American social life. A single organizational structure, one system to accommodate all Chinese of varying cultural and social persuasions, leaves but two choices — to join or to withdraw.

Today's Chinese communities are made up of a diverse and heterogeneous population. Partially as a response to this diversity, Chinese communities have developed an organizational structure manifesting alternative choices. Chinese who wish to continue to participate actively in their Traditionist associations can still do so. Those that find that the Traditionist system can no longer meet their needs can enter into a Modernist network, which caters to their American orientation, yet lets them remain Chinese. Modernist organizations are particularly attractive to marginal men, who desire to maintain a bi-cultural identity. Those young men and women who are satisfied with neither Traditionist nor Modernist rhetoric and activities can join Asian-American groups.

This tripartite system, also, can accommodate the Chinese who wish to participate in more than one cultural arena, but — perhaps, more important — it allows individuals, as they pass through their life cycle from childhood to old age, to retain their ethnic ties, while they shift their cultural outlook.

Thus, as the American-born Chinese increase their participation in American life and shift their reference groups, they, nevertheless, can maintain their Chinese identity. They can continue to be both Chinese and American without sacrificing the psycho-social security that their ethnic identity provides.

Chapter Notes

1. These terms, generally, refer to generational categories (e.g., Traditionists are immigrants from overseas areas, while Modernists are native born.) Newly arrived Chinese immigrants are grouped, often, with Chinese who, although born in Hong Kong or China, have been living in America for many years. American-born persons who live in Chinatown are grouped with Chinese residents who reside in predominantly Caucasian suburbs. My use of these terms refers to their *cultural identity,* rather than age, generation, or residence.

2. "American" refers to basic middle-class, White, Anglo-Saxon, Protestant values and does not encompass present shifts in political and social ideology. Chinese rarely are members of American groups embracing radical philosophies of any nature.

3. All Chinese are, nominally, members of their respective family, district, or linguistic associations. These Traditionist associations are involuntary groups. Active membership (as discussed in this paper) is limited to members who either participate in the decision-making processes of the group or attend most of the group's major functions. Modernist groups are

voluntary associations, and prospective joiners must actively seek membership. Thus, members of voluntary organizations who regularly attend meetings and some major events are considered to be active participants. Most decision making in Modernist groups is conducted at public meetings.

4. Youth groups are voluntary associations. They are described, generally, as either "FOB" (Fresh-Off-the-Boat) or "ABC" (American-Born-Chinese) types. Yet, cultural orientation, rather than place of birth, is the critical key to membership. While they are not always formally associated with adult groupings, they, nevertheless, may follow the same divisions.

5. "The old country" refers, primarily, to the Sze-yap-, but also Sam-yap- and Chung-shan-speaking districts in Kuang-tung province, from which the majority of Chinese immigrants migrated to America (Sung, 1967).

References

Abel, Theodora M., and Hsu, F. L. K. "Some Aspects of Chinese Personality as Revealed by the Rorschach Test." *Research Exchange and Journal of Projective Techniques* XLL, 1949, pp. 285-301.

Barnett, Milton L. "Some Cantonese-American Problems of Status and Adjustment," *Phylon* XVIII, No. 4, 1958, pp. 420-427.

_____. "Alcohol and Culture: A Study of Drinking in a Chinese-American Community." Doctoral dissertation, Cornell University, 1952.

Chen, Eugenia V. "Survey of Chinese Youth and Student Clubs in New York City." Master's thesis, University of Michigan, 1945.

Chen, Ta. *Emigrant Communities in South China*. New York: Institute of Pacific Relations, 1940.

Chen, Wen-Hui Chung. "Changing Socio-Cultural Patterns of the Chinese Community in Los Angeles." Doctoral dissertation, University of Southern California, 1952.

Coser, Lewis A. *The Functions of Social Conflict*. Illinois: The Free Press of Glencoe, 1956.

Crissman, Lawrence W. "The Segmentary Structure of Urban Overseas Chinese Communities." *Man* 2(2), 1967, pp. 185-204.

Dare, Richard Kock. "The Economic and Social Adjustment of San Francisco Chinese for the Past Fifty Years." Master's thesis, University of California, Berkeley, 1959.

Fong, Stanley L. M. "Assimilation of Chinese in America: Changes in Orientation and Social Perception." *American Journal of Sociology* LXXI, No. 3, 1965, pp. 265-273.

Glazer, Nathan, and Moynihan, Daniel. *Beyond the Melting Pot*. Cambridge, Mass.: Harvard University Press, 1963.

Goldstein, Sidney, and Goldscheider, Calvin. *Jewish-Americans: Three Generations in a Jewish Community*. Englewood Cliffs, N.J.: Prentice-Hall, 1968.

Gordon, Milton M. *Assimilation in American Life*. New York: Oxford University Press, 1964.

Grafstein, David I. "A Study in Intragroup Conflict; Some Consequences of the Emergence of an Organization in Boston's Chinatown." *Cornell Journal of Social Relations* Vol. 3, No. 1,, 1968, pp. 15-25.

Heyer, Virginia. "Patterns of Social Organization in New York City's Chinatown." Doctoral dissertation, Columbia University, 1953.

Hambro, Edward. "The Problem of the Chinese

Refugees in Hong Kong." Holland: A. W. Sijthoff-Leyden, 1955.

Kitano, Harry, H. L. *Japanese-Americans: The Evolution of a Sub-Culture.* Englewood Cliffs, N.J.: Prentice-Hall, 1969.

Kwoh, Beulah Ong. "The Occupations of American-Born Chinese Male College Graduates in America." *Journal of Sociology* 53, 1947, pp. 192-200.

Kung, S. W. *Chinese in American Life: Some Aspects of their History, Status, Problems, and Contributions.* Seattle: University of Washington Press, 1962.

Lee, Rose Hum. *The Chinese in the United States of America.* New York: 'Oxford University Press, 1960.

_____. "The Recent Immigrant Chinese Families of the San Francisco-Oakland Area." *Marriage and Family Living* 18, 1956, pp. 14-24.

_____. "The Decline of Chinatown in the United States." *American Journal of Sociology* LIX, 5, 1949, pp. 422-432.

_____. "Chinese Population Trends in the United States." *The Southwestern Journal* 1948, pp. 97-101.

Lyman, Stanford N. "Contrasts in the Community Organization of Chinese and Japanese in North America." *The Canadian Review of Sociology and Anthropology* Vol. 5, No. 2, 1968, pp. 51-67.

Reynolds, C. N. "The Chinese Tongs." *American Journal of Sociology* XL, 1935, pp. 612-623.

Siu, Paul C. P. "The Sojourner." *American Journal of Sociology* Vol. LVIII, No. 1, 1952, pp. 34-44.

Smith, William. "The Second Generation Oriental American." *Journal of Applied Sociology* 10, 1925, pp. 160-168.

Sung, Betty Lee. *Mountain of Gold: The Story of the Chinese in America.* New York: The Macmillan Company, 1967.

Weiss, Melford S. "Conflict and Compromise: The Social Organization of a Chinese Community in America." Doctoral dissertation, Michigan State University, 1971.

Willmott, W. L. "Chinese Clan Associations in Vancouver." *Man* 49, 1964, pp. 33-36.

Wu, Ching-Chao. "Chinatowns: A Study of Symbiosis and Assimilation." Ph.D. dissertation, University of Chicago, 1928.

Yuan, D. Y. "Chinatown and Beyond: The Chinese Population in Metropolitan New York." *Phylon* Vol. 27, No. 4, 1966, pp. 321-323.

25. Community Intervention: Implications for Action

by Stanley Sue

There is increasing recognition among helping professionals that the problems encountered by ethnic minorities cannot be resolved adequately without reference to the community. Attempts to ameliorate difficulties encountered by minorities can be successful only if the wider social milieu in which behavior develops is radically altered. Seen in this light, problems of poverty, unemployment, discrimination, delinquency, and mental illness are only symptomatic of problems in society. These beliefs have given impetus to the formation of community action or intervention programs. This paper examines (1) the problems of Asian communities, (2) the inadequacies of traditional helping services, (3) the types of services which have developed, and (4) the future role of community intervention.

The Problems of Asian Communities

Millions of tourists annually visit American Chinatowns, Little Tokyos, and Manilatowns in order to catch a glimpse of Asian subcultures. In these communities, visitors sample Asian foods, see colorful buildings, hear the inhabitants speak in foreign tongues, and bring back souvenirs of their travels. The problems of Asian communities, however, remain invisible to most tourists. Indeed, the Chinatowns of San Francisco, New York, and Seattle are, essentially, ghetto areas. Jacobs, Landau, and Pell (1971) note that the Chinese in San Francisco's

Chinatown have the highest tuberculosis rate in the city and that the suicide rate is three times higher than the national rate. Forty percent of the families have an income under $4,000 per year. Gangs composed of youths now roam the streets of Chinatown, and ten recent murders have been connected to youthful gangs (*Seattle Post-Intelligencer*, June 28, 1972). Other problems, such as inadequate housing, unemployment, and juvenile delinquency, are also shared by New York's Chinatown (Chin, 1971). The difficulties encountered by immigrants and the elderly have been largely ignored.

Until recently, there were little systematic efforts to alleviate these conditions. The general public believed that Chinatowns represented model minority communities. *U.S. News and World Report* (1966) stated that Chinese were law abiding, hard working, and respectful; Chinatown was relatively free of crime and was flourishing without external help. Even some Chinese businessmen helped to perpetuate the myth that the inhabitants of Chinatowns were experiencing little difficulties (Jacobs, et al., 1971). They represented the views of the business elite, who were interested in maintaining the status quo. Social reform was not in the best interests of employers who could hire workers at minimum wage levels.

Few individuals in Chinatowns have made strong outcries of injustices. Traditional values, emphasizing obedience to authority and the discreet handling of problems, have suppressed public protests. Immigrants who entered the country illegally often face intimidation if they cause "trouble." Thus, a vicious circle is created. Many Chinese have desires to remain among other Chinese or are financially unable to leave Chinatown. Fears of prejudice and discrimination from White Americans, also, serve to keep Chinese in the ghetto. To be sure, youth groups composed of dissatisfied American- and foreign-born Chinese have rebelled against the established business community (Lyman, 1971). Unfortunately, older Chinese often label these groups as juvenile delinquents and dismiss their demands for reform.

Many of these problems are found, also, in Japanese and Filipino areas. The identification of Chinatowns, Little Tokyos, and Manilatowns with Asian communities is quite obvious. The communities not only contain relatively large Asian-American populations but also illustrate the subcultural life styles of the inhabitants. In practice, however, the concept of community must be extended to a broader, and less precise, definition. Community can be defined as a group of Asian-Americans who interact in some manner and feel some degree of commonalty as members of a minority group. Thus, it is both a geographic and psychological concept.

This concept, then, also encompasses the interactions of Asian-American students on college and university campuses. For many years, Asian students, often, were organized into various clubs or organizations. Chinese student clubs, Japanese sororities and fraternities, and Hawaiian clubs have been organized, traditionally, on many college campuses. Currently, a large number of Asian students have come together in an Asian-American movement. Feeling alienated by the lack of courses on the experiences of Asian-Americans, dissatisfied by the "irrelevance" of traditional academic courses, and angered by racism, these students have demanded a more responsive educational experience. They feel motivated to help other Asians caught in ghetto areas, since traditional attempts to resolve problems have failed.

Inadequacies of Current Approaches

The adjustment of individuals depends upon (1) the nature and extent of community demands, and (2) the availability and adequacy of resources (Klein, 1968). Chinatowns throughout the United States can be characterized by high levels of stress and low levels of community resources. The inadequacy of housing, the unemployment, and the ghetto conditions of Chinatowns maintain a high degree of stress. Traditional means of working through emotional problems in individuals seem particularly inappropriate to Asians in their communities. Psychotherapy is geared, often, for White, middle-class individuals who exhibit psychological sophistication. Indeed, inequities exist in the delivery of mental health services, especially to members of minority groups (Hollingshead and Redlich, 1958; Yamamoto, James, and Palley, 1968). Cultural factors, also, limit the applicability of one-to-one psychotherapy, since many Asian-Americans find it difficult to label themselves as mentally ill, to undergo psychotherapy, and to understand the psychotherapeutic process (Kitano, 1970; Sue and Sue, 1972). Even the impact and effectiveness of psychotherapy for individuals have been challenged (Cowen, Gardner, and Zax, 1966). There is a severe manpower shortage in the helping professions to meet current demand for services (Albee, 1965). For Asians, the manpower problem is even more acute, since there is a lack of bilingual therapists. These inadequacies in mental health care have given rise to alternative intervention programs such as prevention, consultation, political organization, and the use of paraprofessionals in the community.

It should be noted that community organization among Asian-Americans is not a new phenomenon. The early Chinese immigrants were organized into family or benevolent associations, Tongs, and business interests. The Japanese Association for Issei and the Japanese-American Citizens' League for the Nisei-Sansei groups played important roles in providing Japanese with legal services, in dealing with discrimination, in sponsoring social affairs, and in maintaining a lobby group in Washington (Kitano, 1969).

The current movement towards community involvement has several features that distinguish it from the older and more traditional Asian-American organizations. First, it is largely a student-initiated movement, which seeks to help all Asian-American groups (Chinese, Filipinos, Japanese, Koreans, etc.) Although increasingly large numbers of Asian professionals and indigenous individuals have contributed to the community, students comprise the major bulk of manpower. Second, emphasis is placed on helping disadvantaged Asians. The problems of the elderly, the recent immigrants, the poor, etc., are given special attention. Finally, there is growing realization that Asian-Americans face prejudice and discrimination, much as other minority groups. Asian students, therefore, seek to expose and actively combat the forces of racism.

Types of Community Programs

Student involvement in Asian-American affairs first started on university campuses, particularly in New York, Hawaii, and the West Coast states. Asian students were quick to follow the examples of the Black and Chicano movements. Ethnic identity and self-awareness became the major goals for Asians. The students wanted to learn more about their immigrant ancestors, about the historical and contemporary forces of racism, and about their own position in society. In response to this demand, courses were offered in Asian-American history, Oriental languages, Asian personality, and Asian communities. Most schools offered these courses as a part of ethnic studies or of an Asian-American department.

Simultaneous with interest in Asian courses,

many students felt a strong desire to help their own people and to actively challenge the racist nature of society. Early attempts to help the community, often, involved the establishment of tutorial services for those who spoke little or no English. Student volunteers would spend a few hours a week trying to improve the English of school children or of the recent Chinese immigrants. Although tutors were providing a much-needed service to the Chinese, their contact with the communities brought a sharper awareness of more urgent problems. Students wanted to improve the conditions faced by many Asian-Americans, i.e., inadequate housing, unemployment, poor health, poverty, and mental health problems.

Some Asians felt that one of the most crucial problems was education. Social and economic reform would have to start with an overhaul of the educational system. On February 14, 1969, a document sponsored by the Concerned Chinese for Action and Change was circulated in San Francisco (see Jacobs, et al., 1971). The following demands were made: (a) establishment of a multiservice English facility for immigrants; (b) incorporation of Asian studies into existing curriculum at all grade levels; (c) initiation of courses in Asian-American history, Asian languages, and Chinatown; (d) recruitment of qualified Chinese immigrant teachers; (e) employment of principals, counselors, and teachers who are, preferably, of Asian descent and who understand and identify with the community; (f) placement of Asian students as counselors and tutors for other students; (g) involvement of the Chinese community in the appointment of faculty and in the development of new educational programs; (h) increasing Chinese adult education classes; (i) assignment of additional compensatory education classes to schools; (j) establishment of pre-school centers in the Chinatown-North Beach area; (k) alleviation of existing overcrowded conditions in schools; (l) declaration of Chinese New Year's Day as a holiday.

These demands reflect the real concern Asian-Americans have over the educational process. Traditionally, schools have ignored the history and experience of Asian-Americans, even in schools with relatively large numbers of Chinese, Japanese, and Filipino students. There is a lack of bilingual teachers who are able to relate to the contemporary problems of students. Thus, many students feel alienated by the lack of relevant courses. Recent immigrants frequently drop out of school because of language difficulties.

Obviously, not all of the demands made by the Concerned Chinese for Action and Change were met, and reforms in the educational system remained a common area of focus. Recently, there was a confrontation between the local school board and the Asian community over the lack of Asian counselors at a Seattle high school. The school board finally agreed to employ Asian counselors, since the school contained a high proportion of Asian students.

While changes in the educational structure and in the relationship between the community and schools represented a social-systems approach, people-centered programs also developed. In Los Angeles, Japanese sponsored a self-help group for Issei in the downtown area. Multiple services were provided, such as social security and welfare information, flu vaccinations, and recreational programs (Tachiki, Wong, Odo, and Wong, 1971). In response to the growing drug problem among Asian-Americans, telephone "hot lines" and walk-in crisis centers have been established.

An interesting program to train more militant minority students to function as counselors was initiated at the University of California, Los Angeles (Sue, in press). The Student Health Psychiatric Clinic, designed to provide treatment for students experiencing emotional problems, was underutilized by minority students. In an attempt to develop more responsive counseling services for minorities, the Clinic staff consulted with the directors of the various ethnic studies programs (Asian, Black, Chicano, and Native-American). The directors felt that many minority students could not relate to the therapeutic services provided by the Clinic and were reluctant to see White therapists. Therefore, the Clinic staff decided to train minority students in counseling and to employ a number of them.

The training program consisted of a one-quarter course in counseling. Two psychiatrists, a counseling psychologist, and two advanced graduate students in clinical psychology served as instructors. At first, many students questioned the purpose of the class. They felt that the counseling of minority individuals was less important than the need for social action. As a compromise, students were given access to various campus services frequently used by minorities. Thus, they could act as referral sources for counselees seeking information about financial aid, tutorial programs, and health services.

The instructors utilized a didactic and experiential approach in the training program. Lectures, discussions, and readings focused on issues such as the cultural background of minorities, crisis intervention, assessment, and helping relationships. Another important part of the training included student participation in small group encounters and in the role playing of counselor-counselee interactions. After the training period, a number of the students were employed as counselors for minority students.

Of the 70 students enrolled in the class, 22 were Asian-Americans. This relatively large number is, perhaps, indicative of a growing interest among Asian students in the social sciences and helping services. Asian-American students have, traditionally, entered fields such as the physical sciences, engineering, or medicine (Sue and Kirk, 1972).

Asians have also become increasingly active in political confrontation. Jacobs, et al., (1971) recount an interesting example of Asian community organization and protestation against injustices. In 1969, Dr. Thomas

Noguchi, the Japanese Chief Coroner for Los Angeles, was asked by the County Chief Administrative Officer to resign. The County Supervisors voted to dismiss Noguchi after he had rescinded his resignation before it was accepted. In an attempt to confront the charges of insanity and cruelty which were lodged against him, Noguchi appealed for a Civil Service hearing. During the hearings, most of the charges were found to be vague and unsubstantiated. Several individuals who testified against Noguchi appeared to harbor some resentment towards him; and some of the alleged "insane" behaviors, such as an almost perpetual smile, were clearly attributable to his Japanese culture.

The Japanese-American community was infuriated by Noguchi's dismissal. Over eighty Japanese organizations sponsored an advertisement in the *Los Angeles Times* newspaper, stating the injustice of the action. In the end, Noguchi was reinstated as Chief Medical Examiner and Coroner.

Many Chinese in San Francisco have organized to protest, not for greater civil rights or social reform, but against the busing and integration of their children. At a public meeting, a crowd of Chinese housewives came "making fists . . . shouting. . . . They stormed the stage. . . . The police were there, ready for trouble, but the poor devils froze. They couldn't have been more astounded. . . ." (Wolfe, 1971, p. 35)

Community intervention programs and demands for social reform often elicit bewilderment or anger on the part of many White Americans. Those who do not understand the problems encountered by Asian-Americans often say, "Asians are getting so militant and are just copying the Blacks," or, "Asians no longer have respect for their traditional values which once made them a model minority." If Asians are imitating the Black movement, it is because they share a minority status; and the lesson learned in the Civil Rights Movement is that one must demand changes. In our society,

being an oppressed group is not, unfortunately, a sufficient condition for obtaining reform. Rather, it is necessary to dramatize the oppression and to actively seek civil rights. Elijah Mohammed stated, "You can't blame the government for not giving you anything when you are not asking for anything." (Lincoln, 1961)

Guidelines for Action

Intervention programs have been achieved on local levels without much co-ordination within and between Asian communities. To be sure, there has been a great deal of communication regarding community organization among Asians, and it is debatable whether more centralized attempts in organizing should be made. Although it is difficult to make generalizations about community programs, several factors appear to facilitate community intervention.

Technical and Social Factors

Ideally, the development of programs must be preceded by an assessment of community needs. What kinds of services are needed? What problems exist? Attempts to answer these questions, often, have been made without any community consultation. Problems of communities, typically, have been defined by outsiders. There is growing realization that the community must be given a strong voice in expressing its needs and in proposing solutions. A program is currently underway in Seattle to assess the difficulties encountered by Chinatown residents. Individuals are administered a survey, written both in English and Chinese. In this way, residents help to determine the direction of community programs. In addition to technical factors which involve assessing the problems and proposing a solution, social factors must be considered. Programs, often, fail because they are not geared to the life style of the community. For example, poverty-stricken families cannot be helped by increasing welfare services, since there is a general resistance among Chinese to use such services. Under the assumption that individuals in Chinatown, Los Angeles, could not financially afford psychiatric hospitalization for personal problems, Resthaven Psychiatric Hospital decided to allow Chinese to receive hospitalization for a drastically reduced fee. (See the paper by Brown, et al.) No one responded to the program, perhaps because of the stigma attached to undergoing psychiatric care. Resthaven, subsequently, has developed community mental health programs. In summary, it is imperative to determine what community services are needed and to initiate programs that adequately respond to the life styles of those being served.

Leadership

Interestingly, Asian communities have lacked the leadership of a national figure. Other groups have been able to point to organizers such as Martin Luther King, Saul Alinsky, Jesse Jackson, and Caesar Chavez. Kitano (1969) notes that very few Japanese leaders have exhibited, traditionally, a dynamic personality, charisma, or a "hero" quality. While Asian leaders do exist, they tend to avoid the spotlight and to work quietly within the ethnic community. Since the planning and execution of community programs require highly trained, politically sensitive organizers (Alinsky, 1971), a new type of political leader may have to emerge. This individual must be able to work in White society as well as to bring together various factions and to have a strong degree of credibility within the Asian community. Unity has been particularly difficult to achieve because of the tremendous differences among Asians. In addition to social and political divisions and to variations among the diverse Asian groups, differences exist, also, in terms of language, area of residence, generation, and degree of assimilation.

Programs

There is a need to develop and maintain a wide diversity of intervention programs. In elementary and high schools with a large number of Asians, special courses on Asian history and contemporary problems should be offered. A serious attempt must be made, also, to identify those students who exhibit educational or language problems. Bilingual Asian tutors should be made available to these students. As mentioned previously, many Asians are reluctant to utilize community projects such as welfare and mental health services. In order to reduce this resistance, it may be wise to have a community multiservice facility, offering traditionally accepted programs as well as newer ones. Medical, legal, recreational, welfare, counseling, language, immigration, and referral aid might be parts of the facility. It must receive the support and encouragement of community leaders and should have members of the community as personnel.

Other projects can also be developed. Coffee houses where Asian youths have the opportunity to discuss their problems with peers and counselors may be able to provide a much-needed service in a relaxed atmosphere. Families should be encouraged to meet and discuss their difficulties. Although organization in Asian communities has been a major problem, more Asians are realizing that it is possible to influence social policy by exerting a united stand. This was demonstrated by Chinese in San Francisco, regarding the busing issue. The likelihood of organizing Asians is increasing, especially since legal and social policies, heretofore ignored by many, are proving to have a strong effect on the lives of Asians.

Research

Community intervention, usually, involves (1) the definition of a problem, (2) the collection of data and re-analysis of the problem, (3) suggestions for action, (4) the implementation of the suggestions, and (5) research concerning the outcome of the project. Most community programs for Asian-Americans have emphasized service and have neglected the systematic study of outcome. Obviously, the success or failure of any program must be determined. Too much money is wasted, often, on programs which do not achieve intended goals. Research is helpful, also, in suggesting how existing programs can be changed to meet the needs of individuals.

Summary

The value of community intervention lies in the use of community resources in response to urgent problems facing Asian-Americans. Many of these problems have been ignored, and previous attempts to meet the needs of individuals have not been adequate. Through the use of community resources, more responsive programs are emerging and greater feelings of unity and self-determination are being developed.

References

Albee, G. W. "Manpower Needs for Mental Health and the Role of Psychology." *Canadian Psychology* 60, 1965, 82-92.

Alinsky, S. "Tactics for the Seventies." In S. Cahill and M. F. Cooper (eds.) *The Urban Reader.* Englewood Cliffs, N.J.: Prentice-Hall, 1971.

Chin, R. "New York Chinatown Today: Community in Crisis." *Amerasia Journal* 1, 1971, 1-24.

Cowen, E. L.; Gardner, E. A.; and Zax, M. (eds.). *Emergent Approaches to Mental Health Problems.* New York: Appleton-Century-Crofts, 1966.

Hollingshead, A. B., and Redlich, F. C. *Social Class and Mental Illness.* New York: Wiley, 1958.

Jacobs, P.; Landau, S.; and Pell, E. *To Serve the Devil — Volume 2: Colonials and Sojourners.* New York: Vintage Books, 1971.

Kitano, H. H. "Mental Illness in Four Cultures." *Journal of Social Psychology* 80, 1970, 121-134.

_____. *Japanese-Americans: The Evolution of a Subculture.* Englewood Cliffs, N.J.: Prentice-Hall, 1969.

Klein, D. C. *Community Dynamics and Mental Health.* New York: Wiley & Sons, 1968.

Lyman, S. M. "Red Guard on Grant Avenue: The Rise of Youthful Rebellion in Chinatown." In S. M. Lyman, *The Asian in the West.* Reno, Nevada, Desert Research Institute, 1971.

Muhammad, E. "The Faith and the Future." In E. C. Lincoln (ed.), *The Black Muslims in America.* Boston: Beacon Press, 1961.

Sue, D. W., and Sue, S. "Counseling Chinese-Americans." *Personnel and Guidance Journal* 50, 1972, 637-644.

_____, and Kirk, B. A. "Psychological Characteristics of Chinese-American Students." *Journal of Counseling Psychology* 6, 1972, 471-478.

Sue, S. "Third-World Student Counselors." *Journal of Counseling Psychology* 1973, in press.

_____, and Sue, D. W. "Chinese-American Personality and Mental Health." *Amerasia Journal* 1, 1972, 36-49.

Tachiki, A.; Wong, E.; Odo, F.; and Wong, B. (eds.). *Roots: An Asian-American Reader.* Los Angeles: Continental Graphics, 1971.

U.S. News and World Report. "Success Story of One Minority Group in U.S." December 26, 1966.

Wolfe, T. "Bok gooi, hok gooi, and T'ang Jen: Or, Why There is No National Association for the Advancement of Chinese-Americans." *New York,* September 27, 1971.

Yamamoto, J.; James, Q. C.; and Palley, N. "Cultural Problems in Psychiatric Therapy." *Archives of General Psychiatry* 19, 1968, 45-49.

26. Whither Ethnic Studies: A Re-examination of Some Issues

by Russell Endo

In the late 1960s, demands for Black studies programs were voiced on many American university and college campuses. For the first time, these institutions were deeply involved in the ethnic protest of the decade. Initially, many were overwhelmed or confused. Some fought back, while others acknowledged the demands in varying degrees and began the difficult task of establishing and financing such programs. During this early period, innumerable issues were raised and debated. The legacy of these discussions are well over seventy essays and commentaries on Black studies.[1] Those unfamiliar with the genesis of these programs and the enormously complex and diverse questions that were raised are encouraged to delve into the literature. Hopefully, this paper will provide the initial stimulus.

Black studies have, in some sense, become synonymous with ethnic studies, though, more recently, the latter term has come to include academic programs focusing on other ethnic groups. Unfortunately, these "other" programs have not received the attention they deserve. This paper will provide a preliminary examination of one of them, Asian-American studies. The paper has two general objectives: to comment upon Asian-American studies programs, and, then, to review a few of the issues raised by ethnic studies, especially Black studies programs, noting, also, the relevance of these issues for Asian-American studies. The discussion

below is primarily based upon the author's participation in two ethnic studies programs and his observations of approximately twenty-five Asian-American programs over the past three years.

The effort was not undertaken in a highly rigorous manner, and, without belaboring the point, the comments may be taken as tentative in nature. Presumably, additional evidence and commentary will soon be forthcoming.

Asian-American Studies

The first Asian-American studies programs were direct outgrowths of the Third World Strike at San Francisco State and the University of California at Berkeley in 1968. Since that time, scores of programs have emerged, primarily in California, though a scattering of programs can be found throughout the West and along the East Coast. The most rapid growth occurred in the succeeding two or three years. On most campuses, programs were established in response to pressures from Asian-American student organizations. These resulted in the creation of experimental courses taught by existing faculty members. The enthusiasm generated by such courses, by the knowledge of programs elsewhere, and by the previous success of Black studies programs usually provided the impetus for the development of additional course offerings.

Other events stimulated the growth and

spread of Asian-American programs. Numerous Asian-American conferences and symposia were held, beginning with the Yellow Identity Symposium in Berkeley in 1969. Bibliographies, readers, journals, newspapers, and various curriculum materials were produced by community groups and on some of the University of California campuses. The general interest in ethnic groups also led to the publication or republication of many books and articles on Asian-Americans. And some mechanisms for pooling materials and conducting exchanges between schools were established.

But, while this period of stimulation produced many new programs, most never managed to expand beyond a small number of courses offered, either on a temporary basis or within regular academic departments such as history, psychology, and sociology. Only a few campuses formed reasonably autonomous and permanent programs within specially created departments or colleges. These programs generally granted degrees in Asian-American or ethnic studies, though a few of the smaller programs co-ordinated their offerings to produce some form of course minors or interdisciplinary majors. Asian-American studies at the college level have been paralleled by the development of courses in a few California secondary schools and by the wider inclusion of materials on Asian-Americans in a significant number of primary and secondary schools.

Newly emerging Asian-American studies programs ran into a number of major problems, and, in most instances, these served to keep the programs at a very modest size. Lack of available funds was a major stumbling block. This can be attributed, depending upon the school, to a lack of commitment to ethnic studies on the part of administrators, greater attention and support devoted to Black demands and courses, refusal to view Asian-Americans as a legitimate minority group, and a lack of knowledge by Asian-Americans on how to exert leverage to obtain funds or their reluctance to do so. In some instances, Asian-American communities

vehemently were opposed to programs that, seemingly, would identify their young with disadvantaged or militant Blacks and Chicanos. Faculty and students, sometimes, did not agree on program objectives, courses, and means of implementation, leading to major conflicts or disillusionment by one or both parties. The early absence of qualified instructors on many campuses and the dearth of curriculum materials also created difficulties. In retrospect, it appears that the most important problems for Asian-Americans were the need to "wait in line" after other ethnic groups; the absence of widespread unity among faculty, students, and community for programs; and the general lack of militance, or, at least, strong advocacy, on the part of proponents.

Some new programs are currently being established and a few are expanding their offerings. But it is abundantly clear that the early period of growth is over. Most campuses are involved in an effort at retrenchment to maintain what they presently have. The retrenchment has resulted from general budget cuts within higher education and the reluctance of universities to expand or even continue what they see as basically innovative and experimental "fringe" programs. One tragic outcome of this situation on several campuses has been the initiation or intensification of political fighting among various ethnic studies programs over limited resources. In such infighting, Asian-American programs often fare poorly and lose to others that are much larger and more politically sophisticated.

At many schools, the retrenchment stems, also, from a decline in student interest. Part of this can be traced to the graduation of the initial group of student participants who helped to establish these programs, and the absence of committed replacements. Part is due to discouragement because of intraprogram conflicts, the constant struggle for recognition and funding, or the development of highly conventional academic programs with little concern for contemporary community problems. Finally, some of the decline in interest might be related to the general slackening of student concern with activism and social problems, including those in the area of race and ethnic relations. The need to maintain student interest is critical, particularly for programs that continue on an experimental basis, and others that were funded under a primary justification of strong student interest.

As a background to further discussion of Asian-American studies programs, some comments will be made about Asian-American activists. Then, comparisons between Black studies and Asian-American studies will be drawn, not only to reveal similarities and differences, but also as a basis for a better understanding of the latter.

The term "Asian-American" encompasses distinct ethnic groups composed of immigrants and their descendents from a number of East Asian societies, including China, Japan, the Philippines, and Korea. Migrants from the first two arrived, primarily, during the periods of 1850-1882 and 1890-1924, respectively, while those from the latter two were more recent newcomers. All of these groups began at the bottom of the economic and social ladder, and all faced intense racial prejudice and oppressive forms of social, political, and economic discrimination. To varying degrees, the early immigrant generations of these groups established ethnic communities, though these changed and, sometimes, declined in importance over the years. Through adherence to norms and values that closely resembled those embodied in the Protestant ethic, they gradually made progress in terms of education, occupation, and income. The basic strategy used was one of accommodation to obstacles, of preparation and hard work until opportunities presented themselves. This was in marked contrast to alternative strategies that emphasize confrontation and the militant advocacy of demands and reforms. For most individuals, assimilation was viewed as an eventual goal.

Today, by conventional indicators of income

and life style, the Japanese-Americans have achieved the most mobility, being primarily a middle-class group. The other ethnic groups present a more mixed picture with varying degrees of mobility and assimilation being apparent. Because of their relative progress and the manner in which it was achieved, Asian-Americans are now being touted as "model" minorities and seen as being basically like middle-class Whites. Portions of some Asian-American communities promote and believe in this new stereotype with all of its implications, but other segments are voicing their opposition. The combating of this stereotype has become one of the general focal points for the activism of young Asian-Americans.

The young activists point out that progress has been accompanied by past suffering and losses, a decline in the traditional communities, an increase in cultural conflicts and identity problems, and an acceptance of middle-class prejudices.[2] The stereotype also ignores major social problems that still beset these groups, such as poverty, delinquency and crime, mental illness, problems of the aged, poor housing and health, and blatant economic discrimination. Even middle-class Asian-Americans face subtle manifestations of racism such as lack of available housing in some areas, reluctance of employers to hire or promote Asians, and infrequent, but existing, discourtesies, slights, and stereotyping that occur in face-to-face interaction. Omission of the Asian-American experience from educational curriculums and the stereotyping of group members in films and on television programs and commercials are further evidence of inequities.

Young activists are working to increase an awareness of these problems among their ethnic groups. They are striving, also, to break with elements of their cultural backgrounds, such as the heavy stress on educational and occupational achievement, the emphasis on obedience and conformity, the sometimes-closed nature of social activities and friendship and marriage patterns, the desire for assimilation, and the existing middle-class notions of security and materialism. Severe criticism has been directed at the previous strategy of accommodation, and, also, at community institutions that maintain the status quo in the face of pressing social and economic issues. The break has necessitated the development of new values and emphases, however diverse or tentative. These include a concern with community organization and action programs, an awareness of problems and discrimination, establishment of unity among Asian-American groups, an identification with Asians abroad (such as the Vietnamese) and their struggles, the creation of new identities and more aggressive political and interpersonal forms of interaction, and attempts to redefine their relationship to American society through a re-examination of Asian-American history and elements of the older, more traditional cultures. The activists are trying to establish alternative organizations such as drop-in centers, legal and medical clinics, newspapers, and a variety of action programs. At least until very recently, one of their key objectives was the development of Asian-American studies programs.

The explicit goals of most Asian-American studies programs are similar to those of Black studies: to provide an understanding of the experiences of the ethnic groups focusing on their communities, their adaptations to oppression and social change, and their contributions to American society; to provide a preprofessional background for persons wishing to pursue occupations within the respective ethnic communities; and to furnish a basis for the creation of a more positive ethnic self-identity. However, if one is willing to generalize across specific programs and ignore for the moment the exceptional cases, there are major differences between Asian-American and Black studies. Asian-American studies programs have, primarily, a sensitizing effect, introducing students, especially young Asian-Americans, to their history and cultural characteristics and to more contemporary issues and problems. For many, this is their first prolonged insight into

these areas, since, generally, they have been ignored, both by Asian-American groups and the society at large. For many young Asian-Americans, the sensitization increases their feelings of group awareness, and, for some, it stimulates strong desires to work on community problems. A number of Asian-Americans begin to question their own identities and feel a sense of cultural marginality. For those who, already, have realized these feelings as the result of other experiences within and outside Asian-American communities, the sensitization may not so much provoke a new awareness as the realization that what were once seen as personal aberrations are, in fact, shared, and that the source may not be the individual himself, but the social structure within which he exists. It may be, partly, in response to these more personal concerns that some courses or entire programs have developed a heavy social-psychological emphasis, probing issues such as alienation, cultural conflict, marginality, value changes, personality development, and psychological approaches to racism. Both the sensitization and the search for new identities and cultural patterns may be promoted by young activists, depending upon their continuing influence in ongoing programs. Both are furthered, also, by some forms of field exercises, such as research or participation in community programs.

A small minority of Asian-American programs go beyond sensitization as described above. These tend to be dominated by various groups of young activists and can be divided into two general strains. Programs of the first type actively work to develop new cultural patterns and alternatives with courses on Asian and Asian-American creative arts and through major efforts to establish and sustain rehabilitative forms of social welfare projects in Asian-American communities. Programs of the second strain may engage in the above activities but can be characterized by their presentation of conflict-oriented ideological and political perspectives. These perspectives view the present condition of ethnic groups, including Asian-Americans, in terms of power differences that exist among societal groups, and are concerned with group-level organization to promote major institutional change. Having characterized these two strains rather briefly, it should be pointed out that there are major variations within each, as well as overlaps. And, although only a few programs have these characteristics, others may contain some of their elements or be influenced by them. However, this is in marked contrast to Black studies programs where the characteristics of these strains are far more predominant.

Black studies programs tend to be different from Asian-American studies because they operate within a different context. Blacks have been more aware of their problems and have been actively engaged in a struggle against blatant racism. Recent years have seen the evolution of militant strategies and efforts to build community institutions and cultural elements based on previous Black experiences and an African heritage. To a far greater extent than Asian-American communities, Black communities have already mobilized and organized for social action. And, while in many respects young Asian-American activists are the mainstays of a still-tentative Asian-American protest movement, young Black students are only one significant part of a more broadly based and ongoing Black protest.

Begun at a time when militant strategies dominated the Black movement, and usually in response to the use of such strategies within the university, Black studies programs provide opportunities for the more activist Black students and academicians to participate in this movement. One of their functions has been to develop and promote rationales for various strategies of social change. Consequently, programs often include an explicit ideological or political content. Black studies programs, also, furnish opportunities for direct action and protest within the university setting and in Black communities. Unlike most Asian-

American programs, they provide more of a link with an extensive network of community action and social welfare programs.

Black studies programs perform the dual role of not only promoting an understanding of Black history and contributions, but also developing and legitimizing new or forgotten elements of the Black experience. This is apparent, for example, in the courses on African history, languages, and the creative arts. These courses and their content are vital elements of the newly emerging American Black culture. In contrast, only a few Asian-American programs contain many courses on East Asian history or culture, and, then, usually only those that are readily available. These are, primarily, a source of complementary background materials, as there is strong sentiment for a movement away from the study of traditional cultures toward a clear emphasis on the Asian experience in America. Asian-American programs also have the effect of legitimizing elements of past group experiences, but active efforts to develop new cultural patterns and emphases are not nearly so extensive nor successful as those within Black studies.

Many Black studies programs provide an important supportive environment for Black students, particularly on predominantly White campuses. Many Blacks, unlike most Asian-American students, are from lower class backgrounds and are on campus as a result of extensive efforts to recruit disadvantaged minority students. Many feel alienated within this setting and have, consequently, pushed for Black studies programs to provide interesting and personally relevant materials and also opportunities to associate with other Black students and faculty. It is, partly, because of this feeling of alienation that demands for programs, sometimes, have been coupled with others for separate residential, eating, and study facilities. Because of the backgrounds of many Black students, remedial programs are more characteristically part of Black studies than Asian-American studies, though, overall, they are in short supply and tend to be very minimal in size. Remedial programs include counseling, tutoring, financial assistance, and training in basic skills such as reading and mathematics.

Both Asian-American and Black studies programs have faced common obstacles such as funding and faculty recruitment, and both have produced a number of different structures. However, Black studies programs have been established on far more campuses, and their offerings, usually, have been more extensive. There are a number of reasons for this, including the relative size of the Black population, the visibility of Black problems over the past decade, and a greater interest on the part of the general population. The militance with which initial demands were made, undoubtedly, forced major concessions at some universities, and feelings of a need to redress past injustices toward Blacks were, probably, a significant factor. Also important was the support of a strong ongoing protest movement, and the fact that Blacks were the first to make demands for ethnic studies programs.

Being the first has also meant that the Blacks had to bear the brunt of the initial debate over the validity and structure of such programs, and they had to fight major political and intellectual battles to become established. Often, program formation was preceded by disruptive demonstrations and the voicing of a variety of "non-negotiable" demands, such as student control over program structure and faculty hiring. Following in the wake of Black studies, a few Asian-American programs emulated the strategies of their predecessors. However, in most instances, Asian-American students approached university administrators in a rather modest fashion and attempted to negotiate very minimal programs. Fortunately, administrators, usually, were highly receptive to these requests because of their previous experiences. Besides being less militant, Asian-Americans presented different rationales for their programs than the Blacks. Blacks emphasized the need to atone for past injustices, often with strong feelings of

moral righteousness, and noted, also, the consequences of noncompliance. Asian-American students tended to emphasize the need for recognition of the generally ignored experiences and contributions of their groups, the numbers of Asian-American and Asian students on the campus, and the precedent set by Black studies. Not being first has, sometimes, meant that little money was left for Asian-American programs, or that severe political infighting for funds had to take place with other ethnic groups. Some Asian-American programs have faced, also, intransigent administrators who were hardened from battles with other ethnic groups and, for various reasons, refused to be cooperative.

A few other differences between Asian-American and Black studies programs will be noted. Where Asian-American programs desired to incorporate materials on traditional cultures, they were often able to do so because of the prior existence of courses on East Asian history or languages within a special department or in a number of departments such as history, anthropology, and languages. In contrast, Black studies programs, generally, had to construct their own courses on African history and cultures. Asian-American programs, initially, relied more heavily upon existing ethnic instructors, while Black studies programs had to recruit new faculty. Because of their small size, many Asian-American programs continue to be carried out by these original instructors. Asian-American courses have been subjected to far fewer criticisms over program quality than Black studies, and some are, perhaps, overly conventional in their formats. These points will be discussed later in more detail.

Finally, it should be noted that, while small Asian-American programs encounter obvious problems, smallness poses an additional burden not found in Black studies. Asian-American studies actually encompass the histories and cultures of a number of distinct ethnic groups. While there, certainly, are important similarities in group backgrounds and experiences, there are, also, major differences. For instance, Asian groups arrived at different points in time and faced somewhat different political and economic circumstances. The communities that they established were not always the same, and there are differences in terms of present status and social problems. Asian-American activists minimize these distinctions in their efforts to foster intergroup unity, while most non-Asian-Americans tend to view these groups as being, basically, alike. However, important differences are apparent and these must be taken into account by programs that strive to be reasonably comprehensive in nature. For small programs, this is a significant problem to overcome.

Selected Issues

In this portion of the paper, some of the issues raised by ethnic studies programs will be reviewed. This discussion is meant to serve as a brief introduction to the arguments surrounding such programs and to provide commentary based upon observations of programs over time. The relevance of issues for Asian-American studies will be noted where appropriate. Unfortunately, all of the ramifications of the various issues cannot be presented because of space limitations, and the reader is urged, again, to consult the ethnic studies literature.

Any discussion of ethnic studies is preceded, necessarily, by the issue of program validity. Though once debated quite extensively, the issue now appears to be a moot question. It is moot, not because such programs have already been established, nor because any discussion offends proponents, who view it as an excuse for nonsupport or inaction. The issue is moot because a high degree of consensus has been achieved on one critical point. The subject matter of ethnic group experiences and contributions has long been absent from the educational process, or it has been presented in a cursory and stereotyping manner. Whether this is due to oversight or some form of racism is

still debatable. What is clear and important is that this subject matter is seen as significant, and not just to those with a personal interest. It is part of the total American experience and, in a broader sense, the experience of man. It, therefore, deserves to be part of the educational process.

Overlooking, for now, such questions as structure and content, ethnic studies programs are attempts to incorporate these materials and, also, to stimulate long-neglected research. Beyond these basic notions, the issue of validity can be related to a number of other issues. Some of these will be noted below, while others are more peripheral because they concern problems of implementation rather than basic validity.

A second general issue is that of program structure.[3] Several of the major features of this issue can be discussed by examining the question of program autonomy. Relatively autonomous programs are those established as academic departments or colleges. Only a minority of Black studies programs and a handful of Asian-American studies programs are structured in this manner. A more common pattern, especially for the latter, are less autonomous structures such as experimental courses within a general studies program, scattered course offerings in standard academic departments, or a loose program of courses coordinated by one department or an interdepartmental committee.

The advantages of relative autonomy are many. It provides greater control by the relevant faculty and students over courses, allows ease in coordinating offerings, and provides centralization to minimize overlaps. Budgetary decisions and allocations can be made, primarily, by those within the program. Autonomy may mean an institutionalized place in the general university budget and a regular source of funds. Autonomous status also, in some sense, may legitimize the program and facilitate the obtaining of money from foundations. The program is able to make decisions in line with its needs, for example, in the recruitment of faculty and the introduction of curriculum innovations. Autonomous programs are relatively permanent and are usually perceived by ethnic group members as an indication of the university's commitment to their courses and problems.

Besides being expensive and difficult to establish, often because of political considerations, autonomous programs suffer from two major drawbacks. Qualified faculty are reluctant to accept appointments in such programs, either because of concerns over their professional futures or because of commitments to their existing academic disciplines. Autonomous programs, also, tend to vest more control in the hands of members of the respective ethnic groups, both faculty and students. Sometimes, the objectives of these members have not been congruent with the expectations of their universities. At times, the ethnic studies programs have been better for this, but, in other instances, the quality of the programs has suffered. The subject of quality is one which will be discussed later. It will only be noted here that, when quality declines, a program can lose its aura of legitimacy within the university. It, then, becomes easy prey for opponents, particularly when resources are scarce.

Ethnic studies programs with less autonomy are more easily established. Existing faculty, generally, are used, or new faculty recruited for joint appointments in the program and in an existing department. This arrangement is more desirable than an appointment only within the program. Since faculty and courses tend to originate from a number of departments, less autonomous programs, at times, achieve more of the interdisciplinary nature characteristic of ethnic studies than autonomous programs. Less autonomous programs can also be run on a trial basis without jeopardizing funds or faculty careers in order to iron out problems or to explore the question of whether the subject matter is sufficient to warrant a separate program. This latter question has been raised,

especially, in connection with Asian-American studies.

Programs with less autonomy suffer from not having the advantages of more autonomous programs such as control of curriculum and money allocations. Their course offerings tend to be sparse and highly related to the particular interests and/or ethnic backgrounds of the available instructors. For example, Asian-American programs have been criticized for their emphasis on the history and problems of Japanese-Americans which is due, partly, to the preponderance of Japanese-American faculty and their interests. Less autonomous programs tend to be impermanent and easy to discontinue or shelve. Some have been established as token responses to ethnic demands without the necessity of having to make a major commitment. Less autonomous programs are, also, more closely under the control of university authorities which may lead to charges of intimidation and co-optation, justified or not, by disgruntled students or people in the community.

A form of program structure that deserves further consideration is that of the research-oriented center or institute. Only a few Black studies programs follow this model, and only one or two Asian-American programs approximate it. A center is supported, largely, from outside grant funds and consists of a group of scholars conducting research in a particular area. Centers are able to provide courses and also generate materials useful in curriculum development. Some are able to offer subject-area minors or to coordinate degree-granting majors in conjunction with existing departments. Being relatively independent, they have many of the advantages of autonomous programs. Centers, sometimes, can obtain additional funds to satisfy new teaching and research needs, and can, often, furnish monies from grants for a variety of community service and action programs. Centers have less difficulty in attracting qualified personnel than autonomous programs, because their activities fit the professional orientations of many faculty, and because joint appointments, often, can be arranged. Apart from offering general courses, centers can involve students in sound research and conduct advanced training for graduate students. Perhaps their greatest advantage over autonomous departments or colleges is the ability to easily maintain academic legitimacy by carrying out research, offering publications, and training students. For this reason, centers may be encouraged and assisted by university administrators and others otherwise opposed to ethnic studies programs. Resistance may be lessened, also, because there is ample precedent for centers focusing on special subject areas, and because the program is willing to fund itself, primarily, from outside sources.

At a time when university funds are becoming tight, this model should be pursued to a greater extent, particularly for relatively new programs such as Asian-American studies. Unfortunately, it can be developed only at larger schools with a major research emphasis, and then only where the requisite faculty interest and skills are present, and resources, such as library materials and ethnic populations are readily available. In addition, the reliance on grant funds can mean a degree of impermanence, especially when the present high funding priority for ethnic research begins to decline. A research orientation, undoubtedly, will be disagreeable to many students, and it may take time for a center to create courses or community projects. There, also, is the probability that a strong research emphasis will preclude instruction for all but a small group of students with special interests. Nevertheless, the advantages of this option beg for its greater consideration.

Related to the issues of program validity and structure are two questions with strong moral and ethical implications. Though they will be discussed here with reference to ethnic studies programs, it should be remembered that they have relevance for a wide variety of efforts designed to alleviate racial and ethnic problems in this society. These questions have not received the serious attention which they deserve because they have been identified as excuses for inaction, or with the racism of those who would continue the discrimination against ethnic groups. However, considered apart from these contexts, they do contain important implications.

For lack of a better label, the first question can be called the "apartheid" issue. It is concerned with the establishment of programs based on racial and ethnic criteria. The fear is expressed that such criteria will only reinforce the use of race and ethnicity to make distinctions among individuals and groups, and that it is also an endorsement of racial and ethnic separation. The additional fear is expressed that ethnic studies programs will always be poor relatives of the standard academic departments. Historically, whenever racial and ethnic criteria were used as an organizing principle for programs or strategies, they always worked to the detriment of the ethnic groups and resulted in "separate and unequal" opportunities and rewards. There is, also, the possibility that ethnic studies programs can become so dominated by the respective groups that they come to be run solely by and for group members. The demands of ethnic students, especially Blacks, to control the content and hiring for their programs reinforces this concern. Ethnic studies, then, would not benefit nongroup members and, easily, could decline in quality. Programs might become a needless duplication, with courses such as ethnic math. Or they might develop a biased point of view to such an extent that courses such as the history of ethnic Americans or the sociology of ethnic Americans become ethnic history and ethnic sociology. In the most extreme situation, ethnic group members might become isolated into their own compartmentalized, inferior departments, without access to outside curriculums that would allow the development of knowledge and skills to be used both for achievement in the society at large and for community action. Ethnic groups, then, would lose an important source of needed technicians and professionals.

Related to the apartheid issue is a second question which is concerned with the use of racial and ethnic criteria to grant preferential treatment to various groups. The preference issue, sometimes called reverse racism or discrimination, has, of course, received wide attention outside the university setting. Here it refers to the use of scarce resources to establish ethnic studies programs rather than putting them to other uses. It refers, also, to preferences that are established, often in connection with implicit or explicit quotas, to recruit and admit or hire ethnic students and faculty, many of whom would not have qualified under standard nonracial and nonethnic criteria. Preference reinforces ethnic criteria, and it is argued that such treatment is patronizing and degrading to the groups involved.

Preferential treatment has allowed Asian-Americans, like other ethnic groups, to establish ethnic studies programs. However, student-faculty quotas have not been uniformly helpful. Some West Coast schools have more Asian-American and Asian students and faculty than a quota, based on their percentage in the local population, would allow. The author is familiar with specific instances in which the establishment of informal quotas, in response to demands for preferential treatment, has resulted in the rejection of prospective Asian-American professional school students and departmental faculty. Some of these individuals might have been admitted or hired had the standard universalistic criteria been used. There, also, have been many instances in which Asian-American demands for preferential treatment have been turned down by universities unwilling to recognize Asian-Americans as a valid minority group. This not only prevents program development but also furthers the stereotype of Asian-Americans as being successful and, basically, like Whites.

Despite the reluctance of ethnic studies proponents to examine these two questions,

they do raise significant points. Also worthy of consideration are some of the counter arguments. Separate programs are, often, the only feasible or expedient means for ethnic groups to gain access and make an initial input into various institutions such as education. They provide, also, a focus for group organization and a chance to develop plans to meet group needs. Separate programs allow ethnic groups to apply constant pressures for change and innovation. Problems such as a decline in quality and ethnic takeover have been characteristic of some programs, especially in the Black studies area, but the evidence is mixed and firm conclusions cannot yet be drawn. It can also be argued that racial and ethnic distinctions are an important fact of life and to ignore them will not make them automatically disappear. Preferential treatment has been an effective means for allowing ethnic groups to make important gains, and it, sometimes, can be rationalized as a kind of retribution for past discrimination. For example, some ethnic group members have benefited from college educations that would have been beyond reach had normal admissions criteria been used. In this instance, preferential admission might be seen as partial compensation for low grades and poor skills resulting from an inferior, segregated education. Also, it can be argued that there has never been a situation of equal opportunity in American society, and that, since various White groups have always been favored in the past, other ethnic groups deserve special consideration in order to redress the balance. Finally, program proponents argue that having resources and being given the chance to do something with them enhances both individual and group feelings of worth, dignity, and pride.

All of the issues discussed above are tied, in some manner, to the general question of program quality. Unfortunately, the concept of quality is difficult to define, and the criteria used depend upon one's basic assumptions about education. A more academic definition views quality programs as providing for intellectual stimulation and growth, and teaching analytic and critical skills of inquiry. Another set of definitions advocate the development of "relevance" in education, creating programs that contribute directly to an individual's personal growth, and that, also, furnish the tools and opportunities to diagnose a variety of problems and undertake corrective actions. The latter definitions are an outgrowth of recent student concerns for educational reform, of which ethnic studies can be seen as one manifestation. Though the two general sets of definitions are not, necessarily, dissimilar or incompatible, the latter attack the "ivory towerism" taken to be implicit in the former.

Individuals adhering to both general definitions of quality, as well as others, have raised significant criticisms of ethnic studies programs. Programs, especially Black studies, have been viewed as having a strong ideological or political content which is, generally, the underpinning for an ethnic movement such as militant Black nationalism. Program proponents either deny this assessment or else note that most academic courses and programs contain inherent biases and implicit ideological assumptions. They argue, also, that ethnic ideologies are necessary to provide direction and unity for group efforts and to furnish alternatives to nonethnic conceptions of issues such as oppression, community action, and social change. Though concerns have been expressed that ideologies breed separatism and contempt for existing institutions, the real problem may not be the presence of ideological content but that, often, only one point of view is represented, which leads to distortions, bias, and selectivity. In this regard, critics have used such terms as "propaganda," "indoctrination," and "chauvanism."

Another criticism of ethnic studies has been that programs have a strong community action orientation which amounts to little more than a misinformed and minor effort to alleviate major problems through some form of rehabilitative model. Communities are not consulted in this undertaking, and the results to date have been minimal. Proponents, however, note that their efforts are only a significant beginning, that they have received community support, and that actual field experiences provide important training and motivation to work on major problem areas. Where the criticism appears to make its strongest point is that programs neglect to provide the necessary analytic and intellectual tools for sound community research and action, and, also, that they strongly emphasize welfare programs to the neglect of alternatives such as basic institutional structural changes. Like the previous criticism, this one appears to have more implications for Black studies programs, but it has been directed at the few Asian-American programs with major community action emphases.

Many critics within the university have charged that, generally, ethnic studies programs have no legitimate academic quality, and that they foster rhetoric and rap sessions but little else. Such programs may have some therapeutic values for the individual as a form of catharsis, although it is questionable whether they can effectively contribute to the development of positive self-identities. Also, they promote and harbor dangerous forms of anti-intellectualism. At best, ethnic studies can be a form of dilettantism, but, at worst, they can generate a social and psychological dependence on ideology, folklore, and action programs. Critics go on to argue that ethnic studies programs attract only a certain type of ethnic student, and that there are strong group pressures for the others to conform and join. Lack of quality may be fostered by a predominance of disadvantaged students admitted under special guidelines and the hiring of ethnic faculty without strong professional orientations. Where control is vested within the program, standards may decline and the curriculum can become an ethnically enclosed social and academic refuge for participants who, otherwise, could not survive in the university setting. Program proponents deny these charges and point out that they are characteristic only of a small minority of programs. They argue that the basic rationales and objectives are sound, and that, if these problems do occur, they are rapidly being overcome. These criticisms are, unfortunately, applicable to a few programs, though recent years have seen the raising of standards and a rise in academic quality.

The criticism of the programs' being an academic refuge for poor students is, perhaps, the most serious one, and it deserves attention wherever it is applicable. A more critical consideration in this regard, however, is the widespread absence of major, comprehensive remedial programs and facilities for high-potential, disadvantaged students, which may leave them with little choice but to seek various academic refuges, or else become seriously alienated from the educational process. The absence of programs might have resulted from the strategies and priorities of proponent ethnic groups. However, in a majority of cases, the blame should be placed on a lack of funds or a low commitment to ethnic group problems by universities.

Again, the highly conventional academic nature of many Asian-American programs removes them from the sphere of these criticisms. Problems of quality arise more from the lack of scope in most small curriculums, and the, sometimes, highly specialized or focused courses taught in lieu of more general ones. In some instances, this conventional academic approach may, itself, be a source of problems. The standard textbook-lecture course, with grades based on rigorously defined point scales derived from quizzes and multiple-choice examinations, may not, necessarily, contribute to learning. In programs of this type, even minor innovations are needed such as guest lecturers, field projects, symposia and discussion sessions, films or tapes, and a wider spectrum of instructional and research materials. Alternative means of student evaluation may be in order. Overly conventional programs might attempt to involve students in the formulation of program objectives and strategies, and allow them to participate in their implementation. Since one feature of ethnic studies has been their push for educational reforms, it would be unfortunate if Asian-American studies could not introduce new methods. The conventionality of some programs, along with the tendency to emphasize history to the exclusion of contemporary problems and community action, has alienated some activist students. Their loss and the consequent movement of action programs away from the university setting will not only promote an unfortunate division in these ethnic groups, but also remove community programs from a source of participants and needed knowledge and training.

A final issue to be briefly outlined concerns the motives of those involved in ethnic studies programs. It would be ideal if the question of motives were not an important consideration, but it has been extensively debated. The motivations of some ethnic studies advocates, especially ethnic group members, have been criticized. A few have been charged with using programs to work out their own personal problems or as a means to "pay their dues" to ethnic protest movements. Advocates have been seen, also, as trying to push a variety of ideological positions under the guise of contributing to the educational process, or of using programs to promote personal plans for community research or action.

The motivations of outside program supporters such as administrators and faculty have also come under scrutiny. Some have been accused of surrendering to political demands under duress, while others have been characterized as supportive because of liberal guilt feelings over past racial injustices. In either case, the basic educational justification for ethnic studies has assumed secondary importance, and serious questions have been raised over the manner in which educational changes should be made. Some apparent supporters have been criticized for establishing only small token programs while offering a variety of excuses. Others have been charged with maintaining tight control over program hiring and content and with attempts to co-opt participants. The most serious accusation in this vein is that ethnic studies supporters have acceded to ethnic group demands in the knowledge that programs would, eventually, lose student interest or so decline in quality and academic legitimacy that they could later be terminated with little opposition. The ramifications of these arguments can get very complex and the variations are numerous. Some accusations may be justified for particular programs. However, it is unfortunate that this issue, often, has been linked to the more basic question of program validity, and that it has, sometimes, distracted attention from other concerns.

There are a number of additional issues that any serious investigator of ethnic studies programs should consider. Among them are the ability of ethnic studies or ethnic curriculum materials to combat and eliminate racism, their ability to promote cultural redefinitions or cultural development, the question of program control, the relationship between programs and ethnic social movements, and the link between ethnic studies and the push for educational reforms.

Conclusion

In conclusion, a few additional comments will be made. First, it is clear that further research on ethnic studies programs is needed to document what has gone on previously and to resolve some of the issues surrounding these programs. Where changes appear to be warranted, these, then, will have to be made. Hopefully, research will move beyond an emphasis on Black studies to include other programs. Research and commentary on Asian-American studies are sorely lacking.

In view of present university budget crises, new means of using existing resources will have to be developed, especially within relatively small programs such as Asian-American studies. Here, there is a need to get away from an emphasis on particular programs and to focus

on better mechanisms of interprogram coordination, such as more effective pooling of curriculum materials and the possible centralization of courses within urban areas that contain several schools. And, as suggested earlier, the model of the research center should be developed in suitable locations.

The basic rationale for initiating ethnic studies was the educational contribution that it would make through the incorporation of new materials and the stimulation of research. A start has been made, but the potential decline of ethnic studies and the degree of ethnic enclosure of some programs threaten this undertaking. Ethnic studies programs should begin to intensify their efforts to push for the inclusion of their materials into other standard curriculums such as history and sociology. Ethnic experiences, after all, are part of the general American experience, and not something separate and inferior. Inclusion will provide for a greater degree of permanence and, also, a wider amount of exposure. It will furnish, also, the context for materials that is, often, so badly needed.

Of course, there will be a great deal of resistance against inclusion by departments and individuals who wish to maintain their perogatives and vested interests. However, if this objective is ever reached, ethnic studies programs may need only to provide a coordinating function, fill in some of the gaps, and conduct research. Until then, they can serve as an important alternative and a source of pressure for educational reforms. It is likely, also, that they will continue for some time to perform their present functions of sensitization and political socialization.

Chapter Notes

1. For an introduction to the literature, see the articles in the topical issues of *The Massachusetts Review* (Autumn 1969), *The American Scholar* (Autumn 1969), *The Black Scholar* (September 1970), *The Journal of Negro Education* (Fall 1969 and Summer 1970), and

The Antioch Review (Summer 1969). Also see Robinson, et al. (1969), Blassingame (1971), Levy (1970), Rosovsky (1969), Draper (1970, 148-167), Bunzel (1968), Genovese (1969), Pentony (1969), Edwards (1970), and Hamilton (forthcoming [1972]). The discussion of issues raised by ethnic studies programs will be done with reference to this literature.

2. This discussion was adapted from Endo (forthcoming [1972]). Some aspects of Asian-American activism can be seen in the articles in Tachiki, et al. (1971) and in *Gidra*, a monthly newspaper of the Asian-American community.

3. Some of these points concerning program structure came to my attention through meetings of the Asian-American Studies Group, University of Washington.

References

Blassingame, John W. (ed.). *New Perspectives on Black Studies*. Urbana, Ill.: University of Illinois Press, 1971.

Bunzel, John H. "Black Studies at San Francisco State." *The Public Interest* 13 (Fall), 1968, 22-38.

Draper, Theodore. *The Rediscovery of Black Nationalism*. New York: Macmillan, 1970.

Edwards, Harry. *Black Students*. New York: Free Press, 1970.

Endo, Russell. "Japanese-Americans: The 'Model Minority' in Perspective." In Rudolph Gomez, et al. (eds.), *Ethnic Minorities*. Lexington, Mass.: D. C. Heath, forthcoming [1972].

Genovese, Eugene D. "Black Studies: Trouble Ahead." *Atlantic Monthly* 233 (June), 1969, 37-41.

Hamilton, Charles V. *They Demand Relevance: Black Students Protest*. New York: Random House, forthcoming [1972].

Levy, Rose W. (ed.). *Black Studies in Schools*. Washington, D.C.: The National School Public Relations Association, 1970.

Pentony, DeVere E. "The Case for Black Studies." *Atlantic Monthly* 233 (April), 1969, 87-89.

Robinson, Armstead L., et al. (eds.). *Black Studies in the University*. New Haven: Yale University Press, 1969.

Resovsky, Henry. *Report of the Faculty Committee on African and Afro-American Studies*. Cambridge: Faculty of Arts and Sciences, Harvard University, 1969.

Tachiki, Amy, et al. (eds.). *Roots: An Asian-American Reader*. Los Angeles: University of California, Los Angeles, Asian-American Studies Center, 1971.

27. Filipinos: A Minority within a Minority

by Nathanial N. Wagner

In considering the situation of Asian-Americans, there is a tendency to concentrate on the Chinese and Japanese and overlook "smaller" and "less important" groups. Filipinos are often thought, incorrectly, to be Orientals; the Orient, traditionally, has been defined as the "Far East" — Japan, China, and Korea. Koreans, also, are an overlooked group, although their approximately 50,000 people in the United States represent a very small percentage of the total population — .025 of 1 percent.

Filipino-Americans are a larger Asian group, 343,060 people, according to the 1970 Census, and, currently, are experiencing considerable growth due to the 1965 revisions of the immigration law. In the year the new law was passed, 1965, only 2,545 Filipinos immigrated to the United States, while in 1971, 28,471 persons immigrated, making the Philippines the second-ranked immigrant nation, after Mexico. This was almost 10 percent of the 1971 total immigration to the United States from all other nations.

As Filipinos have been in this country only a relatively short time — the Census Bureau reported only 160 Filipinos in the United States in the 1910 Census, 5,603 in 1920, and 45,208 in 1930 — many people are unaware of the Philippine history and traditions.

The Philippines is an archipelago with a tropical climate and a mountainous terrain. It is located slightly above the Equator and bounded by the Pacific Ocean, the China Sea, and the Celebes Sea. It lies some 600 miles southeast of the coast of mainland Asia and 7,000 miles west of San Francisco, on a north-south axis, bounded by China on the north and Indonesia and Malaysia to the south and west.

The Philippines consists of 7,100 islands with a total land area of 115,000 square miles, about the size of Italy or the state of Arizona. Although the volcanic origin of the mountains, the extensive river system, and the tropical climate endow the Philippines with fertile agricultural lands, the country, clearly, should be considered in the category of developing nations. It has approximately 40 million people and an exploding birth rate that adds more than 3 percent a year to the population, and a majority of the people live in primitive and backward conditions. Geographically, culturally, and economically, the Philippines has more in common with Indonesia and Malaysia than with the northern developed countries of Japan and China. The Philippine people are, predominantly, of Malay stock and, although many languages and dialects are spoken in the Philippines, Tagalog is the most common native language. English, however, is widely used throughout the Republic and is taught in all schools. More than 80 percent of the people are Roman Catholics and about 10 percent belong to the Philippine Independent Church, organized by a Filipino priest. Members of other Christian faiths, Muslims, and Buddhists make up the rest of the population.

Pre-colonial Filipino history included the influences of many societies and groups. Indonesians and Malays mixed with the early Negrito inhabitants as early as thousands of years before Christ. Hindu and Buddhist influences from India, Chinese traders, and a strong Muslim missionary movement from Arabia marked the time from the eighth century to the fifteenth century.

The country obtained its current name from the Spanish colonials, who named it in honor of Prince Philip of Spain when they began a 333-year rule in 1565. Although at different times the Portuguese, Dutch, and English claimed parts of the Philippines, Spanish rule was maintained until 1896-1898. At that time, there was a genuine national revolution and a proclamation of independence on June 12, 1898. America, however, as a consequence of the Spanish-American war, purchased the Philippines for $10 million by a treaty signed in Paris on December 10, 1898. For the next four years, American military forces were necessary to establish American colonial rule. At this time, Filipinos became subjects — not citizens — of the United States, and some limited immigration of agricultural workers to Hawaii was encouraged. By 1920, it was estimated that 25,000 Filipinos were living in Hawaii, but only about one-fifth of that number had migrated to the continental United States. Around this time, stimulated by labor difficulties on the West Coast, more Filipinos came to California. The Immigration Act of 1924 definitely and specifically excluded the Chinese and Japanese. Filipinos could immigrate, although they could not become citizens. A legislative act in 1925 made Filipinos who had served in the American Navy for three years eligible for citizenship. (See Duff and Arthur's article in this volume.) There were no provisions for Filipino women!

By 1930, the Census Bureau reported 45,208 Filipinos in the United States, excluding

Hawaii. Prejudice and discrimination against this newest minority group began to flare up at this time. Riots occurred in a number of California towns, and the Northern Monterey County Chamber of Commerce at Pajaro, California, passed the following resolution:

> Whereas, any foreign peoples coming to the U.S.A. who, by their customs, habits, and standards of living, prohibit them from assimilating with and adopting our standard of living, are detrimental and dangerous to our social conditions; and Whereas, the unrestricted immigration into the State of California of natives from the Philippine Islands is viewed with alarm from both a moral and sanitary standpoint, while constituting a menace to White labor: Therefore Be It Resolved, that we, the Chamber of Commerce of Northern Monterey County, in regular session, do petition the County, State, and National Governments to adopt such methods and means to prevent further immigration. (Block, 1930, pp. 48)

In 1934, the United States, uncomfortable in its colonial role, passed the Philippine Independence Act, guaranteeing eventual independence to the Philippines. Anti-Filipino groups, such as the Northern Monterey County Chamber of Commerce, succeeded in attaching to the Independence Act an immigration quota of fifty Filipinos a year — amounting to essential exclusion of Filipino immigrants. Subsequent immigration laws slightly opened the door to immigration, and, then, the most recent law change, in 1965, made possible the substantial immigration that occurred in the late 1960s and early 1970s.

The Philippines were granted their independence on July 4, 1946, after a period of occupation by Japan during World War II. Names like Bataan and Corregidor were familiar to all Americans in 1941-1945 when the Japanese and American forces, including Filipinos, fought throughout the islands. Interestingly, a Japanese soldier, who had hidden out in the jungles since the end of the war in 1945, was discovered in 1972. In the same year, in one of the remote sections of the Philippines, anthropologists discovered a group of people who, apparently, had been entirely untouched by civilizing factors and were living in a "stone-age culture." Both these instances speak of the heavy vegetation and unexplored and uncharted nature of parts of the Philippines. Slightly more than 4,000 of the 7,000 islands are still unnamed!

Since independence, the Philippine Republic has experienced many difficulties, as have a number of other developing countries such as Indonesia, Burma, India, and Pakistan. On one hand, there have been sporadic efforts in the Philippines for American statehood as the fifty-first state. On the other hand, there is a developing Communist party, which is viewed by some as weak and ineffectual and by others as the force for revolution in a country they see as the most ripe in Asia for revolution (Guerrero, 1970). Clearly, the standard of living in the United States is superior to that of the Philippines, and many Filipinos would like to immigrate to this country.

The Filipino immigrants to the United States, often, are overshadowed by their Asian brothers from China and Japan. Those northern country immigrants brought skills and traditions that better equipped them to deal with American racism. In many ways, the Filipino has fared more similarly to the Blacks, Chicanos, and Native-Americans, rather than the Japanese or Chinese. This is true of educational attainment, occupational status, and income (Schmid and Nobbe, 1965). In fact, for the state of Washington, Filipinos were below Blacks on these three sensitive socio-economic indicators (Schmid, Nobbe, and Mitchell, 1968).

Unfortunately, at the time of this writing [1972], the 1970 Census socio-economic data have not been analyzed nor published, so it is unclear what effect the current immigrations will have on these factors. Clearly, many of the newer Filipino immigrants are better educated than their countrymen who are unable to emigrate and better educated than the farm workers who came in large numbers around 1930.

These new immigrants report continuing discrimination against them. They state that their educational qualifications are not accepted in this country. They report people with Ph.D.s working as common laborers and many other instances of what, they feel, is outright discrimination against them. There can be no doubt — as of this time, Filipinos have not shared in the American abundance.

As Cordova points out in his chapter, there is a new stirring among Filipinos. As a psychologist who has visited the Philippines and lived for more than a year in a Southeast Asian country with predominantly Malay people (Wagner and Tan, 1971), I am impressed, in a subjective manner, by the gentle, shy, and unassuming traditions of the Filipino. Obviously, much of this is the vestige of centuries of colonialism, but much seems, to this observer, to be indigenous to the culture of this part of the world. As Filipinos become more outspoken in their quest for their fair share of America's wealth, one wonders what changes in personality and style will develop. As a White American who fervently hopes for full Filipino participation, I hope, also, that the uniqueness of the Filipinos can be maintained as they contribute to a truly multiracial, culturally pluralistic society.

References

Block, Louis. *Facts about Filipino Immigration into California.* Washington: U.S. Government Printing Office, 1930.

Guerrero, Amado. *Philippine Society and Revolution.* Hong Kong: Ta Kung Pao, 1971.

Kirk, Grayson. *Philippine Independence.* New York: Farrar and Rhinehart, 1936.

McWilliams, Carey. *Brothers Under the Skin.* Boston: Little, Brown and Company, 1964.

Schmid, Calvin F., and Nobbe, Charles E. "Socioeconomic Differential among Non-White Races. *American Sociological Review* 30, 1965, 909-922.

_____ ; Nobbe, Charles E.; and Mitchell, Arlene E. *Non-White Races: State of Washington.* Olympia: Washington State Planning and Community Affairs Agency, 1968.

Tachiki, Amy; Wong, Eddie; Odo, Franklin; and Wong, Buck. *Roots: An Asian-American Reader.* Los Angeles: UCLA Asian Studies Center, 1971.

Taylor, George L. *The Philippines and the United States.* New York: Frederick A. Praeger, 1964.

Wagner, Nathaniel, and Tan, E. S. *Psychological Problems and Treatment in Malaysia.* Kuala Lumpur: University of Malaya Press, 1971.

Walovits, Sonia Emily. *The Filipinos in California.* Los Angeles: University of Southern California, 1966.

Appendix : 1970 Census Bureau Tables

Appendix
Race of the Population by Division: 1970

Division	Total	White	Negro	Indian	Japanese	Chinese	Filipino	All Other
United States, total	203,211,926	177,748,975	22,580,289	792,730	591,290	435,062	343,060	720,520
New England Division	11,841,663	11,388,774	388,398	10,872	7,485	18,113	6,962	21,059
Middle Atlantic Division	37,199,040	32,921,730	3,955,755	38,594	31,493	97,664	24,462	129,342
East North Central Division	40,252,476	36,160,135	3,872,905	57,732	33,002	31,001	22,375	75,326
West North Central Division	16,319,187	15,481,048	698,645	93,555	9,352	8,342	5,449	22,796
South Atlantic Division	30,671,337	24,112,395	6,388,496	67,126	17,467	19,332	23,914	42,607
East South Central Division	12,803,470	10,202,810	2,571,291	10,363	3,795	4,235	2,473	8,503
West South Central Division	19,320,560	16,104,903	3,010,174	123,733	9,655	10,717	5,592	55,786
Mountain Division	8,281,562	7,798,087	180,382	235,439	20,360	9,245	4,466	33,583
Pacific Division	26,522,631	23,579,093	1,514,243	155,316	458,681	236,413	247,367	331,518

Source: U.S. Department of Commerce, Census Bureau

Cover Photo: "Looking Out" by Irene Poon

Book Design: Barry Ives

Book set in 10/12 theme medium
on IBM Selectric Composer System

Typography by Penguin Cold Type,
Santa Clara, California

Book printed by George Banta Company,
Menasha, Wisconsin